FAITH AND FREEDOM

The one who presents his case first seems right, until someone steps forth to challenge him.

Proverbs 18:17

FAITH AND FREEDOM

*A Complete Handbook for
Defending Your Religious Rights*

Second Edition

Mathew D. Staver

Liberty Counsel • Orlando, Florida

Faith and Freedom:
A Complete Handbook for Defending Your Religious Rights
Second Edition

Cover Design: Cathy Maners

First printing, 1995
Second printing, 1998

Printed in the United States of America

Library of Congress Cataloging-in-Publication Data
Staver, Mathew D., 1956-
    Faith and freedom: a complete handbook for defending your religious rights/Mathew D. Staver
            p.   cm.
    Includes bibliographical references and index.
    1. Church and state-United States. 2. Freedom of religion - United States. 3. Religion in the public schools - Law and legislation - United States. I. Title.
KF4865.S73   1995   342.73'0852-dc20   94-37644
ISBN 0-9662079-0-4

Table of Contents

Acknowledgments

This is the second edition of *Faith and Freedom*. The first edition was published in 1995 by Crossway Books. Since courts are constantly faced with new constitutional challenges, any book addressing constitutional law must be continually updated. In this second edition of *Faith and Freedom* I have included additional case and statutory law. Most of these additions clarify and reinforce propositions outlined in the first edition. I have also added several new chapters. It is my hope that the chapters on Judicial Tyranny and Same Sex Marriage will both challenge and motivate you.

As with any project of this magnitude, no one person can take full credit for the finished product. The staff who work with me are not only colleagues but my best friends. To mention some would leave out others. Those who didn't work directly on the project have supported me in other ways with their prayers and encouragement.

One person I must mention is the one to whom I dedicate this book -- my wife. Anita has always stood by me in both good and bad times. She has been a constant encouragement to me. Without her I my accomplishments would be diminished. Anita has assisted me in so many ways. She recently began her journey into law school. Her vision is the same as mine -- to dedicate her life to defending religious freedom so that the doors of our society remain open to share the gospel. She has been my partner, my wife, and most of all, my best friend. Soon she will be my co-counsel.

Foreword

By Dr. D. James Kennedy

It is always an occasion for rejoicing - to me, at least - when a rock-solid book on the First Amendment appears on the market, either in new or revised form. Mathew Staver's updated handbook of religious rights *Faith & Freedom*, could not have been published at a more propitious time.

The issuance of this scholarly, yet practical, work is timely because of a whole new generation of public unawareness or indifference toward our Bill of Rights, the foundation-stone of American freedoms. The First Amendment is simply not being taught to schoolchildren, along with other basic concepts of our national political history.

More than that, there has never before been such a torrent of convoluted court interpretations of simple Constitutional principles as in the past three decades, accompanied by a flood of extrapolations -- some ridiculous, some frightening -- sponsored by an unending line of hostile pressure groups, all politically motivated by one agenda or another. The result has been to make the First Amendment and other clear enfranchisements of the Constitution seem unintelligible to the average citizen.

Of all the tenets bound in our constitutional system, the First Amendment has become probably the most misunderstood and the most misquoted. Ask the average person on the street what it says, and the vast majority will reply that it says something about a "wall of separation between church and state." Of course, that is not what it says at all. Jefferson's innocent, passing phrase in his letter to the Danbury Baptists (1792) has become, in the minds of perhaps most Americans, a substitute for the First Amendment, which spells out the role of religion in a democratic republic.

The author of this valuable handbook makes it clear that what this opening amendment guarantees in the way of freedoms is specifically (1) freedom of speech, (2) freedom of the press, (3) freedom of assembly, and (4) the right to petition the government concerning grievances, and that it also states explicitly that "Congress shall make no law respecting an establishment of religion, or forbidding the free exercise thereof."

The subject, importantly, is not the church, the school, the ministers, religious people -- it is the Congress. The First Amendment limits what <u>Congress</u> may do. This was written so that the people would have full protection of their rights to free and unrestricted worship. We have seen in our day a 180-degree turnabout from what the First Amendment says, with liberals and secular humanists proclaiming that somehow the First Amendment's purpose is to protect the government from the influence of religion!

The Founding Fathers did not intend to establish a government separated from God, nor does the Constitution suggest such. Neither did it condone a state under the authority of the church, as in medieval Europe, nor a religion under the domination of the state, as in Communist lands. While the church and the state must be separate, the church must be ready to be a prophetic voice to the state and to remind it of its responsibility to God in administering justice. The church is obligated to submit to the civil laws of the state as it honors the divine appointment of the government. However, this submission ends when the state directs the church to act contrary to God's laws or seeks to control the free government of the church.

In *Faith & Freedom*, the reader will discover that the author, a Christian attorney, delineates with unclouded conviction the Biblically oriented relationship between a nation's central government and its churches, schools, courts, and other free institutions. He is in complete agreement with this surprising proclamation by the United States Supreme Court in *The Church of the Holy Trinity v. United States*:

This is a religious people . . . this is a Christian nation.[1]

Thank God that this is not some random, anachronistic idea, but the combined ruling of the most authoritative judicial minds America can muster. Mathew Staver brings together in this user-friendly handbook of Christian rights the true concepts of religious freedom intended and achieved by the Founding Fathers in the First

---

[1] 143 U.S. 457 (1892).

amendment -- as it was adopted rather than as it has been recently interpreted.

- D. JAMES KENNEDY, A.B.,
M.Div., M.Th., D.D., D.Sac.Lit.,
Ph.D., Litt.D., D.Sac.Theol., D.
Humane Let.
Coral Ridge Presbyterian Church
Senior Pastor
Foreward to Second Edition

Foreword

By Professor Charles E. Rice

"Pity the public school principal in December," began the *New York Times* summary. "Between Hanukkah, Christmas and Kwanzaa (a Black-American holiday that celebrates family and community and is based on African harvest festivals), this long last month lays a minefield of grand proportions for educators trying to acknowledge the holidays without bridging the separation of church and state." The object, said one A.C.L.U. official, is "to treat all religions and atheism equally." As one school district framed its policy: "Trees are allowed; religious decorations and Nativity scenes are not. Menorahs are allowed, but there is no daily lighting of candles. Concerts and parties are prefaced with the words holiday or winter instead of Christmas."[1]

One might fairly ask how such distinctions follow from the simple words of the religion clauses of the First Amendment: "Congress shall make no law respecting an establishment of religion, or prohibiting the free exercise thereof. . . ." The short answer is that they don't. The current interpretations of the religion clauses are the product not of constitutional intent but of a bewildering array of Supreme Court decisions, the inventiveness of which is exceeded only by their tendency to secularize the public life of the nation and to work a restrained but taxing persecution on Christian and other religious parents who want to integrate their faith with that public life.

The Supreme Court's erroneous interpretations of the Establishment Clause have institutionalized agnostic secularism as the official national creed. This error has been compounded by the Supreme Court's misinterpretation of the Fourteenth Amendment so as to bind the state and local governments strictly by the Court's interpretation of the Bill of Rights. Through its application of the Bill of Rights strictly against the states, the Supreme Court has claimed for itself the power to determine the meaning and application of virtually all personal and civil rights. The effect of

---

[1] *New York Times*, Dec. 16, 1993, p. B1.

xix

this inventive jurisprudence is nowhere more evident than with respect to the religion clauses of the First Amendment.

Professor Edward S. Corwin accurately summarized the original intent of the Establishment Clause of the First Amendment, that "Congress should not prescribe a national faith, a possibility which those states with establishments of their own—Massachusetts, New Hampshire, Connecticut, Maryland, and South Carolina—probably regarded with fully as much concern as those which had gotten rid of their establishment."[2] Justice Joseph Story, who served on the Supreme Court from 1811 to 1845 and who himself was a Unitarian, said:

> Probably, at the time of the adoption of the Constitution, and of the [First] Amendment to it, . . . the general, if not the universal sentiment in America was, that Christianity ought to receive encouragement from the State, so far as such encouragement was not incompatible with the private rights of conscience, and the freedom of religious worship. An attempt to level all religions, and to make it a matter of state policy to hold all in utter indifference, would have created universal disapprobation, if not universal indignation. . . . The real object of the amendment was, not to countenance, much less to advance Mohammedanism, or Judaism, or infidelity, by prostrating Christianity; but to exclude all rivalry among Christian sects, and to prevent any national ecclesiastical establishment which should give to an hierarchy the exclusive patronage of the national government.[3]

The framers of the First Amendment would have rejected the view of today's Supreme Court, which excludes prayer from public life and forbids even the posting of the Ten Commandments in public schools. The Northwest Ordinance, adopted by the Continental Congress in 1787, provided public support for religious education: "Religion, morality, and knowledge, being necessary to good government and the happiness of mankind, schools and the

---

[2]Edward Samuel Corwin, *The Powers in a Secular State* 102, 106 (1951).

[3]Joseph Story, 2 *Commentaries on the Constitution of the United States* 593 (1833).

means of education, shall forever be encouraged." This enactment was reaffirmed by the First Congress in 1789. After the new Constitution was ratified, the Congress on September 24-26, 1789, did two things. They approved and sent to the states for ratification the First Amendment. And they called on President Washington to "recommend to the people of the United States a day of public thanksgiving and prayer, to be observed by acknowledging, with grateful hearts, the many signal favors of Almighty God." Can you believe that the Congress intended the First Amendment to forbid the sort of prayer it recommended on the same day? Nor was this a result of inadvertence. Representative Thomas Tucker of South Carolina objected that the call for a day of prayer "is a religious matter, and, as such, is proscribed to us." Congress passed the resolution, deliberately overriding the argument the Supreme Court has adopted as doctrine today.[4]

In *The Church of the Holy Trinity v. United States,* in 1892, the Supreme Court unanimously held that a Congressional statute forbidding the immigration of persons under contract to perform labor did not apply to an English minister who entered this country under a contract to preach at a New York church. After reciting the legislative history of the act, the Court said,

> But beyond all these matters no purpose of action against religion can be imputed to any legislation, state or national, because this is a religious people. This is historically true. From the discovery of this content to the present hour, there is a single voice making this affirmation. . . . If we pass beyond these matters to a view of American life as expressed by its laws, its business, its customs and its society, we find everywhere a clear recognition of the same truth. . . . These, and many other matters which might be noticed, add a volume of unofficial declarations to the mass of organic utterances that this is a Christian nation.[5]

---

[4]Annals of Congress 915 (1789).
[5]143 U.S. 457, 470-71 (1892).

The American religious consensus, however, eroded. The Supreme Court in recent years has reflected as well as encouraged that erosion by interpreting the Establishment Clause to require not merely neutrality on the part of government among Christian and other theistic sects, but neutrality between theism and nontheism. It is impossible, however, for government to maintain neutrality on the existence of God. To affirm God is a preference for theism, to deny Him a preference for atheism, and to suspend judgment a preference for agnosticism which is itself a religion.

The Court, nevertheless, requires government at all levels to maintain a neutrality between theism and nontheism. Justice William Brennan argued in his concurrence in the 1963 school prayer case that the words "under God" could still be kept in the Pledge of Allegiance only because they "no longer have a religious purpose or meaning." Instead, according to Brennan, they "may merely recognize the historical fact that our Nation was believed to have been founded 'under god'."[6] This false neutrality would logically prevent an assertion by any government official, whether president or school teacher, that the Declaration of Independence—the first of the Organic Laws of the United States printed at the head of the United States Code—is, in fact, true when it asserts that men are endowed "by their Creator" with certain unalienable rights and when it affirms "the Laws of Nature and of Nature's God," a "Supreme Judge of the world" and "Divine Providence." The result, in practical effect, is a governmental preference for the religion of agnostic secularism.

Generations of public school children have passed through the system in the past three decades without ever seeing the state, in the persons of their teachers, acknowledge that there is a standard of right and wrong higher than the state and that "the Laws of Nature and of Nature's God" are in fact a limit on the power of the state. Moreover, the false rule of neutrality requires that public schools must treat sensitive moral issues such as homosexual activity, promiscuity, abortion, etc., in a "nonjudgmental" manner that cannot help but indoctrinate a relativistic attitude in the students. One result is a potential abridgment of the free exercise of religion of students who do not subscribe to the secular orthodoxy. And the process

---

[6]*School District of Abington Township v. Schempp,* 374 U.S. 203, 304 (1963).

tends to wean the students away from their belief in God. As one writer in *The American Atheist* put it:

> And how does a god die? Quite simply because all his religionists have been converted to another religion, and there is no one left to make children believe they need him.

> Finally, it is irresistible—we must ask how we can kill the god of Christianity. We need only insure that our schools teach only secular knowledge; that they teach children to constantly examine and question all theories and truths put before them in any form; and that they teach nothing is proven by the number of persons who believe a thing to be true. If we could achieve this, god would indeed be shortly due for a funeral service.[7]

What are parents to do in the face of the immersion of public institutions by aggressive secularism? Fortunately, they are not without remedy. Legal avenues remain through which they can fight back in the education of their children and even in the introduction of Christian principle into the public order itself. This book by Mathew D. Staver is a powerful weapon in this fight. Mr. Staver is an expert, perceptive, and properly inventive advocate who is not afraid of a fight. He has provided here a clear and understandable guidebook for all of us who would otherwise be lost in the legalistic maze. More important, he treats the law of the state in proper context. In truth, life and the law come ultimately from God, rather than the state, and they are subject to His dominion. Nor is this a time for pessimism. God is not dead. He is not even tired. We are

---

[7]Bozarth, "On Keeping God Alive," *American Atheist*, Nov. 1977, 7-8.

on the winning side. It is time for us to fight back. Mathew Staver's important book will help mightily in that fight.

—Professor Charles E. Rice
Notre Dame Law School
Foreward to First Edition

Preface

Prior to entering law school, I was in the pastoral ministry. During my days as a pastor, I was continually confronted with the interaction between church and state. At one time I was invited to a pastors' meeting where a film on abortion was shown. I had no position on the issue but presumed that I favored abortion. After viewing this video about the development of the unborn child, I changed my views and became pro-life. Thereupon I began reading the United States Supreme court opinion of *Roe v. Wade*,[1] and the more I learned about the abortion issue, the more I was led to legal issues.

While pastoring, I also became frustrated every year during the Christmas season when one nativity scene after another was challenged in court. These events, among others, formed the background to my law school education. After entering law school and studying constitutional law, I began to realize that there is a great deal of misinformation on religious liberty issues.

In 1989, I founded Liberty Counsel in order to provide education and legal defense on religious liberty matters. I have learned that we lose our religious liberties for three primary reasons: (1) ignorance of the law, (2) hostility toward religion, and (3) apathy. Most of the cases in which Liberty Counsel is involved resolve through education. A minority of cases involve someone who is actually hostile toward religion. In this battle over religious liberty, I frequently encounter a great deal of apathy among Christians and other religious people. Most people would rather run than fight and lose their rights rather than struggle for them. Religious liberty is not simply a legal right —- it is the ability to continue to spread the gospel in a free nation.

The intent of this book is to provide education in areas of free speech and religious liberty. Education is the best weapon against tyranny. The Constitution did not create civil rights. Our civil liberties predate the Constitution. As the signers of the Declaration of Independence would say, our civil liberties are God-given, "self-evident," "unalienable" rights. The government's sole duty is to

---

[1] 410 U.S. 113 (1973).

protect these rights. It is my hope that this book will play a small part in protecting our precious liberties.

RELIGION:
AN ENDANGERED SPECIES

An objective observer cannot escape the conclusion that America was founded upon Judeo-Christian principles. During his travels in the 1830s, Alexis de Tocqueville stated, "On my arrival in the United States the religious aspect of the country was the first thing that struck my attention."[1] The early founders of America came here not so much to flee religious persecution but to evangelize a new continent. The first colonial grant from Queen Elizabeth to Sir Walter Raleigh in 1584 was to enact laws provided "they be not against the true Christian faith."[2] The first charter of Virginia by King James in 1606 was to propagate the "Christian religion to such people, [who] as yet live in darkness."[3] The Mayflower Compact of 1620 was for the "advancement of the Christian Faith."[4]

The signers of the Declaration of Independence in 1776 clearly acknowledged that they were "endowed by their Creator with certain unalienable Rights." In the same year, the Delaware Constitution required an oath from all officers as follows: "[I] profess faith in God the Father, and in Jesus Christ His only Son, and in the Holy Ghost, one God, blessed forevermore: and I do acknowledge the Holy Scriptures of the Old and New Testament to be given by divine inspiration."[5] The Massachusetts Constitution of 1780 spoke of the "right" and "duty" of all citizens to "worship the Supreme Being."[6] The Maryland Constitution of 1807 spoke of the "duty of every man to worship God," noting that no person could be a witness unless he or she "believes in the existence of God."[7] Likewise, the Mississippi Constitution of 1832 stated that one could not hold state office and deny the "being of God, or a future state

---

[1]Alexis de Tocqueville, 1 *Democracy in America* 319.
[2]*The Church of the Holy Trinity v. United States*, 143 U.S. 457, 466 (1892).
[3]*Id.*
[4]*Id.*
[5]*Id.* at 468.
[6]*Id.*
[7]*Id.*

of rewards and punishment."[8] Indeed, John Adams once said, "Our Constitution was made only for a moral and religious people. It is wholly inadequate for the government of any other."[9]

Reviewing this history, the United States Supreme Court stated in 1892 that "this is a religious nation . . . we are a Christian people," and concluded, "this is a Christian nation."[10] When the Constitutional Convention was about to fall apart, Benjamin Franklin stood up and uttered his famous words: "If a sparrow cannot fall without [God's] notice, is it probable that an empire can rise without His aid?"[11]

George Washington distinguished himself as a great general, representative of Virginia, and the first president of the United States. He did not mince words with his convictions regarding religion when he stated: "It is impossible to rightly govern the world without God and the Bible."[12] George Washington also once stated: "Whatever may be conceded to the influence of refined education on minds or peculiar structure, reason and experience both forbid us to expect that the national morality can prevail in exclusion of religious principles. Take away religion, and the country will fail."[13] He warned: "[L]et us with caution indulge the supposition, that morality can be maintained without religion."[14] George Washington also acknowledged God's intervention during his Inaugural Speech to Congress on April 30, 1789:

> [I]t would be peculiarly improper to omit, in this first official act, my fervent supplications to that Almighty Being who rules over the universe, who presides in the councils of the nations and whose providential aids can supply every human defect, . . .

---

[8]*Id.*

[9]John Adams, 1789, *quoted in War and Religious Freedom* 1.

[10]*The Church of the Holy Trinity,* 113 U.S. at 471.

[11]Benjamin Franklin, June 28, 1787, *quoted by* Smyth, *Writings,* IX:600; *quoted by* Alison et al., *The Real Benjamin Franklin* 258-59.

[12]William J. Federer, *America's God and Country* 660.

[13]Washington, Farewell Address, September 17, 1796; *quoted by* Johnson, *George Washington the Christian* 217-18.

[14]*Id.*

****

No people can be bound to acknowledge and adore
the Invisible Hand which conducts the affairs of men
more than the people of the United States.

Every step by which they have advanced to their
character of an independent nation seems to have been
distinguished by some token of providential agency. . .[15]

John Quincy Adams once declared that the "highest glory of
the American Revolution was this: It connected in one indissoluble
bond, the principles of civil government with the principles of
Christianity."[16] Interestingly, a House Judiciary report of March 27,
1854, issued the following statement in response to a petition to
separate Christian principles from government:

If the people, during the Revolution, had a suspicion
of any attempt to war against Christianity, that Revolution
would have been strangled in its cradle.

At the time of the adoption of the Constitution and
the amendments, the universal sentiment was that
Christianity should be encouraged, not any one sect. Any
attempt to level and discard all religion would have been
viewed with universal indignation. The object was not to
substitute Judaism or Mohammedanism, or infidelity, but
to prevent rivalry among the [C]hristian sects to the
exclusion of others.

[Christianity] must be considered as the foundation
on which the whole structure rests. Laws will not have
preeminence or power without the sanction of religious
sentiment, -- without a firm belief that there is a Power

[15]Washington Inaugural Address, April 30, 1789, *quoted by* James D. Richardson, 1 *A Compilation of the Messages and Papers of the Presidents*, 1789-1897 52-53.
[16]John Quincy Adams, July 4, 1821, *quoted by* J. Wingate Thornton, *The Pulpit of the American Revolution 1860* XXIX.

above us that will reward our virtues and punish our vices.

In this age there can be no substitute for Christianity: that, in its general principals, is the great conservative element on which we must rely for the purity and permanence of free institutions. That was the religion of the founders of the republic, and they expected it to remain the religion of their descendants. [17]

In May of 1854, the Congress of the United States passed a resolution in the House which declared: "A great vital and conservative element in our system is the belief of our people in the pure doctrines in divine truths of the gospel of Jesus Christ."[18] On July 13, 1787, the Continental Congress enacted the Northwest Ordinance which stated: "Religion, morality, and knowledge, being necessary to good government and the happiness of mankind, schools and the means of education shall be forever encouraged."[19] On August 7, 1789, after the final agreement on the wording of the Bill of Rights, the newly formed Congress re-enacted the Northwest Ordinance.[20] On September 25, 1789, Congress unanimously approved a resolution asking President George Washington to proclaim a National Day of Thanksgiving,[21] and then on October 3, 1789, President George Washington proclaimed a National Day of Thanksgiving.[22] On June 14, 1954, Congress approved a Joint Resolution which added "under God" to the *Pledge of Allegiance*.[23] Then, on July 20, 1956, Congress passed a Joint Resolution which

---

[17]March 27, 1854, Mr. Meacham's report to the House Committee on the Judiciary, *quoted by* B. F. Morris, *The Christian Life and Character of the Civil Institutions of the United States* 317, 320-327.

[18]*Id.* at 328.

[19]Ord. of 1789, July 13, 1787, Art. A III, *reprinted in Documents Illustrative of the Formation of the Union of American States* 52 (1927).

[20]*An Act to Provide for the Government of the Territory Northwest of the River Ohio (Northwest Ordinance)*, Ch. 8, 1 Stat. 50-51 (Peter's ed. 1845).

[21]September 25, 1789, Congress recommended a National Day of Thanksgiving, *quoted in* 1 *Annals of Congress 1789-1791* 914.

[22]On October 3, 1789, President George Washington issued from New York City, his proclamation for a National Day of Thanksgiving. *Quoted by* James D. Richardson 1 *A Compilation of the Messages and Papers of the Presidents 1789-1897* 64.

[23]Joint Resolution, etc., June 14, 1954, c. 297, 68 Stat. 249, codified, as amended, at 36 U.S.C. § 172 (1978).

adopted Rep. Charles E. Bennett's bill providing the official national motto, "In God We Trust."[24]

The Declaration of Independence unanimously adopted on July 4, 1776, probably contains one of the best outlines for the purpose and place of government. The signers of the Declaration stated as follows:

> When in the Course of human events, it becomes necessary for one people to dissolve the political bands which have connected them with another, and to assume among the powers of the earth, the separate and equal station of which the Laws of Nature and of Nature's God entitle them, a decent respect to the opinions of mankind requires that they should declare the causes which impel them to the separation.

> We hold these truths to be self-evident, that all men are created equal, that they are endowed by their Creator with certain unalienable Rights, that among these are Life, Liberty and the pursuit of Happiness.

> That to secure these rights, Governments are instituted among Men, deriving their just powers from the consent of the governed.

> That whenever any Form of Government becomes destructive of these ends, it is the Right of the People to alter or to abolish it, and to institute new Government, laying its foundation on such principals and organizing its powers in such form, as to them shall seem most likely to effect their Safety and Happiness. Prudence, indeed, will dictate that Governments long established should not be changed for light and intransigent causes; and accordingly all experience hath shown, that mankind are most disposed to suffer, while evils are sufferable, than to right themselves by abolishing the forms to which they are

---

[24]Joint Resolution to Establish a National Motto of the United States, Ch. 795, Pub. L. No. 84-851, 70 Stat. 732 (1957).

accustomed. But when a long train of abuses and usurpations, pursuing invariably the same Object evinces a design to reduce them under absolute Despotism, it is their right, it is their duty, to throw off such Government, and to provide new Guards for their future security.[25]

The signers of the Declaration of Independence understood that there are certain God-given, unalienable rights, among which are life, liberty, and the pursuit of happiness. Government does not establish these rights, cannot modify these rights, and must not infringe these rights. The Constitution did not create these liberties. Like the Declaration of Independence, the Constitution recognizes that these liberties predate our country and supersede any form of government. The *sole* purpose of government is to protect these God-given liberties, and when any form of government fails to protect these liberties, and more particularly, limits these liberties, it is the right of the people, it is their duty, to alter or even abolish that form of government and to create a new government which protects these preexisting liberties. Put into perspective, the sole purpose of government is to protect certain God-given, God-ordained, preexisting liberties. Since these liberties come from God, it is inconceivable that any form of government whose purpose is to protect these liberties would at the same time disavow God and exclude Him from public life. It is inconceivable to separate politics from religion, since politics is supposed to protect religion, and religion is supposed to stabilize politics.

Without question, the early founders did not separate their political beliefs from their religious beliefs. Indeed, this country was based upon Judeo-Christian principles that permeated society. A burning desire of many early pioneers was to develop a society in which religious freedom could flourish. Many sacrificed everything they accumulated, and some even forfeited their lives. Once the pioneers arrived on this continent, they staked out crosses and penned in their original charters their conviction that God had led them to a new country to spread the gospel of Jesus Christ.

Society has changed since those early days. After becoming

---

[25]Declaration of Independence, July 4, 1776, The Organic Laws of the United States of America.

comfortable with their new freedom, many mainline religions became infected by liberal theology. Many churches forsook the gospel and searched for a historical Jesus whom they could not find. These churches became socially-oriented and neglected the very heart of the gospel. They lost the gospel through their liberal interpretation of the Bible, no longer believing in the resurrection of Jesus Christ, in miracles, or in the changing power of the gospel other than through psychology. In response to this liberal trend, some emphasized a purity from within and became repulsed at the liberal agendas of many mainline churches. This backlash resulted in pietism wherein the individual relationship with God was emphasized to the neglect of society. The pendulum swung to the opposite end of extremism.

During this age of pietism, many Christians, fed up with liberal denominations, withdrew from society and public influence, believing association with any social agenda was dirty. As these Christians abandoned society, what remained were secularists in places of public influence, or so-called religionists who forgot their religious roots. The pietistic Christians and the liberal secularists were content to stuff God in a box. God had His own corner reserved within the church; He was hidden within the communion chalice.

This country moves toward secularism at its peril. We have come to accept the standard that where government increases, religion must decrease. We have also come to accept the presumption that government and religion mix like oil and water, that where government treads, religion must flee.

Paul Blanshard, a secular humanist writing in *The Humanist* magazine, once noted that the first seventy-five years of the twentieth century have been "a good seventy-five years, full of rebellion against religious superstition, inspired by developing science, and increasingly open to religious realism."[26] He also stated, "I doubt that any span in human history has carried the world farther along the road to honest doubt."[27] Mr. Blanshard noted that his "primary hero" in moving this nation to a secular society

---

[26]Paul Blanshard, *Three Cheers for Our Secular State*, THE HUMANIST, March/April 1976, p. 17.

[27]*Id.*

was the United States Supreme Court.

Reviewing the first seventy-five years of the twentieth century, and the United States Supreme Court's impact on public education, Mr. Blanshard concluded:

> I think the most important factor moving us toward a secular society has been the educational factor. Our schools may not teach Johnny to read properly, but the fact that Johnny is in school until he is sixteen tends to lead toward the elimination of religious superstition. The average American child now acquires a high school education, and this militates against Adam and Eve and all other myths of alleged history. . . . I am convinced that religious belief of millions of Americans is only nominal. It is warm- hearted service religion, not creedal religion. When I was one of the editors of *The Nation* in the twenties, I wrote an editorial explaining that golf and intelligence were the two primary reasons that men did not attend church. Perhaps I would now say golf and a high school diploma.[28]

Mr. Blanshard continued to describe the engine driving this country toward secularism:

> Indeed, one of the factors moving this country toward a secularist society is the combination of the United States Supreme Court and public schools. Originally the United States Supreme Court had no jurisdiction over First Amendment issues because the First Amendment only applied to restrict the activities of the federal government. The First Amendment was not applicable to the individual states until the 1940s when the Supreme Court said it was applicable to the states.[29]

---

[28]*Id.*

[29]*Id.* The First Amendment Free Exercise Clause was first applied to the states in 1940 and the Establishment Clause was first applied to the states in 19447. *See Cantwell v. Connecticut*, 310 U.S. 296 (1940) (Free Exercise Clause); *Everson v. Board of Education*, 330 U.S. 1 (1947) (Establishment Clause); *Illinois ex rel. McCollum v. Board of Education*, 333 U.S. 203 (1948) (same).

In the early 1960s, the Supreme Court, utilizing the First Amendment, struck down prayer[30] and Bible readings[31] within the public school system. Testimony before the Supreme Court at that time suggested that Bible reading could be psychologically harmful to the child.[32] In 1980, the Supreme Court pulled the Ten Commandments from a classroom bulletin board in the state of Kentucky and thus from all bulletin boards in all public schools throughout the nation.[33] One state court addressing the issue of prayers in public schools lamented that

> an unacceptably high number of citizens who are undergoing difficult times in this country are children and young people. School-sponsored prayer might provide hope to sustain them and principles to guide them in the difficult choices they confront today. But the Constitution as the Supreme Court views it does not permit it. Choices are made in order to protect the interest of all citizens. Unfortunately, in this instance there is no satisfactory middle ground. . . . Those who are anti-prayer thus have been deemed the victors. This is the difficult but obligatory choice this court makes today.[34]

Not only has prayer been struck down in public school classrooms, but one federal court even ruled that invocations delivered before public high school football games violated the Constitution.[35] However, not all prayer has been removed from the public setting. Interestingly, the United States Supreme Court has ruled that state legislatures are permitted to select and compensate legislative chaplains to open legislative sessions with prayer.[36] Other federal courts have approved congressional chaplains[37] and the

---

[30]*Engel v. Vitale*, 370 U.S. 421 (1962).

[31]*School District of Abington Township v. Schempp*, 374 U.S. 203 (1963).

[32]*Id.*

[33]*Stone v. Graham*, 449 U.S. 39 (1980).

[34]*Bennett v. Livermore Unified School District*, 238 Cal. Rpt. 819 (1987).

[35]*Jager v. Douglas County School District*, 862 F.2d 824 (11th Cir. 1989), *cert. denied*, 490 U.S. 1090 (1989).

[36]*Marsh v. Chambers*, 463 U.S. 783 (1983).

[37]*Murray v. Buchanan*, 720 F.2d 689 (D.C. Cir. 1983).

practice of opening city or county board meetings with prayer.[38]

Nevertheless, significant restrictions have been placed upon religious liberty. While federal courts have increasingly removed religion from public places, at the same time, the United States Supreme Court has weakened the First Amendment Free Exercise Clause.[39] This strengthening of the Establishment Clause and concurrent weakening of the Free Exercise Clause has resulted in the rapid loss of First Amendment religious liberty. Notwithstanding, there are many religious freedoms that can still be exercised vigorously. If they are not, the freedoms that remain today will not remain tomorrow.

The Supreme Court tends to wax and wane from generation to generation. The Supreme Court will probably never return to the state of interpretation prior to 1940 when the First Amendment applied only to restrict the federal government. Part of the problem in moving away from the original intent of the First Amendment is that there has been no consistent jurisprudential approach to interpreting the Constitution. This is because under the present system the Supreme Court's interpretation changes from generation to generation instead of remaining consistent and absolute. Within this myriad of varying Supreme Court interpretations, many religious liberty rights still remain. This book is intended to be a guide to those religious liberty rights. It is important that this country continue to remain free and continue to recognize the importance of religious freedom. Once religion is suffocated or stuffed in a box, this country, as President Washington once said, will certainly fail.

The history of the former Soviet Union should teach the United States a lesson. For many years, religion was found mostly in churches turned into museums. However, religious belief and practice continued to operate underground. When the Soviet Communist government failed, the faithful rebounded and now religion flourishes within Russia. At one time, Madalyn Murray O'Hair, the atheist who removed Bible readings from school, wanted to defect to the Soviet Union so that she could live in a country run by atheistic principles. She lost her desire to defect long

---

[38]*Bogen v. Doty*, 598 F.2d 1110 (8th Cir. 1979).
[39]*Employment Division v. Smith*, 494 U.S. 872 (1990).

ago because the United States has certainly changed over the years and, to some extent, is trading places with the former Soviet Union in matters regarding religion. Freedom in this country was bought by sacrifice, and it might just be time for those who want religious freedom to consider the same sacrifices.

2

RELIGIOUS LIBERTY
HANGING IN THE BALANCE

I am concerned with the direction our country is heading. Religion in the public square is becoming an endangered species. I am not an alarmist, nor an extremist, but I am alarmed by attempts to cleanse religion from the public square.

Something needs to be done to protect people of faith from insidious discrimination. We are appalled by the human rights violations in China. Indeed we should be. Yet, in this country, public school students are reprimanded everyday for expressing their faith. Students are often made to feel that their faith is something to be ignored like the plague, something that must be left home, something that is inherently evil. The public needs to be better informed regarding religious liberty. The courts need to be a more hospitable place to people of faith.

Christians and other people of faith are not asking for special privileges. However, religious expression must at least be afforded an equal playing field. Currently, the playing field is not level. Religious expression and practices are treated as second class forms of speech and singled out for discrimination.

In the book, *The Powers in a Secular State*, published in 1951, Professor Edward S. Corwin accurately pointed out that the original understanding of the First Amendment was that Congress should not prescribe a national faith. Justice Joseph Story, who served on the United States Supreme Court from 1811 to 1845, and who was an adherent to the Unitarian faith, stated: "Probably at the time of the of the adoption of the Constitution and of the [First] Amendment to it . . . the general, if not the universal, sentiment in America was that Christianity ought to receive encouragement from the state, so far as such encouragement was not incompatible with the private rights of conscience, and the freedom of religious worship."[1] No one is asking for a Christianized America. However, people of faith should have an equal opportunity to express their convictions as someone who expresses their nontheistic views.

---

[1]Joseph Story, 2 *Commentaries on the Constitution of the United States* 593.

Historical Overview

To understand our present situation, we must consider the past. Oliver Wendell Holmes' statement is apropos: "A page of history is worth a volume of logic."[2] As the first act of the Continental Congress in 1774, the Rev. Mister Duche opened with prayer and read from Psalm 31.[3] From its inception Congress has begun its sessions with an invocation by a paid Chaplain.[4] Courts have historically opened their daily proceedings with the invocation "God save the United States and this Honorable Court."[5] Even the United States Supreme Court has Moses and the Ten Commandments inscribed above the bench recognizing the Biblical foundations of our legal heritage.[6]

George Washington began the tradition of taking the Presidential oath of office upon the Bible. When he assumed office in 1789, he stated, "it would be peculiarly improper to omit in this first official act my fervent supplications to that Almighty Being who rules over the Universe . . . ."[7] An impressive list of presidents subsequent to Washington have invoked the protection and help of Almighty God.[8]

James Madison, the father of the Bill of Rights, was a member of the Congressional committee that recommended the Chaplaincy

---

[2]*New York Trust Co. v. Eisner*, 256 U.S. 345, 349 (1921).

[3]Mr. Duche's prayer was as follows:

> Be Thou present O God of Wisdom and direct the council of this honorable assembly; enable them to settle all things on the best and surest foundations; that the scene of blood may be speedily closed; that order, harmony, and peace may be effectually restored, and truth and justice, religion and piety, prevail and flourish among the people. Preserve the health of their bodies, and the vigor of their minds, shower down on them, and the millions they represent, such temporal blessings as Thou seest expedient for them in this world, and crown them with everlasting glory in the world to come. All this we ask in the name and through the merits of Jesus Christ Thy Son and our Saviour. Amen.

[4]*Marsh v. Chambers*, 463 U.S. 783, 787-89 (1983). *See Lynch v. Donnelly*, 465 U.S. 668, 673-74 (1984).

[5]*Marsh*, 463 U.S. at 786.

[6]*See Lynch*, 465 U.S. at 677.

[7]*Engel v. Vitale*, 370 U.S. 421, 466 (1962) (Stewart, J., dissenting).

[8]*Engel*, 370 U.S. at 446-49.

system.[9] Madison voted for the bill authorizing payment of chaplains.[10] Rev. William Lynn was elected Chaplain of the House of Representatives and paid $500 from the federal treasury.

On September 25, 1789, the day the final agreement was made on the Bill of Rights, the House requested President Washington to proclaim a day of Thanksgiving to acknowledge "the many signal favors of Almighty God."[11] He proclaimed November 26, 1789, a day of Thanksgiving to offer "our prayers and supplications to the great Lord and ruler of nations, and beseech Him to pardon our national and other transgressions."[12] Later President Madison issued four Thanksgiving Day proclamations on July 9, 1812, July 23, 1813, November 16, 1814 and March 4, 1815.[13] Successive presidents have continued this tradition.

"The line we must draw between the permissible and impermissible is one which accords with history and faithfully reflects the understanding of the Founding Fathers."[14] "Government policies of accommodation, acknowledgment, and support for religion are an accepted part of our political and cultural heritage."[15]

In 1892 the United States Supreme Court considered the case of *The Church of the Holy Trinity v. United States*.[16] In that case, the Supreme Court unanimously held that a congressional statute forbidding the immigration of persons under contract to perform labor did not apply to an English minister who entered this country under a contract to preach at a New York church. After reviewing extensive legislative history, the Court concluded:

---

[9]H.R. Rep. No. 124, 33rd Cong., 1st Sess. (1789), *Reprinted in* 2 No. 2 *Reports of Committees of the House of Representatives* 4 (1854).

[10]1 *Annals of Cong.* 891 (J. Gales ed. 1834).

[11]H.R. Jour., 1st Cong., 1st Sess., 123 (1826 ed.); S. Jour., 1st Cong., 1st Sess., 88 (1820 ed.); *Lynch*, 465 U.S. at 675 n.2.

[12]*Id.*

[13]R. Cord, *Separation of Church & State* 31 (1982).

[14]*School District of Abington Township of Pennsylvania v. Schempp*, 374 U.S. 203, 294 (1963) (Brennan, J., concurring).

[15]*County of Allegheny v. American Civil Liberties Union*, 109 S. Ct. 3086, 3135 (1989) (Kennedy. J., concurring in part and dissenting in part).

[16]143 U.S. 457 (1892).

But beyond all these matters no purpose of action against religion can be imputed against any legislation, state or national, because this is a religious people. This is historically true. From the discovery of this continent to the present hour, there is a single voice making this affirmation. . . . If we pass beyond these matters to a view of American life as expressed by its laws, its business, its customs and its society, we find everywhere a clear recognition of the same truth. . . . These, and many other matters which might be noticed add a volume of unofficial declarations to the mass of organic utterances that this is a Christian nation.[17]

Tossing aside the original understanding of the First Amendment, and the volumes of history which document the religious liberty concerns of our founders, in 1989 the Supreme Court in the case of *County of Allegheny v. American Civil Liberties Union*,[18] stated that the purpose of the First Amendment was to mandate that the government remain secular. Justice Joseph Story, as noted above, indicated that the purpose of the First Amendment was to encourage Christianity. In 1892 the Supreme Court recognized the religious heritage of this country, but in 1989 the same Supreme Court found that the purpose of the First Amendment was to mandate that government remain secular. The Supreme Court's understanding of the Constitution has moved from encouragement, to neutrality, to mandating secularism.

In the 1960s the United States Supreme Court focused its attention on public schools. Paul Blanshard, a secular humanist, wrote in *The Humanist* magazine, that his "primary hero" in moving this nation toward a secular society was the United States Supreme Court. Reviewing the impact of the Supreme Court during the first seventy-five years of the twentieth century, Mr. Blanshard concluded that the Supreme Court cases have mandated secularistic teaching and that the most important factor moving America toward a secular society is the educational factor. He noted, "Our schools may not teach Johnny to read properly, but the fact that Johnny is

---

[17]*Id.* at 470-71.
[18]492 U.S. 573 (1989).

in school until he is sixteen tends to lead towards the elimination of religious superstition. The average American child now acquires a high school education, and this militates against Adam and Eve and all other myths of alleged history."[19] Since it struck down prayer[20] and Bible reading,[21] the Supreme Court removed the display of the Ten Commandments from a classroom bulletin board in the state of Kentucky,[22] and then ruled it was impermissible for a rabbi to pray at a public school graduation.[23]

The Establishment Clause And The *Lemon* Test

On its path to mandating a secular society, the Supreme Court developed the so called "Lemon test" as annunciated in its decision known as *Lemon v. Kurtzman*.[24] Under this three-part test, any government interaction with religion is constitutional only if it: (1) has a secular purpose; (2) does not promote or inhibit religion, or more fully defined, does not endorse religion; and (3) does not foster excessive governmental entanglement with religion. Despite repeated criticism of this unworkable test, it is still applied in church-state cases. Justices Scalia and Thomas soundly criticized the *Lemon* test in their stinging critique of the Court as follows:

> Like some ghoul in a late-night horror movie that repeatedly sits up in its grave and shuffles abroad, after being repeatedly killed and buried, *Lemon* stalks our Establishment Clause jurisprudence once again by frightening little children and school attorneys . . . . Its most recent burial, only last Term [in *Lee v. Weisman*] was, to be sure, not fully six-feet under . . . . Over the years, however, no fewer than five of the currently sitting Justices have, in their own opinion, personally driven pencils through the creature's heart . . . .

---

[19]Paul Blanshard, *Three Cheers for Our Secular State*, THE HUMANIST, March/April 1976, p. 17.

[20]*Engel v. Vitale*, 370 U.S. 421 (1962).

[21]*School District of Abington Township v. Schempp*, 372 U.S. 203 (1963).

[22]*Stone v. Graham*, 449 U.S. 39 (1980).

[23]*Lee v. Weisman*, 112 S. Ct. 2649 (1992).

[24]403 U.S. 602 (1971).

The secret of the *Lemon* test's survival, I think, is that it is so easy to kill. It is there to scare us (and our audience) when we wish to do so, but we can demand it to return to the tomb at will . . . . When we wish to strike down a practice it forbids, we evoke it . . . . Sometimes we take a middle ground of course, calling its three prongs "no more than helpful sign posts." Such a docile and useful monster is worth keeping around, at least in a somnolent state: one never knows when one might need him.[25]

Using the convoluted *Lemon* test, the Supreme Court has mandated that in order to pass Constitutional muster, religion must be diluted with secular influences. Thus, a nativity scene standing by itself is unconstitutional, but it magically becomes constitutional when secular symbols of the holiday are placed within its context. Christmas carols at public schools wherein children sing "Silent Night, Holy Night" are unconstitutional, but magically become constitutional, if the same children, during the same presentation, add to their repertoire the song, "Rudolph, The Red-Nosed Reindeer." Using the same test, one court ruled that student-initiated graduation prayers were unconstitutional,[26] while other courts have ruled that the same prayers were indeed constitutional.[27] Yet, the Supreme Court refuses to abandon its convoluted *Lemon* test. The *Lemon* test has created havoc, misunderstanding, and hostility toward religion.

The crisis we face today in protecting religious liberty is two-fold. First, over the past thirty years, the Supreme Court has ignored the original understanding of the First Amendment. Having cut the First Amendment free from its foundational base, the Supreme Court has pliably bent its protections to come in conformance with the majority of the Justices at any one time. Once the First Amendment was wrenched from its foundation, the Court was then

---

[25]*Lamb's Chapel v. Center Moriches Union Free School Dist.*, 113 S. Ct. 2141, 2150 (1993).

[26]*Harris v. Joint School Dist.*, 821 F. Supp. 638 (D. Idaho 1993), *modified*, 41 F.3d 447 (9th Cir. 1994), *vacated*, 115 S. Ct. 2604 (1995).

[27]*Jones v. Clear Creek Independent School Dist.*, 977 F.2d 963 (5th Cir. 1992), *cert. denied*, 113 S. Ct. 2950 (1993). *See also Adler v. Duval County School Bd.*, 851 F. Supp. 446 (M.D. Fla 1994).

forced to develop convoluted rules for its application, and therefore developed the *Lemon* test. The problem with the *Lemon* test is that it injects a great deal of subjectivity into its application, and from the very onset requires that the religious practice be secularized in order to pass constitutional scrutiny. Thus, religion is placed on the defensive, having to secularize its meaning and expression. Though the Court has been asked repeatedly to clarify this test, it has refused to do so.

Second, the lower federal courts have been forced to apply the *Lemon* test. Mass confusion has resulted in its application. For almost every federal district court opinion stating one proposition, one can find another federal district court holding exactly the opposite. Many of these cases have not been appealed through the appellate level, and most have not made their way to the United States Supreme Court. Consequently, many of the federal district court cases still remain and have never been clarified. For practical purposes, many religious liberties have been lost for lack of funds to carry on the battle. Because the Supreme Court has developed such an unworkable test, it has opened the floodgates to religious liberty litigation. Courts have gone in all directions applying the *Lemon* test, and religious adherents have often been frustrated when they first enter the federal district court and are unable to take the case any higher to have it clarified or possibly overturned. To illustrate this point, listed below are a number of conflicting decisions considering the same issue. In most cases only the federal district court cases have been cited simply to illustrate the confusion among those courts. While the propositions stated below may not be the final ruling of the court, as the case may have been appealed to a higher judicial body, the cases are cited to illustrate the religious liberty quagmire.[28]

In the area of release time, courts have allowed students to go off school premises for religious instruction[29] so long as the

---

[28]The cases cited between footnotes 29 and 90 are mostly citations to the federal district courts. These cases are not shepardized and may have been overruled by either a circuit court of appeals or the United States Supreme Court. The cases are listed only as examples of the confusion caused by the *Lemon* test and therefore may not represent the final holding or established law.

[29]*Lanner v. Wimmer*, 662 F.2d 1349 (10th Cir. 1981); *Smith v. Smith*, 523 F.2d 121 (4th Cir. 1975); *State v. Thompson*, 225 N.W.2d 678 (Wis. 1975).

instruction did not take place near the school building.[30] Some courts have ruled it is unconstitutional for students to handcarry attendance slips from the parochial instruction back to the public school.[31] Other courts have ruled that elective credit cannot be given for the parochial course.[32] Some courts have ruled that public school intercoms were permitted in seminary classrooms and public schools could maintain mailboxes for seminary instructors.[33] Schools have been forced to defend the recognition of religious observances[34] and the prohibition of school dances.[35]

A parochial school child can participate in a public school band course,[36] but cannot participate in an all-county band.[37] If a parochial school child needs remedial services, the district may be allowed to fund services at the student's school,[38] but such provision may be void on its face,[39] or funds may be allowed only if services are performed at "neutral sites."[40]

Public funds may be used to lease classroom space from a church related school, but only if public school children are shielded from religious influence.[41] Public schools may[42] or may not[43]

---

[30]*Doe v. Shenandoah County School Board*, 737 F. Supp. 913 (W.D. Va. 1990).

[31]*Lanner*, 662 F.2d at 1349; *Thompson*, 225 N.W.2d at 678.

[32]*Lanner*, 662 F.2d 1349; *See Minnesota Federation of Teachers v. Nelson*, 740 F. Supp. 694 (D. Minn. 1990).

[33]*Id.*

[34]*See Florey v. Sioux Falls School District 49-5*, 619 F.2d 1311 (8th Cir. 1980). *See also Student Members of Playcrafters v. Board of Education*, 424 A.2d 1192 (N.J. 1981) (School board forced to defend policy of prohibiting extracurricular activities on Friday, Saturday, and Sunday).

[35]*See Clayton v. Place*, 884 F.2d 376 (8th Cir. 1989).

[36]*Snyder v. Charlotte Public School District*, 365 N.W.2d 151 (1985).

[37]*Thomas v. Allegheny County Board of Education*, 51 Md. App. 312, 443 A.2d 622 (1982).

[38]*See Walker v. San Francisco Unified School District*, 741 F. Supp. 1386 (N.D. Cal. 1990), *reh'g denied*, 62 F.3d 300 (9th Cir. 1995); *Thomas v. Schmidt*, 397 F. Supp. 203 (D.R.I. 1975).

[39]*Wamble v. Bell*, 598 F. Supp. 1356 (W.D. Mo. 1984); *Viss v. Pittenger*, 345 F. Supp. 1349 (E.D. Pa. 1972).

[40]*Felton v. Secretary*, 739 F.2d 48 (2d Cir. 1984); *Pulido v. Cavasos*, 728 F. Supp. 574 (W.D. Mo. 1989); *Filler v. Port Washington University Free School District*, 436 F. Supp. 1231 (E.D.N.Y. 1977); *Wolman v. Essex*, 417 F. Supp. 1113 (S.D. Ohio 1976).

[41]*Thomas v. Schmidt*, 397 F. Supp. 203 (D.R.I. 1975).

[42]*Spacco v. Bridgewater School Department*, 722 F. Supp. 834 (D. Mass. 1989); *Americans United for Separation of Church & State v. Paire*, 359 F. Supp. 505 (D.N.H. 1973); *Americans United for Separation of Church & State v. Paire*, 348 F. Supp. 506

lease classroom space in parochial schools. Private school students or religious organizations may[44] or may not[45] be permitted to utilize public school facilities. Financial assistance programs for needy students attending private schools have failed the *Lemon* test.[46] Some courts have disqualified private college students from receiving government tuition grants,[47] while other courts have allowed such grants.[48] Some plans have been upheld only when the use of the funds is restricted.[49] Students may receive grants to study philosophy or religion in public schools, but not theology in pervasively sectarian schools failing a 36-prong test.[50] However,

---

(D.N.H. 1972); *Citizens to Advance Public Education v. Porter*, 237 N.W.2d 232 (Mich. 1976) (shared time secular education program).

[43]*See Americans United for Separation of Church & State v. School District of Grand Rapids*, 546 F. Supp. 1071 (W.D. Mich 1982); *Americans United for Separation of Church & State v. Porter*, 485 F. Supp. 432 (W.D. Mich. 1980); *Americans United for Separation of Church & State v. Board of Education*, 369 F. Supp. 1059 (E.D. Ky. 1974).

[44]*Gregoire v. Centennial School District*, 907 F.2d 1366 (3d Cir. 1990); *Parents Association of P.S. 16 v. Quinones*, 803 F.2d 1235 (2d Cir. 1986); *Country Hills Christian Church v. Unified School District*, 560 F. Supp. 1207 (D. Kan. 1983); *Resnick v. East Brunswick Township Board of Education*, 389 A.2d 944 (N.J. 1978); *cf. Chess v. Widmar*, 635 F.2d 1310 (8th Cir. 1980) (University must allow recognized student organizations to use school facilities for religious purposes).

[45]*Lubbock Civil Liberties Union v. Lubbock Independent School District*, 669 F.2d 1038 (5th Cir. 1982); *Lamb's Chapel v. Center Moriches School District*, 736 F. Supp. 1247 (E.D.N.Y. 1990); *Resnick v. East Brunswick Township Board of Education*, 343 A.2d 127 (N.J. 1975); *cf. Wallace v. Washoe County School Board*, 701 F. Supp. 187 (D. Nev. 1988); *Ford v. Manuel*, 629 F. Supp. 771 (N.D. Ohio 1985).

[46]*Wolman v. Essex*, 342 F. Supp. 399 (S.D. Ohio 1972); *People v. Howlett*, 305 N.E.2d 129 (Ill. 1973); *Weiss v. Bruno*, 509 P.2d 973 (1973), *contra Barrera v. Wheeler*, 475 F.2d 1338 (8th Cir. 1973).

[47]*See d'Errico v. Lesmeister*, 570 F. Supp. 158 (D.N.D. 1983); *Smith v. Board of Governors*, 429 F. Supp. 871 (D.N.C. 1977); *Americans United for Separation of Church & State v. Dunn*, 384 F. Supp. 714 (M.D. Tenn. 1974); *Americans United for Separation of Church & State v. Bubb*, 379 F. Supp. 872 (D. Kan. 1974); *Opinion of the Justices*, 280 So. 2d 547 (Ala. 1973); *State v. Swanson*, 219 N.W.2d 727 (Neb. 1974). *But cf. Durham v. McLeod*, 192 S.E.2d 202 (S.C. 1972) (loans constitutional).

[48]*See Americans United for Separation of Church & State v. Blanton*, 433 F. Supp. 97 (M.D. Tenn. 1977); *Lendall v. Cook*, 432 F. Supp. 971 (D. Ark. 1977); *Americans United for Separation of Church & State v. Rogers*, 538 S.W.2d 711 (Mo. 1976); *Cecrle v. Illinois Educational Facilities Authority*, 288 N.E.2d 399 (Ill. 1972).

[49]*See Walker*, 741 F. Supp. at 1386; *Lendall*, 432 F. Supp at 971; *Smith v. Board of Governors*, 429 F. Supp. 871 (D.N.C. 1977); *Americans United for Separation of Church & State Fund, Inc. v. State*, 648 P.2d 1072 (Colo. 1982).

[50]*See Minnesota Federation of Teachers v. Nelson*, 740 F. Supp 694 (D. Minn. 1990); *But cf. In Re Dickerson*, 474 A.2d 30 (N.J. 1983) (testamentary scholarships for ministry students at public institute constitutional).

Veteran's Administration, and some handicap tuition assistance programs, have generally been held valid for recipients attending sectarian schools.[51]

Some courts have ruled that the state may provide bus transportation to private school children,[52] but in Rhode Island, the enabling statute was stricken three times.[53] Public funds cannot be used to provide textbooks to private school students in some states,[54] but in others, it is acceptable for the state to reimburse parochial schools for textbook expenditures.[55] Decisions have limited the provision of educational materials to sectarian schools.[56] In some cases states may not reimburse a sectarian school for costs incurred performing state-mandated tasks, such as testing and record-keeping,[57] but in other cases it is permissible.[58]

State regulation of private schools regarding compulsory attendance,[59] teacher certification,[60] and curriculum[61] have been

---

[51]*Witters v. Washington Department of Service of the Blind*, 474 U.S. 481 (1986); *Bob Jones University v. Johnson*, 396 F. Supp. 597 (D.S.C. 1974).

[52]*Rhode Island Federation of Teachers v. Norberg*, 630 F.2d 855 (1st Cir. 1980) (provision valid but not severable); *Cromwell Property Owners Association v. Toffolon*, 495 F. Supp. 915 (D. Conn. 1979); *Board of Education v. Bakalis*, 299 N.E.2d 737 (1973); *State v. School District*, 320 N.W.2d 472 (Neb. 1982); *Springfield School District v. Department of Education*, 397 A.2d 1154 (Pa. 1979); *cf. Americans United for Separation of Church & State v. Benton*, 413 F. Supp. 955 (S.D. Iowa 1975) (no cross-district transport).

[53]*Members of Jamestown School Committee v. Schmidt*, 699 F.2d 1 (1st Cir. 1983); *Members of Jamestown School Committee v. Schmidt*, 525 F. Supp. 1045 (D.R.I. 1981); *Members of Jamestown School Committee v. Schmidt*, 427 F. Supp. 1338 (D.R.I. 1977).

[54]*California Teachers Association v. Riles*, 632 P.2d 953 (Cal. 1981); *Mallory v. Barrera*, 544 S.W.2d 556 (Mo. 1976); *Paster v. Tussey*, 512 S.W.2d 97 (Mo. 1974); *contra Elbe v. Yankton Independent School District No. 1*, 714 F.2d 848 (8th Cir. 1983); *Wolman v. Essex*, 417 F. Supp. 1113 (S.D. Ohio 1976); *Cunningham v. Lutjeharms*, 437 N.W.2d 806 (Neb. 1989).

[55]*Americans United for Separation of Church & State v. Paire*, 359 F. Supp. 505 (D.N.H. 1973); *Pennsylvania Department of Education v. The First School*, 348 A.2d 458 (Pa. 1975).

[56]*Americans United for Separation of Church & State v. Oakey*, 339 F. Supp. 545 (D. Vt. 1972); *but see Wolman v. Essex*, 417 F. Supp. 1113 (S.D. Ohio 1976).

[57]*Committee for Public Education & Religious Liberty v. Levitt*, 342 F. Supp. 439 (S.D.N.Y. 1972).

[58]*Committee for Public Education & Religious Liberty v. Levitt*, 461 F. Supp. 1123 (S.D.N.Y. 1978); *Thomas v. Schmidt*, 397 F. Supp. 203 (D.R.I. 1975).

[59]*Fellowship Baptist Church v. Benton*, 815 F.2d 485 (8th Cir. 1987); *Attorney General v. Bailey*, 436 N.E.2d 139 (Mass. 1982); *State v. Shaver*, 294 N.W.2d 883 (N.D. 1980).

[60]*Fellowship Baptist Church*, 815 F.2d at 486; *but cf. Bangor Baptist Church v. State*, 549 F. Supp. 1208 (D. Me. 1982); *Johnson v. Charles City Community Schools Board of Education*, 368 N.W.2d 74 (1985); *Sheridan Road Baptist Church v. Department of*

upheld. State employees may not teach or provide remedial services in private schools,[62] but may visit classrooms to observe both secular and religious teaching, suggest teacher replacements, and review accreditation.[63] However, student teachers may not receive credit for teaching at parochial schools.[64]

State inquiry into a religious organization's operating costs violates the Establishment Clause,[65] unless requested by the Internal Revenue Service.[66] The state may enforce compliance with minimum wage laws,[67] the Fair Labor Standards Act,[68] and force participation in FICA and FUTA,[69] despite an organization's

---

Education, 348 N.W.2d 263 (Mich. 1984); *State v. Faith Baptist Church*, 301 N.W.2d 571 (Neb. 1981). *cf. State v. Anderson*, 427 N.W.2d 316 (N.D. 1988) (home schooling parents violated teacher certification requirements).

[61]*New Life Baptist Church Academy v. East Longmeadow*, 885 F.2d 952 (1st Cir. 1989); *Sheridan Road Baptist Church v. Department of Education*, 348 N.W. 2d 263 (Mich. 1984); *State v. Faith Baptist Church*, 301 N.W.2d 571 (Neb. 1981); *cf. New Jersey State Board of Higher Education v. Board of Directors*, 448 A.2d 988 (N.J. 1982) (prohibiting conferring of degree by unlicensed institution applied to a sectarian college whose religious doctrine precluded state licensure).

[62]*Pulido v. Cavazos*, 728 F. Supp. 574 (W.D. Mo. 1989); *Wamble*, 598 F. Supp 1356; *Americans United for Separation of Church & State v. Porter*, 485 F. Supp. 432 (W.D. Mich. 1980); *Americans United for Separation of Church & State v. Board of Education*, 369 F. Supp 1059 (E.D. Ky. 1974); *but see Walker*, 741 F. Supp. at 1386.

[63]*New Life Baptist Church Academy v. East Longmeadow*, 885 F.2d 952 (1st Cir. 1989).

[64]*Stark v. St. Cloud State University*, 802 F.2d 1046 (8th Cir. 1986).

[65]*Surinach v. Pesquera de Busquets*, 604 F.2d 73 (1st Cir. 1979); *Fernandez v. Lima*, 465 F. Supp. 493 (N.D. Tex. 1979). *See also Heritage Village Church & Missionary Fellowship v. State*, 263 A.2d 726 (N.C. 1980) (act requiring only certain religious groups to file information is unconstitutional).

[66]*United States v. Freedom Church*, 613 F.2d 1316 (1st Cir. 1979); *Lutheran Social Service v. United States*, 583 F. Supp. 1298 (D. Minn. 1984); *cf. Hernandez v. Commissioner*, 819 F.2d 1212 (1st Cir. 1987); *St. Bartholomew's Church v. City of New York*, 728 F. Supp. 958 (S.D.N.Y. 1989) (state inquiry into church records does not violate entanglement prong).

[67]*Archbishop of Roman Catholic Apostolic Archdiocese v. Guardiola*, 628 F. Supp. 1173 (D.P.R. 1985); *Donovan v. Shenandoah Baptist Church*, 573 F. Supp. 320 (W.D. Va. 1983).

[68]*Dole v. Shenandoah Baptist Church*, 899 F.2d 1389 (4th Cir. 1990); *E.E.O.C. v. Freemont Christian School*, 781 F.2d 1362 (9th Cir. 1986); *Ninth & O St. Baptist Church v. E.E.O.C.*, 616 F. Supp. 1231 (W.D. Ky. 1985); *Russell v. Belmont College*, 554 F. Supp. 667 (M.D. Tenn. 1982).

[69]*South Ridge Baptist Church v. Industrial Commission*, 911 F.2d 1203 (6th Cir. 1990) (church included within workers' compensation system); *Bethel Baptist Church v. United States*, 822 F.2d 1334 (3d Cir. 1987); *Young Life v. Division of Employment & Training*, 650 P.2d 515 (Colo. 1982) (religious organization subject to unemployment tax); *Baltimore Lutheran High School Association v. Employment Security Administration*, 490 A.2d 701 (Md. 1985) (school subject to unemployment tax); *Contra Grace Lutheran Church v. North Dakota Employment Security Bureau*, 294 N.W. 767 (N.D. 1980) (church not subject to

religious beliefs to the contrary. The National Labor Relations
Board may not be applicable to parochial schools,[70] but a state
labor board may have jurisdiction.[71] Sectarian schools are
prohibited from utilizing CETA workers.[72] Civil rights statutes
have not been enforced against religious organizations,[73] but courts
have split as to whether the "reasonable accommodation"
requirement may be enforced against secular employees.[74] As a
result, religious institutions have been forced to departmentalize
between those employees who carry on the ministry and mission of
the institution from other employees who perform routine tasks.
Thus, while a religious institution may discriminate on the basis of
religion in hiring and firing a school professor, it may not do the
same to a secretary.

Two entanglement triangles arise in the provision of child care.
First, the state may purchase child care services from religiously
affiliated organizations[75] and may consider the religious preference

---

unemployment tax); *The Christian Jew Foundation v. State*, 353 S.W.2d 607 (Tex. 1983)
(organization exempt from unemployment tax); *Community Lutheran School v. Iowa
Department of Job Service*, 326 N.W.2d 286 (Iowa 1982) (school exempt from
unemployment tax).

[70]*Universidad v. N.L.R.B.*, 793 F.2d 383 (1st Cir. 1985); *see also N.L.R.B. v. Salvation
Army*, 763 F.2d 1 (1st Cir. 1985); *N.L.R.B. v. Bishop Ford Central Catholic High School*, 623
F.2d 818 (2d Cir. 1980); *Catholic Bishop v. N.L.R.B.*, 559 F.2d 1112 (2d Cir. 1977);
McCormick v. Hirsh, 460 F. Supp. 1337 (M.D. Pa. 1978); *contra N.L.R.B. v. St. Louis
Christian Home*, 663 F.2d 60 (8th Cir. 1981); *Grutka v. Barbour*, 549 F.2d 5 (7th Cir. 1977).

[71]*Goldsborough Christian Schools, Inc. v. United States*, 436 F. Supp. 1314 (E.D.N.C.
1977); *cf. Catholic High School Association v. Culvert*, 753 F.2d 1161 (2d Cir. 1985).

[72]*Decker v. O'Donnell*, 663 F.2d 598 (7th Cir. 1980) (CETA created entanglement); *see
also, Decker v. Department of Labor*, 473 F. Supp. 770 (E.D. Wis. 1979).

[73]*Dayton Christian Schools v. Ohio Civil Rights Commission*, 766 F.2d 932 (6th Cir.
1985); *Cochran v. St. Louis Preparatory Seminary*, 717 F. Supp. 1413 (E.D. Mo. 1989);
Maguire v. Marquette University, 627 F. Supp. 1499 (E.D. Wis. 1986); *E.E.O.C. v.
Southwestern Baptist Theological Seminary*, 485 F. Supp. 255 (N.D. Tex. 1980); *E.E.O.C.
v. Mississippi College*, 451 F. Supp. 564 (S.D. Miss. 1978); *contra Dolter v. Wahlert High
School*, 483 F. Supp. 266 (N.D. Iowa 1980); *McLeod v. Providence Christian School*, 408
N.W.2d 146 (Mich. 1987); *but see E.E.O.C. v. Pacific Press Publishing Association*, 676
F.2d 1272 (9th Cir. 1982).

[74]*Protos v. Volkswagon of America, Inc.*, 797 F.2d 129 (3d Cir. 1986); *Nottleson v. Smith
Steel Workers*, 643 F.2d 445 (7th Cir. 1981); *E.E.O.C. v. Jefferson Smurfit Corp.*, 724 F.
Supp. 881 (M.D. Fla. 1989); *Gavin v. Peoples Natural Gas Co.*, 464 F. Supp. 622 (W.D. Pa.
1979); *Michigan Department of Civil Rights v. General Motors*, 317 N.W. 16 (Mich. 1982);
American Motors Corp. v. Department of Industry, Labor, & Human Relations, 286 N.W.2d
847 (Wis. 1978).

[75]*Wilder v. Bernstein*, 848 F.2d 1338 (2nd Cir. 1988).

of the parents for placement,[76] but the agency cannot impose its religious doctrine upon a child.[77] Second, religious child care facilities exempted from licensure may or may not be deemed to fail the *Lemon* test.[78] Church-run day care centers are subject to zoning restrictions,[79] but a city may not exempt them from requirements imposed upon commercial operators.[80]

Courts are divided over whether the state may[81] or may not[82] erect a cross as a war memorial. Where a state exercised eminent domain over a cemetery, a court prohibited the state from erecting crosses and a statue of Jesus, but allowed the state to provide and erect religious markers chosen by the descendants.[83] Crosses placed on government property have generally been prohibited,[84] but crosses and religious symbols on official seals may or may not be permissible.[85]

---

[76]*Id.*, *cf. Dickens v. Ernesto*, 281 N.E.2d 153 (N.Y. 1982) (religious affiliation requirements in adoption proceeding constitutional); *Bonjour v. Bonjour*, 592 P.2d 1233 (Alaska 1979) (statute specifying religious needs of child upheld); *Zucco v. Garrett*, 501 N.E.2d 875 (Ill. 1986) (awarding custody based on religious practices is abuse of discretion).

[77]*Arneth v. Gross*, 699 F. Supp. 450 (S.D.N.Y. 1988).

[78]*Forest Hills Early Learning Center v. Lukhard*, 728 F.2d 230 (4th Cir. 1984); *Forte v. Colder*, 725 F. Supp. 488 (M.D. Fla. 1989); *see The Corpus Christi Baptist Church, Inc. v. Texas Department of Human Resources*, 481 F. Supp. 1101 (S.D. Tex. 1979); *Forest Hills Early Learning Center, Inc. v. Grace Baptist Church*, 846 F.2d 260 (4th Cir. 1988); *North Valley Baptist Church v. McMahon*, 696 F. Supp. 578 (E.D. Cal. 1988); *Cohen v. City of Des Plaines*, 742 F. Supp. 458 (N.D. Ill. 1990); *State v. Corpus Christi People's Baptist Church, Inc.*, 683 S.W.2d 692 (Tex. 1984); *State Department of Social Services v. Emmanuel Baptist Pre-School*, 455 N.W.2d 1 (Mich. 1990); *Pre-School Owner's Association v. Department of Children & Family Services*, 518 N.E.2d 1018 (Ill. 1988); *Arkansas Day Care Association v. Clinton*, 577 F. Supp. 388 (E.D. Ark. 1983). *cf. State v. McDonald*, 787 P.2d 466 (Okla. 1989) (religious affiliated "boy's ranch" subject to state licensing requirements).

[79]*First Assembly of God v. City of Alexandria*, 739 F.2d 942 (4th Cir. 1984).

[80]*Cohen v. City of Des Plaines*, 742 F. Supp. 458 (N.D. Ill. 1990); *cf. Arkansas Day Care Association*, 577 F. Supp. 388 (statute disparately treated religious facilities).

[81]*Eugene Sand & Gravel, Inc. v. Eugene*, 558 P.2d 338 (1976).

[82]*Jewish War Veterans v. United States*, 695 F. Supp. 3 (D.D.C. 1988).

[83]*Birdine v. Moreland*, 579 F. Supp. 412 (N.D. Ga. 1983).

[84]*Mendelsohn v. City of St. Cloud*, 719 F. Supp. 1065 (M.D. Fla. 1989); *Hewitt v. Joyner*, 705 F. Supp. 1443 (C.D. Cal. 1989); *ACLU v. Rabun County Chamber of Commerce, Inc.*, 510 F. Supp. 886 (N.D. Ga. 1981); *Fox v. City of Los Angeles*, 587 P.2d 663 (Cal. 1978).

[85]*Saladin v. City of Milledgeville*, 812 F.2d 687 (11th Cir. 1987); *Friedman v. Board of City Commissioners*, 781 F.2d 777 (10th Cir. 1985); *Foremaster v. City of St. George*, 882 F.2d 1485 (10th Cir. 1989); *Harris v. City of Zion*, 927 F.2d 1401 (7th Cir. 1991); *Johnson v. Board of County Commissioners*, 528 F. Supp. 919 (D.N.M. 1981); *Murray v. City of Austin*, 744 F. Supp. 771 (W.D. Tex. 1990).

The Ten Commandments have been removed from schools,[86] but permitted to remain on other public property.[87] A legislature may designate a room for prayer and meditation, but religious decorations or use of the room may be prohibited.[88]

An order of then-Governor Ronald Reagan giving state employees a three hour paid holiday on Good Friday violated the Establishment Clause,[89] but a school district was permitted to designate Good Friday a paid holiday in conjunction with a Union Contract.[90]

As a result of our abandonment of the original understanding of First Amendment and the development of the *Lemon* test, religion has been put on the defensive by forcing it to assume a cloak of secularism.

When there is some form of religious expression that we wish to keep, as Justice Scalia said, we either bury the *Lemon* test, or we interpret it to our own pleasing. For example, Justice William Brennan stated that the phrase "under God" in our Pledge of Allegiance is constitutional because it no longer has a religious purpose or meaning.[91] Under the Supreme Court's rationale, certain religious phrases, such as "In God We Trust," would be constitutional because it is a secular form of religion. In other words, we have used the phrase so many times that it has lost its religious meaning. Under this bizarre analysis, at one time the phrase would probably have been unconstitutional, but because we have used it so much, it has become constitutional under the *Lemon* test.

The Demise Of The Free Exercise Clause

While our Establishment Clause jurisprudence has become schizophrenic, the Free Exercise Clause of the First Amendment has

---

[86]*Ring v. Grand Forks Public School District*, 483 F. Supp. 272 (D.N.D. 1980).

[87]*Anderson v. Salt Lake City Corp.*, 475 F.2d 29 (10th Cir. 1972).

[88]*Van Zandt v. Thompson*, 839 F.2d 1215 (7th Cir. 1988).

[89]*Mandel v. Hodges*, 54 Cal. App. 3d 596 (1976).

[90]*California School Employees Association v. Sequoia Union High School District*, 67 Cal. App. 3d 157 (1977); *cf. Cammack v. Waihee*, 673 F. Supp. 1524 (D. Haw. 1987) (state may declare Good Friday a legal holiday).

[91]*Schempp*, 374 U.S. at 304.

taken a back seat to other constitutional protections. For example, in 1990 the Supreme Court in *Employment Division v. Smith*,[92] ruled that we no longer have the "luxury" in this country to tolerate religious liberty. The Supreme Court ruled that any neutral and generally applicable law which impacts religion will nevertheless be upheld as constitutional.[93] That ruling overturned decades of Supreme Court interpretations that granted special protection to the free exercise of religion. As a result of the *Smith* case, religious liberty has been relegated to second class protection. Now the religious liberty of private citizens is no greater than the religious liberty granted to prisoners.[94] According to Chief Judge Posner of the Seventh Circuit Court of Appeals, "the principle derived from the free-exercise clause of the First Amendment [is] that government must accommodate its laws of general applicability to the special needs of the religious minorities. [T]hat principle is moribund after *Employment Division v. Smith*."[95] In another case the Seventh Circuit again recognized that "*Smith* cut back, possibly to minute dimensions, the doctrine that requires government to accommodate, at some cost, minority religious preferences."[96] Indeed, the *Smith* decision represents "a considerable shift in the

---

[92]494 U.S. 872 (1990).

[93]Prior to the Supreme Court's decision in *Employment Division v. Smith*, 494 U.S. 872 (1990), thirty years of Supreme Court jurisprudence had established that government may not substantially burden the free exercise of religion absent a demonstration that such burden was the least restrictive means of furthering a compelling government interest. *See, e.g., Wisconsin v. Yoder*, 406 U.S. 205 (1972) (state's interest in universal education was not sufficiently compelling to outweigh religious tradition of Amish forbidding formal education past the eighth grade); *Sherbert v. Verner*, 374 U.S. 398 (1963) (compelling state interest did not justify denial of unemployment benefits to Seventh-day Adventist who established working on Saturday would require her to break her Sabbath). Noting that *Smith* "dramatically weakened the Constitutional protection for freedom of religion," S. Rep. No. 111, 103rd Cong., 1st Sess. 3 (1993), Congress passed RFRA "to restore the compelling state interest test as set forth in *Sherbert v. Verner* . . . and *Wisconsin v. Yoder* . . . and to guarantee its application in all cases where free exercise of religion is substantially burdened." 42 U.S.C. § 2000bb(b). The Supreme Court later ruled the Religious Freedom Restoration Act unconstitutional. *City of Boerne v. Flores*, 117 S. Ct. 2157 (1997).

[94]In a prisoner rights case, the Eighth Circuit Court of Appeals stated that "*Smith* does not alter the rights of prisoners; it simply brings the free exercise rights of private citizens closer to those of prisoners." *Salaam v. Lockhart*, 905 F.2d 1168, 1171 (8th Cir. 1990).

[95]*Miller v. Civil City of South Bend*, 904 F.2d 1081, 1102-03 (7th Cir. 1990) (en banc) (citations omitted).

[96]*Hunafa v. Murphy*, 907 F.2d 46, 48 (7th Cir. 1990).

Court's direction in free exercise jurisprudence."[97] Prior to the *Smith* decision, there was a presumption that religious organizations were not intended to be regulated by Congress unless they were specifically included in the statutory language,[98] but after *Smith*, there is a presumption that religious groups are not to receive any special treatment unless specifically stated by the legislature.[99] Since *Smith*, Native American Indians have been prohibited by some courts from using peyote during their worship services.[100] Landmark laws which prohibit a church from expanding its ministry have nevertheless been upheld as constitutional because they are neutral and generally applicable regulations.[101] As a result of the *Smith* decision, neutral zoning laws of general applicability have restricted the ability of churches to either locate their ministry,[102] or to carry on their Biblical mandate and mission to comfort the homeless or feed the hungry.[103]

To counteract the Supreme Court's abandonment of religious liberty, Congress in 1993 passed the Religious Freedom Restoration Act (hereafter "RFRA").[104] Unfortunately, in 1997, the Supreme Court ruled RFRA unconstitutional.[105]

If the *Smith* decision were in existence at the time of

---

[97]*United States v. Board of Education for the School District of Philadelphia*, 911 F.2d 882, 888 n.3 (3rd Cir. 1990).

[98]*N.L.R.B. v. Catholic Bishop of Chicago*, 440 U.S. 490 (1979).

[99]*Intercommunity Center for Justice and Peace v. INS*, 910 F.2d 42 (2d Cir. 1990).

[100]*Peyote Way Church of God v. Thornburgh*, 922 F.2d 1210 (5th Cir. 1991).

[101]*St. Bartholomew's Church v. City of New York*, 914 F.2d 348 (2d Cir. 1990).

It is obvious that the Landmarks Law has drastically restricted the Church's ability to raise revenues to carry out its various charitable and ministerial programs. In this particular case, the revenues are very large because the Community House is on land that would be extremely valuable if put to commercial uses. Nevertheless, we understand Supreme Court decisions to understand that neutral regulations that diminish the income of a religious organization do not implicate the Free Exercise Clause.

Id. at 355.

[102]*Cornerstone Bible Church v. City of Hastings*, 948 F.2d 464 (8th Cir. 1990).

[103]*First Assembly of God v. Collier County*, 20 F.3d 419 (11th Cir. 1993), *opinion modified on denial of reh'g*, 27 F.3d 526 (11th Cir. 1994), *cert. denied*, 115 S. Ct. 730 (1995).

[104]42 U.S.C. § 2000bb.

[105]*City of Boerne*, 117 S. Ct. at 2157.

Prohibition, the Roman Catholic Church would have been prohibited from practicing communion. In other words, the church would be prohibited from taking wine during the communion service because the church would have faced a neutral law of general applicability that forbade the sale and consumption of alcoholic beverages. After *Smith*, Roman Catholic teaching hospitals have been forced to choose between performing abortions contrary to their sincerely held religious beliefs, or forfeiting their teaching hospital status. During the three year reign of terror from 1990 to 1993, religious freedom was significantly damaged. The only way to maintain a religious freedom claim was to link it up to some other form of constitutional protection such as Free Speech or Equal Protection. If that could be done, the religious adherent would have the same protections afforded to the First Amendment Free Speech or Equal Protection Clauses. Standing alone, the Free Exercise Clause is no longer powerful enough to protect the religious liberty of our citizens. Today, religious freedom hangs in a very delicate balance. The Supreme Court has already indicated that we no longer have the luxury of tolerating the free exercise of religion.

The combination of the Supreme Court's convoluted *Lemon* test mandating a secular society with the loss of our free exercise protections, is the reason we need a religious equality amendment. Below is a sampling of cases that people of faith have encountered in the legal religious morass.

Sample Cases

The Supreme Court's interpretation of the Establishment and Free Exercise Clauses of the First Amendment has caused confusion and generated disinformation. Unfortunately, religious liberty is often the loser. Listed below are some examples of discrimination faced by people of faith. All of the examples represent unconstitutional violations of religious liberty. The problem is that these violations occurred at all. Certainly the Supreme Court is partly to blame for this confusion.

The Bible

A fourth-grade student had his Bible confiscated when he brought it to public school. The week prior to this incident he was awarded Student of the Week, and the week of this incident he was awarded the higher honor of Very Special Student. Before the school bell rang, signaling the beginning of another school day, Joshua was silently reading his Bible when his teacher approached him, confiscated the Bible, and stated in front of the entire class, "This is a public school, not a Bible school." The teacher explained this was due to the separation of church and state. On a subsequent day the student brought his Bible back to school. The Bible was closed, sitting by his other books, when the teacher again approached him, pointed to the Bible, and summoned the principal, after stating, "We need to talk to the principal about that thing." The student was taken to the principal's office where he was interrogated for more than an hour. He was asked questions like "Why do you read the Bible?" and "Where do you go to church?" He was then forced to sit in the corner of a room, detained the entire day for the sole "crime" of bringing his Bible to school. When Joshua's father subsequently spoke to the principal, she stated that as soon as students step on the school bus, they are under the school's jurisdiction and they cannot bring their Bible, nor can they share their faith during non-class time because to do so might offend another student. The principal acknowledged that students can talk about politics or read secular books, but religion was a different matter.

* * * *

In another case a Hispanic student by the name of Jesus was told that he could not bring his pictorial Bible to free reading time. With only a few weeks left in the school year, the teacher in charge of the free reading class told the students to bring books from home that they wanted to read during free reading time. Jesus brought his pictorial Bible and was reading it to himself when the teacher approached him, and stated he could not bring the Bible to school because of the separation of church and state. He was forced to put the Bible under his desk, and since he did not have anything else to read, was forced to lay his head down on top of his desk for the remainder of the class. Maria, his mother, had migrated from Cuba to the United States twenty years previously. She stated that she came here for the purpose of freedom and was astounded at what she encountered.[106]

Posters

Peggy has ten children in public schools in Wisconsin. Families were asked to participate in celebration of the twenty-fifth anniversary of the school by making posters on the theme of "Honor the past, embrace the present, prepare for the future." The family's poster has four sections: faith, family, country, and knowledge. In the faith section, there was a picture of a person wearing a t-shirt with the word "Jesus." The family included this picture to highlight the importance of their faith and the faith in the community. The poster was originally displayed, but the principal removed it, while the others remained on display. The poster was removed solely because one of the images was religious. The school had the impression that it must censor this poster because the display was religious.

Show and Tell

A sixth-grade class was assigned the task of doing a book report and reading their reports in front of the entire class. A sixth-grader by the name of Lisa wanted to do her book report on the book of Genesis. None of the other students were required to give disclaimers distancing the class from the book being reviewed, but Lisa was told she has to state a disclaimer to the effect that while she realized everyone in the class was not Christian, these were her own personal views. Lisa gave her book review, but did not state such a disclaimer. Consequently, she was reprimanded by the teacher. No other student was required to publicly give a disclaimer prior to their book reports.

---

[106]For brevity's sake, I have mentioned only two cases involving students bringing Bibles to school. For the record, I have encountered many of these instances throughout the country.

Literature Distribution

On October 30, a fifth-grade student by the name of Amber brought literature to class in a backpack. The literature consisted of an invitation to an after school program, which was an alternative to a Halloween party presented by a church, and a Jews for Jesus gospel tract. She approached her teacher and asked if she could hand out this literature to her fellow classmates during noninstructional time. The teacher summoned the principal, and after the principal came to the classroom and noticed that the material was religious, he took it back to his office. At the end of the school day, Amber asked her teacher if she could have her literature back because she was going to an after school program and wanted to pass out the literature to her friends. The teacher directed her to talk with the principal. When she approached the principal, he told Amber, "I will not have religious literature on my campus." The principal had actually thrown the literature in the garbage and would not return it to Amber. Amber was devastated by this action and began crying. This case resulted in a lawsuit because students were permitted to distribute secular literature but not religious literature. The school lost this lawsuit when the federal court ruled that the principal's actions and the school board policy were unconstitutional, but recent reports indicate that despite the federal court ruling, the school has again taken action against students to prohibit them from bringing religious literature on campus.

* * * *

An eighth-grade student by the name of Jennifer wanted to distribute the religious newspaper, *Issues and Answers*, to her fellow classmates during noninstructional time. When she approached the assistant principal and asked for permission to do so, the assistant principal inspected the newspaper and stated the school prohibited students from bringing Bibles, religious literature, or literature that quotes the Bible because of the separation of church and state. Other students were allowed to distribute secular literature.

Use of Public Facilities

Jim, who operates a ministry known as Victory Outreach Ministry, asked for and received permission to conduct seminars in a public housing facility. These seminars were meant to provide needed training and assistance to those in public housing. Other secular organizations were permitted to conduct seminars within the facilities. During one of the seminars, one of the directors of the facility walked by the classroom and noticed that Jim had a Bible on the front desk as he was teaching the class. This class was free and voluntary to any public resident who wanted to attend. Jim was interrupted during the presentation and asked to see the director after the class finished. He was then told that he would not be able to continue the presentation because the facility would not tolerate this "Jesus stuff" on their premises. Additionally, residents of the facility were allowed to use the common rooms for all sorts of secular meetings. However, one of the residents asked to use the same common room for a Bible study with other residents, but this request was refused.

Graduation Prayer

In Duval County, Florida, the school adopted a memorandum dealing with graduation messages. The memorandum stated that the graduating senior class could have the opportunity for two minutes to present an opening and/or closing message at the graduation ceremony. If they chose to present a message, the senior class would select a student volunteer from the senior class. No outside person could present the message. The school indicated that it would not censor the content of the message, nor would it require a pre-review of the message. Of the seventeen schools, eleven of the graduating senior classes chose to have a student present a message which could be construed as religious. The remaining schools chose either to not have a message, or the message was secular in nature. Notwithstanding, the American Civil Liberties Union brought suit against the school asking the federal court to censor only the religious aspects of the senior messages.

* * * *

In another case, a community college student was elected by her class peers to say a prayer at their nursing school graduation service. The student accepted the invitation from her fellow classmates and her name was printed in the graduation brochure. However, the nursing director told the student that she could not say a prayer, and insisted she say something secular, giving her a poem to recite. When the student refused to read the secular poem instead of saying her prayer, the director revoked the invitation the evening before graduation. The graduation ceremony proceeded with the student's name listed in the program, but the student was prohibited from being on the platform. This graduate was an exemplary student and was well-liked by her classmates. Her classmates realized that faith played a major role in her life, and therefore honored her by asking her to say a prayer. Instead of graduation being a joyous time, the student was devastated and her classmates were disappointed.

Bible Clubs

Notwithstanding the Equal Access Act, student-initiated Bible clubs on public school campuses are still frequent targets of discrimination. For example, schools have allowed secular clubs to meet during the day but require religious clubs to meet only after school hours, which results in low attendance at these clubs because of the inconvenient meeting times.

* * * *

Other schools have allowed students to have secular clubs pictured in the annual while barring religious clubs.

* * * *

Alternatively, schools have allowed secular clubs access to bulletin boards while still censoring access to the board by the religious or pro-life clubs.

* * * *

A new twist occurred in the state of New York where the school adopted a nondiscrimination policy similar to what is currently found in employment discrimination. This particular school forbade a religious club from requiring that its officers be Christian. The nondiscrimination policy states that student clubs cannot discriminate on the basis of race, national origin, sex, religion, creed, or disability. That means that for a Christian Bible Club to operate, it must agree not to require that the officers of the club be Christian. In other words, a Christian club would have to agree that its president could be an Atheist. No similar requirement is being placed upon the secular clubs. The requirement of the Christian clubs is as ludicrous as requiring a black student club to have a white supremacist for its president. Such a nondiscrimination policy would require the Christian club to accept an Atheist as its president.[107]

Religious Symbols

A public park in Columbus, Ohio, permits all forms of secular expression. The city banned the private display of a cross during the Christmas season but allowed the public display of a Jewish Menorah during the same season, reasoning that the cross was a religious symbol but the Menorah was a secular symbol.

I could go on ad infinitum. Suffice it to say that religion is a target of frequent discrimination. In 1994 the Equal Employment Opportunity proposed religious harassment guidelines. If implemented, these proposed guidelines would have cleansed religion from the work place. Although these guidelines were thankfully defeated by Congress, the Internal Revenue Service nevertheless sought to implement similar restrictions on religion in the work place.[108]

It is time to restore and regain our religious liberty. In view of the loss of free exercise rights, and the hostile attitude of the courts

---

[107]*Hsu v. Roslyn Union Free School Dist. No. 3*, 876 F. Supp. 445 (E.D.N.Y. 1995). This case was thankfully reversed on appeal in *Hsu v. Roslyn Union Free School Dist. No. 3*, 85 F.3d 839 (2d Cir. 1996), *cert. denied, Roslyn Union Free School Dist. No. 3 v. Hsu*, 117 S. Ct. 608 (1996).

[108]*See* testimony by Ernest J. Istook, Jr. before the House Judiciary Committee on June 8, 1995.

toward religion when applying the *Lemon* test, it is time that people of faith have protection against discrimination. Such protection need not be in the form of special rights, but equal rights. Religious expression must at a minimum be protected during times and in places where secular expression is permitted. When discrimination against religious expression and religious people has reached such an epidemic proportion, it is time that something be done to protect our God-given religious liberties. To restore our liberties you must first become educated about these liberties. You must then take courage and become engaged in the battle.

3

GENERAL CONSTITUTIONAL PRINCIPLES

The History Of The First Amendment

In order to adequately understand the purpose of the First Amendment, an overview of American history is essential. At one time, I detested history because it did not appear to affect my present day life. History, to me, was made up of names, dates, and facts. However, when I entered college I began to view history as His Story, that is God's story of Himself acting within history, history took on an entirely new meaning for me. In looking back over time, I can see more clearly God's divine will throughout history. Anyone who ignores history is doomed to repeat its mistakes. It's no wonder why American history has been drastically altered in our public schools. We are now suffering the consequences of that revised history, and we will continue to do so as our students become our leaders.

History was extremely important for the Israelite nation. To this day, the famous Shema from Deuteronomy 6:4 is still repeated in Jewish synagogues, "Hear, O Israel, the Lord our God is one." According to the Book of Deuteronomy, the words which God commanded must be taught by the parents to their children while they are sitting, walking, lying down, and rising up. In other words, life is continual education. While today is history in the making, one must never forget the history of the past. The Book of Deuteronomy represents the rehearsing of the law surrounding the birth of the Israelite nation. Moses knew the importance of history, which is why he recounted God's historical intervention in the nation's past as the new generation was about to enter the promised land. This new generation was not a part of the old history, so Moses wanted what God had done for their ancestors to be fresh in their minds. The Shema begins the famous section where Moses commands parents to diligently teach their children about God and His intervention in history. Considering the importance of history, it is no wonder why one major threat to our American culture finds its genesis in historical revisionism.

As a consequence of this revisionist history we have strayed from the correct interpretation of the First Amendment because we have ignored its historical purpose. Looking back into our nation's history, we find Christopher Columbus came to this continent not to flee persecution or for mere exploration, but because he felt God was leading him to spread the gospel in a new land.[1] Later, the Puritans left England because they were impressed that God was leading them to establish the gospel in foreign lands. Public schools were later established in order to teach children how to read the Bible.

After the original thirteen colonies declared independence from Great Britain in 1776, they considered forming a limited federal government for the primary purpose of national security. In order to "secure the blessings of liberty" for future generations, the colonies adopted the Constitution of the United States in 1787. The Constitution established a federal government with very limited and prescribed authority. It set forth three branches of government: the Executive (to carry out the laws), the Legislative (to enact the laws and be accountable to the people) and the Judicial (to interpret the laws). At that time, the Judicial was the weakest of the three branches.

After forming the federal government, the thirteen colonies were concerned that the new government would infringe upon the authority of the individual states by imposing federal bureaucracy into the state system. The colonies wanted to create a limited power that would serve the will of the individual sovereign states. They did not want to lose their identity to a national-based government. To accomplish this goal, the first ten amendments, known as the Bill of Rights, were drafted in 1789 and adopted by the colonies on December 15, 1791. The First Amendment, which pertains to religious liberty, states, "Congress shall make no law respecting an establishment of religion, or prohibiting the free exercise thereof. . . ." These amendments were written for the express purpose of limiting the authority of the federal government. The Tenth Amendment reaffirms this limitation when it states that any authority not specifically granted to the federal government was reserved solely for the individual states.

---

[1]Peter Marshall and David Manual, *The Light and the Glory* 29-48.

The First Amendment explicitly prohibited the federal government from establishing a national church and from prohibiting the free exercise of religion within the states.[2] The federal government had absolutely no jurisdiction over religious matters within the states. If a state established a state-sponsored church or religion, the federal government had no authority to promote or inhibit the practice of religion within the state. Indeed, as late as the Revolutionary War, there were established churches in at least eight of the thirteen colonies and established religions in at least four of the other five.[3] The individual states were regulated by their own individual constitutions or by their own legislative actions, not by the federal government, and certainly not by the United States Supreme Court.

Supreme Court Justice Joseph Story, who died in 1845, wrote that "at the time of the adoption of the Constitution, . . . the general, if not the universal, sentiment in America was, that Christianity ought to receive encouragement from the State so far as such encouragement was not incompatible with the private rights of conscience and the freedom of religious worship."[4]

In 1875, Senator James Blaine, later a Republican candidate for president in 1884, introduced a resolution for a constitutional amendment that read as follows:

No State shall make any law respecting an establishment of religion or prohibiting the free exercise thereof; and no money raised by taxation in any state for the support of public school or derived from any public fund therefor, nor any public land devoted thereto, shall ever be under the control of any religious sect or denomination; nor shall any money so raised or lands so devoted be divided between religious sects or denominations.[5]

This amendment was never added to the Constitution because it did not receive two-thirds majority vote of the Senate.

---

[2]John Eidsmoe, *The Christian Legal Advisor* 97-164.

[3]*Engel v. Vitale*, 370 U.S. 421, 427-48 (1962).

[4]Joseph Story, 2 *Commentaries on the Constitution of the United States* 593.

[5]Alfred W. Meyer, "The Blaine Amendment and the Bill of Rights," HARV. L. REV. 939 (1951).

The first part of the Blaine Amendment is identical to the present First Amendment except that it replaces the word "Congress" with "State." The debates indicate that this amendment would, for the first time, limit the authority of the states in religious matters; whereas previously, only the federal government had been prohibited from acting in state religious matters. Senator Stevenson stated during these debates,

> Friend as he was of religious freedom, [Thomas Jefferson] would never have consented that the states, which brought the Constitution into existence, upon whose sovereignty this instrument rests, which keep it within its expressly limited powers, could be degraded in that the government of the United States, a government of limited authority, the mere agent of the state with prescribed powers, should undertake to take possession of their schools and of their religion.[6]

The issue did not die with the failure of the Blaine Amendment. In 1937, Senator Borah attempted a similar amendment which also failed for lack of two-thirds vote.[7] However, what the legislature failed to do for lack of support, and what the thirteen colonies specifically feared, eventually came to pass in 1940. The year 1940 marks a drastic departure from the intent and purpose of the First Amendment and begins a totally new era in our history. Until 1940, the First Amendment had been specifically written, and properly interpreted, to keep the federal government's hands off religious issues within the states. In other words, since the federal government only had authority to act where the colonies so granted, and since the colonies had stated specifically that the federal government had no authority in matters of religion, the federal government had no jurisdiction to act on religious matters within the states.

Writing for *The Humanist*, Paul Blanshard stated that the primary force changing this country into a secular society was the

---

[6]Cong. Rec. 5589 (1876).
[7]S.J. Res. 92, 75th Cong., 1st Sess. (1937).

United States Supreme Court.[8] I agree with Blanshard when he states that the turning point of American history occurred in 1940.

In 1940, the United States Supreme Court ignored the historical context of the First Amendment and applied the First Amendment Free Exercise Clause to the states in the case of *Cantwell v. Connecticut.*[9] Then, in 1947, the Supreme Court applied the First Amendment Establishment Clause to the states in *Everson v. Board of Education.*[10] In my view, the Court has incorrectly applied the First Amendment to the states by application of the Fourteenth Amendment.[11] Now, instead of the First Amendment erecting a barrier against the federal government at the state border, it has been interpreted to create a bridge to allow the federal government to intrude on state matters pertaining to religion.

Even more amazing than the United States Supreme Court misinterpreting the First Amendment is the fact that there was very little public outcry denouncing its action. Since 1940, the Supreme Court has prohibited schools from composing a prayer to recite before class,[12] prohibited the use of the Lord's Prayer in public schools,[13] and stripped the Ten Commandments from the classroom bulletin board.[14] The Court has also struck down an Arkansas statute that restricted the teaching of evolution by reasoning that the statute had a religious purpose.[15]

Since the Court ignored the clear meaning of the First Amendment and failed to appreciate the Judeo-Christian foundation of the Constitution, the Court has been forced to invent minute distinctions in order to rationalize its unpredictable rulings. For example, in 1989 the Court ruled that a nativity scene was unconstitutional but a Jewish menorah was constitutional.[16]

---

[8]Paul Blanshard, *Three Cheers for Our Secular State*, THE HUMANIST, March/April 1976, p. 17.

[9]310 U.S. 296 (1940).

[10]330 U.S. 1 (1947).

[11]The Fourteenth Amendment was adopted in 1868. Congressional debates on the Blaine Amendment in 1875 reveal that the intent of the Fourteenth Amendment was not to incorporate application of the First Amendment to the individual states.

[12]*Engel v. Vitale*, 370 U.S. 421 (1962).

[13]*School District of Abington Township v. Schempp*, 374 U.S. 203 (1963).

[14]*Stone v. Graham*, 449 U.S. 39 (1980).

[15]*Epperson v. Arkansas*, 393 U.S. 97 (1968).

[16]*County of Allegheny v. American Civil Liberties Union*, 492 U.S. 573 (1989).

Though the Court has upheld the constitutionality of other nativity scenes, the Court reasoned in the *County of Allegheny* case that the nativity scene there violated the First Amendment because it was at the dominant entrance to the county courthouse. The menorah was held constitutional because it was at a different location on the city property and was closer to the other secular symbols of Christmas such as a Christmas tree. The Court suggested that if the nativity scene had been closer in proximity to the Christmas tree, then it would have been constitutional. This nit-picking has no legal basis in the Constitution. The Court has created its own authority and its own quagmire; unfortunately, religious freedom suffers as a result.

The document that was intended to secure religious freedom, in the hands of decision-makers devoid of absolutes, has become the document that often restricts religious freedom. Though history clearly indicates that the First Amendment was never meant to be applicable to the states, the Supreme Court's interpretation since 1940 applying the First Amendment to the states is not likely to change. One federal judge in Alabama ruled that he was unable to decide a First Amendment case because federal courts had no jurisdiction over state religious matters in that the First Amendment was never meant to be applicable to the states.[17] According to Judge Hand, since the First Amendment did not apply to the individual states, the states were free to establish their own religion as they chose and the federal government could not prevent this practice.[18] Judge Hand's decision was quickly and succinctly overruled by the court of appeals, stating that it did not matter how the judge viewed the history of the First Amendment -- the First Amendment was applicable to the states because the Supreme Court said it was, and federal courts must follow court precedent.[19] The federal appeals court indicated that federal "district courts and circuit courts are bound to adhere to the controlling decisions of the Supreme Court."[20] The appeals court also noted that if the federal courts did not follow the precedent of the United States Supreme Court, anarchy would occur, and therefore, the United States

---

[17]*Jaffree v. Board of School Commissioners*, 554 F. Supp. 1104, 1128 (S.D. Ala. 1983), *rev'd* 705 F.2d 1526 (11th Cir. 1983).

[18]*Id.*

[19]*Jaffree v. Board of School Commissioners*, 705 F.2d 1526, 1535-36 (11th Cir. 1983).

[20]*Id.* at 1533 (citing *Hutto v. Davis*, 454 U.S. 370, 375 (1982)).

Supreme Court's decisions "must be followed by the lower federal courts no matter how misguided the judges of those courts may think it to be."[21] Once the case made its way to the United States Supreme Court, the Court ruled that the states "have no greater power to restrain the individual freedoms protected by the First Amendment than does the Congress of the United States."[22] The Supreme Court then reiterated that it believed the First Amendment became applicable to the individual states after the adoption of the Fourteenth Amendment to the United States Constitution in 1868.[23]

Therefore, it is now assumed, without critical analysis, that the First Amendment is applicable to the individual states through the Fourteenth Amendment to the United States Constitution. Subsequent Supreme Court decisions have invented various tests only to expand or ignore these tests when interpreting First Amendment cases. Clearly the Court's attitude toward religion has changed, even to the point of calling the free exercise of religion embodied in the First Amendment a "luxury" which cannot always be accommodated.[24]

When interpreting the First Amendment, the statement of Oliver Wendell Holmes is apropos: "A page of history is worth a volume of logic."[25] The best interpretation of the First Amendment is one that is "illuminated by history."[26] The United States Supreme Court has noted the following in this respect:

> In applying the First Amendment to the states through the Fourteenth Amendment . . . it would be incongruous to interpret that clause as imposing more stringent First Amendment limits on the states than the draftsmen imposed upon the Federal Government.[27]

---

[21]*Id.* at 1533-34 (citing *Davis*, 454 U.S. at 375).

[22]*Wallace v. Jaffree*, 472 U.S. 38, 48-49 (1985).

[23]*Id.* at 48-56.

[24]*Employment Division v. Smith*, 494 U.S. 872 (1990).

[25]*New York Trust Company v. Eisner*, 256 U.S. 345, 349 (1921).

[26]*Lynch v. Donnelly*, 465 U.S. 668, 678 (1984) (citing *Walz v. Tax Commission*, 397 U.S. 664, 671 (1970)).

[27]*Marsh v. Chambers*, 463 U.S. 783, 790-91 (1983).

Therefore, the historical context of the First Amendment is crucial to a proper resolution of any case. A review of the history surrounding the First Amendment indicates that as the first act of the Continental Congress in 1774, the Reverend Mister Duche opened with prayer and read from Psalm 31.[28] From their inception Congress and state legislatures have opened their sessions with an invocation by a paid chaplain.[29] Courts have historically opened their daily proceedings with the invocation, "God save the United States and this Honorable Court."[30] The Supreme Court of the United States itself has the Ten Commandments inscribed above the bench recognizing the biblical foundations of our legal heritage.[31]

George Washington began the tradition of taking the Presidential oath of office upon the Bible. When he assumed office in 1789, he stated, "It would be peculiarly improper to omit of this first official act my fervent supplications to that Almighty Being who rules over the Universe. . . ."[32] Indeed, Washington added the phrase at the end of the Presidential oath, "So help me God." An impressive list of presidents subsequent to Washington have invoked the protection and help of Almighty God.[33]

James Madison, the father of the Bill of Rights, was a member of the Congressional Committee that recommended the chaplaincy

---

[28]Mr. Duche's prayer was as follows:

> Be thou present oh God of wisdom and direct the counsel of this honorable assembly; enable them to settle all things on the best and surest foundation; that the scene of blood may be speedily closed; that order, harmony, and peace may be effectually restored, and truth and justice, religion and piety, prevail and flourish among the people. Preserve the health of their bodies and the vigor of their minds, shower down on them, and the millions they represent, such temporal blessings as Thou seest expedient for them in this world, and crown them with everlasting glory in the world to come. All this we ask in the name and through the merits of Jesus Christ Thy Son and our Savior. Amen.

[29]*Marsh*, 463 U.S. at 787-89. *See Lynch*, 465 U.S. at 673-74.

[30]*Marsh*, 463 U.S. at 786.

[31]*Lynch*, 465 U.S. at 677.

[32]*Engel*, 370 U.S. at 466 (Stewart, J., dissenting).

[33]*Id.* at 446-49. *See also* William J. Federer, *A Treasury of Presidential Quotations.* Mr. Federer has compiled quotations invoking God from every American President beginning with George Washington.

system.[34] Madison voted for the bill authorizing payment of chaplains.[35] Reverend William Lynn was elected chaplain of the House of Representatives and paid $500 from the federal treasury.

On September 25, 1789, the day the final agreement was made on the Bill of Rights, the House requested President Washington to proclaim a Day of Thanksgiving to acknowledge "the many signal favors of Almighty God."[36] He proclaimed November 26, 1789, a Day of Thanksgiving to offer "our prayers and thanksgiving to the great Lord and Ruler of nations, and beseech Him to pardon our national and other transgressions."[37] Later, President Madison issued four Thanksgiving Day proclamations: July 9, 1812; July 23, 1813; November 16, 1814; and March 4, 1815.[38] Successive presidents have continued this tradition.

A correct interpretation of the First Amendment must be in accord "with what history reveals was the contemporaneous understanding of its guarantees."[39] The Supreme Court recognizes "that religion has been closely identified with our history and our government."[40] The history of this country "is inseparable from the history of religion."[41] "The line we must draw between the permissible and impermissible is one which accords with history and faithfully reflects the understanding of the Founding Fathers."[42] The historical setting of the First Amendment should often be reviewed to insure that the court interpretations "comport with what history reveals was the contemporaneous understanding of its guarantees."[43] When adopted, the First Amendment prohibited the federal government from coercively intruding into religion. "Government policies of accommodation, acknowledgment,

---

[34]H.R. Rep. No. 124, 33rd Cong., 1st Sess. (1789), *reprinted in* 2 No. 2 *Reports of Committees of the House of Representatives* 4 (1854).

[35]1 Annals of Cong. 891 (J. Gales, ed. 1834).

[36]H.R. Jour., 1st Cong., 1st Sess., 123 (1826 ed.); S. Jour., 1st Cong., 1st Sess., 88 (1820 ed.); *Lynch*, 465 U.S. at 674 n.2.

[37]*Lynch*, 465 U.S. at 674 n.2.

[38]R. Cord, *Separation of Church and State*, 31 (1982).

[39]*Lynch*, 465 U.S. at 673.

[40]*Abington Township*, 374 U.S. at 212.

[41]*Engel*, 370 U.S. at 434 (1962).

[42]*Abington Township*, 374 U.S. at 294 (Brennan, J., concurring).

[43]*Lynch*, 465 U.S. at 673. *See also Committee for Public Education and Religious Liberty v. Nyquist*, 413 U.S. 756 (1973); *Walz v. Tax Commission*, 397 U.S. 664 (1970); *Marsh*, 463 U.S. at 783.

and support for religion are an accepted part of our political and cultural heritage."[44] Interpreting the First Amendment consistent with history would certainly do a great deal to bring uniformity and reason back to constitutional jurisprudence. On occasion, the courts use history as part of their interpretation, and on other occasions, the courts simply ignore history. Despite these inconsistencies, there still remains clear constitutional decisions by which to guide religious liberty. However, today we face serious threats to our religious liberty.

We have in many ways moved from the First Amendment's intent to create religious prosperity and freedom, to the allegation the First Amendment is designated to mandate "that the government remain secular."[45] History certainly does not bear out this statement that the First Amendment was intended to make government secular, but rather history supports the conclusion that the First Amendment was meant to create religious prosperity, prohibiting government from intruding in religion but allowing religion to flourish within the public square. Indeed, former Supreme Court Justice Joseph Story noted the following about the First Amendment:

> Probably, at the time of the adoption of the Constitution, and of the amendment to it, now under consideration, the general, if not the universal, sentiment in America was, that Christianity ought to receive encouragement from the State, so far as such encouragement was not incompatible with the private rights of conscience, and the freedom of religious worship.[46]

The often quoted expression of Thomas Jefferson regarding the "wall of separation between church and state"[47] has become so popular that many people believe these words are in the Constitution. However, this phrase is not in the Constitution. In fact, Thomas Jefferson was in France at the time the First Amendment

---

[44]*County of Allegheny*, 492 U.S. at 657 (Kennedy, J., concurring in part and dissenting in part).

[45]*Id.* at 574.

[46]Joseph Story, 2 *Commentaries on the Constitution of the United States* 593 (1833).

[47]8 *Works of Thomas Jefferson* 113.

was drafted. Jefferson did not believe that there should be no interaction between church and state. On three occasions, President Jefferson signed into law federal land grants specifically to promote proselytizing among native American Indians.[48] In 1803, President Jefferson proposed to the United States Senate a treaty with the Kaskaskia Indians in which the federal government was to "give annually for seven years one hundred dollars towards the support of a priest" and "further give the sum of three dollars to assist the said tribe in the erection of a church."[49] The treaty was ratified on December 23, 1803, and at Jefferson's request, it included an appropriation for a Catholic Mission.

Moreover, Thomas Jefferson was the first president of the District of Columbia School Board. There the Bible and the Watts Hymnal were used as primary textbooks.[50] As the founder of the University of Virginia, Jefferson believed that religious instruction was important to a proper education. In fact, he stated: "The want of instruction in the various creeds of religious faith existing among our citizens presents, therefore, a chasm in the general institution of the useful sciences."[51]

On July 13, 1787, the Continental Congress enacted the Northwest Ordinance which provided that "Religion, morality, and knowledge being essential to good government and the happiness of mankind, schools and the means of education shall be forever encouraged."[52] On August 7, 1789, after the final agreement on the wording of the Bill of Rights, the newly formed Congress re-enacted the Northwest Ordinance.[53]

History is clearly a good teacher in determining the intent of the First Amendment. The amendment was not intended to erect an impregnable wall between church and state. Indeed, our national

---

[48]R. Cord, *Separation of Church & State,* 41-46 (1982).

[49]*A Treaty Between the United States of America in the Kaskaskia Tribe of Indians,* 7 Stat. 78-79 (Peter's ed. 1846).

[50]J. Wilson, *Public Schools of Washington* 1 Records of the Columbia Historical Society 4 (1897).

[51]*Illinois ex rel. McCollum v. Board of Education,* 333 U.S. 203, 245-46 (1948) (Reed, J., dissenting), (citing 19 *The Writings of Thomas Jefferson* 414-17 (memorial edition 1904)).

[52]Ord. of 1787, July 13, 1787, Art. III, *reprinted in Documents Illustrative of the Formation of the Union of American States* 52 (1927).

[53]An Act to Provide for the Government of the Territory Northwest of the River Ohio (Northwest Ordinance), Ch. 8, 1 Stat. 50-51 (Peter's ed. 1845).

motto declares, "In God We Trust."[54] Not only our currency but also our national anthem contains the national motto.[55] Since 1954, the Pledge of Allegiance has contained the words "One nation *under God.*"[56] Clearly, an objective observer "cannot look at even this brief resumé without finding that our history is pervaded by expressions of religious beliefs."[57] As the United States Supreme Court has recognized, the "real object" of the First Amendment was "to prevent any national ecclesiastical establishment, which should give to an hierarchy the exclusive patronage of the national government."[58]

Governmental Action

When determining whether an individual has a constitutional right under the First Amendment, or any other provision in the Bill of Rights, it is important to note how these constitutional provisions are applied. In reference to the First Amendment it is important to note that this Amendment has two Religion Clauses. The first clause is known as the Establishment Clause, which states: "Congress shall make no law respecting the Establishment of religion. . ." The second clause, known as the Free Exercise Clause, completes the religion clauses by stating: "or prohibit the free exercise thereof. . . ." The entire First Amendment states as follows:

Congress shall make no law respecting an establishment of religion, or prohibiting the free exercise thereof, or abridging the freedom of speech, or of the press, or the right of the people peacefully to assemble, and to petition the Government for a redress of grievances.[59]

---

[54]Joint Resolution to Establish a National Motto of the United States, Ch. 795, Pub. L. No. 84-851, 70 Stat. 732 (1957).

[55]*Engel,* 370 U.S. at 440, 449.

[56]Joint Resolution, etc., Pub. L. No. 94-344, § 1 (19), 90 Stat. 810, 813 (1978), codified, as amended, at 36 U.S.C. § 172 (1978).

[57]*Lynch,* 465 U.S. at 677.

[58]Id. at 678 (quoting J. Story 2, *Commentaries on the Constitution of the United States* 593 (1833)).

[59]U.S. Const. Amend. I.

The First Amendment is meant to protect individuals from government intrusion. Therefore, it provides liberty to individuals and restraint on the government. In order for the First Amendment to be applicable to any situation, two factors must be involved: (1) a person[60] and (2) some form of governmental action. Only a governmental entity is prohibited from establishing a religion and only a governmental entity is prohibited from restricting the free exercise of religion. A private entity can establish a religion, and a private individual can restrict the free exercise of anyone else's religion.

A classic example of how the Constitution works is to compare the difference between a public and a private school. A public school is a governmental entity and therefore is prohibited by the Establishment Clause from establishing a religion. As a governmental entity, the public school is also prohibited from restricting the free exercise of religion. On the other hand, a private school can promote or proselytize in religious matters without any governmental interference, and no matter how offensive the promotion or establishment of a religion may be to an individual, the Constitution through the Establishment Clause has no application to a private school. A private Christian school can require mandatory chapel every day and may also prohibit the distribution of religious literature. However, a public school would violate the Establishment Clause by requiring mandatory chapel every day and would violate the Free Exercise and Free Speech Clause by prohibiting the distribution of religious literature.[61] A public school could not compel a Jehovah's Witness to salute the flag because to do so would violate the student's free exercise of religion.[62] A private Christian school could compel a student to salute the flag.

In summary, there must be some governmental action for the Establishment Clause, the Free Speech Clause, or the Free Exercise Clause to apply in any given situation. Without governmental action, there is no application of the First Amendment.

---

[60]Since corporations are considered legal persons, corporations can bring First Amendment claims.

[61]Nowak, Rotunda, and Young, 3d Ed. *Constitutional Law* 421-48.

[62]*Murdock v. Pennsylvania*, 319 U.S. 105 (1943).

Public Forum Doctrine

Throughout this book the reader will be confronted by the terms "traditional public forum," "limited or designated public forum," and "nonpublic forum." These terms are important in order to determine First Amendment free speech rights. In order to ascertain what limits, if any, may be imposed on free speech rights, the United States Supreme Court has "often focused on the place of that speech, considering the nature of the forum the speaker seeks to employ."[63] The United States Supreme Court has stated that

> [p]ublic places are of necessity the locus for discussion of public issues, as well as protest against arbitrary government action. At the heart of our jurisprudence lies the principle that in a free nation citizens must have the right to gather and speak with other persons in public places. The recognition that certain government-owned property is a public forum provides open notice to citizens that their freedoms may be exercised there without fear of a censorial government, adding tangible reinforcement to the idea that we are a free people.[64]

The "public forum doctrine is to give effect to the broad command of the First Amendment to protect speech from governmental interference."[65] There are three categories of public forums best described as follows: (1) traditional—defined as parks, streets, or sidewalks that have been held in trust for the use of the public and for purposes of assembly, communicating thoughts between citizens, and discussing public questions; (2) designated or limited—which is created when the state intentionally opens public property for use by the public for assembly, speech or other expressive activities; and (3) nonpublic—which exists when the state does not designate public property for indiscriminate expression by

---

[63]*Frisby v. Schultz*, 487 U.S. 474, 479 (1988). *See also Heffron v. ISKCON*, 452 U.S. 640 (1981).

[64]*ISKCON v. Lee*, 112 S. Ct. 2711, 2716-17 (1992).

[65]*Id.* at 2717.

the public at large, by certain speakers, or by certain subjects. Generally the standard of review for a traditional, limited, or designated public forum is a strict or intermediate scrutiny test; whereas, under the nonpublic forum the rational basis or reasonable nexus test is used. For the government to limit the content of speech under the former it must show a compelling interest, and any restriction must be narrowly tailored to achieve that interest; while under the latter, the government must show a reasonable basis for the restriction. Time, place, and manner restrictions are permissible only if content neutral, narrowly tailored to serve a significant government interest, and such restrictions leave open ample alternative channels of expression.[66] A classic example of a time restriction is one that frequently occurs for parade permits. A governmental entity may limit parade permits to a certain time in order to avoid rush hour traffic. This time restriction would be permissible so long as it was content neutral and, therefore, applicable to all permits. However, time, place, and manner restrictions may not be so stringent so as to effectively preclude use of the forum. For example, it would be impermissible to allow a parade permit only at midnight.

Traditional public forums are essentially a closed class consisting of public parks, streets, and sidewalks. These types of public property have immemorially been left open for expressive activity allowing citizens to assemble and communicate with other citizens. By nature of the property, the location is considered a traditional public forum and cannot be closed to public use. A designated or limited public forum is one where the government intentionally opens up the public facility for use by the community. Examples include a public library where outside organizations can meet in various rooms, public school facilities used after hours by outside community organizations, or any other facility open to the public for expressive activity. Once the designated or limited public forum is open to the public, the same strict scrutiny standard that is used for the traditional public forum is applied. The main difference between this classification and a traditional public forum is that a traditional public forum by the nature of the property is always open to the public. A designated public forum need not be open,

---

[66]*See, e.g.,* Perry Education Ass'n v. Perry Local Educators' Ass'n, 460 U.S. 37 (1983).

and at any time can be closed so long as the closure of the facility is done in a nondiscriminatory basis. For example, a public school could close its facilities to all groups in the community. A public library could prohibit all outsiders from using the facilities other than for checking out and reading books. However, a public school or public library cannot close its facilities only to religious but not secular organizations because to do so would discriminate on the content of the speech and would violate the First Amendment. Finally, an example of a nonpublic forum would be an airport, but even in a public airport, all First Amendment activity cannot be prohibited.

Commenting on the traditional and designated or limited public forums, the Supreme Court stated the following:

> In these quintessential public [forums], the government may not prohibit all communicative activity. For the State to enforce a content-based exclusion it must show that its regulation is necessary to serve a compelling state interest and that it is narrowly drawn to achieve that end. . . . The State may also enforce regulations of the time, place, and manner of expression which are content neutral, and are narrowly tailored to serve a significant government interest, and leave open ample alternative channels of communication. [67]

As noted above, the government may place reasonable time, place, and manner restrictions on expression so long as these restrictions are content neutral. Content neutral regulations are those that are "justified without reference to the content of the regulated speech."[68] A time, place, and manner restriction must not be based upon the content of the speech. In other words, the government would violate the First Amendment if, because of the content of the speech being religious, it decided to restrict the time, place, or manner of the religious speech. A neutral regulation would be one that is done in a nondiscriminatory manner regardless of the content

---

[67]*Frisby*, 487 U.S. at 481 (quoting *Perry Education Ass'n*, 460 U.S. at 45).

[68]*Virginia State Board of Pharmacy v. Virginia Citizens Consumer Council*, 425 U.S. 748, 771 (1976).

of speech. A reasonable time regulation in a traditional public forum would be one that permitted use of a street for a parade during hours other than rush hour traffic. Some government facilities try to regulate the place of the speech, yet in doing so, the government must leave open ample alternative channels of communication. The Supreme Court has held that "one is not to have the exercise of his liberty of expression in appropriate places abridged on the plea that it may be exercised in some other place.

The Supreme Court has clearly expressed its disdain for content-based restrictions on free speech. "The First Amendment generally prevents government from proscribing free speech, or even expressive conduct because of disapproval of the ideas expressed. Content-based regulations are presumptively invalid."[69] Undoubtedly, the "First Amendment does not permit [government] to impose special prohibitions to those speakers who express views on disfavored subjects."[70]

Moreover, within a public forum, the government cannot prohibit expressive activity on the basis that the speaker is associated with some other radical or disruptive group. The First Amendment protects freedom of speech and freedom of association. The Supreme Court has noted the following:

> Among the rights protected by the First Amendment is the right of individuals to associate to further their personal beliefs. While the freedom of association is not explicitly set out in the Amendment, it has long been held to be implicit in the freedoms of speech, assembly, and petition.[71]

The interrelationship between free speech and group activity was reaffirmed by the Supreme Court when it stated:

> It should be obvious that the exclusion of any person or group—all-Negro, all-Oriental, or all-white—from public facilities infringes upon the freedom of the individual to

---

[69]R.A.V. v. City of St. Paul, 112 S. Ct. 2538, 2542 (1992).
[70]Id. at 2547.
[71]Healy v. James, 408 U.S. 169, 181 (1972).

associate as he chooses. . . . . "The associational rights
which our system honors permit all white, all black, all
brown, all yellow clubs to be formed. They also permit all
Catholic, all Jewish, or all agnostic clubs to be
established. Government may not tell a man or woman
who his or her associates must be." . . . The freedom to
associate applies to the beliefs we share, and to those we
consider reprehensible. It tends to produce the diversity of
opinion that oils the machinery of democratic government
and insures peaceful, orderly change.[72]

In one case, a school attempted to prohibit the formation of a
student club on a university campus because its national parent or
affiliate organization had been shown to be disruptive and violent
in nature. Thus, the associational free speech rights of the individual
club were violated by the school because the university lumped that
particular student group in with other individuals simply because of
their relationship to the other individuals. To do so violated the First
Amendment according to the United States Supreme Court.[73]
Consequently, a governmental entity cannot prohibit free speech
expressive activities within a public forum on the basis that another
individual or group with which the speaker is affiliated has been
shown to be violent or disruptive in nature.[74] The Supreme Court
has noted that an "individual's freedom to speak, to worship, and to
petition the government for the redresses of grievances could not be
vigorously protected from interference by the state [if] our
correlative freedom to engage in group effort toward those ends
were not also guaranteed."[75]

Though the Supreme Court may be tending to move away from
the public forum doctrine to some extent,[76] the public forum

---

[72]Gilmore v. City of Montgomery, 417 U.S. 556, 575 (1974).

[73]Healy, 408 U.S. at 169.

[74]NAACP v. Claiborne Hardware Co., 458 U.S. 886 (1982).

[75]Roberts v. United States Jaycees, 468 U.S. 609 (1984).

[76]R.A.V., 112 S. Ct. at 2538 (Not using the public forum analysis in a free speech case);
ISKCON v. Lee, 112 S. Ct. at 2711 (Not using a public forum analysis in a free speech case
involving an international airport and discussing whether international airports should be
considered as traditional public forums because of the nature of the airport being similar to
such forums).

doctrine is still well-embedded in constitutional interpretation. It is important to know the difference between a traditional public forum, a designated or limited public forum, and a nonpublic forum. In summary, traditional public forums are public parks, streets, and sidewalks. Such public forums are always open to the public. Designated or limited public forums are those public facilities intentionally open to public use by the government. A nonpublic forum is neither a traditional public forum, nor has it been intentionally opened to outside use. However, not all free speech activities can be excluded from a nonpublic forum. Of course, in speaking about public forums, we are always considering government action and control of the public forum to which the citizen seeks access for First Amendment expressive purposes.

Application of the First Amendment

The three clauses of the First Amendment particularly important for religious liberty include the Establishment Clause, the Free Exercise Clause, and the Free Speech Clause. Applying the First Amendment to any given situation can be simplified by identifying: (1) the parties; (2) the forum; (3) the restriction; and (4) the test.[77]

The Parties

In any constitutional case, there must be a governmental party and a private party. The First Amendment restrains government on the one hand and protects the private liberty of the individual on the other hand. There is no First Amendment application if the adversarial parties are private. One of the adversarial parties must be a governmental actor and one must be a private actor.

The Forum

The three forums include a traditional public forum, a limited or designated public forum, or a nonpublic forum.[78] A traditional

---

[77]See the Appendix entitled First Amendment Outline.
[78]*Perry Education Ass'n. v. Perry Local Educators' Ass'n.*,, 460 U.S. 37 (1983).

public forum includes a street, a sidewalk, or a park. A limited or designated public forum is any public facility intentionally opened to the public by the government for expressive activity. An example of such a forum is a public school which is used by private groups after school hours. A nonpublic forum is public property which the government has not intentionally opened for expressive activity. An example is a utility pole or a public airport.

The Restriction

The third step is to identify the type of restraint. With respect to the First Amendment Free Speech Clause, the various kinds of restraint include a content-neutral restraint, a content based restraint, a viewpoint restraint, or a prior restraint. A content-neutral restraint is a governmental restriction on speech that does not attempt to restrict the content of the message. An example of a content-neutral restriction is a parade permit which requires all applicants to specify the designated time and route of the parade. Such a requirement must be applicable to all speech regardless of the content. A content based restraint is a restriction on a specific category of speech. An example would be where the government permits political speech but attempts to restrict religious speech. A viewpoint restriction is one where the government allows political speech but only from the Democratic rather than the Republican viewpoint. A prior restraint is some type of restriction on speech before it occurs. An example of a prior restraint is where the government requires the speaker to obtain prior permission to speak.

The above analysis of the parties, the forum and the restriction can be outlined as follows:

I.   Identify The Parties.
    A.   Governmental actor, and
    B.   Private actor.
II. Identify The Forum.
    A.   Traditional public forum.
        1.   Streets,
        2.   Sidewalks, or
        3.   Parks.
    B.   Limited Or Designated Public Forum.

    1.   Any facility which the government intentionally opens for expressive activity.

    2.   Government may open any facility for expressive activity but may also close the facility to preserve the facility for its intended purpose.

C.   Nonpublic Forum.

    1.   Any government facility which is not intentionally opened for expressive activity.

    2.   Examples include airports, transportation facilities, or utility poles.

III. Identify The Restriction.

    A.   Content neutral,

    B.   Content based,

    C.   Viewpoint based, or

    D.   Prior restraint.

The Test

Once the actors, the forum, and the restriction are identified, the applicable test can also be identified and then applied. The following outline can be utilized when applying the First Amendment.

1. Establishment Clause

The Establishment Clause test has gone through several variations. Many members of the Supreme Court for the past several years have criticized the most widely used three part *Lemon* test.[79] The Court does not always use the *Lemon* test.[80] Once

---

[79]*Lemon v. Kurtzman*, 403 U.S. 602 (1971). *See also Lee v. Weisman*, 112 S. Ct. 2649 (1992) (Scalia, J., joined by, *inter ailios*, White, J., and Thomas, J., dissenting); *Allegheny County v. American Civil Liberties Union*, 492 U.S. 573, 655-57 (1989) (Kennedy, J., concurring in judgment in part and dissenting in part); *Corporation of the Presiding Bishop of the Church of Jesus Christ of Latter-Day Saints v. Amos*, 483 U.S. 327, 346-349 (1987) (O'Connor, J., concurring); *Wallace v. Jaffree*, 472 U.S. 38, 107-113 (1985) (Rehnquist, J., dissenting); *Id.* at 90-91 (White, J., dissenting); *School District of Grand Rapids v. Ball*, 473 U.S. 373, 400 (1985) (White, J., dissenting); *Widmar v. Vincent*, 454 U.S. 263, 282 (1981) (White, J., dissenting); *New York v. Cathedral Academy*, 434 U.S. 125, 134-135 (1977) (White, J., dissenting); *Roemer v. Maryland Board of Public Works*, 426 U.S. 736, 768 (1976) (White, J., concurring in judgment); *Committee for Public Education & Religious*

during a graduation prayer case the Court used a so-called coercion test,[81] and once when considering legislative prayers, the Court used no test at all but instead looked to the original intent and the history surrounding the First Amendment.[82]

The *Lemon* test is a three part test as follows: (1) there must be a secular purpose; (2) the government action must not primarily promote, endorse, or inhibit religion; and (3) the government action must not foster excessive governmental entanglement with religion. The various Establishment Clause tests are outlined as follows.

I. The *Lemon* Test.
  A. Must have a secular purpose.
  B. The governmental action must not primarily promote, endorse, or inhibit religion.
  C. The governmental action must not foster excessive governmental entanglement with religion.
II. Coercion Test.
  A. Does the governmental action coerce private individuals toward religion.
  B. Sometimes used during graduation prayer cases.
III. The Historical Test.
  A. Review history surrounding the First Amendment.
  B. Determine the original intent of the Amendment.

As noted above, the primary test used by the Supreme Court is the so-called *Lemon* test. If the government fails any one of the three prongs of the test, then the governmental action will be considered unconstitutional. Under the first prong, there need only be a secular purpose, although there may also be a religious purpose. The key here is to have some secular purpose along with the religious purpose. Under the second prong, the government may not primarily endorse, promote, or inhibit religion. Finally, the government may not become excessively entangled with religion. Nativity scenes or Christmas carols best illustrate the application of

Liberty v. Nyquist, 413 U.S. 756, 820 (1973) (White, J., dissenting).

[80]*Lamb's Chapel v. Center Moriches Union Free School District*, 113 S. Ct. 2141, 2150 (1993).

[81]*Lee v. Weisman*, 112 S. Ct. 2649 (1992).

[82]*Marsh v. Chambers*, 463 U.S. 783 (1983).

the *Lemon* test. If a nativity scene sponsored by the government on public property displays only Mary, Joseph, and the Baby Jesus, then it will be considered unconstitutional. This is so because it only has a religious purpose, not a secular purpose. However, if within the same context of a religious nativity scene the government also displays a secular symbol of the holiday such as Santa Claus, reindeer, or the Christmas tree, then the Supreme Court will consider the display to have a secular purpose. The entire context of the display does not have the primary purpose of endorsing or promoting religion. Although religion might be evident, it is not the primary purpose of the display. Finally, there is no excessive governmental entanglement since the administration or maintenance of the display requires very little government involvement. The same holds true for religious Christmas carols in the public school. If students sing only Christian Christmas carols during a Christmas pageant, then the pageant will be considered a violation of the Establishment Clause. However, if secular songs such as "Rudolph, the Red-Nosed Reindeer" are sung alongside "Silent Night, Holy Night," then the presentation will be considered constitutional. This is because the secular songs create a secular purpose. While some songs might endorse or promote religion, the entire pageant does not primarily endorse or promote religion because of the secular songs. Finally, there is very little governmental entanglement since the government is acting neutrally by celebrating both the secular and sacred aspects of the holiday.

2. Free Exercise Clause

The Supreme Court has changed its interpretation with regards to the application of the Free Exercise Clause. Prior to 1990 the applicable test was as follows: (1) there must be a sincerely held religious belief negatively impacted or burdened by some government rule or regulation; (2) the government must have a compelling governmental interest for the restriction; and (3) the government must achieve its interest in the least restrictive means available.[83] After 1990 the Supreme Court weakened the test and changed it as follows: Any law that is (1) generally applicable and

---

[83] *See Wisconsin v. Yoder*, 406 U.S. 205 (1972); *Sherbert v. Verner*, 374 U.S. 398 (1963).

(2) neutral in application will be upheld.[84] The stricter standard that applied prior to 1990 will be used only if the law is found to specifically target religion,[85] or if the First Amendment Free Exercise Clause can be combined with some other constitutional violation.

The basic tests are outlined as follows.

I.   Pre-1990 Test.
     A.   Sincerely held religious belief negatively impacted or burdened by some governmental rule or regulation.
     B.   Must be a compelling governmental interest.
     C.   Must be the least restrictive means available to achieve the governmental interest.
II. Post-1990 Test.
     A.   Any general law of neutral applicability will be upheld.
     B.   Pre-1990 test will be used only in the following circumstances.
          1.   If the law specifically targets religion for discriminatory treatment; or
          2.   The Free Exercise right is combined with some other constitutional right.

3. Prisoner Rights

Whether analyzed under the Free Speech or Free Exercise Clauses, the test for prisoner rights remain the same. The test may be stated as follows: (1) the government must have a legitimate penological interest; and (2) the restriction must be reasonably related to the government interest.[86] Courts are much more deferential to prisons in restricting the rights of prisoners either in their free exercise of religion or in their freedom of speech primarily because of the penological interest at stake. The interest in punishment and security remain high governmental interests to be balanced against the rights of the prisoner. Using this highly

---

[84]*Employment Division v. Smith*, 494 U.S. 872 (1990).
[85]*Church of the Lukumi Babalu Aye, Inc. v. City of Hialeah*, 113 S. Ct. 2217 (1993).
[86]*Turner v. Safley*, 482 U.S. 78 (1987); *O'Lone v. Estate of Shabazz*, 482 U.S. 342 (1987).

deferential standard, the interest of the government almost always defeats the rights of the prisoner. The test for prisoner rights can be best outlined as follows.

I. Prisoner Rights
    A. Government must have a legitimate penological interest.
    B. Restriction must be reasonably related to the governmental interest.

Between 1993 and 1997, when the Religious Freedom Restoration Act[87] was in effect, the rights of prisoners essentially were coextensive to the rights of non-incarcerated individuals. Now that the Religious Freedom Restoration Act has been ruled unconstitutional,[88] the rights of prisoners have reverted back to their pre-1993 status.

4. Free Speech Clause

The Supreme Court has developed more tests for the Free Speech Clause than for the Establishment Clause or the Free Exercise Clause. Any free speech analysis depends upon the forum and the type of restriction. As noted above, there are three separate types of forums in any free speech analysis. Three forums include a traditional, a limited or designated, or a nonpublic forum. It is critical to know whether the speech is taking place in either one of these three types of forums because the analysis depends upon forum. Additionally, within each of these forums there may be four types of restrictions. The various restrictions include a content neutral, content based, viewpoint and prior restraint restriction. Moreover, it is also important to determine whether the restriction is being imposed by a legislatively adopted law or court ordered injunction. The following overviews the Free Speech Clause analysis.

---

[87]42 U.S.C. § 2000bb.
[88]*City of Boerne v. Flores,* 117 S. Ct. 2157 (1997).

I. Content neutral restriction.
   A. Traditional public forum.
      1. Must be a substantial or significant governmental interest.
      2. Reasonable time, place, and manner restrictions must be narrowly tailored.
      3. Must leave open ample alternative means of expression.
   B. Limited or designated public forum.
      1. Must be a substantial or significant governmental interest.
      2. Reasonable time, place, and manner restrictions must be narrowly tailored.
      3. Must leave open ample alternative means of expression.
   C. Nonpublic forum.
      1. Must be a substantial or significant governmental interest.
      2. Restrictions must be reasonable and rationally related to the governmental interest.

II. Content restriction.
   A. Traditional public forum
      1. Must be a compelling governmental interest.
      2. Any restriction must be the least restrictive means available.
   B. Limited or designated public forum.
      1. Must be a compelling governmental interest.
      2. Any restriction must be the least restrictive means available.
   C. Nonpublic forum.
      1. Must be a substantial or significant governmental interest.
      2. Restrictions must be reasonable and rationally related to the governmental interest.

III. Viewpoint restriction.
   A. Traditional public forum.
      1. Prohibited.
      2. Rationale is that government cannot take sides in any debate by allowing one viewpoint to the

exclusion of another.
B.   Limited or designated public forum.
    1.   Prohibited.
    2.   Rationale is that government cannot take sides in any debate by allowing one viewpoint to the exclusion of another.
C.   Nonpublic forum.
    1.   Prohibited.
    2.   Rationale is that government cannot take sides in any debate by allowing one viewpoint to the exclusion of another.

IV. Prior restraint.
A.   Presumptively unconstitutional.
B.   Must have specific time for granting or refusal to grant permit.
C.   Must not permit governmental discretion to grant or deny speech without specific objective standards.
D.   Must provide that the government has the burden to file suit to substantiate any denial of speech.[89]

Sometimes the Supreme Court has used a separate four part test when analyzing symbolic speech. The symbolic speech test arose in the context of flag desecration. The four part test can be summarized as follows: (1) the regulation must be within the Constitutional power of the Government; (2) it must further an important or substantial governmental interest; (3) the government interest must be unrelated to the suppression of speech; and (4) incidental restriction must be no greater than essential to the furtherance of that interest.[90] The Supreme Court has already indicated that this four part test is essentially the same as the time, place, and manner test on content-neutral restrictions.[91] The test for symbolic speech is outlined as follows.

I.   Symbolic Speech.
A.   The regulation must be within the Constitutional power

---

[89]*Freedman v. Maryland*, 380 U.S. 51 (1965).
[90]*United States v. O'Brien*, 391 U.S. 367 (1968).
[91]*Ward v. Rock Against Racism*, 491 U.S. 781 (1989).

of the government.
B.   The regulation must further an important or substantial governmental interest.
C.   The governmental interest must be unrelated to the suppression of speech.
D.   The incidental restriction must be no greater than essential to the furtherance of that interest.

5. Injunctions

An injunction can either be content-neutral or content based. A content-neutral injunction is generally one that targets specific activity rather than speech. Often times a content-neutral injunction is one that attempts to restrain activity of an individual who repeatedly violated the law. A content based injunction is one that specifically targets speech rather than activity. An injunction by its very nature that targets speech is also a prior restraint.

The standard for reviewing content-neutral injunctions requires that a heightened level of scrutiny be applied stricter than the time, place, and manner test. This heightened scrutiny requires that a content-neutral injunction must not burden more speech than necessary to accomplish its objective.[92]

A content based injunction follows the standard content based test as follows: (1) the government must have a compelling governmental interest; and (2) must achieve that interest in the least restrictive means available.[93] Since a content based injunction is also a prior restraint it is presumptively invalid. The test for content-neutral and content based injunctions is outlined as follows.

I.   Content-Neutral Injunction
    A.   Heightened level of scrutiny stricter than the time, place, and manner test.
    B.   Must not burden more speech than necessary to achieve its objective.

---

[92]*Madsen v. Women's Health Center, Inc.*, 114 S. Ct. 2516 (1994).

[93]*Near v. Minnesota*, 283 U.S. 697 (1931); *Better Austin v. Keefe*, 402 U.S. 415 (1971); *New York Times Co. v. United States*, 403 U.S. 713 (1971); *Carroll v. President and Commissioners of Princess Anne*, 393 U.S. 175 (1968).

II. Content Based Injunction
   A. Presumptively invalid.
   B. Must have a compelling governmental interest.
   C. Must be the least restrictive means available.

Summary

The First Amendment is designed to restrain government on the one hand and protect the liberty of private parties on the other hand. The First Amendment is only applicable against the government. It is not applicable to restrain a private party. The several sections of the First Amendment include the Establishment Clause, the Free Exercise Clause, and the Free Speech Clause. The steps to analyze any First Amendment claim is to first identify (1) the parties, (2) the forum, (3) the restriction, and (4) the test. Once the applicable test is determined, that test should be utilized in order to determine if there is a First Amendment violation.

4

FREE EXERCISE RIGHTS

The First Amendment states, "Congress shall make no law respecting the establishment of religion, or prohibiting the free exercise thereof; . . ."[1] The first part of the Amendment is referred to as the Establishment Clause while the second part is referred to as the Free Exercise Clause.

Like the Establishment Clause, the Free Exercise Clause restricts certain governmental activities. The Free Exercise Clause limits the government from restricting religion. In order for the Free Exercise Clause to apply, there must be a governmental entity involved. One party must be acting under governmental authority while the other person or entity must be a private party. A person acting in their private capacity cannot violate the free exercise rights of another person. However, a governmental entity is limited in its ability to restrict the free exercise of religion without a compelling governmental interest to do so. In summary, the First Amendment is a limitation on governmental power.

The interpretation of the Free Exercise Clause remained fairly stable during most of the 1900s. However, in 1990, the United States Supreme Court handed down the decision of *Employment Division v. Smith*,[2] in which the Court severely limited the free exercise rights of all citizens. In 1993, Congress reacted to this dramatic shift in constitutional interpretation by passing what is known as the Religious Freedom Restoration Act (hereafter "RFRA") (pronounced "RIFRA").[3] RFRA restored free exercise rights as they existed prior to the 1990 *Smith* decision. However, on June 25, 1997, the Supreme Court declared RFRA unconstitutional.[4]

This chapter is divided into free exercise rights prior to *Smith*, free exercise rights during the *Smith* era between 1990 and 1993,

---

[1] U.S. Const. Amend. I. For discussion on the origins and historical understanding of the free exercise of religion, see Michael McConnell, *The Origins and Historical Understanding of Free Exercise of Religion*, 103 HARV. L. REV. 1409 (1990).

[2] 494 U.S. 872 (1990).

[3] 42 U.S.C. § 2000bb. See Appendix for the complete text.

[4] *City of Boerne v. Flores*, 117 S. Ct. 2157 (1997).

free exercise rights during RFRA, and free exercise rights after RFRA.

The Pre-*Smith* Era Prior to 1990

Prior to 1990, the Free Exercise Clause found its apex in two cases decided by the United States Supreme Court. The first was a 1963 case known as *Sherbert v. Verner*,[5] which dealt with unemployment compensation, and the second was *Wisconsin v. Yoder*,[6] which considered compulsory education laws.

In *Sherbert*, the South Carolina Employment Security Commission denied unemployment benefits to a Seventh-day Adventist because the claimant refused to perform a job search on Saturday. Seventh-day Adventists have sincerely held religious beliefs that the Sabbath is to be observed on the seventh day of the week, beginning Friday evening at sundown and concluding Saturday evening at sundown. Because of this sincerely held religious belief, Adell Sherbert refused to work on Saturday and, therefore, was denied unemployment benefits on the grounds that her refusal to work on Saturday precluded her from obtaining suitable employment. The Supreme Court ruled that this denial was a violation of her free exercise rights. First, the Court ruled that Ms. Sherbert had a sincerely held religious belief not to do any work on the Sabbath. Second, the state requirement to receive unemployment benefits burdened her sincerely held religious belief by causing her to choose between receipt of unemployment benefits or violating her religious convictions. Third, because of this conflict between the state requirement for unemployment benefits and the claimant's free exercise rights, the Court ruled that the state must have a compelling governmental interest in order to succeed. The Court found that there was no compelling governmental interest. The interest at stake was to preserve the unemployment compensation fund from dilution by false claims, but the state could clearly achieve that interest in a less restrictive manner. Consequently, to deny unemployment benefits to a claimant who refuses to work on

---

[5]374 U.S. 398 (1963).
[6]406 U.S. 205 (1972).

the Sabbath was a violation of the Free Exercise Clause.[7]

In *Yoder*, the Supreme Court ruled that the Wisconsin compulsory attendance law requiring children to attend school until age sixteen violated the free exercise rights of the Old Order Amish faith. Wisconsin, like all fifty states, had a compulsory education law that required students to attend school until age sixteen. However, the religious tenets of the Old Order Amish conflicted with this compulsory attendance law. The Old Order Amish believed that by sending their children to high school, they would not only expose themselves to the danger of censorship by the church community, but they would also endanger their own salvation and the salvation of their children. According to the Old Order Amish heritage, salvation requires life in a church community separate and apart from the world and worldly influence.[8] The Supreme Court observed the following:

> Formal high school education beyond the eighth grade is contrary to Amish beliefs, not only because it places Amish children in an environment hostile to Amish beliefs with increasing emphasis on competition in classwork and sports and with pressure to conform to the styles, manners, and ways of the peer group, but also because it takes them away from their community, physically and emotionally, during the crucial and formative adolescent period of life.[9]

The Court ruled that: (1) the Amish had a sincerely held religious belief which was contrary to compulsory education past the eighth grade; (2) the compulsory state education law placed a significant burden on this sincerely held religious belief; and (3) there was no compelling governmental interest strong enough to violate this sincerely held religious belief. Indeed, "a State's interest in universal education, however highly we rank it, is not totally free

---

[7]*See also Thomas v. Review Board, Indiana Employment Security Division*, 450 U.S. 707 (1981); *Hobbie v. Unemployment Appeals Commission of Florida*, 480 U.S. 136 (1987) (a state cannot withhold unemployment benefits from a Seventh-day Adventist who refuses to work on the seventh-day Sabbath).

[8]*Yoder*, 406 U.S. at 210.

[9]*Id.* at 211.

from a balancing process when it impinges on the fundamental rights and interests, such as those specifically protected by the Free Exercise Clause of the First Amendment."[10] In reaching its conclusion, the Court reviewed the history of the Amish religion and noted that one or two years of formal high school education for an Amish student would do little in view of the informal vocational education long practiced by the Amish community. The Amish formed a very self-sufficient community with no evidence that a lack of one or two more years of education would result in the students becoming burdens on society. Consequently, this compulsory education law was unconstitutional as applied to the Amish religion.

Though not every claim was successful under the Free Exercise Clause,[11] prior to 1990 the test for free exercise rights required two findings: (1) a sincerely held religious belief (2) that is burdened by some governmental action. In light of these two findings, the government must show a compelling governmental interest in order to restrict free exercise rights. In the absence of a compelling interest, free exercise prevails and the government restriction on religion must fail. The Court has already stated that if the compelling interest test means what it says, "many laws will not meet the test."[12]

Any free exercise challenge was therefore analyzed using a

---

[10]*Id.* at 214.

[11]*Reynolds v. United States*, 98 U.S. 145 (1879) (rejecting a claim that criminal laws were unconstitutional as applied against the religious practice of polygamy); *Gillette v. United States*, 401 U.S. 437 (1971) (rejecting a claim that the military selective service system violated the free exercise of religion by conscripting persons who oppose a particular war on religious grounds); *United States v. Lee*, 455 U.S. 252 (1982) (rejecting a claim that the payment of social security tax violated the free exercise rights of the Amish religion); *Bowen v. Roy*, 476 U.S. 693 (1986) (rejecting a claim that obtaining a social security number for the benefit of the applicant's daughter violated free exercise rights); *Lyng v. Northwest Indian Cemetery Protective Association*, 485 U.S. 439 (1988) (ruling that the government's logging and road construction activities took precedence over traditional Indian religious practices); *Goldman v. Weinberger*, 475 U.S. 503 (1986) (rejecting a claim that the prohibition of wearing a yarmulke pursuant to a military dress regulation violated free exercise rights); *O'Lone v. Estate of Shabazz*, 482 U.S. 342 (1987) (sustaining a prison's refusal to excuse inmates from work requirements to attend religious worship services); *Hernandez v. Commissioner*, 109 S. Ct. 2136 (1989) (rejecting a free exercise challenge to payment of income taxes alleged to make religious activities more difficult). In *Lyng, Goldman,* and *O'Lone,* the Court did not apply the *Sherbert* free exercise test.

[12]*Smith,* 494 U.S. at 888.

three step process as follows: Once the individual demonstrates (1) a sincerely held religious belief, (2) that is burdened by some governmental action, then (3) the government is required to show a compelling reason why it must burden this religious belief and must show that the regulation is the least restrictive means of achieving its governmental interest. The government cannot rely on *any* asserted interest or a reason for restricting religious beliefs. It must prove its interest is a *compelling* one. Moreover, the means it chooses to implement its interest cannot be a simple selection of several alternatives, it must be the least restrictive alternative of the means available.

The *Smith* Era from 1990 to 1993

On April 17, 1990, the United States Supreme Court drastically altered its interpretation of the Free Exercise Clause. In *Employment Division v. Smith*,[13] the Court essentially abolished the compelling governmental interest test in free exercise cases. In its place, the Court fashioned a different test that stated if a religious practice is burdened by a general law of neutral applicability, the religious claim will fail and the governmental intrusion on free exercise right will succeed. Prior to 1990, anyone showing a sincerely held religious belief which had been burdened by some governmental activity would be afforded the compelling interest test. If the compelling interest test "means what it says . . . many laws will not meet the test."[14] The compelling interest test meant that most laws under the strict scrutiny standard would be presumptively invalid. The government must show a compelling governmental interest in order to intrude on free exercise rights. In order for the test to be utilized, the only showing was that the individual had a sincerely held religious belief that was burdened by some governmental action.

In 1990, the United States Supreme Court changed its interpretation. Specifically, the Court stated "we cannot afford the luxury of deeming presumptively invalid as applied to the religious objective, every regulation of conduct that does not protect an

---

[13]*Id.* at 872.
[14]*Id.* at 888.

interest of the highest order."[15] In other words, the Supreme Court felt that the past quarter of a century of free exercise rights was a "luxury" the country could no longer afford. Under the *Smith* test, a law that does not single out religion as its object of regulation may be held valid in the face of a free exercise claim. So long as the law applies across the board to religious and nonreligious activities, the law may prevail over the religious objector. Ironically, in 1972 the United States Supreme Court ruled exactly the opposite when it stated the following: "A regulation neutral on its face may, in its application, nonetheless offend the constitutional requirement for governmental neutrality if it unduly burdens the free exercise of religion."[16] In other words, in 1972 the Supreme Court stated that a neutral law could still violate free exercise rights, but in 1990, the Supreme Court stated that a neutral law would not violate free exercise rights. Using the example noted above regarding the unemployment case of *Sherbert,* if that case had been decided between 1990 and 1993, Ms. Sherbert would have lost her free exercise claim. This is because the unemployment law requiring a job search on the seventh-day Sabbath would be a neutral law of general applicability. This law was not made for the purpose of singling out religion. On the contrary, the law applies equally to religious and nonreligious activities. As such, between 1990 and 1993, neutral laws were constitutional; whereas prior to 1990, neutral law of general applicability burdened a sincerely held religious belief, that law would be unconstitutional.

From 1990 to 1993, free exercise rights were dealt a devastating blow. Though the Minnesota Supreme Court ruled that an Amish person's refusal to place an orange triangle on the back of a buggy violated free exercise rights, the United States Supreme Court vacated that decision in light of *Smith.*[17] After *Smith,* many religious rights were lost in cases involving immigration,[18] landmarking,[19] religious clothing,[20] workers' compensation,[21]

---

[15]*Id.*

[16]*Yoder,* 406 U.S. at 220.

[17]*Minnesota v. Hershberger,* 462 N.W.2d 393 (Minn. 1990).

[18]*Intercommunity Center for Justice and Peace v. INS,* 910 F.2d 42 (2nd Cir. 1990).

[19]*St. Bartholomew's Church v. City of New York,* 914 F.2d 348 (2nd Cir. 1990).

[20]*United States v. Board of Education for the School District of Philadelphia,* 911 F.2d 882 (3rd Cir. 1990).

home education,[22] zoning,[23] jurisdiction of the National Labor Relations Board over religious schools,[24] the applicability of the Age Discrimination and Employment Act over religious organizations,[25] and religious objections to autopsies.[26]

According to one court, the Supreme Court's decision in *Smith* "cut back, possibly to minute dimensions, the doctrine that requires government to accommodate, at some cost, minority religious preferences."[27] The United States Supreme Court in *Smith* belittled free exercise rights. Though the term "free exercise" specifically occurs in the First Amendment, the Supreme Court stated that in order to obtain the protection of free exercise rights that existed prior to 1990, any free exercise claim must meet either of the following: (1) the law impacting the religious practice is not a neutral law of general applicability but is one that specifically targets religion,[28] or (2) the free exercise right must be combined with some other implicit or explicit constitutional right. In other words, in order for the compelling interest test to be applicable after *Smith*, the law must specifically target religion, or the free exercise right must be combined with some other constitutional right such as free speech, privacy, or parental rights.[29] This hybrid combination

---

[21]*South Ridge Baptist Church v. Industrial Commission of Ohio*, 911 F.2d 1203 (6th Cir. 1990).

[22]*Vandiver v. Hardin County Board of Education*, 925 F.2d 927 (6th Cir. 1991).

[23]*Cornerstone Bible Church v. City of Hastings*, 948 F.2d 648 (8th Cir. 1990).

[24]*NLRB v. Hanna Boys Center*, 940 F.2d 1295 (9th Cir. 1991).

[25]*Lukaszewski v. Nazareth Hospital*, 764 F. Supp. 57 (E.D. Pa. 1991).

[26]*Montgomery v. County of Clinton*, 743 F. Supp. 1253 (W.D. Mich. 1990); *You Vang Yang v. Sturner*, 728 F. Supp. 845 (D.R.I. 1990).

[27]*Hunafa v. Murphy*, 907 F.2d 46 (7th Cir. 1990).

[28]*Church of the Lukumi v. City of Hialeah*, 113 S. Ct. 2217 (1993)(a law specifically enacted against the Santeria religion violated free exercise rights because it was required to meet a compelling interest test since the law was not neutral and of general applicability).

[29]Pursuant to the analysis in *Smith*, combining a free exercise of religion with some other federally recognized right such as free speech brings the standard of protection to its highest level. *Id.* at 1601. *Hobbie v. Unemployment Appeals Commission of Florida*, 480 U.S. 136 (1987) (unemployment benefits); *Thomas v. Review Board, Indiana Employment Security Div.*, 450 U.S. 707 (1981) (unemployment benefits); *Wooley v. Maynard*, 430 U.S. 705 (1977) (invalidating compelled display of a license plate slogan that offended individual religious beliefs); *Wisconsin v. Yoder*, 406 U.S. 205, (1972) (invalidating compulsory school attendance laws as applied to Amish parents who refused on religious grounds to send their children to school); *Sherbert v. Verner*, 374 U.S. 398 (1963) (unemployment benefits); *Follett v. McCormick*, 321 U.S. 573 (1944) (same); *Murdock v. Pennsylvania*, 319 U.S. 105 (1943) (invalidating a flat tax on solicitation as applied to the dissemination of religious ideas); *West*

would then equate to the same standard utilized by the Court prior to 1990. This simply belittled free exercise rights by requiring free exercise to be combined with some other constitutional recognition. In reaction to this limitation on free exercise rights, Congress took action in 1993 by enacting the Religious Freedom Restoration Act.

The Post-*Smith* Era Under RFRA from 1993 to 1997

Because religious freedom rights were dealt a devastating blow by the *Smith* decision that reigned between 1990 and 1993, Congress passed what is known as the Religious Freedom Restoration Act.[30] The major portion of RFRA states as follows:

(a) IN GENERAL—Government shall not burden a person's exercise of religion even if the burden results from a rule of general applicability, except as provided in subsection (b).

(b) EXCEPTION—Government may substantially burden a person's exercise of religion only if it demonstrates that application of the burden to the person—

(1) is in furtherance of a compelling governmental interest; and

(2) is the least restrictive means of furthering that compelling governmental interest.[31]

RFRA recreated the constitutional standard that existed prior to the 1990 *Smith* decision. Thus, all of the Supreme Court's decisions noted above involving free exercise rights prior to the *Smith* decision were revived by RFRA. The three-year reign of

---

Virginia Board of Education v. Barnette, 319 U.S. 624 (1943) (invalidating compulsory flag salute statue challenged by religious objectors); *Cantwell v. Connecticut*, 310 U.S. 296 (1940) (invalidating a licensing system for religious and charitable solicitations under which the administrator had discretion to deny a license to any cause he deemed nonreligious); *Pierce v. Society of Sisters*, 268 U.S. 510 (1925) (directing the education of children).

[30]42 U.S.C. § 2000bb.

[31]42 U.S.C. § 2000bb-1.

terror was over. Free exercise rights were again recognized as deserving specific protection. The First Amendment to the United States Constitution specifically recognized and protected free exercise rights, but the First Amendment was ignored by the Supreme Court in 1990. Between 1993 and 1997 free exercise was primarily protected by legislative enactment rather than the Constitution. The standard required the showing of (1) a sincerely held religious belief, (2) which is burdened by some governmental action. If these two factors were present, the government was required to show a compelling governmental interest and further show that the restriction on the religious practice was the least restrictive means of achieving that compelling governmental interest. Remember, once the compelling governmental interest test is applicable, the Supreme Court has already recognized that "many laws will not meet the test."[32]

Prior to the passage of the Religious Freedom Restoration Act, the National Right to Life Committee opposed RFRA unless it contained an abortion-neutral amendment. Specifically, National Right to Life argued that the amendment would be used to justify abortion. Though some courts were requested to grant an abortion in the face of governmental restrictions to the contrary based on a free exercise right,[33] the United States Supreme Court previously rejected such a claim under the Free Exercise Clause of the Constitution.[34]

The Post-RFRA Era After 1997

Though RFRA ended the three year reign of terror for religious liberty, the Supreme Court no longer considers it good law. On June 25, 1997, the United States Supreme Court found the federal statute unconstitutional.[35] The battle over the constitutionality of RFRA originated in the city of Boerne, Texas, located some 28 miles northwest of San Antonio. Situated in this hill city is St. Peter

---

[32]*Smith*, 494 U.S. at 888.

[33]*McCrae v. Califano*, 491 F. Supp. 630 (E.D.N.Y. 1980).

[34]*Harris v. McCrae*, 100 S. Ct. 2671 (1980). *See* Bopp, *Will There Be a Constitutional Right to Abortion After the Reconsideration of Roe v. Wade?*, 15 J. Contemporary L. 131 (1989).

[35]*City of Boerne*, 117 S. Ct. at 2157.

Catholic Church built in 1923. The church's structure replicates the
mission style of the region's earlier history. The church is built to
accommodate approximately 230 worshippers, but the congregation
outgrew its sanctuary. Each Sunday approximately 40 to 60
parishioners were turned away from the Sunday masses. In order to
accommodate its growing congregation, the archbishop of San
Antonio gave permission to enlarge the sanctuary. A few months
later the Boerne city council passed an ordinance which authorized
the city's Historic Landmark Commission to prepare a preservation
plan with proposed historic landmarks and districts. Under this
ordinance the Commission was required to preapprove construction
affecting any historical landmark.

The archbishop applied for a building permit to enlarge the
church sanctuary. Relying on the city ordinance and the fact that the
church was located in a designated historical district, city authorities
denied the application. The archbishop then filed suit claiming that
the church's religious free exercise was violated under RFRA.

When the case finally made its way to the United States
Supreme Court, the city argued that RFRA was unconstitutional
because it exceeded Congress' authority to pass substantive
legislation regarding the free exercise of religion.

When Congress passed RFRA, it relied upon Section 5 of the
Fourteenth Amendment to the United States Constitution. Section
1 of the Fourteenth Amendment provides the following:

> No State shall make or enforce any law which shall
> abridge the privileges or immunities of citizens of the
> United States; nor shall any State deprive any person of
> life, liberty, or property, without due process of law; nor
> deny to any person within its jurisdiction equal protection
> of the laws.[36]

Section 5 of the Fourteenth Amendment states as follows: "The
Congress shall have power to enforce, by appropriate legislation, the
provisions of this article."[37] The Fourteenth Amendment was
enacted after the Civil War to ensure equal protection of all

---

[36]U.S. Const. Amend. 14, sec. 1.
[37]U.S. Const. Amend. 14 sec. 5.

citizens. The genre of the amendment was to provide protection among the individual states to all citizens, regardless or race. However, the amendment was not limited solely to race but applied to all privileges or immunities and prohibited states from depriving any person of life, liberty, or property without due process of law, and also provided equal protection to the laws to be applied to all citizens. Section 5 of the Fourteenth Amendment empowered Congress to enact appropriate legislation that would be remedial in nature. In other words, Congress could pass legislation that would put in practice the actual dictates of the Fourteenth Amendment. Therefore, Section 5 was a "positive grant of legislative power"[38] to Congress to enact legislation which would put in practice the specific dictates of the Fourteenth Amendment. In fact, the Supreme Court stated the following about Section 5 of the Fourteenth Amendment:

> Whatever legislation is appropriate, that is, adapted to carry out the objects the amendments have in view, whatever tends to enforce submission to the prohibitions they contain, and to secure to all persons the enjoyment of perfect equality of civil rights and the equal protection of the laws against State denial or invasion, if not prohibited, is brought within the domain of congressional power.[39]

However, the Supreme Court has also noted that "[a]s broad as the congressional enforcement power is, it is not unlimited."[40] The Supreme Court agreed that Congress has the authority to enforce the Free Exercise Clause through the Fourteenth Amendment but defined this power as remedial in nature, not substantive. The Supreme Court went on to state the following:

> Legislation which alters the meaning of the Free Exercise Clause cannot be said to be enforcing the Clause. Congress does not enforce a constitutional right by changing what the right is. It has been given the power "to

---

[38]*Katzenbach v. Morgan*, 384 U.S. 641, 651 (1966).
[39]*Ex Parte Virginia*, 100 U.S. 339, 345-46 (1880).
[40]*Oregon v. Mitchell*, 400 U.S. 112, 128 (1970).

enforce," not the power to determine what constitutes a constitutional violation. Were it not so, what Congress would be enforcing would no longer be, in any meaningful sense, the "provisions of [the Fourteenth Amendment]."[41]

To determine whether RFRA was remedial or substantive, the Court used circular reasoning by harkening back to its 1990 *Smith* decision. Congress obviously passed RFRA to overcome the devastating blow the 1990 *Smith* decision dealt to religious liberty. The Supreme Court concluded that RFRA was attempting to enact substantive legislation regarding religious liberty and was therefore contrary to its *Smith* decision which weakened religious liberty. The court then went on to state the following:

> Our national experience teaches that the Constitution is preserved best when each part of the government respects both the Constitution and the proper actions and determinations of the other branches. When the Court has interpreted the Constitution, it has acted within the province of the Judicial Branch, which embraces the duty to say what the law is. When the political branches of the Government act against the background of a judicial interpretation of the Constitution already issued, it must be understood that in later cases and controversies the Court will treat its precedents with the respect due them under several principles, including *stare decisis*, and contrary exceptions must be disappointed. RFRA was designed to control cases and controversies, such as the one before us; but as the provisions of the federal statute herein invoked are beyond congressional authority, it is this Court's precedent, not RFRA, which must control.[42]

The Court found RFRA unconstitutional because it concluded Congress exceeded its authority in passing substantive legislation regarding the free exercise of religion. The Court concluded that

---

[41]*City of Boerne*, 117 S. Ct. at 2159.
[42]*City of Boerne*, 117 S. Ct. at 2172 (citation omitted).

only it had the sole province to determine what the law is, and once it determined the meaning of the Constitution, no other branch of government had authority to alter its decision.

The proposition cited by the Supreme Court is somewhat arrogant. The Court determined long ago that it is the sole interpreter of the Constitution and has the final say regarding constitutional principles. However, both the executive and the legislative branches similarly have the obligation to support the Constitution no less than the judicial branch. The problem created with the Free Exercise Clause was initiated by the Supreme Court in 1990 when it handed down the *Smith* decision. Congress had very little choice but to respond to the Court by enacting appropriate legislation. Whether this legislation is remedial or substantive is up to debate, but the point is that this legislation was supported by both liberals and conservatives, Christians and Jews, because the Supreme Court in its "wisdom" essentially abrogated the First Amendment Free Exercise Clause. Striking a blow to religious freedom once is reprehensible. Doing it twice plants the seed from which revolution may spring forth.

Now that RFRA has been ruled unconstitutional, the reign of terror for religious liberty during the time period of 1990 to 1993 has again been resurrected. We again live under the tyranny of the 1990 *Smith* decision. To understand the status of religious liberty today, a simple example best illustrates the point. For this purpose, I will use the example of the time period of prohibition during which the sale and consumption of alcohol was forbidden.

If a church faced a prohibition law pertaining to the sale or consumption of alcohol prior to 1990, the church could bring suit under the Free Exercise Clause claiming that the law burdened their exercise of religion. Under the pre-*Smith* analysis, the church would win. For example, the church would first argue that it has a sincerely held religious belief to consume wine as part of its communion service. The government would then have the burden to show it had a compelling governmental reason to enact the prohibition. It might be debatable whether the government has a compelling reason, the only reason the government could come up with would be based upon health, safety and welfare due to the effects of intoxication. The government would then be required to show that it used the least restrictive means available to meet its compelling governmental interest. If the real reason is the protection of the health, safety and welfare, the government could still achieve this interest by controlling the sale of alcohol much like a prescription drug, or by limiting intoxication levels. Consequently, a flat ban covering communion use would be unconstitutional because there would be no risk to the health, safety, or welfare of the citizens. A flat ban would therefore not be the least restrictive means and consequently the church would win.

However, under the post-1990 *Smith* legislation, the church would lose and the government would win. While the church would argue that it has a sincerely held religious belief, the government would rely up on *Smith* to state that the law is general and that it is applied to both religious and nonreligious uses therefore is neutral in application. Since the law covers a broad class, religious and nonreligious, and since it does not target any specific religious practice to the exclusion of other practices, the government would win. So long as the law governed both religious and nonreligious uses, and did not specifically target only religion, the law would be upheld against a constitutional challenge. The only way the law would be considered unconstitutional is if the government targeted religion by prohibiting only the consumption of alcohol during communion while allowing the general public to consume alcohol.[43]

As you can see, under the *Smith* interpretation of the Free Exercise Clause, religion will almost always be the loser. As in the *City of Boerne*, the Court preferred the preservation of architecture over the preservation of religious freedom. Any zoning regulation that applies to secular and nonsecular practices, will usually be upheld against a constitutional challenge. For example, historically churches have been permitted to locate in residential areas primarily based upon the free exercise of religion and the concept that churches are beneficial to the community. While a business cannot locate in a residential area, churches have historically enjoyed this privilege. Under *Smith*, churches would not be able to locate in a residential area because businesses cannot locate there. Also, zoning

---

[43]The only other possibility is to come up with some other constitutional right and then combine this right with the Free Exercise Clause. If no other constitutional right could be found, the Free Exercise claim alone would not benefit the church.

regulations pertaining to schools, daycare centers, or ministries to the hungry and homeless will have a negative impact on religion. Many church schools, daycare centers, and ministries to the hungry and homeless will be denied because they will face laws that are general and neutral in their application. Licensing laws pertaining to counseling may also negatively affect pastoral ministries. Since pastors engage in a form of counseling, it is very likely that licensing laws pertaining to counseling will be upheld against constitutional challenges since these laws are general and neutral in their application. If the pastor raises a constitutional objection, the Supreme Court will respond: "Too bad."

Constitutionally, the only way to restore religious liberty under the present Supreme Court interpretation is to argue that the law being challenged specifically targets religion to the exclusion of other practices, or to combine the claim of religious liberty with some other constitutional right. To argue that a law specifically targets religion will be very difficult since the cautious legislator will attempt to negate a true motive by drafting a general law. Alternatively, it is possible in some situations to combine religious free exercise challenges with a free speech, equal protection or a parental rights analysis. For example, a person who wants to hand out religious literature in a public park can argue under the Free Speech Clause and the Free Exercise Clause. However, this is apparently useless because adding the free exercise argument to the free speech argument adds no additional constitutional protection. The free speech argument already raises the issue to a stringent constitutional standard irrespective of the free exercise argument. Thus, tacking on free exercise to a free speech argument adds very little to a claim. In other words, once you have a free speech claim, you do not need free exercise. Moreover, churches generally do not have a free speech right infringed in the area of zoning or other potential challenges. Therefore, there will be many cases where no other constitutional right can be appended to the free exercise right. Essentially this has caused civil liberty groups to abandon free exercise challenges and search the Constitution for other religious liberty protections. In practice, the Free Exercise Clause has become essentially nonexistent under the Supreme Court's ruling.

There are several possible recourses to the Supreme Court's reprehensible behavior. First, some argue that what the Supreme

Court really said in the *City of Boerne* is that Congress may not enact legislation affecting the states with regards to a substantive matter of religious liberty. However, some argue that Congress may enact legislation restricting its own activity with respect to religious liberty. In other words, some argue that Congress may reenact the RFRA legislation to restrict only the federal government from infringing on free exercise rights, but may not restrict the states from infringing on these rights. It seems if this were true, then the Supreme Court would have suggested such an approach but they made no mention of a dichotomy between the state versus the federal application. Moreover, most restrictions on religious liberty originate from the state, not the federal branch, and therefore even if this were true, it would still leave most free exercise challenges unprotected.

A second approach suggested by some is impeachment. This issue is addressed in another chapter. However, it seems unlikely that Congress would engage in an impeachment debate, and it is further unlikely that Congress would garner enough support to begin picking off judges like clay ducks.

The third approach is to enact a form of RFRA state by state. This would require each state and territory to enact its own version of RFRA. It is not at all clear whether the Supreme Court would even continence this aspect of protecting religious liberty. However, it is a viable alternative for a state to enact its own RFRA version which would restrict the state government from infringing on free exercise of religion. The state versions of RFRA would not affect the federal government. It is potentially possible to combine a federal statute wherein Congress restricts its own ability to infringe on free exercise with individual state legislation that restricts the state government from infringing on the free exercise of religion. This would be an enormous task because all fifty states plus the territories including the federal government would have to enact their own legislation.[44]

The fourth alternative is to pass a constitutional amendment specifically protecting free exercise of religion. This is probably the only viable approach to the Supreme Court's decision. On the one hand, it is distasteful to even talk about adopting a constitutional

---

[44]See Appendix for Liberty Counsel's suggested state version of RFRA.

amendment to protect religious freedom. Why would we need to do that when the very first amendment to the Constitution specifically protects the free exercise of religion? The only reason is the Supreme Court's abdication of the very principles that underscore the First Amendment. Adopting a new amendment to protect religious freedom would make the First Amendment Free Exercise Clause a useless appendage to the Constitution. On the other hand, absent a constitutional amendment, it is practically a useless appendage under the Supreme Court's ruling.

There seems to be a great deal of support for protecting religious liberty both from the conservative and the liberal political parties. This support is widespread from Christian and Jewish organizations as is evidenced by the broad based support for RFRA in 1993.

The history of religious liberty in this country parallels the history of judicial tyranny. It is frustrating to guess from day to day about one's constitutional rights. It is sad to say that the constitutional rights we enjoyed in 1990 are no longer enjoyed after 1997. The religious liberty protections we all took for granted have been evaporated by the stroke of a pen. This is not how a constitutional form of government is supposed to operate. The Constitution is supposed to be immutable, unchangeable, and above our fluctuating human philosophies. However, if the Supreme Court has the authority to determine what the law is, and if this Court is not dedicated to the original understanding of the Constitution, then the Constitution has lost its uniqueness.

Summary

Prior to 1990, the Free Exercise Clause was a powerful constitutional protection for religious freedom. If an individual had (1) a sincerely held religious belief, (2) which was burdened by some governmental regulation, then (3) the government had to show a compelling governmental interest in order to limit the free exercise of religion and must achieve its interest with the least restrictive means available. If there was no compelling governmental interest, then the individual free exercise right won. If there was a compelling governmental interest, but there was a less restrictive means to achieve that interest, again, the individual's free exercise of religion would triumph. According to the Supreme Court, if the compelling interest test means what it says, "many laws will not meet the test."[45] In other words, once an individual showed that a sincerely held religious belief was burdened by a governmental regulation, most governmental regulations would fail in light of the Free Exercise Clause.

In 1990, the interpretation of the Free Exercise Clause was drastically altered by the *Smith* decision. The Supreme Court ruled in 1990 that individual free exercise would fail if the governmental regulation was a neutral law of general applicability. In other words, if the governmental regulation applied equally to religious as well as nonreligious practices, the free exercise right would lose. The only time the compelling governmental interest test would arise is if (1) the regulation specifically singled out religion for discriminatory treatment or (2) the free exercise right was combined with some other implicit or explicit constitutional protection. Thus, by combining two constitutional provisions, free exercise with some other constitutional provision, the free exercise right would then reach the level of protection it enjoyed prior to 1990. Free exercise in and of itself no longer demanded the strict compelling governmental interest. Free exercise rights were dealt a devastating blow between 1990 and 1993.

Reacting to this drastic change in the interpretation of the Free Exercise Clause, the Religious Freedom Restoration Act was passed in late 1993. This federal law restored free exercise rights to the level of protection that existed prior to 1990. Thus, if an individual had (1) a sincerely held religious belief, (2) which was burdened by some governmental regulation, then (3) the government was required to demonstrate a compelling interest to restrict the religious exercise and to achieve that compelling governmental interest in the least restrictive manner. Unfortunately, in 1997, the Supreme Court ruled RFRA unconstitutional. We now live under the dreadful *Smith* decision. A law or regulation burdening religion will generally be upheld so long as the law is a general law of neutral applicability. The only chance of success against a contrary law is to prove that it is specifically aimed at religious suppression, or to combine the free exercise claim with some other recognized constitutional right.

---

[45]*Smith*, 494 U.S. at 888.

Something needs to be done to restore our religious liberty. We should not stand by idly while our "masters" in black robes carve the heart out of our nation as it gasps for its final breath.

5

RELIGIOUS BIAS IN PUBLIC SCHOOL TEXTBOOKS

Bias in public school textbooks poses a significant threat to religious liberty. Whether motivated by intentional hostility, or fueled by a misunderstanding of church and state, the result is the same -- a distorted presentation of history which suggests that religion has no place in American culture. Modern public school textbooks either demean religion, or worse, pretend as though history was not shaped by religion. This vacuum in our public school textbooks teaches a silent message that religion is irrelevant, that it is best confined to the sanctum of the inner mind. Censoring religion is a far cry from neutrality. Acting as though religion had nothing to do with shaping American history is outright hostility. Hostility toward religion is forbidden by the First Amendment Establishment Clause.

Some time ago the so-called "Scopes II" trial in Greenville, Tennessee received significant media attention.[1] The media portrayed the controversy as one involving fanatical "fundamentalist" christians objecting to textbooks such as the *Wizard of Oz*, *Macbeth*, and the *Diary of Anne Frank*. Unfortunately, the real issues are far more serious than the media is willing to admit.

Statistical Analysis

One of the most extensive content analysis of public school textbooks to date was conducted by Dr. Paul C. Vitz, a professor of psychology at New York University. The study was funded by the federal government through the National Institute of Education, a branch of the Department of Education. The results were published in Dr. Vitz's book, *Censorship: Evidence of Bias in Our Children's Textbooks*.[2]

Using scientific methods, Dr. Vitz examined ninety widely

---

[1]*Mozert v. Hawkins County Public Schools*, 647 F. Supp. 1194 (E.D. Tenn. 1986).
[2]Paul C. Vitz, *Censorship: Evidence of Bias in Our Children's Textbooks* (1986).

used social studies texts, high school history texts, and elementary readers. The data consisted of information received directly from state-adopted textbook lists.[3] The variables included, *inter alia*, primary and secondary references to religion; primary references being some form of worship (in text or picture), and secondary references consisting of the mere mention of religious words (in text or picture), such as the word "God" inscribed on a tombstone, or even a Christmas tree or Easter eggs. All pages of the texts were evaluated by a panel of three external judges.[4] Intercoder agreement was nearly one hundred percent (100%) throughout various portions of the study. The publisher at issue in the "Scopes II" case, Holt, Rinehart & Winston, was part of the study.[5]

Some of the results include, but are not limited to, the following:

•In the sixty books grades 1-4, and twenty books grades 5-6, not one word refers to any child or adult who prayed, or who went to church or temple.[6]

•Only eleven pictures refer to religious activity in roughly 15,000 pages grades 1-4, yet not one image depicts any

---

[3]*Id.* pp. 5-9, 46, 62. The state-adopted textbook lists include California and Texas. These two states alone account for 9.9% and 7.0% of the student population in the United States, or a combined 16.9% of the total student population. The official adoption lists of fifteen other states were also provided by Educational Products Information Exchange (EPIE): Alabama, Arkansas, Florida, Georgia, Idaho, Indiana, Mississippi, New Mexico, Nevada, North Carolina, Oklahoma, Oregon, South Carolina, Utah, Virginia, and West Virginia. The available adopted lists varied slightly from one category to another, e.g., the category of grades 1-4, grades 5-6, and high school. Of course, not every state uses state-adopted textbook lists. However, the textbooks used in this study based primarily on adopted lists provide ample representation.

[4]According to Dr. Vitz, the accuracy of the scoring of the different religious categories was checked by having the texts scored by a panel of independent judges provided by EPIE. See Vitz, *Censorship: Evidence of Bias in Our Children's Textbooks* 10.

[5]*Mozert*, 647 F. Supp. at 1195. The publishers include: Allyn & Bacon (formerly Follett); D.C. Heath (formerly American Book Co.); Holt, Rinehart & Winston; Laidlaw Brothers; Macmillan; McGraw-Hill; Riverside (formerly Rand McNally); Scott, Foresman & Co.; Silver Burdett; Silver-Vaughn (formerly Scholastic); Addison Wesley; Globe; Harcourt Brace & Jovanovich; Houghton Mifflin; Economy (Keytexts); and Lippincott. *See* Vitz, *Censorship: Evidence of Bias in Our Children's Textbooks* 7, 12-13, 22-26, 28-29, 31, 46, 48-56, 63, 130-37.

[6]Vitz, *Censorship: Evidence of Bias in Our Children's Textbooks* 5-20.

form of contemporary representative Protestantism.[7]

•In a total of 670 stories from third and sixth grade readers not one reference to representative Protestant religious life is found.[8]

•The few references to religion occur during the sixteen and seventeen hundreds, leaving the impression that religion has become extinct as a modern societal force.[9]

•Thanksgiving is presented without stating that the Pilgrims gave thanks to God. When the Pilgrims are mentioned there is no reference to their Puritan religious faith. They are misleadingly described as people who take long journeys. Though all the early colonial charters state that God led the Pilgrims to America to spread the gospel, not a word of this well-established historical fact is mentioned anywhere in any of these books.[10]

---

[7] *Id.* at 1-2, 5-20.

[8] *Id.* at 3, 61-76.

[9] *Id.* at 15, 20-36, 48-60, 65-70, 75-76.

[10] *Id.* at 18-19. For example, the First Charter of Virginia providing for the settlement of Jamestown and dated A.D. 1606 declared:

We greatly commending, and graciously accepting of, their Desires for the Furtherance of so noble a Work, which may, by the Province of Almighty God, hereafter tend to the Glory of His Divine Majesty, in propagating the Christian Religion to such People, as yet live in Darkness and miserable ignorance of the true Knowledge and Worship of God, living in those Parts, to human Civility, and to a settled and quiet Government. . . .

After the Pilgrims landed at Cape Henry in April of 1607, they erected a large wooden cross and prayed to God. The Pilgrims then sailed on the Mayflower to Plymouth Rock. On November 11, 1620, the Pilgrims signed the Mayflower Compact, stating:

Having undertaken for the glory of God, and advancements of the Christian faith, and honor of our kind and country, a voyage to plant the first colony in the Northern parts of Virginia, does by these present solemnly and mutually in the presence of God, and one another, covenant and combine ourselves together into a civil body politic. . . .

The New England Confederation was signed on May 19, 1643 and stated:

•When Martin Luther King, Jr. is mentioned for his efforts against racism, the books seldom mention the importance religion had on his life; if religion is mentioned at all, the most that is said is that he was a minister.[11]

•Joan of Arc is described, but there is no reference to any religious aspect of her life.[12]

•Major Catholic, Protestant, and Jewish historical events are not covered, such as the First and Second Great Awakenings, the Reformation, the Catholic founding of private schools,[13] the christian origins of American

---

Whereas we all came into these parts of America with one and the same end and aim, namely to advance the Kingdom of our Lord Jesus Christ and to enjoy the liberties of the Gospel in purity with peace....

The first Pennsylvania Charter of Privileges clearly gives the religious character of the early colonial settlers and their stated purpose for coming to America:

And Almighty God being the only Lord of Conscience, Father of Lights and Spirits; and the Author as well as Object of all divine Knowledge, Faith and Worship, who only doth enlighten the Minds, and persuade and convince the Understandings of People....And that all Persons who also profess to believe in Jesus Christ, the Saviour of the World, shall be capable (notwithstanding their other Persuasions and Practices in Point of Conscience and Religion) to serve this Government in any Capacity, both legislatively and executively. . . .

[11]Vitz, Censorship: Evidence of Bias in Our Children's Textbooks 23-24, 25, 27, 51, 55-56, 57. Clearly, Martin Luther King, Jr. used many religious motifs when addressing his audience about slavery and equality. Religious themes pervaded his speeches. To ignore the importance of religion in his life as it pertains to civil rights is nothing less than religious censorship.

[12]Id. at 3, 36. Joan of Arc (1412-1431), is a French national heroine and saint of the Roman Catholic Church who led the French army to victory at the siege of Orleans in 1429, thus liberating the city of Orleans from the English. She died a martyr's death on May 30, 1431, in the city of Rouen. She was later beatified by Pope Pius Calixtus III in 1456 (beatification is the first step toward canonization). She was then declared a saint by Pope Benedict XV in 1920. A feast is celebrated throughout France in memory of her death an May 30. To accurately describe Joan of Arc the religious aspect of her life cannot be overlooked. Judging by the description of Joan of Arc in these books the only probable reason she is included at all is to emphasize feminism.

[13]Possibly an additional reason why the founding of a private school system by the Catholic Church is not mentioned is because of the fear of competition between public and private education, a competition the National Education Association greatly abhors.

education (e.g., Harvard, Princeton, etc.),[14] the Jewish celebration of Hanukkah, etc.[15]

•The neglect of Catholic, Protestant and Jewish religion is not due to a total avoidance of all religion, for the textbooks covered Indian, Egyptian, and Greek religions, including magic and some occult forms.[16]

•The family is often mentioned in social studies books, grades 1-4, but there was not one text reference to "marriage" or "wedding." In fact, neither the word "husband" nor "wife" occurs once in any of these books. The words "housewife" or "homemaker" never occur in these books. One second grade book published by Laidlaw states that "a family is a group of people" and the teacher's edition elaborates on this definition so as to describe a family as a group of people "who identify themselves as family members."[17]

•One high school history book published by Houghton Mifflin defines "fundamentalism" as rural people who "follow the values or traditions of an earlier period."[18] Thus the impression is made that christians who have been termed by the media as "fundamentalists" follow a way of life that is now antiquated. This same textbook lists in an appendix 642 important historical dates. Only six events refer to religion: (1) 1649--Religious Toleration Act in Maryland; (2) 1661--First Bible published in America; (3) 1692--Salem Witch Trials; (4) 1769--Spanish missions in California; (5) 1858 [sic]--

---

[14]The first 126 colleges in the United States were Christian colleges. Clearly, the educational roots of America are planted in Christian soil.

[15]Vitz, *Censorship: Evidence of Bias in Our Children's Textbooks* 11-20, 27, 30-36, 48-60, 64-70.

[16]*Id.* at 15-20, 32-36, 64-70, 75-76.

[17]*Id.* at 36-39. Such a loosely defined definition of "family" leaves open the possibility of a homosexual "family" and delimits the importance of marriage in the traditional sense.

[18]*Id.* at 53.

Religious revivals;[19] and (6) 1875--Hebrew Union College founded in Cincinnati, Ohio. The list has nothing on religion since 1875, yet it deems the following important: (1) 1893--Yale introduces ice hockey; (2) 1897--First subway completed in Boston; (3) 1920--United States wins first place in Olympic Games, (4) 1930--Irish Sweepstakes becomes popular; (5) 1960--Pittsburgh Pirates win World Series; and (6) 1962--A popular dance craze developed known as the Twist.[20]

•An example of the religious bias is provided by a story of the Nobel laureate and Jewish writer Isaac Bashevis Singer. In Singer's original story the main character was a boy who prayed "to God" during a blizzard, and when the blizzard ended by what the boy believed was God's answer to his prayer' he remarked, "Thank God." A sixth grade reader presented a revised version of the story by excising the words "to God" and changing "Thank God" to "Thank goodness."[21]

Conflict Between Secular Humanism And Christianity

The list of religious bias could continue for pages. A prior study conducted by Dr. Donald Oppewal, professor of education at Calvin College, came to essentially the same conclusions as did Dr. Vitz.[22] A recent study by Dr. Robert Bryan, whose doctorate is in church history, focused on the *way* in which religion was mentioned rather than simply *when* it was mentioned. He noted that Christianity was presented as having no historical presence in America after the year A.D. 1700. He concluded "*[t]hese textbooks are written to propound the thesis that America was settled for the sake of religious freedom, and that religious freedom means the*

---

[19]The date of 1858 is incorrect. No major religious revival occurred during this period. The First Great Awakening is dated c. 1740; the Second Great Awakening is dated 1830-1840; and the Pentecostal Movement is dated 1880-1910.

[20]Vitz, *Censorship: Evidence of Bias in Our Children's Textbooks* 53-54.

[21]*Id.* at 3-4.

[22]Donald Oppewal, *Religion in American Textbooks: A Review of the Literature* (Part of Final Report: NIE-G-84-0012; Project No. 2-0099. Equity in Values Education).

absence of religion."[23] This determined bias against religion, especially Christianity, is clearly evident when viewed against the religious heritage of American culture.[24]

For example, Alexis de Tocqueville, an astute foreign observer of the United States, commented in the 1840s after visiting this country:

> The religious atmosphere of the country was the first thing that struck me on arrival in the United States. The longer I stayed in the country, the more conscious I became of the important political consequences resulting from this novel situation.

> Religion, which never intervenes directly in the government of American society, should therefore be considered as the first of their political institutions. . . .[25]

The checkered history of public school education has been well documented by Samuel Blumenfeld in his poignant expose entitled, *NEA: Trojan Horse in American Education.*[26] Blumenfeld focuses particularly on the National Education Association (hereafter "NEA"). He notes that John Dewey probably influenced public education more than any other individual.[27] Dewey's goal was to socialize the students by indoctrinating them with his humanistic faith, which faith was grounded solidly in Darwinian evolution, stressing the centrality of man to the exclusion of God.[28] Dewey was the driving force behind the *Humanist Manifesto I.*[29]

---

[23]Robert Bryan, *History, Pseudo-History, Anti-History: How Public School Textbooks Treat Religion* (Washington, D.C.: Learn, Inc., The Education Foundation, ca. 1984).

[24]*Church of Holy Trinity v. United States*, 143 U.S. 452 (1892) (Justice David J. Brewer declared that America "is a Christian nation."); *McCollum v. Board of Education*, 333 U.S. 203 (1948); *Zorach v. Clauson*, 343 U.S. 306, 313 (1952) (Justice William O. Douglas stated, "We are a religious people whose institutions presuppose a Supreme Being."); *Engle v. Vital*, 370 U.S. 421 (1962). *See also* John Whitehead, *The Second American Revolution* 25-32; John Eidsmoe, *The Christian Legal Advisor* 97-164.

[25]Alexis de Tocqueville, 1 *Democracy in America* 292, 295 (1945).

[26]Samuel Blumenfeld, *NEA: Trojan Horse in American Education* 55.

[27]*Id.* at 49-50, 53-55.

[28]John Dewey, *A Common Faith* 87. *See also* John Whitehead, *The Stealing of America* 16-20; John Whitehead, *The End of Man* 59-60.

[29]Paul Kurtz, ed., *Humanist Manifestos I and II.*

Published in 1933, this humanistic creed had the stated purpose of establishing a new religion, the religion of Secular Humanism.[30] Secular Humanism holds that: (1) the universe is self-existing; (2) man has evolved by a continuous process from lower life forms; (3) there is no God or supernatural being, (4) there are no absolutes and therefore no eternal truths by which to live ethical and moral lives; and (5) man can save himself by controlling the environment and directing societal evolution by technological and scientific methods.[31] Dewey attempted to disseminate these humanistic ideas through the public school system, for he believed society's world view could be molded into a common humanistic faith by social evolution, and what better place to begin than the public schools? Public schools provided Dewey with a captive audience filled with impressionable young minds. He desired to systematically shape and alter the student's value systems.

Dewey's impact on public education cannot be underestimated. The humanistic foundation that undergirds public school education today is in some measure attributable to Dewey and those he influenced.[32] No wonder there is evidence of religious bias in the textbooks, for Christianity stands in absolute antithesis to Secular Humanism and the clash between the two world views is inevitable.

Paul Blanshard, a secular humanist, wrote an article in *The Humanist* magazine entitled "Three Cheers for Our Secular State." In this article he said the following about public education:

> I think that the most important factor moving us toward a secular society has been the educational factor. Our schools may not teach Johnny to read properly, but the fact that Johnny is in school until he is sixteen tends to lead toward the elimination of religious superstition. The average American child now acquires a high-school education, and this militates against Adam and Eve and all other myths of alleged history. Just how pious or impious we are is impossible to say scientifically although it is certain that religious affiliation is declining. . . .

---

[30]*Id.* p. 8.
[31]*Id.* pp. 8-10.
[32]Blumenfeld, *NEA: Trojan Horse in American Education* 55.

When I was one of the editors of *The Nation* in the twenties, I wrote an editorial explaining that golf and intelligence were the two primary reasons that men did not attend church. Perhaps I would now say golf and a high-school diploma.[33]

John Dunphy, also a humanist, understood the importance of education in shaping the future of the Nation when he declared in *The Humanist* magazine:

I am convinced that the battle for humankind's future must be waged and won in the public school classroom by teachers who correctly perceive their role as the proselytizers of a new faith; a religion of humanity that recognizes and respects the spark of what theologians call divinity in every human being. These teachers must embody the same selfless dedication as the most rabid fundamentalist preachers, for they will be ministers of another sort, utilizing a classroom instead of a pulpit to convey humanist values in whatever subject they teach, regardless of the education level--preschool day care or large state university. *The classroom must and will become an arena of conflict between the old and the new--the rotting corpse of Christianity, together with all its evils and misery, and the new faith of humanism,* resplendent in its promise of a world in which the never-realized Christian ideal of "love thy neighbor" will finally be achieved.[34]

The religious bias in public school textbooks is the logical result of the conflict between the two distinct world views of Secular Humanism and Christianity. The bias against Christianity is evidenced by the clear distortion of early and contemporary American history. The textbooks have censored out important

---

[33]Paul Blanshard, *Three Cheers for Our Secular State*, THE HUMANIST (March/April, 1976), p. 17.

[34]John J. Dunphy, *A Religion for a New Age*, THE HUMANIST (January/February, 1983), p. 26 (emphasis added).

historical religious events, distorted religious history, and placed emphasis upon ideologies that are hostile to religious beliefs.[35] For example, because Secular Humanism places man as the measure of all things, and stresses that absolutes have been replaced by relativism, it follows that public schools channeling humanistic values would inculcate the philosophy of situation ethics. Leading the way in teaching relativism are Sidney Simon and Lawrence Kohlberg, both Secular Humanist's who developed Values Clarification and moral reasoning.[36]

An example of Values Clarification used in public schools is the "life boat" game. The students are asked to pretend they are shipwrecked with only one life boat available. The problem is that the life boat cannot accommodate everyone. The dilemma posed then causes the students to evaluate the worth of each potential survivor. The person having the least worth to the community is then sacrificed for the sake of the others. This technique teaches that human value is relative and may vary according to individual contribution to society.

Another example of valueless education is illustrated by federally funded sex education curricula.[37] The following questionnaire was prepared for eighth grade students, asking them to give the minimum age at which each of the behaviors listed is considered appropriate or acceptable in their own value system: holding hands; kissing; French kissing; petting; (masturbation) petting but not all the way; love-making with a person of the same sex; staying out all night with a sex partner; talking with the opposite sex about sex; talking with parents about sex; smoking tobacco; smoking marijuana; drinking booze; getting drunk or stoned; using swear words; seeing explicit sex in movies; seeing violence in movies; having intercourse; having a variety of sexual partners; living together; getting married; creating a pregnancy,

---

[35]Mel and Norma Gabler, *What are They Teaching Our Children?* 47-64.

[36]Louis Rath, et. al., *Values and Teaching: Working with Values in the Classroom*; Maury Smith, *A Practical Guide to Values Clarification*; Alan Lockwood, *A Critical View of Values Clarification*, THE ELEMENTARY SCHOOL JOURNAL 1, Vol 77, Columbia University (Sept., 1975); Martin Eger, *The Conflict in Moral Education: An Informal Case Study*, EDUCATION: ANNUAL EDITIONS 1983-84, Fred Shultz, ed. 98-106.

[37]*See generally, Citizens For Parental Rights v. San Mateo County Board of Education*, 51 Cal. App. 3d 1 (1975).

having an abortion; taking birth control pills; and becoming sterilized.[38] The instructions to the teacher ask that the classroom be divided into two sections representing before and after age fourteen. As instructed, the students are to get up from their seats and move to the side of the room which indicates whether they believe the above mentioned activities are appropriate or acceptable before or after age fourteen.[39]

A final example of Secular Humanism's influence on values education is provided by the controversial federally funded textbook series entitled, *Man: A Course of Study* (hereafter "MACOS").[40] Developed by the National Science Foundation, MACOS was designed to have students question their value systems by comparison with those of other cultures.[41] Students were taught about cannibalism, infanticide, wife-swapping, mating with animals, and murder. The instructions often asked the students to role play the various cultural value systems and they were discouraged from critically judging these values, because each cultural value was neither "right" nor "wrong" and to judge another value system is to unjustifiably impose one's own relative viewpoint.

In response to the humanistic approach to values education, a federal law was passed entitled, *Protection of Pupil Rights Amendment* (hereafter "Pupil Rights Amendment").[42] Passed in 1978, the *Pupil Rights Amendment* could not be implemented until the Department of Education issued enabling regulations. These regulations were not issued until September 6, 1984. The *Pupil Rights Amendment* allows a parent or guardian to inspect instructional material which will be used in connection with any survey, analysis or evaluation. If consent is not given by an adult student or an emancipated minor, or consent in writing by a parent in the case of an unemancipated minor, the student may be exempted from any survey, analysis or evaluation that reveals information concerning: (1) political affiliations; (2) mental or psychological problems potentially embarrassing to the student or

---

[38]Phyllis Schlafly, ed., *Child Abuse in the Classroom* 39.

[39]Such coercive tactics obviously create undue peer pressure and are designed to alter value systems.

[40]John Conlan, *The MACOS Controversy*, SOCIAL EDUCATION (October, 1975), p. 29.

[41]Gabler, *What are They Teaching Our Children?* pp. 124-25.

[42]20 U.S.C. §1232h.

family) (3) sex behavior and attitudes; (4) illegal, anti-social, self-incrimination and demeaning behavior; (5) critical appraisals of other individuals with whom respondents have close family relationships; (6) legally recognized privileged and analogous relationships, such as those of lawyers' physicians, and ministers; or (7) income (other than that required by law to determine eligibility for participation in a program or for receiving financial assistance under such program).

The *Pupil Rights Amendment* has at least recognized that a serious problem exists in the public schools with regard to humanistic values and social engineering. However, the effectiveness of the federal law is limited. First, the amendment only applies to surveys, analysis or evaluations. Second, most parents are unaware that the federal law exists and therefore do not exercise their legal rights. Third, some educators are unaware of the law, and many who are aware of the Amendment do not abide by its restrictions.[43] It is important to note that educational agencies and institutions are required to give parents and students notice of their rights under the *Pupil Rights Amendment*.[44]

Despite the *Pupil Rights Amendment*, Values Clarification is still actively promoted through public school textbooks. Values Clarification promotes the notion that values are relative and that student values need not conform to parental authorities. Values Clarification expressly forbids teaching absolute ethical or moral standards.[45] The students are therefore placed in a valueless vacuum to be filled by circumstantial relativism. Of course, such an approach to ethical and moral teaching is unquestionably biased against the Judeo-Christian religion.

The public school textbook controversy is merely a struggle between two competing religions: Christianity and Secular Humanism. The Supreme Court of the United States has interpreted the First Amendment to forbid the establishment of a state sanctioned religion. All too frequently this interpretation has been used by extreme church separation groups to banish any vestige of

---

[43]Ann Dellinger, *Experimentation in the Classroom: Use of Public School Students As Research Subjects*, 12 JOURNAL OF LAW AND EDUCATION 347 (1983).

[44]20 U.S.C. 1232h(c).

[45]Arnold Burron, et. al., *Classrooms in Crisis* 50-74. *See also* Kathleen Gow, *Yes, Virginia, There is Right and Wrong.*

Christianity from the public school classroom. Ironically, the Supreme Court has also interpreted the First Amendment to forbid the establishment of theistic *and* non-theistic religions. Specifically, the Court has recognized that Secular Humanism is a religion.[46] Yet the Court has inconsistently excluded Christianity from the public schools while allowing the religion of Secular Humanism to enter unscathed. The textbook controversy is simply Secular Humanism clothed in a book cover.

The issues involved in the so-called "Scopes II" trial are real and will not go away by the media's attempt to label parents as fanatics or "fundamentalists." To deny religion (particularly Christianity) a place in American education is to deny part of American history and culture. Teaching about religion is not to be equated with indoctrination, but teaching the absence of theistic religion is nothing less than state sanctioned Secular Humanism.

---

[46]*Torcaso v. Watkins*, 367 U.S. 488, 495 (1961); *School District of Abington Township v. Schempp*, 374 U.S. 203, 225 (1963); John Whitehead and John Conlan, *The Establishment of the Religion of Secular Humanism and its First Amendment Implications*, 10 TEXAS TECH L. REV. 1 (1978); Charles Rice, *Conscientious Objection to Public Education: The Grievance and the Remedies*, 1978 B.Y.U.L. REV. 847, 853-861.

6

TEACHERS' RIGHTS ON PUBLIC SCHOOL CAMPUSES

Classroom As The Battleground

Teachers in today's public schools often find themselves in difficult positions. Most teachers sincerely want the best for their students. They unfortunately work in a very litigious, often aggressive, environment. For the most part, discipline has all but disappeared under the threat of lawsuits. Child abuse allegations against public school teachers have increased. Trying to protect their school, administrators often side with parents rather than teachers in student-teacher disputes. The classroom is becoming more violent and disruptive. One study found that over 130,000 students bring guns to school every day. Many school administrators are so cautious that they have erroneously erased all traces of religion. Some have run roughshod over teachers. Others have attempted to squelch all discussion of religion.

The public school has become a battleground for religion. John Dunphy, a secular humanist, wrote in *The Humanist* magazine:

I am convinced that the battleground for humankind's future must be waged and won in the public school classroom by teachers who correctly perceive their role as the proselytizers of a new faith: a religion of humanity that recognizes and respects the spark of what theologians call divinity in every human being. These teachers must embody the same selfless dedication as the most rabid fundamentalist preacher, for they will be ministers of another sort, utilizing a classroom instead of a pulpit to convey humanist values in whatever subjects they teach regardless of the educational level —- preschool daycare or large state university. The classroom must and will become an arena of conflict between the old and the new —- the rotting corpse of Christianity together with all its adjacent evils and misery and the new faith of humanism, resplendent in its promise of a world in which the never realized Christian idea of "love thy neighbor" will be finally achieved.[1]

John Dewey, the so-called father of modern education, hoped to replace sectarian religion with "a religious faith that shall not be confined to sect, class, or race."[2] Some have referred to the religion envisioned by John Dewey as a religion of secular humanism. Indeed, the Supreme Court has recognized secular humanism as a religion.[3] As a result of the secularization of public education, many teachers have the mistaken view that religion is forbidden on public school campuses.

Notwithstanding the confusion over religion, teachers still have constitutionally protected liberties and should exercise them. Teachers play a critical role in educating our future generation. Indeed, schools were originally founded to instill religious principles. With the exception of the University of Pennsylvania, every collegiate institution prior to the Revolutionary War was established by some branch of the Christian church.

Aristotle understood the importance of teaching when he stated "all who have meditated on the art of governing mankind are convinced that the fate of empires depends on the education of youth." Martin Luther once stated that he was "afraid that schools will prove to be great gates of hell unless they diligently labor in explaining the Holy Scriptures, engraving them in the hearts of youth. I advise no one to place his child where the Scriptures do not reign paramount. Every institution in which men are not increasingly occupied with the word of God must become corrupt." However, Martin Luther was not operating under the present day interpretations of the United States Supreme Court.

Teachers are in a unique position to inculcate values for the next generation. Under the present constitutional makeup, teachers still have great latitude in reviewing religious topics. The United States Supreme Court has observed the following: "It can hardly be argued that either students or teachers shed their constitutional

---

[1]John Dunphy, *A Religion for a New Age*, THE HUMANIST, January/February 1982, p. 26.
[2]*A Common Faith* 86, 87.
[3]*Torcaso v. Watkins*, 367 U.S. 488 (1961).

rights to freedom of speech or expression at the schoolhouse gate."[4]

Teacher As Individual And State Agent

Though the First Amendment of the Constitution initially restricted the authority of the federal government and not the states, the United States Supreme Court in 1940 nevertheless applied the First Amendment to the states through the Fourteenth Amendment.[5] The First Amendment is now interpreted to protect the free exercise of religion of individuals and to prohibit the establishment of religion by state and federal entities.

Teachers are in a unique position because they are both individuals and agents of the state. Consequently, the First Amendment serves to protect their freedom of speech and free exercise of religion, and to prohibit them from establishing a religion.[6] In other words, since teachers are employees of the state, they are, in a sense, an extension of the state. As such, the First Amendment Establishment Clause, prohibiting the government from establishing a religion, places certain restrictions on teachers' activities in matters of religion. On the other hand, teachers do not lose their constitutional free speech and freedom of religion rights simply because they are employees of the state.

The First Amendment has been interpreted to mean that a state may not affirmatively promote or proselytize a particular religious viewpoint, but neither may the state be hostile toward religion.

---

[4]*Tinker v. Des Moines Independent School District*, 393 U.S. 503, 506 (1969).

[5]*Cantwell v. Connecticut*, 310 U.S. 296 (1940) (Free Exercise Clause); *Everson v. Board of Education*, 330 U.S. 1 (1947) (Establishment Clause); *Illinois ex rel. McCollum v. Board of Education*, 333 U.S. 203 (1948) (same).

[6]Originally the term "establishment of religion" referred to the federal government establishing a national religion or national church. The First Amendment prohibited the federal government from establishing such a national church. While the individual states could establish their own religion, the federal government had no jurisdiction in this matter. However, this term has been interpreted over time by the United Supreme Court to mean endorsement or promotion of religion. Essentially, the Supreme Court has required that the government remain neutral in matters of religion, neither inhibiting, nor promoting religion. Applying this concept of neutrality to the public school teacher means that the teacher must not only be neutral but objective when overviewing religious topics. Consequently, a teacher should not ignore, nor should a teacher actively proselytize, a particular religion or faith. To ignore, censor, or denigrate religion is just as prohibited by the Supreme Court's interpretation as is active promotion or proselytizing of religion by government.

Thus, while teachers may not encourage students to have a saving faith in Jesus Christ, teachers may objectively overview the teachings of Jesus as long as the overview is consistent with the subject matter being taught.

Asserting Your Rights

The teacher is protected by the Constitution and should assert constitutional protection when deemed appropriate. A teacher can assert not only constitutional rights but also the status of tenure, which should at least guarantee notice and reason for a hearing in the event of a complaint.[7]

Freedom Of Speech

Teachers have the constitutional right to free speech while on a public school campus.[8] Neither students nor teachers "shed their constitutional rights to freedom of speech or expression at the schoolhouse gate."[9] A teacher can discuss religious topics with other teachers in the school lounge or between classes. If a school allows its facilities to be used by teachers for meetings unrelated to the curriculum, it probably cannot prohibit teachers from meeting with other teachers during noninstructional time solely on the basis of religion.[10]

Clearly, during nonschool hours and while off school property, teachers are individual citizens and not actors of the state. As such, they enjoy the affirmative protection of the Free Speech and Free Exercise clauses. In this context, they are not actors of the state and therefore do not have the restrictions imposed by the First Amendment Establishment Clause.

---

[7]On occasion the Apostle Paul utilized his status as a Roman citizen to his benefit. Acts 22:25. Indeed, Paul used his status as a Roman citizen to have his case heard in Rome before Caesar where he stated "I am standing before Caesar's tribunal, where I ought to be tried." Acts 25:10.

[8]*Tinker*, 393 U.S. at 506.

[9]*Id.*

[10]*Cf. Widmar v. Vincent*, 454 U.S. 263 (1981); *May v. Evansville-Vanderbaugh School Corporation*, 787 F.2d 1105 (7th Cir. 1986); *Police Department of Chicago v. Mosley*, 408 U.S. 92 (1972).

While on school campus but before or after school hours, teachers may have certain restrictions imposed by the First Amendment Establishment Clause. In this context, some courts have looked at the age of students and their impressionability. The younger the student, the more careful the teacher must be in matters of religion. The courts have reasoned that younger students are not able to easily separate the acts of the teacher from the acts of the school. The courts have considered that older students have the capability of making a distinction between the teacher as an individual and the actions of the school. Unfortunately, no clear line has been drawn as to when this age differential changes. No matter the age, however, teachers may not proselytize students in a captive setting. Thus, for example, if several teachers were to congregate before school in a classroom to pray, the teachers could not invite students and could not publicize the meeting to the students. To do so may give the impression that the school is affirmatively promoting religion. However, a teacher does not have to be so paranoid as to avoid a student's religious inquiry.

Academic Freedom

Academic freedom means "the principle that individual instructors are at liberty to teach what they deem to be appropriate in the exercise of their professional judgment."[11] According to the Supreme Court, academic freedom "is a special concern of the First Amendment."[12] However, academic freedom is not absolute. A teacher cannot use the classroom to indoctrinate students in religious faith, but a teacher is free to disseminate information in an objective manner so long as the information is reasonably related to the subject matter being taught in the curriculum.[13] Therefore, academic freedom, or the right to free speech, permits an objective discussion of religion as it relates to the curriculum. In fact, no subject can be thoroughly taught without some discussion of religion.

---

[11]*Edwards v. Aguillard,* 482 U.S. 578, 586 n.6 (1987).

[12]*Keyishian v. Board of Regents,* 385 U.S. 589, 603 (1967).

[13]Free speech or academic freedom is not unlimited. *Cf. Krizek v. Cicero-Stickney Township High School District,* 713 F. Supp. 1131 (N.D. Ill. 1989) (school did not renew the contract of a nontenured teacher who showed an R-rated film during class).

The teacher would probably be prohibited from talking about a biblical reason for sexual abstinence before marriage in a math class, but a teacher in a health class may discuss sexual abstinence, including various religious views on sexual abstinence. Biblical literature could be discussed in literature class, but probably not in a math class. However, it is permissible to discuss numerology in math class. The Egyptians used mathematics as part of their religion. Both Old and New Testaments use numbers and mathematical formulas to represent symbolic meanings.[14] If the content of speech is consistent with the course being studied, the teacher may objectively overview religious contributions and viewpoints dealing with the issue.

Certainly schools have "important, delicate and highly discretionary functions" to perform.[15] These functions, however, must be performed "within the limits of the Bill of Rights."[16] "The vigilant protection of constitutional freedoms is nowhere more vital than in a community of American schools."[17] Since the "classroom is peculiarly the market place of ideas,"[18] teachers may lead robust discussions and present information, including religious information, in an objective manner.

One of my teacher friends taught space technology in a public

---

[14]For example, the number 3 and 7 occur throughout the Bible. The number 12 is also frequently used. This number plays an integral role when describing the new heaven, which when measured, forms a perfect cube. *See* Revelation 21:9-21. Some ancient Hebrews often assigned mathematical significance to the Hebrew alphabet. This is done in different ways. One way is to assign a number to each successive letter of the alphabet. One example is the name David. In Hebrew it is spelled Dwd. The Daleth or "d" is the fourth letter in the Hebrew alphabet. The Waw or "w" is the eighth letter in the Hebrew alphabet. When added together, David's name equates to the number 14. This is probably the reason that the first chapter of Matthew describes three series of fourteen generations, fourteen from Abraham to David, fourteen from David to the Babylonian deportation, and fourteen from the Babylonian deportation to Christ. *See* Matthew 1:1-17. Actually, there are more than fourteen generations if every individual is counted, but when one understands how genealogies were counted in the Old Testament, the number 14 makes perfect sense. Counting genealogies did not mean counting every single individual in the lineage. Rather, genealogies highlight certain individuals throughout time which show a link from the past to the present. One final example of numerology used in the Bible is the infamous "666," which is the number of a man, and is the mark of the beast. *See* Revelation 13:18.

[15]*West Virginia State Board of Education v. Barnette*, 319 U.S. 624, 637 (1943).

[16]*Id.* at 637.

[17]*Shelton v. Tucker*, 364 U.S. 479, 487 (1967).

[18]*Keyishian*, 385 U.S. at 603 (1967).

high school. His innovation earned him teacher of the year. He used innovative approaches in the classroom, including having his class directly linked to the space shuttle and communicating with the astronauts on board. This class addressed topics related to space technology, including the technology used in laser guided bombs during the Persian Gulf War, astronomy, satellite hookups, and other forms of technology.

During the Persian Gulf War, this teacher focused on the technology used by the military. During one discussion, he brought up the issue of war in the Middle East, which naturally led to a discussion regarding the various confrontations among the warring religious sects. It is virtually impossible to address the Persian Gulf War without looking at the religious and cultural issues involved.

This teacher also focused on astronomy, and as such, must addressed the Big Bang theory and the origin of the universe. Not long ago the Big Bang theory was brought into question by scientists. This theory is replete throughout many science books, and even after its repudiation by some well known scientists, many science books continue to rely on this theory. A good teacher brings up this information, critiques it, and then the natural question arises as to what other theories have been put forth regarding the origin of the universe. Within this context, the teacher may overview theories of abrupt appearance. As Wendell Bird has shown in his two volume work entitled *The Origin of the Species Revisited*,[19] abrupt appearance can be taught as science. The theory of abrupt appearance is a classic example of an issue that can be objectively overviewed in class.[20] Abrupt appearance does not need to use the

---

[19]Wendell R. Bird, 2 *The Origin of the Species Revisited*.

[20]The United States Supreme Court struck down the State of Arkansas' anti-evolution statute which prohibited the teaching of evolution within public schools because the court found that the primary purpose of this statute was religious and had no objective secular basis. *Epperson v. Arkansas*, 393 U.S. 97 (1968). The Supreme Court ruled in *Edwards v. Aguillard*, 482 U.S. 578 (1987), that a state could not mandate the teaching of creationism by requiring that creation theories be taught whenever evolutionary theories are taught. The principle in this case was that the state statute had primarily a religious and not a secular aspect which indeed required the teaching of creationism. It is an entirely different matter when a teacher objectively overviews origin of the universe theories without religious advocacy. A federal appeals court has ruled that a principal may prohibit a teacher from teaching nonevolutionary theories of creation in the classroom without violating the teacher's First Amendment rights. *Webster v. New Lenox School District*, 917 F.2d 1004 (7th Cir. 1990). In the *Webster* case, the issue was not so much whether teaching evolutionary creation

Bible as the textbook. However, when overviewing theories of the origin of the universe, the astute teacher may present evidence proffered for evolution and for abrupt appearance. In the final analysis, neither can be scientifically proven. Both theories must be accepted by faith. However, when discussing the scientific data, in order to adequately overview the entire subject, cultural and religious views may be discussed in an objective manner. Many religions have theologies regarding creation in addition to the Judeo-Christian religion. Egyptian theology on this matter can be found in *The Memphite Theology of Creation*.[21] Likewise, the Akkadians, as well as those in the Far East, had creation epics.

Similarly, when studying geographical topography such as the Grand Canyon, the theory of deluge must be overviewed. The Sumerians, the Akkadians, and the Babylonians all had similar flood stories.[22] To ignore this rich religious and cultural history is to neglect the topic and to cheat the students of a broad education.[23]

No topic can be adequately studied without objectively overviewing religious contributions. When studying sociology, demographic studies may be brought in showing the geographical distribution of the various religious faiths. Glenmary Research Center in Atlanta,[24] publishes demographic maps of the United States showing the distribution of religious faiths within the states. This is certainly relevant to sociology and is a permissible form of teaching. Religious contributions and musical compositions may be studied in music class. Religious art may be studied in art class.

---

violates the First Amendment Establishment Clause, but whether a principal had the right to control the curriculum within the school contrary to the individual desires of teachers within that school. The court noted the essence of the case was that "an individual teacher has no right to ignore the directives of duly appointed education authorities." *Id.* at 1008. The court further noted that the teacher had "not been prohibited from teaching any nonevolutionary theories or from teaching anything regarding the historical relationship between church and state" but that the teacher was merely prohibited from "religious advocacy." *Id.* at 1006.

[21] James B. Pritchard, ed., 1 *The Ancient Near East* 1.

[22] *Id.* at 28, 31; N. Bailkey, ed., *Readings In Ancient History From Gilgamesh To Diocletian* 12.

[23] One of the best videos addressing a modern day catastrophe which may give insight to the theory of deluge has been produced by the Institute for Creation Research regarding the eruption of Mount St. Helens. The video on Mount St. Helens is worth viewing and is highly recommended. Information may be obtained from ICR by writing to PO Box 2667, El Cajon, California 92021 or by calling (619) 448-0900.

[24] Glenmary Research Center, 750 Piedmont Avenue, NE, Atlanta, Georgia, 30308.

History and political science cannot be studied properly without considering the Roman Catholic, Protestant, evangelical, or charismatic impacts. Literature cannot be adequately studied without considering religious influences. For example, today's book format arose out of Christian evangelization. Prior to the formation of books, Old Testament scriptures were contained on bulky scrolls. The New Testament Christians cut these scrolls in pieces and sewed the edges together to form what was called a codex, which is now known as a book. Printing presses were developed primarily to reproduce the Bible. In short, no subject matter can be taught adequately without considering and overviewing the impact of religion. Teachers have a constitutional right to teach about religion and should not shirk their responsibility to do so.

Teaching About Religion

In *School District of Abington Township v. Schempp*,[25] the Supreme Court stated that study of the Bible or religion when presented objectively as part of a secular program of education is consistent with the First Amendment. The Bible could be studied as literature in a literature course. One recommended book that analyzes the Bible as literature is Leland Ryken's *The Literature of the Bible*.[26] Religious literature can be used in any course in which the message is relevant to the subject matter.

The Bible is an excellent literary source. For example, the entire Book of Lamentations is written in acrostic form. An acrostic is a mnemonic device utilizing the twenty-two letters of the Hebrew alphabet. Chapter one of Lamentations contains twenty-two verses, each verse successively begins with the corresponding letter of the alphabet. Verse one begins with the aleph (A), the first letter of the alphabet. Verse two begins with the beth (B), the second letter of the alphabet. Verse twenty-two ends with a tau (T), the last letter of the Hebrew alphabet. Chapter two continues this sequence and also contains twenty-two verses. Chapter three, the middle chapter, triplicates the Hebrew alphabet. This chapter contains sixty-six verses, the alphabet multiplied by three. These verses follow the

---

[25]374 U.S. 203 (1963).
[26](Grand Rapids, Mich.: The Zondervan Corp.).

alphabet in sequence but are grouped in three's. Verses one, two, and three begin with the first letter of the alphabet while verses four, five, and six begin with the second letter of the Hebrew alphabet and so on. Chapter four again contains twenty-two verses, each starting with the successive letter of the alphabet. Chapter five, though containing twenty-two verses, departs from the acrostic pattern.

The most famous acrostic of all is Psalm 119. This psalm contains twenty-two sections, each section containing eight verses. The first eight verses begin with the first letter of the Hebrew alphabet while the second series of eight verses begin with the second letter of the Hebrew alphabet and so on.

Hebrew literature also contains parallelisms. Approximately one-third of the Old Testament and parts of the New Testament are written in poetry. By and large there is no rhyme in terms of sound as we know it in English. Hebrew rhyme is based on thought parallelisms. For example, synonymous parallelism is found in Isaiah 1:3 where the same thought is expressed in successive stichs: "The ox knows its owner, and the ass its master's crib." The "ox" is equivalent to the "ass" and the "owner" is equivalent to the "master." Another example is found in Amos 5:24. Antithetic parallelism means that the second stich is in contrast to the first, as found in Psalm 1:6, "For the Lord knows the way of the righteous, but the way of the wicked will perish." In Matthew 7:18, Jesus stated: "A sound tree cannot bear evil fruit, nor can a bad tree bear good fruit." The most famous one of all is in Matthew 10:19 where Jesus declared: "He who finds his life will lose it, and he who loses his life for my sake will find it." Formal or synthetic parallelism contains neither repetition nor contrasted assertions but is where the first stich is carried further in thought through the second stich. Psalm 14:2 is an example, "The Lord looks down from heaven, upon the children of men." Climatic parallelism is found in Psalm 28:1 where the second stich echoes or repeats the first part of the stich and adds to it an element of thought such as the following: "Ascribe to the Lord, oh heavenly beings, ascribe to the Lord glory and strength." These examples are what is known as Internal Parallelism. Examples of External Parallelism are found between dystichs, such as that found in Isaiah 1:27-28:

Zion shall be redeemed by Justice,
And those in her who repent, by righteousness.
But rebels and sinners shall be destroyed together,
And those who forsake the Lord shall be consumed.

The first stich (first two lines) speaks of redemption using synonymous terms of "justice" and "righteousness." The second stich (second two lines) contrasts the thought of the first stich and speaks of destruction using synonymous terms such as "destroyed" and "consumed."

Hebrew poetry also has meter with the most frequent pattern being 3:3, that is a dystich with three stressed syllables in each stich. An example is found in Job 14:1-2. The shorter 2:2 meter is used to convey intense emotion and urgency as found in Isaiah 1:16-17. The 3:2 pattern is known as the Qinah or the Lament or dirge meter. This is the prevailing meter used in the book of Lamentations. An example is also found in Amos 5:2. Other but less frequently used patterns are 4:4, 2:2:2, and 3:3:3. In the original Hebrew, alliteration is found in Psalm 122:6-7, where the effect of the passage is gained by juxtaposition of words or syllables which begin with the same consonant.

Assonance is found in Psalm 90:17, where the same vowel sound is often deliberately repeated. An interesting concept is found in Judges 5:2 known as onomatopoeia, where the writer uses words which actually sound like the described activity. This is the Song of Deborah describing the galloping of horses. The Hebrew words when spoken together sound like the galloping of horses' hooves. Paranomasia, or a play on words, is aptly found in Isaiah 5:7. There, Isaiah says that God looked for "justice" (mishpat), but instead he found only "bloodshed" (mispah); he looked for "righteousness" (sedhaqah) but instead found only a "cry" (seaqah).

Clearly the Bible is a fascinating literary book. The *Chronicles of Narnia* is also a work that can be studied from a literary point of view. When studying religious works from a literary standpoint, the teacher should be objective. Indeed, to ignore religious literature, including the Bible, ignores a vast amount of educational material that ultimately is the detriment of the student.

Symbols, Music, Art, Drama And Literature

The constitutional principle regarding symbols, music, art, drama, or literature, whether in public school or in association with other public entities, is simple -- mix the secular and the sacred. In other words, if a public entity, or a teacher as an agent of that entity, displays or presents a secular aspect or purpose along with the religious symbol, music, art, drama, or literature, then the display or the presentation is considered constitutional. For example, a publicly sponsored nativity scene without any other accompanying symbols on public property would be unconstitutional. However, the same nativity scene becomes constitutional when secular symbols of the holiday are presented in the same context. A nativity scene in the classroom follows the same principles. A school sponsored Christmas concert on a public school campus containing only Christian music would be unconstitutional, but Christian Christmas songs mixed with secular songs of the holiday mixes the secular and the sacred and consequently the presentation is considered constitutional.[27] In art class the teacher can overview religious art so long as secular art is also overviewed. Religious literature can be read and studied so long as it is objective and combined with other secular aspects of literature.

Probably the best illustration of the permissibility for the use of symbols, music, art, drama, and literature within the public school system is the school board policy of Sioux Falls School District in Sioux Falls, South Dakota. This policy has been court tested and serves as an example to other schools. The school policy begins by stating that tolerance and understanding should be promoted and that "students and staff members should be excused from participating in practices which are contrary to their religious beliefs" unless there are clear overriding concerns that would prevent excusal.[28]

The policy goes on to state the following:

1. The several holidays throughout the year which have a

---

[27]See *Bauchman v. West High School,* 1997 WL 778108 (10th Cir. 1997).

[28]*Florey v. Sioux Falls School District 49-5,* 619 F.2d 1311, 1319 (8th Cir.), *cert. denied* 449 U.S. 987 (1980).

religious and a secular basis may be observed in the public schools.

2. The historical and contemporary values and the origin of religious holidays may be explained in an unbiased and objective manner without sectarian indoctrination.

3. Music, art, literature, and drama having religious themes or basis are permitted as part of the curriculum for school-sponsored activities and programs if presented in a prudent and objective manner and as a traditional part of the cultural and religious heritage of the particular holiday.

4. The use of religious symbols such as a cross, menorah, crescent, Star of David, creche, symbols of Native American religions or other symbols that are part of a religious holiday [are] permitted as a teaching aid or resource provided such symbols are displayed as an example of the cultural and religious heritage of the holiday and are temporary in nature. Among these holidays are included Christmas, Easter, Passover, Hanukkah, St. Valentines' Day, St. Patrick's Day, Thanksgiving and Halloween.

5. The school district's calendar should be prepared so as to minimize conflicts with religious holidays of all faiths.[29]

The same school board policy also correctly addresses religious literature in the curriculum as follows:

Religious institutions and orientations are central to human experience, past and present. An education excluding such a significant aspect would be incomplete. It is essential that the teaching about and not of religion be conducted in a factual, objective and respectful manner.[30]

---

[29]*Id.* at 1319-20.
[30]*Id.* at 1320.

The policy then goes on to outline the following:

1. The District supports the inclusion of religious literature, music, drama, and the arts in the curriculum and in school activities provided it is intrinsic to the learning experience in the various fields of study and is presented objectively.

2. The emphasis on religious themes in the arts, literature and history should be only as extensive as necessary for a balanced and comprehensive study of these areas. Such studies should never foster any particular religious tenets or demean any religious beliefs.

3. Student-initiated expressions to questions or assignments which reflect their beliefs or non-beliefs about a religious theme shall be accommodated. For example, students are free to express religious belief or non-belief in compositions, art forms, music, speech and debate.[31]

The above cited school board policy of the Sioux Falls School District is presented here because it concisely and correctly outlines the parameters for the celebration of religious holidays, the display of symbols, the performance of music, art, or drama, and the study of religious literature within the public school system. The constitutionality of this school board policy has been upheld by the Eighth Circuit Court of Appeals. As for the issue of music, the United States Supreme Court has acknowledged that "[m]usic without sacred music, architecture minus the Cathedral, or painting without the Scriptural themes would be eccentric and incomplete, even from a secular view."[32] As it pertains to religious literature within the public school system, the United States Supreme Court declared that the "study of the Bible or of religion, when presented objectively as a part of a secular program of education," is

---

[31]*Id.*
[32]*McCollum*, 333 U.S. at 206 (Jackson, J., concurring).

consistent with the First Amendment.[33] Indeed, the Supreme Court has reiterated that the Bible may constitutionally be used as an appropriate study of history, civilization, ethics, comparative religion, or the like.[34] In other words, a public school teacher may teach about religion in an objective manner, but should avoid promoting belief in a particular religion and should likewise avoid degrading or showing hostility toward any religion.

In summary, religious symbols, music, art, drama, and literature may clearly be taught and presented in public school so long as the presentation is done in an objective manner consistent with the topic or the holiday occasion. Contrary to some popular opinion, religious Christmas carols are still permitted in the public school, religious art, drama, and literature are still permitted as part of the curriculum, and religious symbols are still permissible. The key is to present the information, display, or performance objectively and in combination with other secular aspects surrounding the holiday or subject matter. To exclude religion from public school creates an atmosphere of hostility, rather than neutrality, toward religion. Clearly, the First Amendment demands accommodation and absolutely forbids hostility.

Religious Holidays

The Supreme Court has upheld the display of religious symbols on public property if the context of the religious symbols have other nonreligious symbols which acknowledge the secular aspects of the holiday.[35] The classic example is a nativity scene in the context of a Christmas tree, a menorah, or Santa Claus. All these symbols should be in close proximity to each other.

The Eighth Circuit Court of Appeals ruled in 1980 that a

---

[33]*Abington Township,* 374 U.S. at 225.

[34]*Stone v. Graham,* 449 U.S. 39, 42 (1980). The Supreme Court in *Stone* struck down the display of the Ten Commandments on a classroom bulletin board because, standing alone in the absence of a secular context, it was not integrated into the school curriculum, where the Bible may constitutionally be used as an appropriate study of history, civilization, ethics, comparative religion, or the like. Presumably, if the Ten Commandments were displayed on the bulletin board in association with other secular symbols of law-based society, the Supreme Court may well have ruled the display to be constitutional.

[35]*Lynch v. Donnelly,* 465 U.S. 668 (1984); *County of Allegheny v. American Civil Liberties Union,* 492 U.S. 573 (1989).

school Christmas program may include religious carols so long as they are presented "in a prudent and objective manner and as a traditional part of the cultural and religious heritage of the particular holiday."[36] The Supreme Court has long ago acknowledged that "[m]usic without sacred music, architecture minus the cathedral, or painting without the Scriptural themes would be eccentric and incomplete, even from a secular view."[37] Teachers should not shun celebrations of religious holidays. This includes permitting students to give reports, whether oral or written, on religious holidays or topics. This also includes the display of a nativity scene within the classroom setting. A nativity scene is certainly permissible in a classroom setting if, within the same nativity scene setting, secular symbols of Christmas are also displayed. For example, a teacher can display a nativity scene so long as secular symbols are displayed within the same, such as a Christmas tree, Santa Claus or reindeer. Jewish celebrations of Hanukkah may also be displayed. The background of Hanukkah can be found by reading the Apocryphal book of Maccabes, which describes the Jews taking back and cleansing the temple from the Syrians on Kislev 25, or the ninth month of the Jewish calendar.[38]

Unfortunately, teachers and administrators have mistakenly concluded that students are not permitted to sing religious Christmas carols during the Christmas season. However, Christmas carols, including Christian carols such as "Silent Night, Holy Night," are permissible within a public school setting so long as other secular songs of Christmas are included, such as "Rudolph the Red Nosed Reindeer".[39]

Clothing And Jewelry

Teachers should be permitted to wear religious symbols. Like the students in *Tinker v. Des Moines Independent School District*, a federal appeals court permitted teachers to wear black arm bands

---

[36] *Florey*, 619 F.2d at 1311 (8th Cir. 1980).
[37] *McCollum*, 333 U.S. at 206 (Jackson, J., concurring).
[38] 1 Maccabes 4.
[39] For more information, see the model school board policy in Appendix B.

in symbolic protest to the Vietnam war.[40]

In contrast to a student's ability of free expression through articles of clothing, a teacher has a few limitations. If the content of the message is not religious, a teacher probably has greater latitude to wear clothing with inscribed words. However, the First Amendment Establishment Clause places certain restrictions on a teacher with respect to promoting religion. Nevertheless, a teacher should be able to wear religious articles of clothing or jewelry. Articles of clothing with religious writing moves a little bit more into a gray area. The more objective the writing without promoting a religious view, the more likely the teacher is able to wear the article of clothing.

In one case, a school allowed teachers to wear T-shirts to class on "Spirit Day." Spirit Day was a time when students and teachers acknowledged the various student-initiated clubs on campus. Teacher-sponsors and others were permitted to wear T-shirts of the various clubs, but the school prohibited some teachers from wearing the Fellowship of Christian Athletes' T-shirt, claiming to allow teachers to wear these shirts would violate the "separation of church and state." Liberty Counsel intervened. The teachers were then allowed to wear the Fellowship of Christian Athletes shirts just like other teachers were allowed to wear the secular club T-shirts. In this case, to discriminate against the teacher solely because of the content of the message, while allowing other teachers to wear secular messages, violated the First Amendment. Whether clothes or jewelry, Christian teachers should receive equal treatment as that afforded other teachers who wear articles of clothing or jewelry with secular messages.

Outside Speakers

Teachers may bring in outside speakers to present views on a particular topic. The teacher can even utilize a debate format to present both sides of an issue. This avoids the problem of the school endorsing the speaker and allows for experts in various areas to present information to students. However, a debate format is not

---

[40]*James v. Board of Education,* 461 F.2d 566 (2d Cir. 1972), *cert. denied,* 409 U.S. 1042 (1972), *reh'g denied,* 410 U.S. 947 (1973).

necessary for a teacher to bring an outside speaker on campus to present a particular view. A teacher may bring an outside speaker to present a view opposing the teacher, or a view in support of the teacher. There is no requirement that both sides of a topic be presented. Since the outside speaker is not an agent of the state, the speaker may address controversial topics and state their opinion on these topics. The teacher should avoid a regular pattern of inviting outside speakers to present only one viewpoint. The school should not pay for or sponsor the outside speaker.[41] However, the school may pay a speaker to come on campus to present a message dealing with sexual abstinence or drug abuse. Such a message, while having moral and social concerns, also has religious concerns. The speaker may talk about all the concerns touching this topic. The only time a school should avoid paying for a speaker is if the speaker is brought to campus for the sole purpose of presenting a specific sectarian view that could be construed as proselytizing or evangelism.

Student Bible Clubs

According to the Equal Access Act, schools may require that student-initiated Bible Clubs have a teacher sponsor. Schools may require a sponsor for religious clubs but only if the same requirements are made of secular clubs. According to the Equal Access Act, the provision of a school sponsor, whether an employee, agent, or otherwise, does not mean that the school is actually endorsing the club.[42] Moreover, the employee or agent of the school should be present at such religious meetings "only in a nonparticipatory capacity."[43] This "nonparticipatory" attendance means that the teacher should not actively lead or direct the group. The club must be student-initiated and student-led. The activity must primarily be the activity of the students, not of the school. Teachers or other school employees certainly may be in attendance but should not take active leadership roles in these clubs. Sponsors can give advice and counsel, but the clubs should remain

---

[41]*Wilson v. Chancellor*, 418 F. Supp. 1358 (D. Or. 1976).
[42]20 U.S.C. § 4072(2).
[43]20 U.S.C. § 4071(c)(3).

student-initiated and student-led. However, teachers may invite the students to their homes, and in the off-campus setting, teachers may take an active role.

Some teachers have requested the opportunity to pray with students during the annual "See You at the Pole" event. Constitutionally this is probably risky. Like Bible Clubs, "See You at the Pole" should be primarily student-initiated and student-led. If teachers desired, they could meet separately in a room out of the view of the public to offer prayers for the school. However, under current Supreme Court interpretations, it would probably not be advisable to meet with the students to openly pray on the campus during school hours in the presence of the student body.

Summary

Teachers on public school campuses are protected by the First Amendment Free Speech and Free Exercise Clauses. Teachers are also limited by the First Amendment Establishment Clause. Teachers retain the constitutional right to bring information to the classroom that is related to the curriculum being taught. The more relevant the information to the curriculum, the stronger the constitutional protection. Teachers may objectively instruct about religion but should be careful not to proselytize. Every subject taught in public school has in some way been impacted by religion. To ignore religion is to render a disservice to the curriculum being taught and to the students.

7

STUDENTS' RIGHTS ON PUBLIC SCHOOL CAMPUSES

Freedom Of Speech

Students on public school campuses enjoy constitutional protection of free speech and free exercise of religion. Student speech can be prohibited only when speech activities "substantially interfere with the work of the school, or impinge upon the rights of other students."[1] In *Tinker v. Des Moines Independent School District*, the United States Supreme Court stated:

> In our system, state-operated schools may not be enclaves of totalitarianism. School officials do not possess absolute authority over their students. Students in school as well as out of school are "persons" under our Constitution. They are possessed of fundamental rights which the State must respect, just as they themselves must respect their obligations to the State. In our system, students may not be regarded as closed-circuit recipients of only that which the State chooses to communicate. They may not be confined to the expression of those sentiments that are officially approved. In the absence of a specific showing of constitutionally valid reasons to regulate their speech, students are entitled to freedom of expression of their views.[2]

The Supreme Court further stated: "It can hardly be argued that either students or teachers shed their constitutional rights to freedom of speech or expression at the schoolhouse gate."[3] The Court recognized that when a student is "in the cafeteria, or on the playing field, or on the campus during the authorized hours, he may express his opinions."[4] Students may exercise their constitutional right to

---

[1] *Tinker v. Des Moines Independent School District*, 393 U.S. 503, 509 (1969).
[2] *Id.* at 511.
[3] *Id.* at 506.
[4] *Id.* at 512-13.

free speech while on public school campuses before and after school, in between class, in the cafeteria, or on the playing field. Students have a constitutionally protected right to freedom of speech during noninstructional time. However, during class instruction, students must conform their speech to the relevant topic being studied. While a student may talk to another student during noninstructional times about politics or religion, the student should refrain from such discussion with another student during class time unless it is relevant to the topic being studied and is done in an orderly fashion.

Students have a guaranteed right to free speech on public school campuses. When students walk on the premises of any public school, kindergarten through college, they carry with them the First Amendment protection of free speech and free exercise of religion.[5] These students do not shed their Constitutional rights when they enter the schoolhouse gate.[6]

The facts in the *Tinker* case involve students in grade two through eleven who came to school wearing black armbands to symbolically protest America's involvement in the Vietnam war. The emotional reaction was certainly strong. Some of the students and faculty no doubt had family or friends who either died in the Vietnam war or who were then stationed in Vietnam. These people no doubt bristled at the sight of the black armbands. The students were told to remove the armbands. When they refused, they were threatened with suspension. These students took the case all the way to the United States Supreme Court, where the Court ruled in 1969 that students have a constitutional right to freedom of speech. Just because other students find their speech repulsive is no basis to censor their speech. The only basis to restrict student free speech during noninstructional time is if it materially and substantially

---

[5]The students in *Tinker* involved an eight-year-old second grader, an eleven-year-old fifth grader, a thirteen-year-old eighth grader, and a fifteen and a sixteen-year-old in the eleventh grade. The students in *Board of Education v. Mergens*, 110 S. Ct. 2356 (1990), involved a public secondary school. Public secondary schools, depending on state law, include middle schools and/or junior high schools and high schools. The students in *Widmar v. Vincent*, 454 U.S. 263 (1981), involved college students. Though the latter two cases pertained to student clubs within a public secondary school or college, these cases were based on student free speech rights.

[6]*Tinker*, 393 U.S. at 506.

interferes with the ordinary operation of the school or with the rights of others.

Federal courts have the duty "to apply the First Amendment mandates in our educational system" in order "to safeguard the fundamental values of freedom of speech and inquiry."[7] Indeed, the Supreme Court has specifically stated that students may express themselves all the way "from kindergarten through high school."[8] This statement was made prior to the Supreme Court's decisions dealing with speech on college campuses, and thus, it can now rightfully be said that students have free speech rights from kindergarten through college.

Some opponents of student free speech have attempted to restrict student rights by arguing that public schools are closed, limited, or designated public forums. In using this terminology, opponents of student free speech argue that student speech activities are limited to that type of speech condoned by the school. Some erroneously argue that schools may allow secular speech but prohibit all religious speech so long as the prohibition on speech is applied against all religious speech. Others argue that student speech can be prohibited so long as it is equally prohibited across the board, both secular and religious. This is the same kind of argument that is used regarding student-initiated clubs. However, the analysis for student-initiated clubs is different than the analysis for student speech where students are not requesting use of school facilities. As for student-initiated clubs, schools can prohibit all student clubs so long as the prohibition applies equally to secular and religious clubs. However, this is in the context where students are requesting the use of school facilities.[9] In the context of free speech, students are not requesting use of school facilities. To the contrary, they are commanded by law to be on the public school campus, and once there under mandate of law, schools cannot flatly prohibit their speech.

Public schools are unique within American culture. School is the only place where citizens are commanded to be until the age of

---

[7]*Epperson v. Arkansas*, 393 U.S. 97, 104 (1968).

[8]*Tinker*, 393. U.S. at 516.

[9]*But see DeNooyer v. Livonia Public Schools*, 799 F. Supp. 744, 752 (E.D. Mich. 1992), aff'd sub nom, *DeNooyer v. Merinelli*, 1 F.3d 1240 (6th Cir. 1993).

sixteen. All fifty states have compulsory education laws. These laws require compulsory education up to the age of 16. Compulsory education can be satisfied by either attending a public, private, or home school. For many Americans there is very little freedom of choice between public and private school because of the monetary considerations involved. Consequently, most Americans have been trained in the public schools. This training is not voluntary, but mandatory. Failure to attend school until the age of sixteen will result in civil or criminal penalties. Since school is the only place in America where attendance is demanded, it would be incongruous not to recognize that students in attendance at public schools have constitutional liberties.

The basic constitutional liberty of freedom of speech is not only a protected right but is common sense. We would all agree that when exiting the school bus on the way to class, a student has the right to converse with another student. One student can say to another student, "I like you." The same student could go even further and say, "I love you." Moreover, this student could invite a friend to their house after school for a birthday party or to some other after school program. The freedom to speak is not only constitutionally correct, it just makes common sense. Whatever can be verbally spoken can be transferred to print. For example, this same student could give out a Valentines' card with the "I love you" message. There is no difference between verbal or written speech. The only difference is one creates litter and the other doesn't. However, the Supreme Court has already indicated that instead of punishing all speech under the guise of prohibiting litter, the appropriate course is to punish the litter bug.[10] Everyone would

---

[10]There is no difference between oral and written expression except litter. *See Organization for a Better Austin v. Keefe*, 410 U.S. 415 (1971); *Martin v. City of Struthers*, 319 U.S. 143, 145 (1943); *Jamison v. Texas*, 318 U.S. 413, 416 (1943); *Schneider v. New Jersey*, 308 U.S. 147, 162 (1939); *Lovell v. Griffin*, 303 U.S. 444, 452 (1938). Clearly, a ban handbilling suppresses "a great quantity of speech that does not cause the evils that it seeks to eliminate." *Ward v. Rock Against Racism*, 491 U.S. 781, 799 n.7 (1989). Leafletting is a "form of religious activity [that] occupies the same high estate under the First Amendment as do worship in churches and preaching from the pulpits." *Murdock v. Pennsylvania*, 319 U.S. 105, 108-09 (1934). Because literature distribution is synonymous with pure speech, students have the right to distribute religious literature during noninstructional times as long as their activities do not disrupt the orderly operation of the school. *See Tinker*, 393 U.S. at 509.

acknowledge that a student can engage in secular speech. The same student can engage in Christian or religious speech. For example, one student could tell another that "Jesus Christ loves you," and could further invite that student to an after school church program. This verbal message could also be transmitted in print through a gospel tract or a church invitation. A student does not lose the constitutional right to freedom speech when the message is transferred to print, and further does not lose the right to free speech when the message changes from secular to sacred topics.

One court has stated the following:

> [P]ublic schools are dedicated, in part, to accommodate students during prescribed hours for personal intercommunication. Unless the students' speech is curriculum-related, the speech cannot be limited during those hours on the school campus without a strong showing of interference with school activities or with the rights of other students. As the Court stated, 'Dedication to specific uses [including student interpersonal communication] does not imply that the constitutional rights of persons entitled to be there are to be gauged as if the premises were purely private property.'[11]

According to the Supreme Court's ruling in *Tinker*, the "principle use to which schools are dedicated is to accommodate students during prescribed hours for the purpose of certain types of activities. Among those activities is personal intercommunication among the students."[12] "The holding in *Tinker* did not depend upon a finding that the school was a public forum."[13] *Tinker* clearly acknowledged that schools by virtue of their very existence are dedicated to personal intercommunication among the students. Thus, in a sense, schools are by their very nature a designated or limited public forum for student speech and can be none other than a limited or designated public forum by virtue of the fact that they

---

[11]*Slotterback v. Interboro School District*, 766 F. Supp. 280, 293 (E.D. Pa. 1991) (quoting *Tinker*, 393 U.S. at 512 n.6).

[12]*Tinker*, 393 U.S. at 512.

[13]*Rivera v. East Otero School District*, 721 F. Supp. 1189, 1193 (D. Colo. 1989).

are dedicated "to accommodate students during prescribed hours."[14] Recently one federal district court recognized this important aspect of *Tinker* by declaring,

> In the light of *Tinker*, I conclude that government intent to create public secondary schools as limited public forums, during school hours, for the first amendment personal speech of the students who attend those schools, is intrinsic in the dedication of those schools. Only when the schools cease operating is that intent negated.[15]

In other words, it is improper to analyze student-initiated speech under a forum framework, and to state, in turn, that schools can limit the public forum and thus prohibit student speech. First, students are commanded by law to be on public school campuses. Once there, the government cannot restrict their speech unless it disrupts the ordinary operation of the school or interferes with the rights of other students. Schools may not prohibit student speech simply because another student objects to the content of the message. "If school officials were permitted to prohibit expression to which other students objected, absent any further justification, the officials would have a license to prohibit virtually every type of expression."[16] Additionally, the phrase "interferes with the rights of other students" found in *Tinker* means student speech that is sexually explicit, libelous or defamatory toward another student.[17] Second, even if a public forum analysis were used within a public school context, the Supreme Court and other federal cases suggest that by their very nature, schools are dedicated to student interpersonal communication. Only when schools cease being schools is that public dedication extinguished. Just as schools could not prohibit students from verbally speaking to one another between class, on the playing field, in the cafeteria, or during noninstructional times before or after class sessions, schools cannot

---

[14]*Tinker*, 393 U.S. at 739.

[15]*Slotterback*, 766 F. Supp. at 293.

[16]*Clark v. Dallas Independent School District*, 806 F. Supp. 116, 120 (N.D. Tex. 1992) (citing *Rivera*, 721 F. Supp. at 1189; and *Slotterback*, 766 F. Supp. at 280).

[17]*Hazelwood School District v. Kuhlmeier*, 484 U.S. 260, 274 (1988); *Bethel School District v. Fraser*, 478 U.S. 675 (1986).

prohibit other forms of student expression. "In the absence of a specific showing of constitutionally valid reasons to regulate their speech, students are entitled to freedom of expression of their views."[18] Indeed, the "vigilant protection of constitutional freedoms is nowhere more vital than in the community of American schools."[19]

The Supreme Court has already rejected arguments that a school may prohibit student speech simply because others might find it offensive. The Supreme Court could not make this point any clearer in *Tinker*:

> Any departure from absolute regimentation may cause trouble. Any variation from the majority's opinion may inspire fear. Any word spoken, in class, in the lunchroom, or on the campus, that deviates from the views of another person may start an argument or cause a disturbance. But our Constitution says we must take this risk and our history says that it is this sort of hazardous freedom -- this kind of openness -- that is the basis of our national strength and of the independence and vigor of Americans who grow up and live in this relatively permissive, often disputatious, society.[20]

Regardless of the arguments presented by opponents of student-initiated speech, the Supreme Court in "*Tinker* made clear that school property may not be declared off limits for expressive activity by students. . . ."[21]

Literature Distribution

The Supreme Court has long recognized "that the right to distribute flyers and literature lies at the heart of the liberties guaranteed by the Speech and Press Clauses of the First Amendment."[22] "It is axiomatic that written expression is pure

---

[18]*Clark*, 806 F. Supp. at 119 (quoting *Tinker*, 393 U.S. at 511).

[19]*Shelton v. Tucker*, 364 U.S. 479, 487 (1967).

[20]*Tinker*, 393 U.S. at 508-09 (citations omitted).

[21]*Grayned v. City of Rockford*, 408 U.S. 104, 118 (1972).

[22]*ISKCON v. Lee*, 112 S. Ct. 2711, 2720 (1992).

speech."[23] Well-settled constitutional law confirms "that the guarantee of freedom of speech that is enshrined in the First Amendment encompasses the right to distribute peacefully."[24] "From the time of the founding of our nation, the distribution of written material has been an essential weapon in the defense of liberty."[25]

The right of free speech includes the right to distribute literature.[26] In fact, the distribution of *printed* material is considered pure speech.[27] Consequently, peaceful distribution of literature is protected speech.[28] Literature distribution includes anything in printed format such as brochures, pamphlets, newspapers, cards, stamps, books, and pictures that are not considered obscene.

Religious speech enjoys the same protection as political speech.[29] Indeed, the right to persuade, advocate, or proselytize a religious viewpoint is protected by the First Amendment. The Supreme Court has stated that "free trade in ideas means free trade and the opportunity to persuade, not merely to describe facts."[30] The burden on the government (public school) to justify an exclusion of free speech requires the government to show that the denial of speech is necessary to serve a compelling state interest and that complete denial is the least restrictive alternative to achieve that end.[31] Mere disagreement with the content of the speech is not sufficient reason to deny student speech.[32]

The Supreme Court has held that a school principal may

---

[23]*Slotterback*, 766 F. Supp. at 288.

[24]*Id.*

[25]*Paulsen v. County of Nassau*, 925 F.2d 65, 66 (2d Cir. 1991).

[26]*Martin v. City of Struthers*, 319 U.S. 141 (1943).

[27]*Texas v. Johnson*, 491 U.S. 397, 406 (1989) ("The Government generally has a freer hand in restricting expressive conduct than it has in restricting the written or spoken word.")

[28]*United States v. Grace*, 461 U.S. 169, 176 (1983) ("Leafletting is protected speech."); *Lovell v. City of Griffin*, 303 U.S. 444, 451-52 (1938) ("Liberty of circulating is as essential to [freedom of speech] as liberty of publishing; indeed, without circulation, the publication would be of little value.").

[29]*Widmar v. Vincent*, 454 U.S. 263, 269 (1981) (citing *Heffron v. ISKCON* 452 U.S. 640 (1981)). *See also Niemotko v. Maryland*, 340 U.S. 268 (1951); *Saia v. New York*, 334 U.S. 558 (1948).

[30]*Thomas v. Collins*, 323 U.S. 516, 537 (1945).

[31]*Carey v. Brown*, 447 U.S. 455, 461, 464-65 (1980); *Widmar*, 454 U.S. at 270.

[32]*Clark*, 806 F. Supp. at 120.

restrict the content of a school-sponsored newspaper which was published as part of the course work for a journalism class because the newspaper was not a public forum, was part of the educational curriculum, and was a regular classroom activity.[33] However, the Court distinguished the newspaper case from literature distribution by stating:

> The question whether the First Amendment requires a school to tolerate particular student speech -- the question that we addressed in *Tinker* -- is different from the question whether the First Amendment requires a school affirmatively to promote particular student speech. The former question addresses educators' ability to silence a student's personal expression that happens to occur on the school premises. The latter question concerns educators' authority over school-sponsored publications, theatrical productions, and other expressive activities that students, parents, and members of the public might reasonably perceive to bear the imprimatur of the school. These activities [that is, writing an article in a school-sponsored newspaper,] may fairly be characterized as part of the school curriculum, whether or not they occur in a traditional classroom setting, so long as they are supervised by faculty members and designed to impart particular knowledge or skills to student participants and audiences.[34]

---

[33]*Hazelwood School District v. Kuhlmeier,* 484 U.S. 260 (1988). In *Desilets v. Clearview Regional Board of Education,* 630 A.2d 333 (N.J. Sup. Ct. 1993), a New Jersey state appeals court ruled that a school violated the First Amendment Free Speech Clause when it censored from a school-sponsored newspaper a student's movie reviews of the R-rated films *Mississippi Burning* and *Rainman.* The court reasoned that the censorship was based on the content of the movie reviews and was not associated with pedagogical concern such as grammar, writing, research, bias or prejudice, or vulgar or profane language. Since the censorship was purely based on the content of the movie being R-rated, the school violated the student's free speech right. The court ruled that any school newspaper censorship case must be read in light of the Supreme Court's decision in *Tinker,* 393 U.S. at 503. The court also ruled that if the school was concerned about the appearance that it endorsed R-rated movie reviews, the school could add a disclaimer to the newspaper.

[34]*Hazelwood,* 484 U.S. at 270-71.

The same distinction makes literature distribution different from *Bethel School District v. Fraser*,[35] in which the Court ruled that a student was appropriately disciplined by the school authorities for the offensive tone of a nominating speech at a school assembly.[36]

The difference between the Supreme Court decision in *Hazelwood* (school-sponsored newspaper), *Fraser* (an offensive nominating speech at a school assembly), and *Tinker* (student-initiated speech) is important. The Court in *Hazelwood* ruled that a school could censor student speech when that speech occurred in a school-sponsored newspaper. There were two reasons the Court allowed the school to censor this speech. First, the student speech occurred in a school-sponsored newspaper. This school newspaper was clearly a school-sponsored publication in which other faculty members participated in the production thereof, and the school newspaper contained the school logo, thus giving the appearance that the school sponsored the content of the newspaper. The second reason was that the article dealt with a fellow student who had become pregnant. The article did not name the student, but so specifically described the circumstances that everyone within the school would know to whom the article was referring. As such, this article could have been defamatory toward the student and thus interfered with the right of a particular student under the *Tinker* analysis. Similarly, the student nominating speech in *Fraser* was also somewhat defamatory or libelous. In this particular case the student gave a nominating speech and used sexual innuendoes, describing as it were, a sexual act between himself and the student body. Moreover, the speech occurred during a school-sponsored convocation during which the speaker was addressing a captive audience.

The Supreme Court, however, indicated that there is a clear difference between "whether the First Amendment requires a school

---

[35]478 U.S. 675 (1986).

[36]Another federal court of appeals ruled that "civility" is a legitimate pedagogical concern of a school and therefore school officials could declare a high school student ineligible to run for student office as a sanction for an offensive campaign speech delivered at a school assembly in which the student ridiculed an assistant principal. *Poling v. Murphy*, 872 F.2d 757 (6th Cir. 1989), *cert. denied*, 493 U.S. 1021 (1990).

to tolerate particular student speech [as was addressed in *Tinker*] from the question of whether the First Amendment requires a school affirmatively to *promote* particular student speech [the question addressed in *Hazelwood*]."[37] The reason the school could censor the content of the student newspaper was in part because the production of that newspaper was "supervised by faculty members and designed to impart particular knowledge or skills to student participants and audiences."[38] However, student interpersonal communication, either verbally or through printed format, has no supervision of faculty and is not designed to impart knowledge or skills to other participants or audiences. As such, the school has no reason to censor this form of student speech unless the student speech interrupts the ordinary operation of the school or interferes with the rights of other students. Students may therefore distribute literature during noninstructional time -- before, after, and between classes. As *Tinker* stated, when a student is "in the cafeteria, or on the playing field, or on the campus during the authorized hours, he may express his opinions."[39] The only compelling reason to prohibit literature distribution is when such activities substantially interfere with the work of the school or impinge upon the rights of other students.[40]

The distribution of religious literature is a powerful evangelization tool. Students should not be intimidated from using this form of expression. Students may distribute religious literature before or after school while students are arriving on the campus. Bus stops and hallways are prime areas for the distribution of literature. Students may also distribute literature or verbally express themselves between classes. Other times appropriate for student expression include lunchtime, in the cafeteria, or on the playing field. During noninstructional time students have the right to express

---

[37]*Hazelwood*, 484 U.S. at 270-71 (emphasis added).

[38]*Id.* at 271. A federal court of appeals ruled that a school board could properly reject Planned Parenthood's advertisement for publication in high school newspapers and other school publications because in such a school-sponsored publication, the school had the right to maintain a position of neutrality on controversial issues. *Planned Parenthood of Southern Nevada, Inc. v. Clark County School District*, 941 F.2d 817 (9th Cir. 1991).

[39]*Tinker*, 393 U.S. at 512-13.

[40]*Id.* at 509, 511. *Accord Baughman v. Freienmuth*, 478 F.2d 1345 (4th Cir. 1973); *Quarterman v. Byrd*, 453 F.2d 54 (4th Cir. 1971); *Rivera*, 721 F. Supp. at 1189.

themselves. Students should not attempt to distribute literature during class time. However, outside of class time, a flat "ban on the distribution of student-initiated religious literature cannot be constitutionally justified."[41]

Sometimes the bigotry and ignorance of some school officials is astonishing. One eighth grader brought the religious newspaper *Issues and Answers* to school, planning to distribute this literature to her fellow students during noninstructional time. She asked the assistant principal for permission to distribute the literature. After reviewing the contents of the literature and noting that it was religious and contained Bible verses, the assistant principal responded that students were not permitted to bring Bibles, religious literature, or literature that quoted the Bible on public school campuses. Therefore, the request for distribution was flatly denied. Liberty Counsel represented this student and filed suit against the school board for denial of the student's free speech rights. The day after filing suit, one school board member was quoted by the media as saying that religion had no place on public school campuses and that students had no right to bring religious literature to school. This statement by the school board member was later retracted when the school board agreed with Liberty Counsel's position and further agreed that the student had a First Amendment right to distribute her literature before and after class, in between classes, in the cafeteria, or on the playing field.

Following school board policy, the principal for the Milwaukee High School for the Arts, told students that they could no longer refer to their Bible club as Christian Fellowship because the word "Christian" violated the separation of church and state. Instead, the school advised the students they must refer to themselves as "CF." As if that were not enough, when Heather, Jolie and Sarah sought

---

[41]*Widmar*, 454 U.S. at 269-70. It should be noted that distribution of literature by outside groups is treated differently than distribution of literature by students. Though some courts have ruled in favor for Gideons, others have ruled that Gideons may not come on public school campuses for the purpose of distributing Bibles. *Cf. Meltzer v. Board of Public Instruction of Orange County*, 548 F.2d 559 (5th Cir. 1977) and 577 F.2d 311 (5th Cir. 1978) (en banc) (Gideons may distribute Bibles on public school campuses); *Peck v. Upshur County Board of Educ.*, 941 F. Supp. 1465 (N.D. W.Va. 1996) (same); *Schanou v. Lancaster County School Dist.*, 863 F. Supp. 1048 (D. Neb. 1994) (same) *with Berger v. Rensselaer Central School Corporation*, 992 F.2d 1160 (7th Cir.), *cert. denied*, 113 S. Ct. 2344 (1993) (Gideons may not distribute Bibles on public school campuses.)

permission to hang a poster on the club bulletin board and to distribute a pledge card to other students on Valentines' Day in support of a "True Love Waits" campaign, school officials denied permission because the pledge contained the word "God." Throughout the country many high school students were promoting the "True Love Waits" campaign which was designed to encourage other students to remain sexually abstinent until entry into a biblical marriage. The card pledged support to family, friends, future spouse, future children, and to God. Though the other clubs were allowed to put up secular posters on the bulletin board and distribute secular literature, school board policy stated that no religious literature could be posted on bulletin boards or distributed by students. Fortunately Liberty Counsel was able to intervene on behalf of these students. On February 12, it became apparent that the school would not budge in its position. Several attorneys began working on this case in the late afternoon on February 12 and worked around the clock throughout the entire night until midday on February 13. A federal lawsuit containing approximately one and one-half inches of typed legal research was sent via the internet to a local Milwaukee law firm. The documents were printed, signed by the parties, and delivered to the federal court at 4:15 p.m., fifteen minutes before court closed. On the morning of February 14 at 11:15 a.m., a federal judge entered an emergency restraining order which allowed the students to hang their posters and distribute the pledge cards. At the end of the day one girl approached Sarah expressing interest in the pledge, but during the course of the conversation the student hung her head down and said, "I can't sign the pledge because I'm not a virgin." Sarah responded that God forgave her past, and she could pledge from that time forward to remain sexually abstinent until she entered a biblical marriage. At that moment the girl's face lit up and she signed the pledge. Certainly literature distribution is a powerful tool, and in this case, at least one student may have begun a new chapter in her life.

Some schools have attempted to regulate student literature distribution by requiring that all literature be reviewed by school officials prior to distribution. However, the requirement of giving advance notice of a student's intent to speak inherently inhibits free speech.[42] The Supreme Court has stated that prior notification is "quite incompatible with the requirements of the First Amendment."[43] Indeed, the "simple knowledge that one must inform the government of his desire to speak and must fill out appropriate forms and comply with applicable regulations discourages citizens from speaking freely."[44] Certainly the "delay inherent in advance notice requirements inhibits free speech by outlawing spontaneous expression."[45] The Supreme Court has further noted that when "an event occurs, it is often necessary to have one's voice heard promptly, if it is to be considered at all."[46]

Most of these school policies requiring advance notice prior to distribution are insufficient because they lack specific guidelines. These policies often leave so much discretion to the school officials so as to allow the school officials to censor the speech without using objective criteria. These pre-distribution review requirements are presumptively invalid because, essentially, they require a license from the government prior to speaking.[47] One case concluded that a one day advanced notification requirement was unconstitutional.[48] In striking down an advanced notification requirement, a federal court noted that "a policy which subjects all nonschool sponsored communications to pre-distribution review for content censorship violates the First Amendment. . . . [N]o . . . content control is justified for communication among students which is not part of the educational program."[49] The "majority of courts

---

[42]*NAACP v. City of Richmond*, 743 F.2d 1346 (9th Cir. 1984).

[43]*Thomas v. Collins*, 323 U.S. 516, 540 (1945).

[44]*City of Richmond*, 743 F.2d at 1455 (citing *Rosen v. Port of Portland*, 641 F.2d 1243 (9th Cir. 1981)).

[45]*City of Richmond*, 743 F.2d at 1355.

[46]*Shuttlesworth v. City of Birmingham*, 394 U.S. 147, 163 (1969).

[47]"It is well established that in the area of freedom of expression an overbroad regulation may be subject to review and invalidation, even though its application in the case under construction may be constitutionally unobjectable." *Forsyth County v. Nationalist Movement*, 112 S. Ct. 2395, 2400 (1992). *See also Secretary of State of Maryland v. Joseph Munson Company*, 467 U.S. 947 (1984); *Shuttlesworth v. Birmingham*, 394 U.S. 147 (1969); *Freedman v. Maryland*, 380 U.S. 51 (1965); *Talley v. California*, 362 U.S. 60 (1960); *Abramson v. Gonzalez*, 949 F.2d 1567 (11th Cir. 1992); *Sentinel Communications Company v. Watts*, 936 F.2d 1189 (11th Cir. 1991).

[48]*Rosen v. Port of Portland*, 641 F.2d 1243 (9th Cir. 1981) (dealing with an international airport).

[49]*Burch v. Barker*, 861 F.2d 1149 (9th Cir. 1988).

of appeals considering policies similar to the one at issue here [a pre-distribution review policy] found them violative of the First Amendment because they were overly broad and inadequately focused on avoidance of disruption and interference with school discipline."[50]

Reviewing a pre-distribution review literature distribution policy within the context of the public school, a federal court found such a policy unconstitutional because it gave school officials "unfettered discretion."[51] The court went on to state that such a policy gave

> the government the power to suppress speech in advance, while imposing no time limits or other procedural obligations on school officials that would insure that speech is suppressed to the minimum extent possible, or that the speech is supported for good and expressed reasons, rather than at the whim of the school officials. This policy gives the school authorities the power to

---

[50]*Id.* at 1157. The Seventh Circuit stated in *Fujishima v. Board of Education*, 460 F.2d 1355, 1358 (7th Cir. 1972), that "*Tinker* in no way suggests that students may be required to announce their intentions of engaging in a certain conduct beforehand so school authorities may decide whether to prohibit the conduct." The First Circuit invalidated a policy requiring literature distribution to be pre-approved. *Riseman v. School Committee*, 439 F.2d 148 (1st Cir. 1971). The Second Circuit also found that a prior review policy was a prior restraint and noted it could only be permitted if accompanied by elaborate procedural safeguards. *Eisner v. Stamford Board of Education*, 440 F.2d 803 (2nd Cir. 1971). The Fourth Circuit found that a rule which required prior permission from the principal before distributing any material was unconstitutional. *Quarterman v. Byrd*, 453 F.2d 54 (4th Cir. 1971). The same "basic vice" was present in *Vaughman v. Board of Education*, 478 F.2d 1345 (4th Cir. 1973). Failure to provide a reasonable time on the review of materials renders the prior review unconstitutional. *Nitzderg v. Parks*, 525 F.2d 378, 383-85 (4th Cir. 1975). *But see Bystrom v. Fridley High School*, 822 F.2d 747 (8th Cir. 1987) (school may prohibit written material pervaded or characterized by four-letter words which may be considered unprintable); *Shanley v. Northeast Independent School District*, 462 F.2d 960 (5th Cir. 1972) (a prior review policy is not per se unconstitutional). We have already pointed out that other federal district courts have found prior review policies unconstitutional. *See Muller v. Jefferson Lighthouse School*, 98 F.3d 1530 (7th Cir. 1996), *cert. denied*, 117 S. Ct. 1335 (1997); *Hedges v. Wauconda Community Unit School Dist. No. 118*, 9 F.3d 1295 (7th Cir. 1993); *Johnston-Loehner v. O'Brien*, 859 F. Supp. 575 (M.D. Fla. 1994); *Slotterback v. Interboro School District*, 766 F. Supp. 280 (E.D. Penn. 1991); *Rivera v. Board of Regents*, 721 F. Supp. 1189, 1197 (D. Col. 1989); *Sullivan v. Houston Independent School District*, 333 F. Supp. 1149 (S.D. Tex. 1971); *Zucker v. Panitz*, 299 F. Supp. 102 (S.D. N.Y. 1969).

[51]*Rivera*, 721 F. Supp. at 1198.

extinguish the right of students to speak through inaction and delay.[52]

One school district argued that all literature brought on campus by students must be approved by the school superintendent prior to distribution. In a case brought on behalf of a fifth-grade student whose literature was confiscated by a school principal, Liberty Counsel argued that the policy placed an impermissible restraint on free speech. The school argued that it must pre-review the literature for religious content. The court stated the following:

> It is beyond dispute that the school policy imposes a prior restraint on speech. It is also beyond dispute that the restraint is based on content, for only after reviewing content does the school decide whether particular materials may be distributed.[53]

Recognizing that students on public school campuses, including fifth-grade students, are protected by the constitutional right to free speech, the court declared:

> In order for the State in the person of school officials to justify prohibition of a particular expression of opinion, it must be able to show that its action was caused by something more than a mere desire to avoid the discomfort and unpleasantness that always accompany an unpopular viewpoint. . . .

Following *Tinker*, a school seeking to impose a content-based prior restriction on student speech must show that the restricted speech would materially and substantially interfere with school operations or with the rights of other students. Mere fear of possible interference is not sufficient to sustain a content-based prior restraint on student speech.[54]

The courts have disdained pre-distribution review policies

---

[52] *Id.*

[53] *Johnston-Loehner v. O'Brien*, 859 F. Supp. 575, 579 (M.D. Fla. 1994).

[54] *Id.* at 580.

because they essentially allow the government to suppress speech in advance. Policies which do not contain time limits in which the government official has to grant or deny the request essentially allow the government to suppress speech either through inaction or delay. One federal court of appeals stated that "*Tinker* in no way suggests that students may be required to announce their intentions of engaging in certain conduct beforehand so school authorities may decide whether to prohibit the conduct."[55] These pre-distribution review policies are essentially a licensing law, and the Supreme Court has made "clear that a person faced with such an unconstitutional licensing law may ignore it and engage with impunity in the exercise of the right of free expression for which the law purports to require a license."[56] Clearly, a policy which requires students to present their literature for pre-distribution review is flatly unconstitutional.[57]

Going back to the common sense approach mentioned earlier regarding student free speech, it would be laughable for any school to require students to reveal the content of their verbal communication to public officials prior to engaging in discussion during noninstructional time. Certainly when a student gets off the bus that student is not required to announce to the principal the content of all verbal speech that will occur for the day. A student does not need permission to tell another student, "I like you." It would not only be unconstitutional but ludicrous for a school to impose such a requirement. Additionally, it is likewise unconstitutional and ludicrous to require prior review of speech simply because it is transformed to the printed page.

A final way schools have attempted to restrict student distribution of literature is to require that the literature be placed at a designated location. Some schools argue that their restrictive policies do not violate student free speech so long as the students

---

[55]*Fujishima*, 460 F.2d at 1358.

[56]*Shuttlesworth*, 394 U.S. at 151.

[57]*But see Muller v. Jefferson Lighthouse School*, 98 F.3d 1530 (7th Cir. 1996), *cert. denied*, 117 S. Ct. 1335 (1997); *Hedges v. Wauconda Community Unit School Dist. No. 118*, 9 F.3d 1295 (7th Cir. 1993). This *Hedges* case upheld a policy requiring prior review of literature distributed in quantities greater than ten. However, this decision is flawed and is inconsistent with Supreme Court cases regarding prior literature distribution. Moreover, the majority of the federal appellate courts are not in agreement with the Seventh Circuit.

can exercise their free speech off campus on the public sidewalks surrounding the school, or so long as they can place their literature in a designated rack within the school. However, the Supreme Court has stated that "one is not to have the exercise of his liberty of expression in appropriate places abridged on the plea that it may be exercised in some other place."[58] Actually, requiring students to place literature at a designated location creates a First Amendment Establishment Clause conflict rather than alleviating such a problem. This is so because the designated location, like a school newspaper, carries with it a seal of sponsorship, endorsement, or approval by the school facility. Student speech does not violate the Establishment Clause or raise any church-state issues. However, one school argued that it must prohibit student distribution of literature because to allow it would violate the Establishment Clause or the so-called separation of church and state. Therefore, the school instead allowed the distribution of literature, but only if it were placed at a specific designated location. A court reviewing this situation ruled that the designated location restriction created an Establishment Clause problem which the school attempted to avoid.[59] It is unreasonable to require students to speak only at a designated location. Just as it would be ridiculous to require students to go to a designated location in order to pass out a love note or directions, it is unreasonable to require students to place their religious literature at a designated location. Remember, verbal speech is equivalent to written speech, and the two should be treated equally. The only difference between the two would be a concern involving litter. However, schools should prohibit the one who litters and not use littering or some other invalid reason to restrict speech in general.[60] A ban on handbilling would suppress "a great quantity of speech that does not cause the evils that it seeks

---

[58]*Schneider v. New Jersey*, 308 U.S. 147 (1939).

[59]*Johnston-Loehner v. O'Brien*, 859 F. Supp. 575 (M.D. Fla. 1994). The Establishment Clause is not implicated by student-initiated literature distribution during noninstructional time. When the school sought to restrict student literature distribution by requiring that the literature be "distributed" only in a placement rack provided by the school, the school created, rather than avoided, an Establishment Clause violation.

[60]*See Organization for a Better Austin v. Keefe*, 410 U.S. 415 (1971); *Martin v. City of Struthers*, 319 U.S. 143, 145 (1943); *Jamison v. Texas*, 318 U.S. 413, 416 (1943); *Schneider v. State*, 308 U.S. 147, 162 (1939); *Lovell v. Griffin*, 303 U.S. 444, 452 (1938).

to eliminate."[61] Leafletting is a "form of religious activity [that] occupies the same high estate under the First Amendment as do worship in churches and preaching from the pulpits."[62]

Some schools have attempted to restrict student-initiated speech on the basis that it violates the Establishment Clause of the First Amendment, or the so-called "separation of church and state." For example, Liberty Counsel brought suit on behalf of Amber against one school district which claimed it had to prohibit a fifth grade student's distribution of religious literature to her fellow students. The school argued that allowing this distribution would violate the Establishment Clause. In this case, a principal confiscated and destroyed religious tracts which Amber wanted to distribute to her fellow students during noninstructional time. The school argued that if it allowed Amber to distribute material to her fellow classmates, the other students would perceive that the school was endorsing the message within these tracts, and since the school was prohibited from endorsing or promoting religion, the distribution of these tracts would violate the Establishment Clause. Thus, in order to avoid a constitutional problem on behalf of the school, the school took the position that it must prohibit all religious expression by students. The federal court ruled that the school board's "asserted interest in avoiding a violation of the Establishment Clause is invalid because permitting student distribution of religious materials does not violate the Establishment Clause."[63]

The school district's reasoning was, of course, flawed. Students as well as school officials have the affirmative protection of the First Amendment Free Speech and Free Exercise Clauses. However, only teachers and school officials have the restriction of the Establishment Clause and are restricted in their promotion of religion. The Establishment Clause applies only to governmental entities. It does not apply to individuals who are not associated with the government. Therefore, students do not have the restriction imposed by the Establishment Clause. Students cannot establish a religion, only governmental entities and their agents can establish a religion. Consequently, students have all the affirmative protection

[61]*Ward*, 491 U.S. at 789, 799n.

[62]*Murdock v. Pennsylvania*, 319 U.S. 105, 108-09 (1934).

[63]*Johnston-Loehner v. O'Brien*, 859 F. Supp. 575 (M.D. Fla. 1994).

of the Free Speech and Free Exercise Clauses of the First
Amendment and do not have any restriction or prohibition of the
First Amendment Establishment Clause. While schools and their
agents are prohibited from actively promoting and proselytizing a
particular religious tenet, students have absolutely no prohibition in
this regard. The Supreme Court has already recognized that "there
is a crucial difference between *government* speech endorsing
religion, which the Establishment Clause forbids, and *private* speech
endorsing religion, which the Free Speech and Free Exercise
Clauses protect."[64]

Voluntary, student-initiated, student-led distribution of religious
literature on public school property has never been prohibited by the
courts on the basis that it violates the separation of church and state.
"It is only when individuals seek to observe their religion in ways
that unduly involve the government that their expressive rights may
be circumscribed."[65] There has never been any case in which
student initiated speech has constituted a violation of the
Establishment Clause.

A Texas court flatly rejected the Establishment Clause
argument on the basis that the Establishment Clause "is not a
restriction on the rights of individuals acting in their private
lives."[66] Another court has also rejected this argument by stating
the following:

> The Establishment Clause is a limitation on the power of
> governments; it is not a restriction on the rights of
> individuals acting in their private lives. The threshold
> question in any Establishment Clause case is whether
> there is sufficient governmental action to invoke the
> prohibition. In *Bethel* and *Hazelwood*, the Supreme Court
> recognized a distinction between school-affiliated speech
> and the private speech of students. It is clear that the mere
> fact that student speech occurs on school property does
> not make it government supported. It is undisputed in this

---

[64]*Mergens*, 110 S. Ct. at 2360.

[65]*Berger v. Rensselaer Central School Corporation*, 992 F.2d 1160, 1168 (7th Cir. 1993).

[66]*Clark*, 806 F. Supp. at 121. *Accord Mergens*, 110 S. Ct. 2356 (1990); *Rivera*, 721 F.
Supp. at 1195.

case that the students are not government actors, are not acting in concert with the government, and do not seek school cooperation or assistance with their speech. Accordingly, the Establishment Clause simply is inapplicable.[67]

The Supreme Court has already recognized a distinction between student-initiated speech and school-sponsored speech.

The question whether the First Amendment requires the school to tolerate a particular student speech -- the question that we addressed in *Tinker* -- is different from the question of whether the First Amendment requires the school affirmatively to promote particular student speech. The latter question concerns educators' authority over the school-sponsored publications, theatrical productions, and other expressive activities that the students, parents and members of the public might reasonably perceive to bear the imprimatur of the school.[68]

One federal court has clearly recognized the difference between school-sponsored and student-initiated speech when it pointed out that the "standard for reviewing the suppression of...school-sponsored speech [is governed] by *Hazelwood*, and all other speech by *Tinker*."[69]

Clothes

Expressive activity through the wearing of clothes that have writing or articles of clothing such as crosses or religious jewelry which do not substantially interfere with the work of the school or impinge upon the rights of other students also retains First Amendment protection. The *Tinker* case involved students wearing black armbands to school as a symbolic protest to the Vietnam War.

---

[67]*Rivera*, 721 F. Supp. at 1195. *See also Clark*, 806 F. Supp. at 121; *Thompson v. Waynesboro Area School District*, 673 F. Supp. 1379 (N.D. Pa. 1987).

[68]*Hazelwood*, 484 U.S. at 270-71.

[69]*Chandler v. McMinnville School District*, 978 F.2d 524, 528 (9th Cir. 1982).

The Supreme Court held that such expression was protected by the First Amendment.[70]

The analysis used for clothing should be the same analysis used for literature distribution. Courts have already established that students have free speech rights on public school campuses. Printed words on clothing such as T-shirts is a form of free speech. Just like the students in *Tinker* who wore black armbands protesting involvement in the Vietnam War, students have the right to wear printed words or symbols on their clothing. Student expression may be limited only if it interferes with the ordinary operation of the school or with the rights of other students. In the case of interfering with the rights of other students, the issue is whether the wording is defamatory or libelous to another student, not whether it is offensive.[71] Simply because another student disagrees with the content of the message does not permit the school to restrict the wearing of the shirt.

One student contacted Liberty Counsel after listening to a national radio broadcast on this topic. The student apparently had worn a T-shirt to school with a pro-life message. The principal ordered her to change clothes and not wear the shirt again. The shirt had the message "God created woman with a womb, not a tomb." Liberty Counsel instructed the student that she should respect those in authority over her, but this situation involved her religious conviction and her right to speak under the First Amendment. Therefore, the student was advised that she had a right to wear the shirt to school. When she later showed up at school wearing the shirt, the principal questioned her, stating, "Why are you wearing that T-shirt again?" The student responded, "Because my attorney said I have a constitutional right to do so." That was the end of the discussion. After contacting the superintendent, the principal agreed that the student had a right to wear the shirt.

In one case, junior high school students designed T-shirts on the back of which were the words: "The best of the night's adventures are reserved for people with nothing planned."[72] School

---

[70]*Tinker*, 393 U.S. at 506, 511.

[71]*Clark*, 806 F. Supp. at 120.

[72]*McIntire v. Bethel Independent School District*, 804 F. Supp. 1415, 1421 (W.D. Ok. 1992).

officials told the students to remove the T-shirts because the officials believed the message promoted an alcohol advertisement. However, the students contended that the T-shirt was meant to convey a message of being spontaneous and having fun. The federal court found that students' speech was "presumptively protected by the First Amendment."[73] The court further noted that the t-shirts worn during regular school hours did not bear the imprimatur or sponsorship of the school and therefore neither the *Hazelwood* case (the school newspaper case) nor the *Fraser* case (the nominating speech case) applied. Finally, the court ruled that a forum analysis was not appropriate and that the proper test was to apply *Tinker*.[74] The court therefore concluded that the students had a First Amendment right to wear the T-shirts, and they could not be prohibited unless there was evidence of "substantial disruption or material interference with school activities."[75]

One shirt that is particularly intriguing was created by a pro-life group in Orlando, Florida. On the front of the shirt are the words "CHOOSE LIFE." The word "CHOOSE" is written across the top of the shirt. Underneath, in big letters approximately eight inches tall, is the word "LIFE." On the back of the shirt is the following:

4,352 babies Killed in abortions each day in U.S.A. · 18 days after conception the child's heart starts beating · In the year 2,000, over ½ of our population will be 50 and older · 1 out of every 3 pregnancies end in abortion · 99% of all abortions performed are for social reasons · Less than 1% of all abortions are for rape, incest & medical reasons · Only half the people that go into abortion clinics come out alive · Mother's womb: the most dangerous place on earth · Abortions are performed legally through all 9 months of pregnancy · All of the unborn child's organs are formed and functioning at 2

---

[73]*Id.* at 1424. *See also Roth v. United States*, 354 U.S. 476, 484 (1957) ("All ideas having even the slightest redeeming social importance—unorthodox ideas, controversial ideas, even ideas hateful to the prevailing climate of opinion, have the full protection of the guarantees [of the First Amendment].")

[74]*McIntire*, 804 F. Supp. at 1427.

[75]*Id.* at 1420.

months · Child is dependent on mother's body; not part of it · Genetic code is set from moment of conception · Brainwaves are detected at 40 days · Nervous system functioning before 12 weeks · Birth is merely changing place of residence, dining habits, and airwaves · Abortion: the worst form of child abuse · Just because it's legal, doesn't make it right.

Below this inscription are the words: "This is dedicated to all those whose lives were brutally ended by abortion. We mourn their deaths, but know their souls are with God."

This message is written in black interspersed with red highlighted words to break up the paragraph. As a student sits in class, the student behind the classmate with the T-shirt obviously sees the writing. During class, discussion about the writing is probably not appropriate, but after class or in between class, discussion of the message is appropriate. This shirt provides an outstanding opportunity for students to discuss pro-life issues.

Hair

Though hair is an issue that will not often arise as a religious liberty matter, the length of hair is clearly important to certain religious beliefs. School dress codes requiring males to have short hair may conflict with the beliefs of some Native American students. One federal court ruled that it is unconstitutional for a school to require Native American male students to have short hair contrary to their religious belief, for some Native Americans short hair may only be worn to show mourning when a close family member dies. Since wearing long hair for males of certain religious beliefs may actually be a First Amendment expressive activity, some dress codes may be ruled unconstitutional.[76] In order to object to a dress code, the student must have a sincerely held religious belief that is negatively impacted by the code. The school should then take efforts to accommodate the student's religious belief.

---

[76]*Alabama and Coushatta Tribes of Texas v. Trustees of the Big Sandy Independent School District*, 817 F. Supp. 1319 (E.D. Tex. 1993).

Class Discussions And Reports

The issue often arises as to whether students may ask questions or even challenge teachers during class when the subject matter being taught is disagreeable to the student. Another interesting question arises as to whether students may give religious verbal or written reports.

Again, student speech, whether verbal or written, is protected by the First Amendment. A student cannot stand up in a math class and begin speaking about religion if the speech has no relation to the topic being studied. However, if the subject matter is evolution, the student can certainly ask questions regarding creation science or abrupt appearance, and can even express disagreements with the teacher. The student may express views on any subject being taught so long as it is consistent with the subject matter being discussed at that time. Moreover, if students are asked to give verbal or written reports, students may give these reports on religious matters, so long as it falls within the parameters of the context of study. For example, in a literature class, if students are required to read a book and give a written or oral report, a student may read a religious book and give a report on this book. If a teacher prohibited the student from giving the report simply because the content of the report was religious, this would be a violation of the student's free speech and free exercise rights.[77]

One person called Liberty Counsel and advised that students were required to give a written report on the fall season. The student wrote in the report that God created the fall season. When the student presented this paper to the teacher and the teacher realized that it contained information regarding God, the teacher

---

[77]*But see DeNooyer v. Livonia Public Schools*, 799 F. Supp. 744 (E.D. Mich. 1992), *aff'd sub nom, DeNooyer v. Merinelli*, 1 F.3d 1240 (6th Cir. 1993) (A school may prohibit a second grade student from showing during show and tell time a videotape of herself singing a proselytizing religious song and advocating accepting Jesus Christ as Savior because the school teacher believed that showing the videotape was inappropriate in that it was inconsistent with the purpose of the class, which was designed to develop self-esteem through oral presentations in the classroom.); *Duran v. Nitsche*, 780 F. Supp. 1048 (E.D. Pa. 1991) (A fifth grade teacher may prohibit a student from giving an oral presentation to her class about her belief in God because, even though the teacher allowed oral presentations, the classroom was not open for all forms of discussion.).

ripped up the paper and threw it away, stating that it violated the separation of church and state. This is clearly a bigoted action and violative of the First Amendment.

In another case, a parent contacted Liberty Counsel stating that his seventh grade son had been told he could not use the word "God" in his oral presentation to the class because it would violate the separation of church and state. Incredibly, the teacher required the seventh grade boy to reverse the "d" with the "G" every time the word appeared. Though the other students were allowed to give their oral presentations without censorship, this student was required to say "Dog" every time his written speech mentioned "God." Unbelievable as it seems, this is the battlefield into which public school students enter every day. The teacher was unquestionably wrong in her actions and unfortunately sent a horrible message to the entire class.

In addition, students may object to participating in certain kinds of class activities if the activity violates a sincerely held religious belief. If a class project, assignment, or activity violates a student's sincerely held religious beliefs, the student may opt out and request alternative accommodations.

Students and parents may object to various curriculum on several grounds. One challenge to religiously objectionable curriculum is to raise a free exercise claim. The student or parent must first have a sincerely held religious belief that is negatively impacted or burdened by the curriculum being taught. If the sincerely held religious belief is burdened or negatively impacted by the curriculum, the school is then required to show that it has a compelling reason to present the curriculum, and that the curriculum is being presented in the least restrictive manner possible. Generally a school should be required to allow the student to opt out of religiously objectionable instruction. Challenges to the entire curriculum are generally not successful but challenges to portions of classroom instruction may be appropriate.

Courts have generally rejected challenges to the entire curriculum. One federal court rejected challenges brought by parents to the entire school curriculum on the basis that the curriculum promoted the religion of secular humanism.[78] Challenges to the

---

[78] *Mozert v. Hawkins County Board of Education*, 827 F.2d 1058 (6th Cir. 1987).

entire curriculum based upon allegations that it promotes the religion of secular humanism have failed for two reasons. First, courts have found the task of defining secular humanism difficult. Second, courts are reluctant to strike down an entire curriculum since that would substantially interfere with the educational process and create a huge void with nothing to fill the instructional time. Moreover, courts are reluctant to strike down an entire curriculum based upon one person's religious belief for fear that another person will have a different religious viewpoint and the schools will be caught in a quagmire.

Not only are courts reluctant to strike down the entire curriculum, courts are also reluctant to rule unconstitutional specific courses. A federal court of appeals ruled against parents challenging curriculum on the basis that the students were required to learn witchcraft and create poetic chants.[79]

In probably the most egregious case, a federal appeals court rejected the challenge of parents who claimed that their parental rights were violated when their children were subjected to a sexually explicit presentation put on by a private organization called Hot, Sexy and Safer Productions, Inc.[80] The parents complained that their children had been mentally raped when they were required to go to a mandatory convocation reportedly on sex education. However, instead of objectively overviewing sex education issues, the outside organization called students from the audience, placed huge condoms over their entire body and then licked the condoms. Comments were also made regarding the kinds of pants boys should wear, their physical features, genitalia, masturbation and homosexuality. The students were shocked and horrified, and yet the court rejected the constitutional challenge that parental rights had been violated by subjecting these students to this unwarranted mental rape. Challenges to entire curriculum, or even to an entire class, have met with little success. Additionally, challenges relying upon the Fourteenth Amendment due process or parental rights claim generally have not been successful. The best challenge is to raise a freedom of religion defense and opt out of a portion of the class. However, it is possible in certain situations to look to

---

[79] *Brown v. Woodland Joint Unified School Dist.*, 27 F.3d 1373 (9th Cir. 1994).
[80] *Brown v. Hot, Sexy and Safer Productions, Inc.*, 68 F.3d 525 (1st Cir. 1995).

individual state law to challenge offensive curriculum. A New York State court ruled that a condom distribution program violated state law when the schools failed to get the parents prior consent to distribute the condoms.[81]

Additionally, certain sex education programs may be challenged on state law grounds because many states require that sex education be abstinence based. However, many schools have ignored their state legislation and have presented sex education programs that are not abstinence based.

Though not raising religious objections, two federal courts ruled that compulsory community service requirements do not violate due process or parental rights.[82] In both of these cases, the school boards enacted regulations requiring students to perform community service prior to graduation. The students and parents raised objections based upon due process, interference with parental rights, and violation of the Thirteenth Amendment, which prohibits involuntary servitude. The courts found that none of these claims had merit. However, these cases did not raise religious objections, and it may be arguable in some cases that mandatory community service would violate sincerely held religious beliefs. This would certainly be true if the choices presented for community service required the student to participate in religiously objectionable activities.

Access To Books And Films

The Supreme Court has declared that a student's "right to receive ideas is a necessary predicate to the recipient's meaningful exercise of his or her own right of speech."[83] While a school may not be forced to place a book in the library, once a book is placed there, the discretion to remove the book is circumscribed by the First Amendment. The book may not be removed simply because

---

[81] *Alfonso v. Fernandez*, 606 N.Y.S.2d 259 (1993) (Court ruled that the condom distribution fell under the state statute dealing with health services which required parental consent).

[82] *Imnediato v. Rye Neck School Dist.*, 73 F.3d 454 (2nd Cir. 1996); *Herndon v. Chapel Hill-Carrboro City Board of Education*, 89 F.3d 174 (4th Cir. 1996).

[83] *Board of Education, Island Trees Union Free School District No. 26 v. Pico*, 457 U.S. 853, 867 (1982).

the school disagrees with the content. However, the book could be removed if it lacked "educational suitability" or if it contained pervasive vulgarity.[84] Similarly, the Bible cannot be removed from a library on the basis of its religious content.[85] Finally, although a school has wide latitude in the selection and retention of curriculum, content-neutral criteria may be necessary to remove a book or film from part of the curriculum.[86]

One student called Liberty Counsel because her library did not have any pro-life literature. She obtained certain books and donated them to her school library, and the library accepted the books and placed them on the library shelves. Once accepted, the library has certain restrictions on removing the books. These books cannot be removed simply because the content of the speech is disagreeable or offensive. The so-called political correctness movement wants to remove certain speech that offends various classes of society. This is an absolute violation of the First Amendment and should be resisted. One individual contacted Liberty Counsel and stated that the school principal told her that a Bible could not be in the school library because it violated the so-called separation of church and state. This is absolutely untrue. Schools may and should have religious literature in their libraries. Schools that remove religious material simply because the content is religious violate the First Amendment because such decisions are based on the content of the literature.

Student Fees

Any student who has attended college is familiar with mandatory student fees. These fees are paid by students and are used by the school for a multitude of reasons. Students have two constitutional rights regarding the payment and receipt of fees. First, schools may not discriminate in the disbursement of the fees. Second, students may choose to opt out of paying a portion of the fees based on objections regarding the use of these fees.

The University of Virginia is one of the Nation's oldest

---

[84]*Id.* at 871.

[85]*But see Roberts v. Madigan,* 702 F. Supp. 1505 (D. Colo. 1989).

[86]*Pratt v. Independent School District,* 670 F.2d 771 (8th Cir. 1982).

schools. Like other schools, the University of Virginia imposed mandatory student fees. Recognized student groups were entitled to apply for funds from the Student Activities Fund to assist their student club. Though the University funded 15 student newspapers along with a Jewish and a Muslim student group, it refused to fund a newspaper published by Wide Awake Productions on the basis that it was Christian.[87] The University took the position that the Jewish and Muslim clubs were not religious but cultural. The school then took the position that it was prohibited by the Constitution from funding any religious organization. The United States Supreme Court rejected the University of Virginia's argument and ruled that the University must fund the Christian publication because failure to do so would violate the First Amendment. The Court noted:

> It is axiomatic that the government may not regulate speech based on its substantive content or the message it conveys. Other principles follow from this precept. In the realm of private speech or expression, government regulation may not favor one speaker over another. Discrimination against speech because of its message is presumed to be unconstitutional. These rules informed our determination that the government offends the First Amendment when it imposes financial burdens on certain speakers based on the content of their expression. When government targets not subject matter but particular views taken by speakers on a subject, the violation of the First Amendment is all the more blatant. Viewpoint discrimination is thus an egregious form of content discrimination. The government must abstain from regulating speech when the specific motivating ideology or the opinion or perspective of the speaker is the rationale for the restriction.[88]

The University of Virginia then argued that this case involves the disbursement of funds, and since funds are scarce, the

---

[87]*Rosenberger v. Rector and Visitors of the University of Virginia*, 115 S. Ct. 2510 (1995).

[88]*Id.* at 2516 (citations omitted).

University is justified in restricting funds from certain groups. However, the Supreme Court rejected this argument, stating that "government cannot justify viewpoint discrimination among private speakers on the economic fact of scarcity."[89] The Court then stated the following:

> Vital First Amendment speech principles are at stake here. The first danger to liberty lies in granting the State the power to examine publications to determine whether or not they are based on some ultimate idea and if so for the State to classify them. The second, and corollary, danger is to speech from the chilling of individual thought and expression. That danger is especially real in the University setting, where the State acts against a background and tradition of thought and experiment that is at the center of our intellectual and philosophic tradition. In ancient Athens, and, as Europe entered into a new period of intellectual awakening, in places like Bologna, Oxford, and Paris, universities began as voluntary and spontaneous assemblages or concourses for students to speak and to write and to learn. The quality and creative power of student intellectual life to this day remains a vital measure of a school's influence and attainment. For the University, by regulation, to cast disapproval on particular viewpoints of its students risks the suppression of free speech and creative inquiry in one of the vital centers for the nation's intellectual life, its college and university campuses.[90]

The Supreme Court found that allowing the Christian student group access to student fees would not violate the Establishment Clause of the First Amendment. Disbursement of the student fees is neutral toward religion in that the fees are available to all student clubs. The University would not be singly funding religion. Moreover, these fees come from students, not the University.[91] The Court pointed out the following:

---

[89]*Id.* at 2519.
[90]*Id.* at 2520 (citations omitted).
[91]*Id.* at 2522.

> It does not violate the Establishment Clause for a public
> university to grant access to its facilities on a religion-
> neutral basis to a wide spectrum of student groups,
> including groups which use meeting rooms for sectarian
> activities, accompanied by some devotional exercises. This
> is so even where the upkeep, maintenance, and repair of
> the facilities attributed to those uses is paid from a student
> activities fund to which students are required to contribute.
> The government usually acts by spending money.[92]

The Court noted that there is no constitutional violation for a
university to allow access to its facilities on a neutral basis. If a
school created a printing room and allowed access to the printers by
secular groups, it must allow access to the same printers by
Christian groups. Moreover, if the school takes student funds and
pays a third-party off campus to print student newspapers for
secular groups, it must also provide the same funds to pay other
third-party printers off campus to print a newspaper for a Christian
group.[93]

The Supreme Court's decision is clear. Public schools, whether
at the college or university level or lower, may not discriminate in
the disbursement of student funds. Christian groups have just as
much right to apply for and receive student funds as secular student
groups.

Another aspect of receiving student funds is payment of student
funds. Some students may object to the payment of a portion of
their student fees because of how these funds are used. For
example, some student funds are used to provide health insurance
for students which may include coverage for abortion. Other
portions of the funds may go to political causes advocated by the
school which are contrary to sincerely held religious beliefs.
Students may raise objections to the portion of the mandatory funds
contrary to their sincerely held religious beliefs. The school should
remit that portion of the mandatory student fee which is used to

---

[92]*Id.* at 2523 (citations omitted).
[93]*Id.* at 2523-2524.

promote the objectionable activity.[94]

Advertisements in School Newspapers and Yearbooks

Frequently a public school newspaper or yearbook will print paid advertisements submitted by either students or nonstudents. In *Yeo v. Lexington*,[95] the Lexington School Committee decided to distribute condoms and informational packets regarding "safe sex" to high school students without parental consent. This issue caused extensive controversy and generated a great deal of public debate. The high school newspaper took up the issue and began following the story. In an editorial, the newspaper took a position in favor of making condoms freely available to high school students. Individuals opposed to the condom distribution program gathered enough signatures to place the school's condom distribution policy on the town ballot. These same individuals then sought to place an ad in the school yearbook that stated as follows:

> We know you can do it!
> ABSTINENCE:
> The Healthy Choice
> Sponsored by:
> Lexington Parents Information Network (LEXNET)
> Post Office Box 513, Lexington, MA 02173

The same advertisement was later submitted to the school newspaper with only slight modifications. Neither the yearbook nor the newspaper agreed to print the ad, stating that any ad was subject to approval of the editorial staff.

To analyze the case the court considered the question of whether the school newspaper and yearbook became a public forum for advertisements when it opened the newspaper and yearbook for outside advertisement placement. The court noted the following:

---

[94]But see *Goehring v. Brophy*, 94 F.3d 1294 (9th Cir. 1996) (students failed to establish that the University's health insurance system imposed a substantial burden on their free exercise of religion).

[95]1997 WL 748667 (1st Cir. 1997).

While selective access to government facilities does not a
public forum make, we cannot accept the proposition that
government can selectively, and with sole and absolute
discretion, open its facilities or avenues of communication
along purely content-based lines, and thus determine to
admit the messages it likes and choose to exclude the
messages it dislikes on no basis beyond the messages'
content. It is axiomatic that the government may not
regulate speech based on its substantive content or the
message it conveys. As we have noted, once the state has
created a forum, it may not condition access to the forum
on the content of the message to be communicated.[96]

The court found that both the yearbook and the newspaper
accepted paid advertisements and that neither publication had ever
rejected any proffered ad, regardless of content. The court found
that the school newspaper and yearbook ultimately rejected the
abstinence ads because they found them "objectionable" or
"controversial." The court therefore found that by rejecting the ads,
the school violated the First Amendment right to free speech.

Release Time

Release time programs allow public school students a certain
time each week to leave school to attend religious instruction.[97]
The instruction must be given by non-school personnel off
campus.[98] Portable instruction sites must not be on school premises
and no academic credit should be given for such instruction.[99]
Finally, the printing cost of attendance cards should be borne by the

---

[96]*Yeo*, see slip op. 11 (citations and quotations omitted). Note the First Circuit Court of
Appeals and the *Yeo* case disagreed with the Ninth Circuit Court of Appeals decision in
Planned Parenthood of S. Nev. v. Clark County School Dist., 941 F.2d 817 (9th Cir. 1991)
(*en banc*). The Ninth Circuit in *Planned Parenthood* ruled that a school-sponsored
publication does not display the requisite intent to create a public forum when they opened
their ad pages to the public but retained discretion to deny any ad submitted by a business
or individual that is not in the school's "best interest."

[97]*Zorach v. Clauson*, 343 U.S. 306 (1952).

[98]*Lanner v. Wimmer*, 662 F.2d 1349 (10th Cir. 1981).

[99]*Doe v. Shenandoah County School Board*, 737 F. Supp. 913 (W.D. Va. 1990).

religious institution providing the instruction,[100] and elective credit should not be given.[101]

The Pledge Of Allegiance

The Pledge of Allegiance has been attacked in two forms. The first attack has been from a free exercise standpoint, and the second has been from an Establishment Clause position. The first type of challenge has been upheld while the second has been rejected.

Jehovah's Witnesses have a sincerely held religious belief against saluting flags, which they consider to be idols. The United States Supreme Court ruled that a Jehovah's Witness should be excused from the requirement of saluting the flag.[102] Indeed, anyone who opposes saluting the flag should be excused from the requirement without regard to whether their refusal is based on religious or nonreligious grounds. To compel a student to salute the flag may violate exercise rights and free speech rights by virtue of the state compelling a specific type of speech.

The United States Supreme Court case deciding the flag salute issue with regard to Jehovah's Witnesses occurred in 1943. However, in 1954, the Pledge of Allegiance was amended to add the phrase "under God." In 1992, an atheist brought suit against an Illinois school board claiming that the flag salute was an unconstitutional establishment of religion by the state because it required individuals, at the direction of the state, to confess belief in God. The federal appeals court found that the pledge was "a secular rather than sectarian vow" and therefore did not violate the First Amendment Establishment Clause.[103] The court, therefore, ruled that the pledge was constitutional, merely recognizing "the historical fact that our Nation was believed to have been founded 'under God'."[104] The court went on to say that "reciting the pledge may be no more of a religious exercise than the reading

---

[100]*Lanner*, 662 F.2d at 1349.

[101]*Id. See Minnesota Federation of Teachers v. Nelson*, 740 F. Supp. 694 (D. Minn. 1990).

[102]*West Virginia State Board of Education v. Barnette*, 319 U.S. 624 (1943).

[103]*Sherman v. Community Consolidated School District*, 980 F.2d 437 (7th Cir. 1992), *cert. denied*, 113 S. Ct. 2439 (1993).

[104]*Id.* at 447.

allowed of Lincoln's Gettysburg Address, which contains an allusion to the same historical fact."[105] Students in public schools should have the option to refuse to say the Pledge of Allegiance. Without this option, there may be a constitutional violation.

Equal Access On Public School Campuses

The Equal Access Act of 1984 (hereafter the "Act")[106] has been affirmatively upheld by the Supreme Court in *Board of Education v. Mergens*.[107] If the public secondary school receives federal funds and allows one or more noncurriculum-related student groups to meet on campus, then the school cannot prohibit other noncurriculum-related student groups from meeting on campus unless such clubs "materially and substantially interfere with the orderly conduct of educational activities within the school."[108] A noncurriculum-related student group is interpreted broadly to mean "any student group that does not *directly* relate to the body of courses offered by the school."[109] The Court indicated that "a student group directly relates to a school's curriculum if the subject matter of the group is actually taught, or will soon be taught, in a regularly offered course; if the subject matter of the group concerns the body of courses as a whole; if the participation in the group is required for a particular course; or if participation in the group results in academic credit."[110] Examples of noncurriculum-related groups are chess clubs, stamp collecting clubs, or community service clubs.

Equal access means exactly what it says -- equal access to every facility of the school which is used by at least one or more other noncurriculum-related student groups, which would include use of classroom facilities, copy machines, intercom systems, bulletin boards, school newspaper, yearbook pictures, and annual

---

[105]*Id.*
[106]20 U.S.C. §§ 4071-74. This Act is reproduced in the Appendix.
[107]110 S. Ct. 2356 (1990).
[108]*Id.* at 2364, 2367.
[109]*Id.* at 2366.
[110]*Id.*

club fairs.[111]

The application of the Act is simple -- all groups must be treated equally without discrimination. Religious and political groups must be treated equally with other social or activity groups. According to the United States Supreme Court in *Mergens*, Congress passed the Act in order "to prevent discrimination against religious and other types of speech."[112]

In the *Mergens* case the Westside High School already allowed a Christian club to meet informally in the school facilities after school hours. However, the Christian club was denied official recognition which allowed other student clubs to be a part of the student activities program and allowed access to the school newspaper, bulletin boards, the public address system, and the annual club fair. According to *Mergens*, since the Westside High School officially recognized other non curriculum related student groups, allowed those groups access to the school newspaper, bulletin boards, public address system and the annual club fair, but did not allow the same privileges to the Christian club, the school violated the Act. Thus, if any club is given the opportunity of access to use school facilities, then a school must allow the same access to other groups. As one group is treated, all groups must be treated.

Following the *Mergens* case, one school decided that it would try to get around *Mergens*. This school reluctantly allowed the Christian club to meet on campus, but informed the club that it could only meet after school hours while the secular student clubs could meet throughout the school day. The school argued that it allowed equal access to school facilities just at different times. However, the Federal Court of Appeals easily saw through this thinly guised form of discrimination and ruled that equal access means student clubs must be treated equally. In other words, if the school allows the secular clubs to meet during the day, it must also allow the Christian clubs to meet throughout the day.[113]

---

[111]As for use of bulletin boards and yearbooks, the school can designate space to "noncurriculum-related student clubs" thus avoiding the appearance of school endorsement.

[112]*Mergens*, 110 S. Ct. at 2371.

[113]*Good News/Good Sports Club v. School Dist. of City of LaDue*, 28 F.3d 1501 (8th Cir. 1994), *cert. denied, School Dist. of City of LaDue v. Good News/Good Sports Club*, 115 S. Ct. 2640 (1995).

Additionally, another Federal Court found that a high school discriminated against Christian clubs when it allowed the secular clubs to meet during the lunch hour but denied the Christian clubs the same right. The Court ruled that lunch time was considered noninstructional time, and therefore since the school allowed the secular clubs to meet during the lunch hour, it must also allow the Christian clubs to meet during the same time period.[114]

In another case, the school board developed a nondiscrimination policy, requiring that no student-initiated club could discriminate against any person wishing to hold office on the basis of race, sex, national origin, and *religion*. The policy prohibited discrimination on the basis of race, color, national origin, creed or religion, marital status, sex, age, or handicap condition.

When the Christian group refused to put this nondiscrimination clause in their constitution, the school refused to allow the club access. The school argued that it treated all clubs equally, and that all clubs were prohibited from discriminating against potential officers. However, the Christian club argued that if it were not allowed to discriminate on the basis of religion, then the Christian club could essentially face a situation where someone running for office to lead their Christian club could be an atheist or a Satanist. Fortunately, the Federal Court agreed and found this nondiscrimination policy unconstitutional because it would essentially obliterate the unique essence of a Christian club.[115]

Application of Equal Access

The Act provides a safe harbor in which a school may operate. The Act should be viewed as a floor and not a ceiling. In other words, it presents the bare minimum that a school may provide to student groups, but a school may grant even more rights to student groups than the Act requires.

The Act applies to any (1) public secondary school (2) which receives federal funds and (3) which has a limited open forum.

---

[114] *Ceniceros v. Board of Trustees of the San Diego Unified School Dist.*, 106 F.3d 878 (9th Cir. 1997).

[115] *Hsu v. Roslyn Union Free School Dist. No. 3*, 85 F.3d 839 (2d Cir. 1996), *cert. denied, Roslyn Union Free School Dist. No. 3 v. Hsu*, 117 S. Ct. 608 (1996).

Identifying a public school providing secondary education which receives federal funds is easy. A limited open forum occurs "whenever such school grants an offering to or opportunity for one or more noncurriculum-related student groups to meet on school premises during noninstructional time."[116]

The Supreme Court in *Mergens* defined a noncurriculum-related student group "broadly to mean any student group that does not *directly* relate to the body of courses offered by the school."[117] The Court further stated that

> a student group directly relates to a school's curriculum if the subject matter of the group is actually taught, or will soon be taught, in a regularly offered course; if the subject matter of the group concerns the body of courses as a whole; if participation in the group is required for a particular course; or if participation in the group results in academic credit.[118]

A student government group would generally relate directly to the curriculum to the extent that it addresses concerns or solicits opinions and formulates proposals pertaining to the body of courses offered by the school. If participation in the school band or orchestra were required for the band or orchestra classes, or resulted in academic credit, then such groups would directly relate to the curriculum.

On the other hand, some examples of noncurriculum-related student groups include, but are by no means limited to, the chess club, a stamp collecting club, a community service club, camera club, diving club, music groups, Key Club, debate groups, business groups, political groups, and religious groups.[119]

---

[116]20 U.S.C. § 4071(b).

[117]*Mergens*, 110 S. Ct. at 2366.

[118]*Id.*

[119]*See Mergens*, 110 S. Ct. at 2366; *Bender v. Williamsport Area School District*, 741 F.2d 538, 539 n.18 (3rd Cir. 1984), *vacated on other grounds*, 475 U.S. 534 (1986); *Student Coalition for Peace v. Lower Merion School District*, 633 F. Supp. 1040, 1042 (E.D. Pa. 1986); 130 Cong. Rec. H 7732 (daily ed. July 25, 1984) and 130 Cong. Rec. S 8365 (daily ed. July 27, 1984).

Organizing a School Club

Under the Act a student club must be initiated by the students. Once initiated, the student group, no matter the size, must be given equal treatment as all other existing clubs. If the school requires a constitution or a statement of purpose from the other clubs, then a constitution or a statement of purpose may also be required of the new club.[120] The school may require a faculty member or any other school employee to be a sponsor of the group if a sponsor is required of the already existing groups. The school faculty member or employee may attend the student meetings. The basic principle is that the student group must be initiated and predominantly led by students, although the students may on occasion bring in outside speakers.

Equal Access and Disruptive Clubs

A concern that was brought up during the legislative hearings on the Act was that equal access would allow groups in public schools which are racist, hate groups, or disruptive.[121] However, the Act has been in effect since 1984; yet, an influx of disruptive hate groups disturbing schools has not occurred.

The Act specifically indicates that it "shall not be construed to limit the authority of the school, its agents or employees, to maintain order and discipline on school premises, to protect the well-being of students and faculty, and to assure that attendance of students at meetings is voluntary."[122] If a group substantially interferes with the normal operation of the school or is disruptive, the school under the Act is free to prohibit such a group from meeting on campus. The school must be able to show that the group is, in fact, disruptive. A simple fear that a group may be disruptive in the future is not enough to support denial of equal access, but the actual disruption or a threatened disruption by a group may be enough to restrict equal access. Satanic, occultic, racist, and hate

---

[120]Liberty Counsel has produced a model constitution which can be used as an example. This constitution is reproduced in the Appendix.

[121]See U.S. Code Congressional and Administrative News, P.L. 95-561 Vol. 5 pp. 4971-5226 (1978).

[122]20 U.S.C. § 4071(f).

groups may at some time cause disruption, but time has shown that schools have not seen an influx of these groups. Simply because some students or faculty disagree with the content of a group's speech is not enough to prohibit that group from equal access. However, if such a group is disruptive to the ordinary operation of the school, then the administrators retain the authority under the Act to maintain an orderly operating school. A school cannot deny access to a group simply because the content of the group's speech is distasteful or offensive. Moreover, a school cannot deny access to a group merely because an affiliate or parent organization at some other location has been shown to be disruptive.[123] The United States Supreme Court has stated:

Among the rights protected by the First Amendment is the right of individuals to associate to further their personal beliefs. While the freedom of association is not explicitly set out in the Amendment, it has long been held to be implicit in the freedoms of speech, assembly, and petition.[124]

The Supreme Court has also observed the following,

It should be obvious that the exclusion of any person or group—all-Negro, all-Oriental, or all-white—from public facilities infringes upon the freedom of the individual to associate as he chooses. . . . The associational rights which our system honors permit all white, all black, all brown, and all yellow groups to be formed. They also permit all Catholic, all Jewish, or all agnostic clubs to be established. Government may not tell a man or woman who his or her associates must be. . . . The freedom to associate applies to the beliefs we share, and to those we consider reprehensible. It tends to produce the diversity of opinion that oils the machinery of democratic government

---

[123]*Healy v. James*, 408 U.S. 169 (1972).
[124]*Id.* at 181.

and insures peaceful, orderly change.[125]

On one university campus, a school tried to prohibit the formation of a student group because its national affiliate or parent organization was known to have violent or disruptive behavior. However, there was no evidence that the local student group had created any violent or disruptive behavior. The school denied access to the student group simply because of the affiliation with its national parent. The United States Supreme Court ruled that denying access to this student group based upon the activities of other individuals was a violation of the First Amendment.[126] Consequently, though school administrators have the right to maintain an orderly process on campus, mere distaste for the content of the student group's speech or an undifferentiated fear of disruption is not enough to prohibit access. Moreover, it is not enough to prohibit access simply because some other parent or affiliate organization similar to the one seeking access is known to be violent or disruptive. Certainly schools can prohibit violent or disruptive groups, but the school must have specific information to support the violent or disruptive behavior of the particular group requesting access.

Equal Access and the Constitution

On June 4, 1990, the Supreme Court of the United States upheld the constitutionality of the Act.[127] Specifically, the *Mergens* case ruled that the Act was not prohibited by the First Amendment Establishment Clause. Although the Supreme Court in 1986 hinted that the Act was constitutional in the case of *Bender v. Williamsport Area School District*,[128] the *Mergens* case in 1990 left no doubt as to the constitutionality of the Act.[129]

Although the United States Supreme Court in 1990 clearly upheld the constitutionality of the Act, some schools still have not

---

[125]*Gilmore v. City of Montgomery*, 417 U.S. 556, 575 (1974) (quoting *Moose Lodge No. 107 v. Irvis*, 407 U.S. 163, 179-80 (1972) (Douglas, J., dissenting)).

[126]*Healy*, 408 U.S. at 169.

[127]*Mergens*, 110 S. Ct. at 2356.

[128]*Bender*, 475 U.S. at 534.

[129]*Mergens*, 110 S. Ct. at 2356.

heard the message. In one situation, Liberty Counsel was contacted by a concerned parent because the school discriminated against religious clubs. Religious clubs were allowed to meet, but only after school hours, while the secular clubs were allowed to meet during school hours. Fortunately the situation was resolved by sending one of Liberty Counsel's brochures to the school officials. After reading the brochure, the school officials agreed that they had wrongly discriminated against the clubs and decided to allow them to meet during the school hours as they allowed the secular clubs. In one month, the Youth Alive club grew from six to sixty students and the Fellowship of Christian Athletes club doubled in size. The rate of growth of these clubs was so enormous that school officials requested assistance from other teachers to be sponsors of these clubs.

In another case, Liberty Counsel was contacted because the school would not allow the religious clubs to be pictured in the school annual. Though the other secular clubs had their pictures in the school annual, the school stated it would not allow the religious clubs to be pictured in the annual because to do so would violate the so-called separation of church and state. After several weeks of negotiation and a trip to the school board, the school agreed that it had violated the Act and decided to treat the clubs equally. Consequently, the school allowed the religious clubs to have their picture in the annual just like they allowed the secular clubs.

Students should take advantage of student-initiated Bible clubs. Much can be accomplished through these clubs. Through these clubs students may announce religious activities such as the annual "See You at the Pole" event. If the other secular clubs are allowed to use the intercom system or bulletin boards, then the religious clubs can use these same facilities to make announcements. Periodically students may work through these clubs to bring outside events onto campus.

Guidelines for Starting a Club

The following are suggested steps for starting a club. These steps are not required by the Act but are presented here to illustrate practical guidelines.

(1) A club must be initiated by a student. One student should talk to friends to see if there is an interest in starting a club. The students should share ideas about the club. What will the club do? What will the name of the club be? What is the purpose? How often will the club meet?

(2) After the idea of the club has been formulated, one or two students should ask a school employee to be its sponsor. Meet with the sponsor to share your ideas. Not all schools require a sponsor, so talk to members of other clubs to see if they have a sponsor.

(3) Prepare a constitution which states the club's name and purpose. A constitution can be anything from one paragraph to several pages. If you need assistance, Liberty Counsel's model constitution is reproduced in the Appendix.

(4) One or two student leaders of the club should meet with the principal or one of the vice principals in charge of clubs. Present your request to form a club and your constitution at this meeting.

(5) The school should then consider your request and give you guidance for beginning your meetings.

Summary

In summary, students on public school campuses do not shed their constitutional rights at the schoolhouse gate. Before, after, in between classes, during the lunch period and on the playing field, students have the First Amendment right to free speech and freedom of religion. Student speech can be exercised during noninstructional time so long as it is not disruptive to the ordinary operation of the school. Students can communicate with each other verbally, through literature, through jewelry, or through clothing with inscribed messages.

During class discussions, students have a constitutional right to ask questions and discuss religious issues so long as the question or discussion is related to the curriculum being studied. Students have the First Amendment right to express themselves through projects or reports. To allow other students to present secular reports while prohibiting religious reports is to show hostility toward religion, which the Constitution forbids.

The First Amendment rights of students also permit them to have access to various books and films. Schools may not remove books or films from libraries if the decision to remove the book or film is based upon the content of the message. Students also have free exercise of religion rights which would permit a school to provide for release time allowing students to leave campus for off-site religious instruction.

Since students have First Amendment free speech and free exercise of religion rights, schools cannot compel a student to say a pledge of allegiance to a flag if the student has a sincerely held religious belief prohibiting the student from saying a pledge or simply objects to the pledge for nonreligious reasons.

Finally, the First Amendment permits students to gather together in student clubs. The Equal Access Act requires schools to treat all clubs equally. Even if the Equal Access Act was not in existence, the First Amendment still grants First Amendment free speech rights for students to form noncurriculum-related student clubs. If a school allows any noncurriculum-related club, it must allow all noncurriculum-related student clubs, even if the content of their speech is religious. All clubs must be treated equally.

Students are clearly protected by the Constitution while on public school campuses and may exercise their religious rights by sharing their faith with other students.

8

PARENTAL RIGHTS TO DIRECT THE EDUCATION OF CHILDREN

Constitutional Claims for Parental Rights

Parental responsibility reaches its apex in the duty to train and educate children. Parents form the critical link between the past and the future. History and heritage is transmitted from one generation to the next through the medium of parents. Our future depends in part upon the transmission of religious and moral values to our children. The "family is the basis of our society"[1] and the epicenter of our culture.

The right of parents to train and educate their children according to their religious and moral objectives is of paramount importance. The seminal Supreme Court case addressing parental rights began with the 1923 decision of *Meyer v. Nebraska.*[2] In *Meyer* an instructor at Zion Parochial School was charged and convicted with unlawfully teaching the subject of reading in the German language to a ten-year old student who had not yet passed the eighth grade. Nebraska law forbade instruction in a language other than English to any student who had not yet successfully passed the eighth grade. At issue was whether the Nebraska law unreasonably infringed on the liberty guaranteed by the Fourteenth Amendment, which states in pertinent part: "No state. . . shall deprive any person of life, liberty or property without due process of law."[3] While the Court conceded that it had not yet attempted to define the liberty interest protected by the Fourteenth Amendment, the Court concluded,

> [w]ithout doubt, it denotes not merely freedom from bodily restraint but also the right of the individual to contract, to engage in any of the common occupations of

---

[1] *In re: Guardianship of Faust*, 123 So.2d 218, 221 (Miss. 1960).
[2] 260 U.S. 390 (1923).
[3] U.S. Const. Amend. 14.

life, to acquire useful knowledge, to marry, establish a home and bring up children, to worship God according to the dictates of his own conscious, and generally to enjoy those privileges long recognized at common law as essential to the orderly pursuit of happiness by free men.[4]

The Court stated that the liberty protected by the Fourteenth Amendment may not be interfered with by state legislative action which is arbitrary or without reasonable relation to some legitimate state interest.[5] The Court acknowledged that parents have the "natural duty" to educate their children suitable to their situation in life.[6] The Court then concluded that state legislation which prohibits instruction in a language other than English violates the Fourteenth Amendment because it has no reasonable relationship to any legitimate state interest.

Two years later the Supreme Court returned to the issue of parental rights in the case of *Pierce v. Society of Sisters*[7]. *Pierce* addressed an Oregon statute that required students between eight and sixteen years of age to attend public schools. The only exceptions were for children who were "not normal," who had completed the eighth grade, or whose parents are private teachers residing at considerable distances from any public school, or for parents who hold special permits from the county superintendent.[8] The Court pointed out the following:

The fundamental theory of liberty upon which all governments in this Union repose excludes any general power of the state to standardize its children by forcing them to accept instruction from public teachers only. The child is not the mere creature of the state; those who nurture him and direct his destiny have the right, coupled with the high duty, to recognize and prepare him for additional obligations.[9]

---

[4]*Id.* at 399 (citations omitted).
[5]*Id.* at 399-400.
[6]*Id.*
[7]268 U.S. 510 (1924).
[8]*Id.* at 530-531.
[9]*Id.* at 535.

The Supreme Court found the Oregon legislation unconstitutional under the Fourteenth Amendment because it had no reasonable relationship to any legitimate state interest. The Court concluded that the legislation "unreasonably interferes with the liberty of parents and guardians to direct the upbringing and education of their children under their control."[10]

The next major Supreme Court decision involving parental rights to educate their children occurred in the 1972 decision known as *Wisconsin v. Yoder*.[11] This case involved a Wisconsin compulsory education law that required children to attend public or private school until the age of sixteen. The two children in the *Yoder* case were ages fourteen and fifteen. They were members of the Old Order Amish religion. Fundamental to the Amish belief is that salvation requires life in a church community separate and apart from the world and any worldly influence.[12] Amish beliefs require members of the community to make their living by farming or closely related activities. Amish objection to formal education beyond the eighth grade is a fundamental aspect of their religious faith and practice. The Court observed the following with respect to the Old Order Amish religion:

> They object to high school and higher education generally, because the values they teach are values of the Amish way of life; they view secondary school education as an impermissible exposure of their children to a 'worldly' influence in conflict with their beliefs. The high school tends to emphasize intellectual and scientific accomplishments, self-distinction, competitiveness, worldly success, and social life with other students. Amish society emphasizes informal learning-through-doing; a life of 'goodness,' rather than a life of intellect; wisdom, rather than technical knowledge, community welfare, separation from, rather than integration with, contemporary worldly society.

---

[10]*Id.* at 534-535.
[11]406 U.S. 205 (1972).
[12]*Id.* at 210.

> Formal high school education beyond the eighth grade is contrary to Amish beliefs, not only because it places Amish children in an environment hostile to Amish beliefs with increasing emphasis on competition and classwork and sports and with pressure to conform to the styles, manners and ways of the peer group, but also because it takes them away from their community, physically and emotionally, during the crucial and formative adolescent period of life.[13]

The Amish do not object to education through the first eight grades as a general proposition because they agree their children must have certain basic skills but they object to education beyond the eighth grade. Testimony presented in the *Yoder* case indicated that compulsory high school attendance could not only result in great psychological harm to Amish children, but would also ultimately result in the destruction of the Old Order Amish Church community as it exists in the United States.[14]

The Supreme Court began its decision by stating that the state had a high responsibility to educate its citizens and to impose reasonable regulations for the control and duration of basic education.[15] However,

> a State's interest in universal education, however highly we rank it, is not totally free from a balancing process when it impinges on fundamental rights and interests, such as those specifically protected by the Free Exercise Clause of the First Amendment, and the traditional interest of parents with respect to the religious upbringing of their children so long as they, in the words of *Pierce*, 'prepare (them) for additional obligations.'[16]

Though the Court pointed out that the state's compulsory education law conflicted with the twin interests of free exercise of

---

[13]*Id.* at 210-211.
[14]*Id.* at 212.
[15]*Id.* at 213.
[16]*Id.* (citing *Pierce*, 268 U.S. at 535).

religion and parental rights, the Court thereafter focused only on the free exercise of religion under the First Amendment. The Court pointed out that "only those interests of the highest order . . . can over balance legitimate claims to the free exercise of religion."[17] The State of Wisconsin argued in favor of the legislation because it applied uniformly to all citizens, and did not, on its face, discriminate against any religion or particular religious practice. However, the Court observed:

> A regulation neutral on its face may, in its application, nevertheless offend the constitutional requirement for governmental neutrality if it unduly burdens the free exercise of religion. The Court must not ignore the danger that an exception from a general obligation of citizenship on religious grounds may run afoul of the Establishment Clause, but that danger cannot be allowed to prevent any exception no matter how vital it may be to the protection of values promoted by the right of free exercise.[18]

We should note that it appeared the *Yoder* decision based its ruling primarily on the free exercise of religion although it did mention parental rights one time. The basis of the decision seemed to turn on the religious free exercise rights of the Old Order Amish religion claimed by the parents. Despite the fact that the law was a general law of neutral applicability, the Supreme Court found it nevertheless burdened a sincerely held religious belief of the Old Order Amish religion.[19]

Wisconsin argued that the state's interest in compulsory education was so compelling that even the established religious

---

[17]*Yoder*, 406 U.S. at 215.

[18]*Id.* at 220-221 (citations omitted).

[19]Note that in the Supreme Court decision of *Employment Division v. Smith*, 494 U.S. 872 (1990), the Supreme Court ruled that any general law of neutral applicability will be upheld against a religious objection to the contrary. Despite the fact that it appears the *Smith* decision is contrary to the *Yoder* decision, the *Smith* court nevertheless did not overrule *Yoder*. *Smith* (unconvincingly) distinguishes *Yoder* on the basis that *Yoder* involved a free exercise and parental right claim. Therefore, by combining parental rights with the free exercise of religion, the state must have a compelling governmental interest and achieve that interest in the least restrictive manner before the legislation will be held constitutional.

practices of the Old Order Amish must give way. The Supreme Court disagreed and found that the compulsory education statute as applied to the Old Order Amish religion was unconstitutional. The Court found that the intrusion into the Old Order Amish beliefs was severe. Moreover, the interest advanced by the state in educating a responsible citizenry was extremely weak as applied to the Old Order Amish which had a history of independence and successful social functioning. The balance tipped quite favorably on the side of the Amish.

Several factors can be gleaned from the Supreme Court's trilogy involving parental rights in education. First, the state has a recognized interest in educating its citizenry.[20] Second, parents have a constitutionally protected liberty interest under the Fourteenth Amendment to educate their children. Finally, parents have a constitutionally protected religious right under the First Amendment to educate their children. Parents may object to certain educational requirements apart from any religious objection by utilizing the Fourteenth Amendment liberty interest. However, parents may also find that certain educational requirements directly collide with their sincerely held religious beliefs and may rely upon the First Amendment as additional protection.

While challenges to an entire curriculum have not met with much success,[21] parents may successfully raise challenges to

---

[20]*Yoder*, 406 U.S. at 213 ("providing public schools ranked at the very apex of the function of a State").

[21]In *Fleischfresser v. Directors of School District 200*, 15 F.3d 680 (7th Cir. 1994), the Seventh Circuit Court of Appeals also upheld a challenge to the Impressions curriculum. In *Brown v. Woodland Joint Unified School Dist.*, 27 F.3d 1373 (9th Cir. 1993), parents objected to portions of Impressions, a teaching aid, used in the first through sixth grade. The parents objected to 32 of the 59 books used in the series, stating that the books promoted the religion of Wicka and asked students to discuss witches or create poetic chants as well as to pretend that they were witches and sorcerers and further asked them to engage in role-play. The court assumed that Wicka was a religion. The case was analyzed under the Establishment Clause. The court then found that an Establishment Clause violation does not arise every time a student believes a school practice either advances or disapproves of religion. The court then upheld the curriculum against the parental challenges. Note that the parents used the First Amendment Establishment Clause as their basis for their challenge. Similarly, in *Grove v. Meade School District No. 354*, 753 F.2d 1528 (9th Cir. 1985), the Ninth Circuit Court of Appeals rejected a challenge to The Learning Tree against the allegation that it advanced the religion of secular humanism. The court observed that the "Supreme Court has stated clearly that literary or historic study of the Bible is not prohibited religious activity." *Id.* at 1534. One judge also pointed out that "'Luther's Ninety-Nine Theses' are hardly balanced or

portions of curriculum and request opt out or other alternative accommodations.

Federal Claims for Parental Rights

A former educator and United States Senator, Samuel I. Hayakawa, warned the United States Senate in 1978 that schools had become vehicles for a "heresy that rejects the idea of education as the acquisition of knowledge and skill," and stated that schools regarded their "fundamental task in education as therapy."[22] Congress responded the same year by amending the General Education Provisions Act to include a section entitled *Protection of Pupil Rights Amendment* (hereafter "Pupil Rights Amendment").[23]

Notwithstanding the passage of the so-called Pupil Rights Amendment, educators never implemented this federal law until September 6, 1984, when the Department of Education promulgated rules after conducting extensive hearings. These hearings revealed that schools were using federal funds to implement experimental testing programs to make personal inquiries into students' individual personal, sexual, family, and religious lives.

The Pupil Rights Amendment requires that all instructional material, including teacher manuals, films, tapes, or other supplementary instructional material that are used in connection

---

objective, yet their pronounced and even vehement bias does not prevent their study in a history class' exploration of the Protestant Reformation, nor is protestantism itself 'advanced' thereby." *Id.* at 1540 (Canvy, J. concurring). In *Smith v. Board of School Commissioners of Mobile County*, 827 F.2d 684 (11th Cir. 1987), the Eleventh Circuit Court of Appeals rejected a challenge brought by parents to the school's use of textbooks that they characterized as endorsing the religion of secular humanism. The court noted that while the books contained ideas consistent with the tenets of secular humanism, it nevertheless concluded that the textbooks did not violate the Establishment Clause because "mere consistency with religious tenets is insufficient to constitute unconstitutional advancement of religion." *Id.* at 692. The court reached a similar conclusion in *Mozert v. Hawkins County Public Schools*, 647 F. Supp. 1194 (E.D. Tenn. 1986). However, in *Malnak v. Yogi*, 592 F.2d 197 (3rd Cir. 1979), the Third Circuit Court of Appeals found unconstitutional student participation in a ceremonial offering to deities as part of a regularly scheduled public school course noting that participation crossed the boundary and therefore violated the Establishment Clause.

[22]Phyllis Schlafly, ed., *Child Abuse in the Classroom* 13 (1985).

[23]20 U.S.C. § 1232h. The Pupil Rights Amendment is reproduced in the Appendix.

with any survey, analysis or evaluation, be made available for inspection by the parents or guardians of the children involved in such program or project.[24]

The Pupil Rights Amendment further states that without the prior consent of the student, or in the case of an unemancipated minor, without the prior written consent of the parent, no student shall be required to submit to a psychiatric examination, testing, or treatment, or psychological examination, testing, or treatment in which the primary purpose is to reveal information concerning: (1) political affiliation; (2) mental and psychological problems potentially embarrassing to the student or his family; (3) sex behavior and attitudes; (4) illegal, anti-social, self-incriminating and demeaning behavior; (5) critical appraisals of other individuals with whom respondents have close family relationships; (6) legally recognized privileged and analogous relationships, such as those of lawyers, physicians, and ministers; or (7) income (other than that required by law to determine eligibility for participation in a program or for receiving financial assistance under such program).[25]

Educational agencies and institutions are required to give students and parents notice of their rights under the Pupil Rights Amendment. Parents and students should avail themselves of the right to prior notice, prior consent and the right to inspect instructional materials.

Reading the testimony received by the Department of Education in 1984 is enlightening and concerning. One parent who testified in the state of Washington stated that the guidance counseling program asked the following questions of the students:

Do you believe in a God who answers prayer?
Do you believe that tithing—giving one-tenth of one's earnings to the church—is one's duty to God?
Do you pray about your problems?
Do you read the Bible or other religious writings regularly?
Do you love your parents?

---

[24]20 U.S.C. § 1232h(a).
[25]20 U.S.C. § 1232h(b).

Do you believe God created man in His own image?
If you ask God for forgiveness, are your sins forgiven?[26]

A parent from Oregon stated that her son was required to participate in a Magic Circle where the students would hold hands and divulge personal information about their thoughts, feelings, values, and beliefs. The student was also given a questionnaire asking whether he drank alcohol, used drugs, lied to his parents, or believed in God.[27] One question asked "Are you going to practice religion just like your parents?" Another question queried "What is your parents' income?" Surprisingly, one question discussed in third grade asked, "How many of you ever wanted to beat up your parents?"[28]

In another school, one course, entitled Risk Taking, required students to arrange themselves in small groups and roll dice to determine which category of questions they would discuss. Some of the questions they were to discuss in the personal and social category required the students to consider swimming in the nude at a private beach with friends, not telling your parents the truth about where you are going and what you will be doing, and having sexual intercourse with your boyfriend or girlfriend. The grade level for these questions was seventh through ninth grade.[29]

Another parent testified during these hearings that a *Values Clarification Handbook* used by the teacher indicated that the purpose of the program was to have students "begin to realize that on most issues there are many shades of gray, and they are more likely to move away from either/or black-and-white thinking which often occurs when controversial issues are discussed in the classroom."[30]

The Department of Education received testimony from a Michigan parent where senior high school teachers were instructed to administer the following program:

[26]Schlafly, ed., *Child Abuse in the Classroom* 29-30.
[27]*Id.* at 55-56.
[28]*Id.* at 57.
[29]*Id.* at 72-73.
[30]*Id.* at 95.

> First ask the students to relax, feel comfortable and close their eyes. Then ask them to fantasize and design a form of birth control that they would enjoy using. If possible, they should include in their design how the contraceptive would work to prevent pregnancy, but this is not necessary.[31]

In another case, students were divided up into three groups representing eight and nine-year-olds, twelve and thirteen-year-olds, and young adults. They discussed abortion, teenage pregnancies, contraceptives, and seeing a person of the opposite sex naked.[32] A vocabulary brainstorming program was conducted by dividing the class up into groups of five or six to list as many synonyms in three to five minutes using such words as "penis, vagina, intercourse, [or] breast."[33]

After being subjected to this kind of social behavior testing, one student testified as follows:

> I was severely depressed. I didn't know what I believed about myself. I didn't know who I was or anything. Even things I was positive about earlier, I just didn't know. I had to learn to know myself all over again. I had to learn what I believed all over again, using all the sources that the school taught me were outdated, such as my mom and dad, my pastor, and my Bible. I had to learn to make decisions again, the hardest part of all, and one that now, four years later, I am still having problems with.[34]

Psychological and behavior modification is not new to the public school system. The Pupil Rights Amendment is designed to return some student and parental control over these types of intrusions into private lives. Students and parents should become familiar with the Pupil Rights Amendment and utilize it when necessary.

---

[31]*Id.* at 146.
[32]*Id.* at 147-48.
[33]*Id.* at 148.
[34]*Id.* at 124.

School administrators often act as if the Pupil Rights Amendment does not exist. Students and parents should insist on schools abiding by the Pupil Rights Amendment. In addition to this federal law, many states have laws requiring public schools to reveal all records, which includes teaching materials, to parents upon request. If schools refuse this request, oftentimes state laws provide for the award of attorney's fees if a parent has to retain an attorney to obtain such documents.

Consequently, the Pupil Rights Amendment and parental rights may be utilized to restrict a school's intrusion into personal and parent-student relationships.

State Claims for Parental Rights

In addition to constitutional and federal protection of parental rights, parents in some cases may also assert parental rights based on state law. Whenever parental rights are threatened, parents should always look to at least three separate sources of protection: constitutional, federal, and state law.

Parents successfully combined both constitutional and state law protection of parental rights to prohibit the distribution of condoms throughout the New York public schools. In September of 1987, the New York State Commission of Education directed that all elementary and secondary schools include, as part of health education programs, instruction concerning the Human Immunodeficiency Virus (HIV) which causes Acquired Immune Deficiency Syndrome (AIDS). In late 1990 the chancellor of the New York City Board of Education suggested enlarging the HIV/AIDS curriculum to include the distribution of condoms to high school students upon request. When complaints by parents fell on deaf ears, several parents filed suit in state court. These parents claimed that the distribution of condoms constituted health services rather than education and therefore violated state law which prohibited health services to minors without parental consent, and furthermore that the distribution violated the due process rights of parents to direct the upbringing of their children under the

Fourteenth Amendment of the United States Constitution.[35]

The New York state court began its decision by noting that at common law it was "for parents to consent or withhold their consent to the rendition of health services to their children."[36] The court pointed out that historically children are considered as legal incompetents and therefore unable to consent to medical treatment or to enter into contracts except in certain situations such as when children marry, are able to support themselves, are inducted into the military, or their parents abandon or fail to support them. The court then stated that condom distribution "is not merely education, but it is a health service to prevent disease by protecting against HIV infection."[37] Although there may be certain exceptions to parental consent, in the state of New York, for minors to receive health services required parental consent and it was for the legislatures, not the courts, to make any additional exceptions.[38]

The court correctly observed that parents have the right to rear their children and noted the following:

> The petitioner parents are being compelled by State authority to send their children into an environment where they will be permitted, even encouraged, to obtain a contraceptive device, which the parents disfavor as a matter of private belief. Because the Constitution gives parents the right to regulate their children's sexual behavior as best they can, not only must a compelling State interest be found supporting the need for the policy

---

[35]*Alfonso v. Fernandez*, 195 A.D.2d 46 (N.Y. App. Div. 1993).

[36]*Id.* at 50.

[37]*Id.* at 52.

[38]*Id.* at 54. The *Alfonso* court reviewed certain federal laws that provided federal funds for family planning programs and specifically required that adolescents be treated confidentially. The court pointed out that the Supreme Court of the United States invalidated state regulations that mandated parental consent for family planning services to otherwise eligible minors. *Jones v. T. H.*, 425 U.S. 986 (1976). *See also Planned Parenthood Assn. of Utah v. Dandoy*, 810 F.2d 984 (10th Cir. 1987); *Jane Does 1 through 4 v. State of Utah Dept. of Health*, 776 F.2d 253 (10th Cir. 1985); *State of New York v. Heckler*, 719 F.2d 1191 (2nd Cir. 1983). However, the court noted that these statutes were merely legislatively-enacted exceptions to the requirement of parental consent. The court then concluded: "It is for the Congress or the Legislature, not the courts -- and certainly not the State Commissioner of Education or a Board of Education -- to provide the exceptions to parental consent requirements." *Alfonso*, 195 A.D.2d at 54.

at issue, but the policy must be essential to serving the interests as well. We do not find the policy is essential. No matter how laudable its purpose, by excluding parental involvement, the condom availability component of the program impermissibly trespasses on the petitioners' parental rights by substituting the [school board] *in loco parentis* [in place of the parents], without a compelling necessity therefore.[39]

The court correctly noted that parents "enjoy well-recognized liberty interests in rearing and educating their children in accord with their own views. . . . Intrusion into the relationship between parent and child requires a showing of overriding necessity."[40] Contrary to the school board's contention that the provision of condoms was merely education, the court stated that students "are not just exposed to talk or literature on the subject of sexual behavior; the school offers the means for students to engage in sexual activity. . . ."[41] In ruling the condom distribution unlawful under both state and constitutional authority, the court concluded as follows:

[I]n determining whether this program intrudes on parental rights in the first instance the issue is not one of purpose but one of effect. We must take great care not to be blinded by the concept that the end justifies the means. In accord with the foregoing, we conclude that the policy intrudes on [the parents'] rights by interfering with parental decisionmaking in a particularly sensitive area. Through its public schools the City of New York has made a judgment that minors should have unrestricted access to contraceptives, a decision which is clearly within the purview of the [parents'] constitutionally protected right to rear their children, and then has forced that

---

[39]*Alfonso*, 195 A.D.2d at 56.
[40]*Id.*
[41]*Id.* at 57.

judgment on them.[42]

Despite the importance of HIV and AIDS education, the court noted the following:

> The primary purpose of the Board of Education is not to serve as a health provider. Its reason for being is education. No judicial or legislative authority directs or permits teachers and other public school educators to dispense condoms to minor, unemancipated students without the knowledge or consent of their parents. Nor do we believe that they have any inherent authority to do so.[43]

The court concluded that by excluding parental involvement, the condom availability program "impermissibly trespasses" on parental rights.[44]

In addition to constitutional and federal protection of parental rights, parents should always consider whether there is additional

---

[42]*Id.* at 57-58. However, the federal appeals court in *Brown v. Hot, Sexy and Safer Productions, Inc.*, 68 F.3d 525 (1st Cir. 1995), distinguished the *Alfonso* case on the basis that the distribution of condoms did not constitute education but rather a health service, whereas the discussion of sexual activity was education and could not be prevented by parents. In the case of *Hot, Sexy and Safer Productions*, students were required to attend a mandatory, school-wide assembly which consisted of a 90 minute presentation by an individual who was affiliated with *Hot, Sexy, and Safer, Inc.* During this presentation the students were told by the representative of Hot, Sexy, and Safer that they were going to have a "group sexual experience with audience participation." The presenter used profane, lewd, and lascivious language to describe body parts and excretory functions, advocated and approved oral sex, masturbation, homosexual activity, and condom use during promiscuous premarital sex, simulated masturbation, characterized the loose pants worn by one minor as "erection wear," referred to being in "deep sh__" after anal sex, had a male minor lick an oversized condom with her, after which she had a female minor pull it over the male minor's entire head and blow it up, encouraged a male minor to display his "orgasm face" with her for the camera, informed a male minor that he was not having enough orgasms, closely inspected a minor and told him that he had a "nice butt," and made eighteen references to orgasms, six references to male genitals, and eight references to female genitals. Unbelievably, the federal appeals court found that the parental liberty interest to raise and direct the rearing of children did not encompass "a fundamental constitutional right to dictate the curriculum at the public school to which they had chosen to send their children." *Id.* at 533.

[43]*Alfonso*, 195 A.D.2d at 56.

[44]*Id.*

state law that affords protection for parents to train and educate their children. Sometimes the state law allows parents to inspect curriculum and imposes penalties whenever the educational institution prohibits inspection. State law may also require parental consent. In addition, parents may find protection under their state constitution. Whatever the source, parental rights must be protected. Parents, not the state, have the primary duty to train and educate their children.

9

PAROCHIAL SCHOOL STUDENTS AND PUBLIC BENEFITS

Controversy continues to fuel the debate regarding parochial school students receiving taxpayer funded benefits. Not surprisingly, the Supreme Court's past precedents muddied the waters. However, the Supreme Court categorically altered its interpretation in this area and specifically overruled some of its prior decisions.

When considering the constitutionality of parochial schools receiving public benefits, both clauses of the First Amendment come into play. The first question to be addressed is whether the Establishment Clause[1] prohibits the government from diverting public funds to parochial schools. Under this analysis, the question is whether the Establishment Clause prohibits the government from extending public benefits to parochial schools or their students.

The second question to address is whether parochial school students may affirmatively claim under the Free Exercise Clause that the government must divert public funds to finance their education.[2] Under this analysis, the question is whether a parochial school student may force an unwilling government to divert public funds.

Under current jurisprudence, the question of the Establishment Clause is now pretty well settled. As pointed out later, extending public funds to students enrolled in a parochial school receiving neutral instruction is not prohibited by the Establishment Clause. However, the question of whether a parochial school may affirmatively force the government to extend funds while enrolled in a parochial school has been met with both positive and negative results.

Title I

Congress enacted Title I of the Elementary and Secondary

---

[1]"Congress shall make no law respecting an establishment of religion. . . ." U.S. Const. Amend. I.

[2]"Congress shall make no law respecting an establishment of religion, *or prohibiting the free exercise thereof*; . . ." U.S. Const. Amend I (emphasis added).

Education Act of 1965[3] to "provide full educational opportunity to every child regardless of economic background."[4] Title I channels federal funds through the states to "local educational agencies" (hereafter "LEA's").[5] The LEA's spend these funds to provide remedial education, guidance, and job counseling to eligible students and they use the funds to provide "conflict mentoring, and other pupil services."[6]

According to Title I, an eligible student is one (1) who resides within the attendance boundaries of a public school located in a lower income area,[7] and (2) who is failing, or is at risk of failing, the State Student Performance Standards.[8]

According to the language of Title I, the funds must remain available to all eligible children, regardless of whether they attend public schools,[9] and the services provided the children attending private schools must be "equitable in comparison to services and other benefits for public school children."[10]

Title I funds extended to students enrolled in private schools may be provided only to those private school students eligible for aid, and cannot be used to provide services on a "school-wide" basis.[11] The LEA must retain complete control over the Title I funds, retain title of all materials used to provide Title I services, and provide those services through public employees or other persons independent of the private school and any religious institution.[12] Services provided under Title I must be "secular, neutral, and nonideological,[13] and may supplement, but "in no case supplant, the level of services" already provided by the private

---

[3] 20 U.S.C. § 6301 *et seq.*

[4] S. Rep. No. 146, 89th Cong., 1st Sess. 5 (1965).

[5] 20 U.S.C. §§ 6311, 6312. Title I has been reenacted in various forms over the years, most recently in the Improving America's Schools Act of 1994. 108 Stat. 3518.

[6] 20 U.S.C. §§ 6315(c)(1)(A) and 6314(b)(1)(B)(i), (iv).

[7] 20 U.S.C. § 6313(a)(2)(B).

[8] 20 U.S.C. § 6315(b)(1)(B).

[9] 20 U.S.C. § 6312(e)(1)(F).

[10] 20 U.S.C. § 6321(a)(3); *see also* 20 U.S.C. § 6321(a)(1); 34 C.F.R. §§ 200.10(a), 200.11(b)(1996).

[11] *Cf.* 34 C.F.R. § 200.12(b) *with* 20 U.S.C. § 6314 (allowing "school-wide" programs at public schools).

[12] 20 U.S.C. §§ 6321(c)(1), (2).

[13] 20 U.S.C. § 6321(a)(2).

school.[14]

The history of Title I funds with respect to the Supreme Court began with the Board of Education of the City of New York. In 1966, the year after Congress adopted Title I, the New York City School Board arranged to transport children attending sectarian schools to the public schools for after school Title I instruction. However, this program was largely unsuccessful because attendance was poor, as it obviously made for a very long day. The New York school board then altered its provision of Title I services. Under this revised plan, school board employees went directly to the sectarian schools to provide Title I instruction and counseling. Assignments to the private schools were voluntary. The school employees were given written and oral instructions emphasizing the secular purpose of Title I and setting out the rules to be followed. However, several individuals sued the school board claiming that the use of their tax money to provide Title I instruction at a sectarian school violated the Establishment Clause. In 1985, the Supreme Court in *Aguilar v. Felton*[15] "held that the Establishment Clause of the First Amendment barred the city of New York from sending public school teachers into parochial schools to provide remedial education to disadvantaged children pursuant to a Congressionally mandated program."[16] After the Supreme Court's ruling, the New York City School Board reverted to its prior practice of providing instruction at public school sites, leased sites, and in mobile instructional units parked near the sectarian schools. The Supreme Court noted the financial burden of its *Aguilar* decision:

> It is not disputed that the additional costs of complying with *Aguilar*'s mandate are significant. Since the 1986-1987 school year, the Board has spent over $100 million providing computer-aided instruction, leasing sites and mobile instructional units, and transporting students to those sites.[17]

---

[14]34 C.F.R. § 200.12(a)(1996).
[15]473 U.S. 402 (1985).
[16]*Agostini v. Felton*, 117 S. Ct. 1997, 2003 (1997).
[17]*Id.* at 2005.

The so-called "*Aguilar* costs" therefore reduced the amount of Title I money an LEA had available for remedial education. LEA's were forced to cut back on the number of students who received Title I benefits, with some estimates noting that the increased cost resulted in a decline of about 35 percent in the number of private school children who were served.[18]

On June 23, 1997, the United States Supreme Court stated that *Aguilar* is no longer good law and therefore reversed its decision, holding that the Establishment Clause of the First Amendment does not bar a public school from sending teachers into parochial schools to provide remedial education to disadvantaged children pursuant to a Congressionally mandated program under Title I. The Court stated that *Aguilar* has been eroded by its subsequent Establishment Clause jurisprudence.

The Court pointed out that *Aguilar* rested upon several judicial decisions and outdated constitutional presumptions. *Aguilar* relied in part upon *School Dist. of Grand Rapids v. Ball*[19] and *Meek v. Pittenger.*[20] In the *Meek* case, the Court reviewed a program in which full-time public employees provided supplemental "auxiliary services" involving remedial and accelerated instruction, guidance counseling and testing, and speech and hearing services to nonpublic school children on the site of the nonpublic school. The Court found this program unconstitutional because "the teachers participating in the programs may become involved in intentionally or inadvertently inculcating particular religious tenants or beliefs."[21] According to the Court, the presence of the public school teachers on parochial school grounds created a "graphic symbol of the 'concert or union or dependency' of church and state."[22]

In *Ball* the Supreme Court evaluated a Shared Time program wherein classes were taught during regular school hours on the premises of nonpublic schools by public school teachers using materials purchased with public funds. The Shared Time courses

---

[18]*Id.* at 2005-2006.

[19]473 U.S. 373 (1985).

[20]421 U.S. 349 (1975).

[21]*Id.* at 385. *Cf. Wolman v. Walter*, 433 U.S. 229, 248 (1977).

[22]*Id.* at 391 (quoting *Zorach v. Clauson*, 343 U.S. 306, 312 (1952)).

were in subjects designed to supplement the "core curriculum" of the nonpublic schools. In *Ball*, the Court found the Shared Time program violated the Establishment Clause because it had the impermissible effect of advancing religion.[23]

The Supreme Court's previous conclusion that the Shared Time program in *Ball* had the impermissible effect of advancing religion, rested on three assumptions: (1) a public school employee working on the premises of a sectarian school is presumed to inculcate religion; (2) the presence of a public school employee on a private school campus creates a symbolic unity between church and state; and (3) any public aid that directly benefits the educational function of a sectarian school impermissibly finances religious indoctrination, even if that aid reaches the school as a consequence of the student's private decision making. Moreover, the *Aguilar* decision added a fourth assumption, mainly that the Title I program necessitated an excessive governmental entanglement with religion because public employees who teach on the premise of a religious school must be closely monitored to insure that they do not inculcate religion.[24]

Since its 1985 *Aguilar* decision, the Supreme Court has altered its Establishment Clause jurisprudence. First, the Court "abandoned the presumption erected in *Meek* and *Ball* that the placement of public employees on parochial school grounds inevitably results in the impermissible effect of state-sponsored indoctrination or constitutes a symbolic union between government and religion."[25] Second, the Court "departed from the rule relied on in *Ball* that all government aid that directly aids the educational function of religious schools is invalid."[26] In 1993, the Court decided in *Zobrest v. Catalina Foothills School Dist.*,[27] that under the Individuals With Disabilities Education Act, the Establishment Clause did not bar a state-employed sign-language interpreter provided to a student enrolled in a Roman Catholic high school. The Court "refused to presume that a publicly employed interpreter

---

[23]*Ball*, 473 U.S. at 385.
[24]*Agostini*, 117 S. Ct. at 2008.
[25]*Id.* at 2010.
[26]*Id.* at 2011.
[27]509 U.S. 1 (1993).

would be pressured by the pervasively sectarian surroundings to inculcate religion by 'add[ing] to [or] subtract[ing] from' the lectures translated."[28]

> *Zobrest* therefore expressly rejected the notion -- relied on in *Ball* and *Aguilar* -- that, solely because of her presence on private school property, a public employee will be presumed to inculcate religion in the students. *Zobrest* also implicitly repudiated another assumption on which *Ball* and *Aguilar* turned: that the presence of a public employee on private school property creates an impermissible "symbolic link" between government and religion.[29]

In *Agostini*, the Court noted that it has now "departed from the rule relied on in *Ball* that all government aid that directly aids the educational function of religious schools is invalid."[30] In *Witters v. Washington Dept. of Servs. for the Blind*,[31] the Supreme Court held that "the Establishment Clause did not bar a State from issuing a vocational tuition grant to a blind person who wished to use the grant to attend a Christian college and become a pastor, missionary, or youth director."[32] Even though the parochial school student used the public funds to obtain a religious education, the Court observed that the grants were "'made available generally without regard to the sectarian-nonsectarian, or public-nonpublic nature of the institution benefited.'"[33] According to the Supreme Court, the grants were distributed directly to the students and used to pay for tuition at the educational institution of their choice. In the Supreme Court's view, "this transaction was no different from a State's issuing a paycheck to one of its employees, knowing that the employee would donate part or all of the check to a religious

---

[28]*Agostini*, 117 S. Ct. at 2010-11 (quoting *Zobrest*, 509 U.S. at 13.)

[29]*Id.* at 2011.

[30]*Id.*

[31]474 U.S. 41 (1986).

[32]*Agostini*, 117 S. Ct. at 2011.

[33]*Witters*, 474 U.S. at 487 (quoting *Committee for Public Ed. & Religious Liberty v. Nyquist*, 413 U.S. 756, 782-783, n.38 (1973)).

institution."[34]

According to the 1997 *Agostini* Supreme Court decision, "[i]nteraction between church and state is inevitable, and we have always tolerated some level of involvement between the two."[35]

In *Agostini*, the Court stated that the Title I program implemented by New York in which public school employees deliver Title I instruction on parochial campuses does not run afoul of the Establishment Clause or any of their three primary criteria which they currently use to evaluate whether government aid has the effect of advancing religion. First, the Court stated that the program did not result in governmental indoctrination. Second, the Title I program did not define its recipients by reference to religion. Finally, the Title I program did not create an excessive entanglement with religion.[36]

> We therefore hold that a federally funded program providing supplemental, remedial instruction to disadvantaged children on a neutral basis is not invalid under the Establishment Clause when such instruction is given on the premises of sectarian schools by government employees pursuant to a program containing safeguards such as those present here.[37]

Individuals With Disabilities Education Act

Under the Individuals with Disabilities Education Act (hereafter "IDEA"), a state receiving federal funds for the education of handicapped children must provide those children with a "free appropriate public education."[38] A "'free appropriate public education' consists of educational instruction designed to meet the unique needs of the handicapped child, supported by such services as necessary to permit the child 'to benefit' from the instruction."[39]

---

[34]*Agostini*, 117 S. Ct. at 2011.
[35]*Id.* at 2015 (citation omitted).
[36]*Id.* at 2014-16.
[37]*Id.* at 2016.
[38]20 U.S.C. § 1412(a).
[39]*Board of Education v. Rowley*, 458 U.S. 176, 188-89 (1982).

The special education must be "meaningful" and not trivial or de minimis.[40]

The centerpiece of IDEA's education delivery system for disabled children is the Individualized Education Program (hereafter "IEP").[41] "'The IEP consists of a detailed written statement arrived at by a multi-disciplinary team summarizing a child's abilities, outlining the goals for the child's education and specifying the services a child will receive.'"[42] The instruction and services offered by the state "must be provided at public expense, must meet the state's educational standards, must approximate the grade levels used in the state's regular education, and must comport with the child's IEP."[43]

Federal rules implementing IDEA funding prohibit the use of federal funds to pay for "[r]eligious worship, instruction, or proselytization."[44] In any administrative or judicial proceeding brought by a parent challenging the school's implementation of IDEA, the school district bears the burden of proving the appropriateness of the IEP it has proposed for the child.

> If a court determines that a school has offered an inappropriate education for a child, and an aggrieved parent has unilaterally chosen to place her child in an appropriate placement, appropriate relief may be ordered. Courts have often approved relief in the form of tuition reimbursement to the parent for the costs of educating her child during the period in which the school district failed to offer a free appropriate public education in accordance with its obligations under the IDEA. However, a parent who chooses to educate her child in a placement other than that offered by the school does so at her own financial risk in the event that the school's offered placement is determined to be

---

[40]*Polk v. Central Susquehanna Intermediate Unit 16*, 853 F.2d 171, 184 (3rd Cir. 1988).

[41]*Honig v. Doe*, 484 U.S. 305, 311 (1988).

[42]*Overti v. Board of Education*, 995 F.2d 1204, 1213 and 1216 (3rd Cir. 1993) (quoting *Polk*, 853 F.2d at 173).

[43]*Rowley*, 458 U.S. at 204-05.

[44]34 C.F.R. § 76.532(a)(1).

appropriate.[45]

In *Zobrest v. Catalina Foothills School Dist.*,[46] the United States Supreme Court held that the Establishment Clause does not prohibit a public school from providing the services of an interpreter under IDEA to a student attending a sectarian school.[47] The Supreme Court pointed out the following:

> We have never said that "religious institutions are disabled by the First Amendment from participating in publicly sponsored social welfare programs." For if the Establishment Clause did bar religious groups from receiving general government benefits, then a "church could not be protected by the police and fire departments, or have its public sidewalk kept in repair." Given that a contrary rule would lead to such absurd results, we have consistently held that government programs that neutrally provide benefits to a broad class of citizens defined without reference to religion are not readily subject to an Establishment Clause challenge just because sectarian institutions may also receive an attenuated financial benefit.[48]

---

[45]*Christen G. v. Lower Merion School Dist.*, 919 F. Supp. 793, 798-99 (E.D. Penn. 1996) (citations omitted).

[46]113 S.Ct. 2462 (1993).

[47]Note this case was based solely on the Establishment Clause. By the time the case made its way to the United States Supreme Court, the parents had abandoned their Free Exercise claim.

[48]*Zobrest*, 113 S. Ct. at 2466 (quoting *Bowen v. Kendrick*, 487 U.S. 589, 609 (1988) and *Widmar v. Vincent*, 454 U.S. 253, 263, 274-75 (1981)). The Court pointed that in *Mueller v. Allen*, 463 U.S. 388 (1983), and in *Witters v. Washington Dept. of Servs. for the Blind*, 484 U.S. 481 (1986), it clearly upheld government programs offering general educational systems even though it indirectly benefited religion. In *Mueller*, the Court rejected an Establishment Clause challenge to a Minnesota law allowing taxpayers to deduct certain educational expenses in computing their state income tax, even though the vast majority of the deductions went to parents whose children attended sectarian schools. In *Witters* the Court upheld against an Establishment Clause challenge to the State of Washington's extension of vocational assistance (as part of a general state program) to a blind person studying at a private Christian college to become a pastor, missionary, or youth director.

In *Zobrest*, the Court stated that the services provided under
IDEA were "part of a general government program that distributes
benefits neutrally to any child qualifying as 'disabled' under the
IDEA, without regard to the 'sectarian-nonsectarian, or public-
nonpublic nature' of the school the child attends."[49] The Court
pointed out the following:

> By according parents freedom to select a school of
> their choice, the statute insures that a government-
> paid interpreter will be present in a sectarian school
> only as a result of the private decision of individual
> parents. In other words, because the IDEA creates
> no financial incentive for parents who choose a
> sectarian school, that interpreter's presence there
> cannot be attributed to state decisionmaking.[50]

Under the IDEA, "no funds traceable to the government
ever find their way into sectarian schools' coffers."[51] According to
the Court, the only economic benefit a sectarian school might
receive from IDEA funding "is the disabled child's tuition."[52]

Because the government funds flowing from IDEA are
neutrally provided benefits to a broad class of citizens defined
without reference to religion, IDEA funding does not violate the
Establishment Clause. Moreover, the IDEA funds do not go directly
to the sectarian school. The funds instead go to the individual
student, who freely chooses to attend either a public or nonpublic
school.

In *Zobrest*, the Court answered the question as to whether
the government may extend IDEA funding to students attending
sectarian schools. The Court unequivocally ruled that the First
Amendment does not bar such funding. However, the question of
whether the government is required to extend benefits under IDEA
to a student attending a sectarian school under the student's free
exercise of religion claim has not yet been answered by the

---

[49]*Zobrest*, 113 S. Ct. at 2467.
[50]*Id.*
[51]*Id.*
[52]*Id.* at 2468.

Supreme Court.

In *Goodall v. Stafford County School Board*,[53] a federal appeals court ruled that the Free Exercise Clause of the First Amendment does not require state funds to be provided to a student attending a sectarian school.[54]

Apart from the free exercise claim, other federal courts have ruled that by its own terms IDEA may require state funded services to individuals attending sectarian schools. In each case the question to be addressed is whether the public schools are able to provide a comparable education to that which is offered in the sectarian school for a child who otherwise qualifies for IDEA funding.[55] Now that the United States Supreme Court has ruled the Religious Freedom Restoration Act unconstitutional,[56] a free exercise claim attempting to force federal funding may be difficult. However, it may be possible to combine a free exercise claim with a parental

---

[53] 60 F.3d 168 (4th Cir. 1995).

[54] Note the previous case of *Goodall v. Stafford County School Board*, 930 F.2d 363 (4th Cir. 1991), was overruled by *Zobrest*. In the 1991 *Goodall* decision, the Court ruled that the Establishment Clause prohibited the provision of funds to a student requiring a cued speech interpreter at a private religious school. After that case was overruled by *Zobrest* in 1993, the same parents brought another action claiming that the state was affirmatively required to fund the interpreter on the basis that the Free Exercise Clause compelled such funding due to the economic burden born by the parents for choosing to place their student in a religious school. The *Goodall* court in 1995 rejected that argument. In *Miller v. Benson*, 68 F.3d 163 (7th Cir. 1995), the Court was faced with a free exercise challenge similar to that brought forth in *Goodall*. However, by the time it made its way to the Seventh Circuit Court of Appeals, the free exercise challenge was moot and therefore the court did not reach the merits of the case.

[55] *Russman v. Sobol*, 85 F.3d 1950 (2nd Cir. 1996) (IDEA requires school district to provide a student with a consultant teacher and teacher's aid at a parochial school); *K.R. v. Anderson Community School Corp.*, 887 F. Supp. 1217 (S.D. Ind. 1995) (IDEA requires public school to provide benefits to disabled private school students that are "comparable" to benefits provided to disabled public school students and therefore IDEA requires the public school in this case to provide the disabled student with an instructional assistant at a private parochial school); *Shelter v. Cape Girardeau School Dist.*, 810 F. Supp. 1062 (E.D. Mo. 1993) (student was entitled to transportation, as related service to her individualized education program, from the sidewalk of her parochial school to her special education classes at a public school); *McNair v. Cardimone*, 676 F. Supp. 1361 (S.D. Ohio 1987), *aff'd sub. nom. McNair v. Parochial Local School Dist.*, 872 F.2d 153 (6th Cir. 1989); *Work v. McKenzie*, 661 F. Supp. 225 (D.D.C. 1987) *But see Foley v. Special School Dist. of St. Louis County*, 927 F. Supp. 1214 (E.D. Mo. 1996) (under the facts of the case, IDEA did not require school district to provide special education services at private parochial school in which the student had been unilaterally placed by her parents so long as the services are made available at a public school).

[56] *City of Boerne v. Flores*, 117 S. Ct. 2157 (1997).

rights or equal protection claim. Under such a claim, the parent could argue that any neutrally funded program denied to a parent whose child attends a parochial school violates parental rights to direct the raising and upbringing of the child and also violates equal protection as well as religious freedom. Such a claim would argue that a school is affirmatively required under the Constitution to provide equal treatment, and equal funding, to otherwise qualified students who choose to attend a parochial school. This issue has not yet been decided by the United States Supreme Court.

Other Funding Programs

There are many other state or federal funded programs that may indirectly benefit religion other than Title I or IDEA funding. Some funding schemes might include loaning textbooks and equipment,[57] transportation,[58] or vouchers.

Apart from any state constitutional provision, any of these programs should be constitutional so long as the programs "neutrally provide benefits to a broad class of citizens defined without reference to religion."[59]

Though the state or federal government may voluntarily provide these benefits without violating the Establishment Clause or the First Amendment, the question as to whether the state or federal government is required to provide such funding under the Free Exercise Clause or any other constitutional provision has not yet been settled.

[57]*Walker v. San Francisco Unified School Dist.*, 46 F.3d 1449 (9th Cir. 1995); *reh'g denied*, 62 F.3d 300 (9th Cir. 1995).
[58]*Helms v. Cody*, 856 F. Supp. 102 (E.D. La. 1994).
[59]*Zobrest*, 113 S. Ct. at 2466.

10

GRADUATION PRAYER IN PUBLIC SCHOOLS

The United States Supreme Court decision in *Lee v. Weisman*[1] has caused some confusion as to whether prayers are permissible at public school graduation ceremonies. While prayers have been restricted at public school graduations, they have not been completely prohibited. It is important to know what the Court did and did not say.

What Is Prohibited?

To understand what is presently prohibited by the United States Supreme Court decision in *Lee v. Weisman*, it is important to know some of the history regarding the case. The Supreme Court focused on the following three factors: (1) the school principal decided that an invocation and benediction would be given at the ceremony and placed prayer on the agenda; (2) the principal chose the religious participant; and (3) the principal provided the clergyman with a copy of *Guidelines for Civic Occasions*, produced by the National Council of Christians and Jews, outlining suggestions for delivering nonsectarian prayers. Justice Kennedy found that these three factors placed the school in the position of guiding and directing the prayer during a public ceremony, and based upon his opinion, this participation and guidance of the prayer was a violation of the First Amendment Establishment Clause.

What the Supreme Court prohibited can be summed up as follows: School officials cannot direct that prayer be part of a public school graduation ceremony, specifically select a religious participant to say a prayer during a public graduation ceremony, and give guidelines on how to say a nonsectarian prayer during a public graduation ceremony. In practical terms, a public school cannot invite a clergyman to say a prayer at a graduation ceremony and direct the clergy on how to say the prayer. As an additional note, the *Lee* decision does not affect graduation prayers at

---

[1] 112 S. Ct. 2649 (1992).

post-secondary schools, that is the college or university level.[2]

Clearly the Supreme Court did not say that all prayers at graduation were flatly prohibited. In fact, the Court stated that its ruling was limited to the facts of that particular case.[3] Therefore, any change in the factual situation presented in *Lee* could change the outcome. Justice Scalia wrote in his dissenting opinion that merely adding a disclaimer to the graduation program would make the same set of facts constitutional.[4] Justice Scalia stated the following:

> All that is seemingly needed is an announcement, or perhaps a written insertion at the beginning of the graduation program, to the effect that, while all are asked to rise for the invocation and benediction, none is compelled to join in them, nor will be assumed, by rising, to have done so. That obvious fact recited, the graduates and their parents may proceed to thank God, as Americans have always done, for the blessings He has generously bestowed on them and on their country.[5]

Obviously the United States Supreme Court has not taken the position that all graduation prayer is unconstitutional. Indeed, the Court noted the following:

> We recognize that, at graduation time and throughout the course of the educational process, there will be instances when religious values, religious practices, and religious persons will have some interaction with the public schools and their students.[6]

The United States Supreme Court recognized that "[a]

[2]*Tanford v. Brand*, 104 F.3d 982 (7th Cir. 1997) (students at university level are mature enough to understand that a prayer delivered by a clergy at a state university graduation ceremony is not an establishment of religion and therefore such prayer is constitutional). *See also Chaudhuri v. Tennessee*, 1997 WL 713533 (6th Cir. 1997).

[3]*Id.* at 2655.

[4]*Id.* at 2685 (Scalia, J., dissenting).

[5]*Id.*

[6]*Lee*, 112 S. Ct. at 2661.

relentless and all-pervasive attempt to exclude religion from every aspect of public life could itself become inconsistent with the Constitution."[7]

What Is Permitted?

Prayer is still permissible during public school graduation. Post-secondary schools (colleges and universities) may continue to invite clergy to deliver a prayer at graduation. While secondary schools (middle, junior high and high school) face more restrictions than post-secondary schools, they still retain a number of options for the continuation of prayer.[8]

---

[7]*Id.*

[8]After the *Lee v. Weisman* decision in the summer of 1992, some schools attempted to prohibit student-initiated prayer at graduation ceremonies. In one case, a community college student was elected by her class peers to say a prayer at their graduation service. However, the nursing director prohibited the student from saying the prayer and instead insisted that she must say a secular poem. The student refused to say a secular poem and, therefore, was not part of the graduation ceremony although her name was printed in the bulletin. Liberty Counsel negotiated with the community college, and the president of the college eventually realized that the student had been deprived of her First Amendment right to speak. The president then wrote the following acknowledgment and apology:

> Please accept this letter as my personal apology and that of the staff of . . . Community College for any embarrassment that you suffered as a result of the decision of the nursing staff of the college to not allow you to offer the invocation which you wrote at the request of your fellow students for the Pinning Ceremony. . . . I hope that you will also accept my representation that they thought that they were doing what they were required to do under the law as they understood it at the time. They did not have the benefit of either the legal memoranda that your attorneys of the Liberty Counsel have since furnished to the college or the recent Supreme Court decision that essentially confirmed the Liberty Counsel position.
>
> It may be possible that unfortunate incidents work out for the best in the long run. I have always been a strong supporter of the provisions of the First Amendment, especially as it relates to the educational process. Because of this situation having come to my attention, I have asked our college attorney to draft a policy for the college that should prevent any future occurrence of this nature.

In the spring of 1993, many schools allowed student-initiated graduation prayer. Approximately four schools nationwide were sued by students objecting to student-initiated graduation prayer. The reported cases include *Harris v. Joint School District No. 241*, 821 F. Supp. 638 (D. Idaho 1993), *modified*, 41 F.3d 447 (9th Cir. 1994), *vacated*, 115 S. Ct. 2604 (1995); *Adler v. Duval County School Board*, 851 F. Supp. 446 (M.D. Fla. 1994),

Option One
Outside Speaker Selected By Religion-Neutral Criteria

If a school avoided placing prayer on the agenda and avoided selecting a clergy for the sole purpose of delivering a prayer, it would avoid two of the Supreme Court's major concerns. Consequently, school officials could use neutral criteria for selecting the participants. A neutral criteria would simply be one that does not specifically look for someone who is a religious participant to say a specific religious message. If a school chose a speaker because of some contribution the speaker made to society and not because the speaker happened to be a clergyman, then the school would avoid one of the concerns of the Supreme Court. In short, school officials could choose a speaker or participant because of some recognized contribution to society. A clergyman could be a participant as long as the selection was made using neutral criteria and not solely because the participant is religious.

An individual selected using neutral criteria could then participate in the public graduation ceremony and could voluntarily offer a prayer or make religious comments. In this way, the school does not specifically select a religious person for the purpose of offering prayer. For the school to forbid this participant from saying a prayer may be a violation of that person's First Amendment right to freedom of expression. Furthermore, if a school prohibited such a person from saying a prayer, either before or after the fact, the school might violate the First Amendment Establishment Clause because the school would be showing hostility, rather than neutrality, toward religion. In summary, a school could select a participant using neutral or secular criteria, and that participant could voluntarily pray or offer religious comments.

---

vacated, 112 F.3d 1475 (11th Cir. 1997); and *ACLU v. Black Horse Pike Regional Board of Education*, 84 F.3d 1471 (3rd Cir. 1996). In the *Adler* case, the ACLU represented three Jewish students in an attempt to prohibit student-initiated prayer. Liberty Counsel intervened on behalf of eleven other students, grades seven through eleven. These students became co-defendants with the school board. This is one of the first cases of its kind in the country where students have been allowed to intervene in a case to defend their right to free speech. The federal court ruled that students have the constitutional right to pray. To censor their speech because of religious content would violate their right to free speech.

Option Two
Students Selected By Religion-Neutral Criteria

Similar to option one, another option includes a valedictorian, salutatorian, president of the senior class, or any other student participant chosen based on academic criteria or other secular standards, to be a part of the graduation ceremony. When addressing the senior class, this person could voluntarily offer a prayer or religious message. In this circumstance, the school would not specifically be placing prayer on the agenda and would not be selecting the student for the specific purpose of prayer. The school may not even know that the participant would pray until the participant actually stood up and did pray. Again, under this particular option, if the school prohibited this student participant from praying, it could violate the First Amendment Free Speech and Establishment Clauses in that the school would be restricting speech based on the content of the message and showing hostility toward religion.

In one case, Liberty Counsel was contacted by a high school senior class president who was chosen to be the keynote speaker at graduation. The class president wanted to thank God in his speech. When he spoke to the principal, the principal warned the student not to mention anything regarding religion. After discussing this situation with Liberty Counsel, we advised that, of course, he must have respect for his authorities, but this issue dealt with the expression of his religious conviction and the First Amendment. We advised that he had the right to speak about his relationship with Jesus Christ. He was rightfully there on the platform by virtue of his position as a class officer, and while there, he had the right to speak freely, so long as he did not speak libelous or defamatory remarks toward other students. When he did speak during the graduation ceremony, he acknowledged and thanked God for his accomplishments. At the end of the speech, he got a standing ovation. Afterwards, he received numerous cards from students and parents congratulating him for having the courage to speak about God. The response was so overwhelming that the principal, who originally warned against speaking about . God, also wrote the student a thank you card.

In one school, the valedictorian sneezed after giving the

valedictory address. All of the students in unison responded, "God bless you." Of course, this is a humorous way of acknowledging God during a ceremony. Nowhere does the Constitution require students to resort to these tactics in order to acknowledge God. When student speakers enter the podium during a graduation ceremony, they do not shed their constitutional rights to freedom of expression, just like they do not shed these rights when they enter the schoolhouse gate.[9]

Option Three
Student Class Officers

Similar to option two, prayer can still be conducted at a graduation ceremony if the student body elects a student chaplain as a class officer. This chaplain could be elected by the student body in the same way that the student body elects class officers. Some class sections already elect student chaplains along with the election of other class officers. As part of the graduation ceremony, the student chaplain could address the student body along with the other officers of the class, and the address could include a prayer. In this manner, the school would not be directly endorsing the school officers since they would be elected by the student body. The student chaplain could certainly be placed on the agenda, and the school should avoid any efforts to guide or direct the prayer or address given by the student chaplain. While not required, the chaplain could announce, or the bulletin could state, that while all are asked to rise for the invocation and benediction, none are compelled to do so. If this option is chosen, the bulletin should state that the school does not control, review, promote, or endorse the content of student messages.

Option Four
Parent or Student Committee

The Court in *Lee* was concerned that school officials specifically placed prayer on the agenda, selected a clergy, and gave the clergyman guidelines for saying nonsectarian prayers. If these

---

[9]*Tinker v. Des Moines Independent School District*, 393 U.S. 503, 506 (1969).

factors were avoided, prayers would be permissible. One way that these factors could be avoided is for school officials to allow a parent and/or student committee to create the agenda for graduation ceremonies. This student committee could then come up with its own agenda, which could include prayer. This committee could specifically choose a religious participant to say a prayer and could, in fact, discuss the prayer with the participant. By permitting a parent and/or student committee to create the agenda and select the participants, the school would avoid any appearance of sponsorship. The school could note that the graduation ceremony was not actually sponsored by the school, but rather was sponsored by the parents and students. The parents and students could request to use the school facilities in order to conduct the graduation ceremonies.

A federal court of appeals ruled in *Jones v. Clear Creek Independent School District* that "a majority of students can do what the State acting on its own cannot do to incorporate prayer in public high school graduation ceremonies."[10] It is important to note that the *Jones* case was decided in November of 1992, *after* the Supreme Court's decision in *Lee*. In fact, the *Jones* (student prayer) case discusses the *Lee* (clergy prayer) decision and states that its situation is clearly distinguishable from that presented in *Lee*. In *Jones*, the school district passed a resolution permitting the high school graduating seniors to vote whether or not to have a fellow student lead the graduating class in prayer. Quoting the Supreme Court's decision in *Board of Education v. Mergens*, the *Jones* court stated that "there is a crucial difference between *government* speech endorsing religion, which the Establishment Clause forbids, and *private* speech endorsing religion, which the Free Speech and Free Exercise Clauses protect."[11] In other words, what the government cannot do through its school officials, individual students can do acting on their own. If this option is chosen, the bulletin should state that the school does not control, review, promote, or endorse the content of student messages.

---

[10]*Jones v. Clear Creek Independent School District*, 977 F.2d 963, 972 (5th Cir. 1992), *cert. denied*, 113 S. Ct. 2950 (1993).

[11]*See Board of Education v. Mergens*, 110 S. Ct. 2356, 2360 (1990). Though the school district in *Jones* required the student prayers to be nonsectarian, schools should avoid this requirement because it injects the school into religion by mandating that school officials monitor the prayer.

The Supreme Court has clearly stated that students on public school campuses do not "shed their constitutional rights to freedom of speech or expression at the schoolhouse gate."[12] The Court recognized that students have free speech rights "in the cafeteria, on the playing field, or on campus during authorized hours."[13] Therefore, a student clearly has the First Amendment right to lead fellow students in a prayer during a graduation ceremony. First, in allowing a student to pray during a graduation ceremony, there would be no church-state problem as encountered in *Lee* because the prayer would be conducted by a private individual rather than school officials. Second, to prohibit the student from saying a prayer would actually result in a violation of the student's free speech rights. Prohibiting prayer in this context could subject the school to lawsuits.

Some confusion has arisen as to constitutionality regarding a school policy that specifically provides for student-initiated prayer at graduation ceremonies. As noted above, the Fifth Circuit Court of Appeals in *Jones v. Clear Creek Independent School Dist.* ruled that such a policy providing for student-initiated prayer is constitutional.[14] The Fifth Circuit Court of Appeals has reaffirmed its opinion.[15] However, the Ninth Circuit Court of Appeals ruled that a similar policy was unconstitutional.[16] This ruling was set aside by the United States Supreme Court based upon the fact that the high school student had graduated by the time the case reached the Supreme Court level and therefore the case was moot.[17] The Supreme Court did not make any ruling on the substantive issue of whether students have the right to pray during graduation. However, the Supreme Court did set aside and vacate the Ninth Circuit ruling so that it is null and void and has no precedential value. The Third Circuit Court of Appeals then decided a case known as *American Civil Liberties Union v. Blackhorse Pike Regional Board of Education*.[18] This case directly conflicts with the Fifth Circuit

---

[12]*Tinker*, 393 U.S. at 506.

[13]*Id.* at 512-513.

[14]977 F.2d at 963.

[15]*Insevretsen v. Jackson Public School Dist.*, 88 F.3d 274 (5th Cir. 1996).

[16]*Harris v. Joint School Dist. No. 241*, 41 F.3d 447 (9th Cir. 1994).

[17]*Joint School Dist. No. 241 v. Harris*, 115 S. Ct. 2604 (1995).

[18]84 F.3d 1471 (3rd Cir. 1996).

Court of Appeals in *Jones*, and contrary to *Jones*, ruled that a policy allowing students to vote on whether to have another student voluntarily pray at graduation is unconstitutional. This case was not appealed to the United States Supreme Court.[19]

Whether a school can enact a policy that specifically provides for student-initiated prayer at graduation depends upon where the school is located and what court is governing the school district. However, we should make here two very important observations. First, the court which struck down the school policy that provided for student-initiated prayer would likely not interfere with a student praying at graduation in the absence of a policy. In other words, if a school creates a policy which only provides one option on the issue of whether to include prayer during the graduation, the school may well have injected itself into the issue of prayer. Students do not need a policy in order to pray. As noted above, students who are rightfully on the platform can deliver prayer or a religious message. Additionally, in the absence of a policy, students can on their own organize part of the graduation ceremony and on their own decide to include prayer. If this occurred there would be no official school participation. There would be no policy to challenge. As noted in another chapter, the First Amendment only applies on behalf of a person against a public entity. If somebody sued to prevent students from praying at graduation in the absence of a policy where the school has not taken any action, there would be essentially no state action and no state involvement and consequently no basis for a suit. If a school chose not to have a policy it would essentially be taking a hands off position and

---

[19]Other lower federal courts have split over the issue regarding the constitutionality of student-initiated prayer at graduation. *Cf. Freiler v. Tangipahoa Parish Board of Education*, 975 F. Supp. 819 (E.D. La. 1997) (School policy allowing student-initiated graduation prayer is constitutional); *Stein v. Plainwell Community Schools*, 610 F. Supp. 43 (W.D. Mich. 1995) (Invocations and benedictions do not violate the Establishment Clause); *and Adler v. Duval County School Board*, 851 F. Supp. 446 (M.D. Fla. 1994) (Court upheld the school policy allowing students to have two minutes of uncensored messages which include secular and sacred content), *with Gearon v. Loudoun County School Board*, 844 F. Supp. 1097 (E.D. Va. 1993) (Unconstitutional to allow graduating senior class to vote on whether to include prayer in the graduation ceremony). *See also Lundberg v. West Monona Community School Dist.*, 731 F. Supp. 331 (N.D. Ia. 1989) (School district voted to ban invocations and benedictions at high school graduation ceremonies, and court later rejected a lawsuit brought on the basis that the school was violating the plaintiff's right to free speech by excluding prayer from the graduation ceremony).

allowing the students to act on their own without any school involvement or suggestion. Moreover, if a school chose to create a policy, it should create the policy along neutral lines. The policy should address speech, not prayer. Such a policy would provide that students have an opportunity to speak. The student could obviously choose to speak on secular or sacred topics. This option is outlined further below.

Option Five
Student Messages

Similar to options three and four, a school could choose to allow student-initiated, student-led messages. This option does not mention prayer but instead focuses on student messages. The students are then permitted to choose whatever topic they wish to address. This method is actually preferable to one focusing on student-initiated prayers. The difference between this option and option four is that option four states that students may choose to include *prayer* in the graduation, whereas this option states that students may choose to present a *message* during graduation.

One school district developed the following guidelines:

1. The use of a brief opening and/or closing message, not to exceed two minutes, at high school graduation exercises shall rest within the discretion of the graduating senior class.

2. The opening and/or closing message shall be given by a student volunteer, in the graduating senior class, chosen by the graduating senior class as a whole.

3. If the graduating senior class chooses to use an opening, and/or closing message, the content of that message shall be prepared by the student volunteer and shall not be monitored or otherwise reviewed by school officials, its officers, or employees.[20]

---

[20]*Adler v. Duval County School Board,* 851 F. Supp. 446, 449 (M.D. Fla. 1994).

During the first year in which the above policy was operative within the school district, ten of the seventeen high schools opted for messages that constituted various forms of religious prayer. The remaining seven schools had either no message at all or their message was entirely secular in nature.[21] A policy allowing student messages truly focuses on the initiation of the student to choose the contents of the message. Moreover, the policy restricts all forms of review or censorship of the message by school officials. Students may say whatever they wish with impunity. In the case in which this policy arose, the American Civil Liberties Union sued the school board requesting that the policy be declared unconstitutional. Liberty Counsel intervened on behalf of students ranging from seventh through twelfth grade to defend the school. A federal court ruled that the policy was constitutional and that students have First Amendment rights to free speech during the graduation ceremony. As in options three and four, it is advisable for the bulletin to note that the school does not control, review, promote, or endorse the content of student messages.

Option Six
Privately Sponsored Graduation

Under the above options one through five, prayer could still be conducted during public school graduation ceremonies. The First Amendment permits prayer as noted above but does not require prayer. In other words, prayer could still be conducted under the circumstances presented above, but the First Amendment would not require the speaker or participant to pray, the student to pray, or the school officials to allow a parent-student committee. Under options one through five, there may be some years when prayer would be conducted and other years when it would not be conducted. In order to insure that prayer would be conducted on a consistent basis during public school graduations, community leaders and churches could privately sponsor graduation ceremonies. Currently many schools are not large enough to conduct public graduation ceremonies. Such schools often use outside facilities, and many use church auditoriums. Churches throughout the community could

---

[21]*Id.* at 449-450.

organize public graduation ceremonies or baccalaureate services. The time, place, and manner could be organized by the churches or other community leaders, and student groups could publicize the event through their on campus clubs. Public school students along with teachers and staff could be invited to participate in the ceremony designed and choreographed by nonschool officials.

School officials could participate in ceremonies conducted at churches as long as they were not necessarily organizing it as part of a sponsorship of the local school. At such a service, there would be no prohibition against inviting a religious speaker to address the students.

If a public school allows use of its facilities by outside secular organizations, then the public school must allow use of the same facilities by religious organizations including use for religious purposes. Such a purpose can be the performance of a graduation or baccalaureate ceremony. In one case, a United Methodist Church sued a school board because it wished to rent the facilities for a graduation ceremony. The school refused, and an Alabama federal court ruled that disallowing use of the facilities by the Methodist church was a violation of the First Amendment Free Speech Clause because the school allowed use of its facilities to other outside secular organizations.[22] Indeed, the United States Supreme Court stated that "if a State refused to let religious groups use facilities open to others, then it would demonstrate not neutrality, but hostility toward religion."[23] In another case, a group of parents and graduating senior students requested use of a high school gymnasium to conduct a baccalaureate ceremony. The baccalaureate ceremony was privately-sponsored and open to the public. Participation by the students was completely voluntary. However, the school board decided not to rent the gymnasium because its use would be for a religious purpose. The school board had on other occasions allowed use of its facilities to outside secular organizations. A federal court in Wyoming ruled that refusal to rent

---

[22]*Verbena United Methodist Church v. Chilton County Board of Education*, 765 F. Supp. 704 (M.D. Ala. 1991).

[23]*Mergens*, 110 S. Ct. at 2371. *See also Grace Bible Fellowship, Inc. v. Maine School Admin. District #5*, 941 F.2d 45 (1st Cir. 1991); *Gregoire v. Centennial School District*, 907 F.2d 1366 (3rd Cir. 1990), *cert. denied*, 111 S. Ct. 253 (1993); *Concerned Woman for America v. Lafayette County*, 883 F.2d 32 (5th Cir. 1990).

the gymnasium to the parents and students to conduct the religious baccalaureate service was an unconstitutional violation of the First Amendment.[24]

Summary

Prayers at public secondary school graduations have been limited by the United States Supreme Court. These limitations apply only to secondary schools. Prayer at the college or university level has not been circumscribed by the Supreme Court. The courts addressing prayer on college or university campuses have distinguished the Supreme Court ruling on the basis of the maturity level of the students, who are perceptive enough to understand that such prayer is not an establishment of religion. However, for elementary or high school graduation ceremonies, the tradition that can be dated back as far as July of 1868, when the first public school graduation is officially documented, will no longer continue as it has for so many years. However, prayer is still permissible at public school graduation ceremonies.

The Supreme Court has ruled that a school cannot place prayer on the agenda of a public graduation ceremony, cannot select a religious participant for the purpose of praying, and cannot give guidelines to a religious participant as to how that participant should pray. However, prayer is still permissible if a school selects a participant using secular criteria and the participant voluntarily prays. Prayer is also permissible if a student participant who was selected to be a part of the graduation ceremony based upon some outstanding achievement voluntarily prays. Prayer could also be conducted by a student chaplain or speaker elected by the student body in the same way class officers are elected. Additionally, prayer is permissible if the school officials permit a parent and/or student committee to create the agenda and to select the participants. In this instance, the school should avoid any sponsorship of the ceremony and may even want to place in the bulletin that the ceremony is

---

[24]*Shumway v. Albany County School District #1*, 826 F. Supp. 1320 (D. Wyo. 1993); In *Pratt v. Arizona Board of Regents*, 520 P.2d 514 (Ariz. 1974), the Arizona Supreme Court ruled that the rental of the Sun Devils Stadium on a university campus to an evangelist for a religious service did not violate the First Amendment Establishment Clause.

being sponsored by the parents and students. Prayer is also permissible if the school has a policy allowing a volunteer student from the senior class to present an uncensored message, be it secular or sacred. Such a policy will not mention prayer but rather provides for the opportunity to present a message. Under this policy, the student may present a message on any topic. Finally, prayer at a public school graduation ceremony is permissible if organized and conducted by nonschool officials, without school sponsorship, and on or off school premises.

11

PRAYERS AT PUBLIC ASSEMBLIES

Although prayer at public meetings predates our Constitution, and although prayer is replete throughout America's historical documents, since the 1960s prayer at such meetings has taken on a somewhat checkered history. Prior to the early 1960s there was little controversy regarding prayer at public meetings. There had been no successful judicial challenge to prohibit prayer at any public meeting. However, in the past thirty years courts have come to conflicting conclusions regarding the constitutionality of prayer. These conclusions often depend largely on circumstances surrounding the prayer. These circumstances include the particular event in question, the audience, and the participants. This chapter overviews prayers in public school classrooms, athletic events, graduation prayers, prayers in the courtroom, legislative prayers, and prayers offered before county, municipal or school board meetings.

Public School Classrooms

There are three types of public school classroom prayers. The first includes prayers composed by public school officials. The second deals with statutes authorizing a moment of voluntary prayer. The final type involves statutes, rules, or policies authorizing a moment of silence.

State-Composed or State-Led Prayers

The first case dealing with school prayer reached the United States Supreme Court in 1962. The case, known as *Engel v. Vitale*,[1] involved a prayer composed by the Board of Regents for the New York public schools. The prayer stated as follows: "Almighty God, we acknowledge our dependence upon thee, and we beg Thy blessings upon us, our parents, our teachers and our

---

[1]370 U.S. 421 (1962).

Country."[2] The parents of ten students brought suit against the
public school and the Board of Regents arguing that the
state-composed prayer was a violation of the Constitution. The
Supreme Court agreed by stating the following:

> [W]e think the constitutional prohibition against laws
> respecting an establishment of religion must at least mean
> that in this country it is no part of the business of
> government to compose official prayers for [students] to
> recite as part of a religious program carried on by
> government.[3]

From 1962 to the present, the United States Supreme Court has
consistently ruled that state-composed and state-led prayers in the
public school classroom violate the First Amendment Establishment
Clause.

In 1963 the United States Supreme Court considered a case
involving state required Bible readings and the recitation of the
Lord's Prayer by a state official at the beginning of the school day.
In *School District of Abington Township v. Schempp,*[4] the Supreme
Court ruled that it was unconstitutional for state officials to read the
Bible to public school students followed by the recitation of the
Lord's Prayer at the beginning of each day.[5] School officials were
charged with selecting various Bible verses and reading these verses
at the beginning of each school day. The students were then asked
to recite the Lord's Prayer in unison. The Court ruled that both of
these practices violated the First Amendment Establishment
Clause.[6] However, the Court ruled that the Bible itself could be
studied as literature and religion could be studied in a history of
religions class.

---

[2]*Id.* at 422.
[3]*Id.* at 425.
[4]374 U.S. 203 (1963).
[5]*Id.* at 211.
[6]*Id.* at 223.

Moment of Voluntary Prayer

The major case involving voluntary prayer decided by the Supreme Court is *Wallace v. Jaffree.*[7] In *Wallace,* the state of Alabama in 1978 passed a law authorizing a one minute period of silence in all public schools "for meditation." In 1981, the state passed another law authorizing a period of silence "for meditation or voluntary prayer," and in 1982, the state amended the law to authorize teachers to lead "willing students" in a prescribed prayer to "almighty God . . . the Creator and Supreme Judge of the world."[8] Prior to reaching the United States Supreme Court, a federal court ruled that the statute allowing a time for meditation was constitutional.[9] This part of the decision was never appealed and, therefore, not before the Supreme Court for determination. The two parts of the statute which were before the Supreme Court involved the 1981 statute authorizing meditation or voluntary prayer and the 1982 statute authorizing teachers to lead willing students in a prescribed prayer.

In reviewing the statute, the Supreme Court considered the state legislative debates prior to its adoption. Apparently Senator Donald Holmes was one of the main sponsors of the bill. He stated on the legislative floor that his intent behind the statute was "to return voluntary prayer" to the public schools.[10] The Court, therefore, ruled that the Alabama state law was merely an attempt to get around its 1962 and 1963 opinions in *Engel* and *Schempp* and struck down the laws in violation of the First Amendment Establishment Clause.

It is extremely important to note the exact parameters of the United States Supreme Court's opinion. The Supreme Court did not rule on the constitutionality of a moment of silence. The issue before the Supreme Court was a moment of "voluntary prayer" and another statute dealing with authorization of teachers to lead students in a specific state-composed prayer. Both of these statutes were struck down as unconstitutional.

---

[7]472 U.S. 38 (1985).
[8]*Id.* at 40.
[9]*Jaffree v. James,* 554 F. Supp. 727, 732 (S.D. Ala. 1982).
[10]*Wallace v. Jaffree,* 472 U.S. at 57.

Moment of Silence

Though the United States Supreme Court has never directly
ruled on a moment of silence statute, its 1985 opinion in *Wallace
v. Jaffree*[11] suggests that moment of silence statutes, rules, or
policies will be held constitutional. Justice Stevens wrote the
opinion in *Wallace v. Jaffree* striking down the state laws requiring
a moment of voluntary prayer and a law authorizing teachers to lead
students in a state-composed prayer. However, in a concurring
opinion, Justice Powell stated that he fully agreed with Justice
Sandra Day O'Connor's "assertion that some moment-of-silence
statutes may be constitutional."[12]

In *Wallace v. Jaffree*, Justice O'Connor stated that the prior
Supreme Court opinions of *Engel* and *Schempp* were not dispositive
of the constitutionality of moment of silence laws.[13] In this regard,
she stated the following:

> A state-sponsored moment of silence in the public schools
> is different from state-sponsored vocal prayer or Bible
> reading. First, a moment of silence is not inherently
> religious. Silence, unlike prayer or Bible reading, need not
> be associated with a religious exercise. Second, a pupil
> who participates in a moment of silence need not
> compromise his or her beliefs. During a moment of
> silence, a student who objects to prayer is left to his or
> her own thoughts, and is not compelled to listen to the
> prayers or thoughts of others. For these simple reasons, a
> moment of silence statute does not stand or fall under the
> Establishment Clause according to how the court regards
> vocal prayer or Bible reading.[14]

Justice O'Connor cites Justice Brennan's concurring opinion in
Schempp as follows:

---

[11] *Id.* at 38.
[12] *Id.* at 62.
[13] *Id.* at 71.
[14] *Id.* at 72.

[T]he observance of a moment of reverent silence at the opening of class "may serve" the solely secular purpose of the devotional activities without jeopardizing either the religious liberties of any members of the community or the proper degree of separation between the spheres of religion and government.[15]

As noted above, the United States Supreme Court has never directly addressed a statute dealing with a moment of silence, but Justice O'Connor's opinion regarding the constitutionality of a moment of silence found support from a majority of the Court. In fact, Chief Justice William Rehnquist went so far as to suggest that the Supreme Court should recede from its 1962 and 1963 opinions which struck down state-led and state-composed prayers.[16]

In 1996 the Georgia legislature enacted the Moment of Quiet Reflection in Schools Act.[17] Under the Act, the teacher in charge of the public school classroom at the opening of each school day was required to conduct "a brief period of quiet reflection for not more than 60 seconds with the participation of all peoples who were assembled."[18] Prior to the start of the 1994-95 school year, a school teacher in the Gwinnett County School District expressed concerns about implementing the Act. The teacher then wrote a letter to the superintendent who in turn sent the teacher a letter that had been sent to all the school principals. In the letter the superintendent advised the principals to remind teachers and administrators not to suggest or imply that students should or should not use this time for prayer. Students were free to use this time for prayer if they chose but the school did not tolerate any coercion or overbearing by school officials in this manner. At the beginning of the school day on August 22, 1994, the principal for South Gwinnett High School made various announcements over the intercom. Following the announcements, the principal stated: "Let us take a few moments to reflect quietly on our day, our activities, and what we hope to accomplish."[19] In contravention of the Act,

---

[15]*Id.* (quoting *Abington Township*, 374 U.S. at 281.)

[16]*Wallace v. Jaffree*, 472 U.S. at 91.

[17]O.P.G.A. §20-2-1050 (1996).

[18]O.P.G.A. §20-2-1050(a).

[19]*Bown v. Gwinnett County School Dist.*, 112 F.3d 1464, 1468 (11th Cir. 1997).

the school teacher told his class that each student may do as they wished, but he was going to continue with his lesson. The teacher was later fired for failure to comply with the Act.

The teacher then brought suit against the school board alleging that the Quiet Reflection Act violated the First Amendment Establishment Clause. The federal court of appeals found the Act constitutional.[20]

In summary, state-composed and state-mandated prayers in public schools have been ruled unconstitutional. Moments of voluntary "prayer" have been ruled unconstitutional. However, a moment of silence statute or policy would be considered constitutional.

Student-Led Classroom Prayer

Even after the Supreme Court decision in 1962, many public schools in the State of Mississippi continued to allow prayer in the classroom. For example, students in Pontotoc County regularly offered prayer over the intercom. At North Pontotoc Attendance Center, the Aletheia Club announced the times and places of its meeting over the intercom and also offered prayers and read devotionals. In 1996, a Mississippi federal court ruled that prayer delivered by students via intercom to the classrooms was unconstitutional.[21] The court found that the students in the classroom were a captive audience and that the school intercom had not been generally opened to student speech. Though the court acknowledged that in some cases a school "may have a valid argument that it has created a forum to permit announcements at the school and student activities,"[22] the facts in the Pontotoc case indicated that the school had not allowed the intercom system to be

---

[20]The court found that the Act had a secular purpose, that it did not have the primary effect of advancing religion, and that it did not foster excessive governmental entanglement with religion. The court stated that "[e]ven if some legislators were motivated by a conviction that religious speech in particular was valuable and worthy of protection, that alone would not invalidate the Act, because what is relevant is the legislative purpose of the statute, not the possibly religious motives of the legislators who enacted the law." *Bown*, 112 F.3d at 1471-72 (quoting *Board of Education of Westside Community Schools v. Mergens*, 496 U.S. 226, 249 (1990)).

[21]*Herdahl v. Pontotoc County School Dist.*, 933 F. Supp. 582 (N.D. Miss. 1996).

[22]*Id.* at 589.

used as a "soap box for the religious, social or political expressions of members of the student body who want to preach, teach or politicize over the intercom system."[23]

The legislature and the student body quickly reacted to the judge's ruling. The Mississippi legislature passed a statute that purported to permit prayer on any public school property so long as it was nonsectarian, non-proselytizing, student-initiated voluntary prayer. The legislation attempted to do what the students did through the intercom system. However, a federal court of appeals found that statute unconstitutional.[24]

The student body was not content with the result of the court or legislative remedies. Representatives of the student body approached school officials requesting permission to use the auditorium or gymnasium to hold voluntary student prayer meetings in the morning before the start of the school day.[25] The students therefore began using the gymnasium and auditorium for these large prayer meetings. The school board voted to move the school day back several minutes to allow the students to meet prior to the start of the official day. There is approximately a 95% attendance ratio of the entire student body. These students in Pontotoc County meet every day to begin their school day with prayer and devotions. As a result of the litigation, more students now take prayer more seriously as is evident by the overwhelming participation. Since this is student-led, voluntary, and held outside mandatory class hours, it is clearly constitutional.

Athletic Events And Assemblies

In 1989 a federal court of appeals ruled that prayer at a public high school football game was unconstitutional.[26] In this case a

---

[23]*Id.*

[24]*Ingebretsen v. Jackson Public School District*, 88 F.3d 274 (5th Cir. 1996), *cert. denied,* 117 S. Ct. 388 (1996).

[25]Actually, the *Herdahl* case, which struck down the intercom prayer and ruled that no forum had been created through the intercom system, added language that suggested the students could voluntarily meet together to pray. This could include the younger students so long as they had parental consent.

[26]*Jager v. Douglas County School District*, 862 F.2d 824 (11th Cir. 1989), *cert. denied,* 490 U.S. 1090 (1989).

student was a member of the Douglas County High School marching band and objected to pregame invocations delivered at home football games. The invocations began with the words "Let us bow our heads" or "Let us pray," and the prayers frequently invoked reverence to Jesus Christ or closed with the words "In Jesus' name we pray."

From 1947 to 1986, an announcer introduced the invocation speaker and usually identified the church affiliation. The student government originally invited the invocation speakers, but in 1950 local ministers began to give the invocations. In the early 1970s, an assistant football coach delegated the task of furnishing invocation speakers to a Presbyterian clergyman. From the early 1970s to 1986 the same clergyman recruited invocation speakers from the Douglas County Ministerial Association, whose membership consisted exclusively of Protestant Christian ministers. In 1986, in response to a complaint by a student, a so-called equal access plan was developed permitting the various school clubs and organizations to designate club members to give the invocation, including any student, parent, or school staff member. Under this plan, the student government was to randomly select the invocation speaker and no minister was to be involved in the selection process or in the delivering of the invocations. Notwithstanding this random selection process, the federal court of appeals still ruled that the prayers before high school football games violated the First Amendment Establishment Clause.[27]

Another federal court addressed the issue of prayer led by coaches of athletic teams and came to a similar conclusion as did the court regarding prayers before public high school football games. In *Doe v. Duncanville Independent School District,*[28] a girls' basketball coach regularly began and ended practice with a team recitation of the Lord's Prayer. At one of the first basketball games, the Lord's Prayer was recited in the center of the court at the end of the game, the girls on their hands and knees with the coach standing over them having their heads bowed. During away games, the coach would lead the team in prayer prior to leaving the school premises as well as before exiting the bus upon the team's

---

[27]*Id.* at 832-33.
[28]994 F.2d 160 (5th Cir. 1993).

return. A seventh grade basketball player objected to these prayers and filed suit. The court ruled that the recitation of the Lord's Prayer in this manner violated the First Amendment Establishment Clause because the coach, as an agent of the school, had actually "composed" a prayer.[29]

Another federal court ruled that the First Amendment did not permit the student counsel to open up assemblies with prayer.[30] In this case, the student counsel officers conducted various assemblies throughout the school year under the guidance and direction of the school principal. Students who did not wish to attend could report to a supervised study hall. With the permission of the principal, the student counsel was permitted to open their assemblies with prayer and Bible readings of their choosing. A time was set aside on the agenda, and the student counsel selected one member of the student body to say a prayer. Nevertheless, the court ruled that prayer in this context was unconstitutional.

When considering the above rulings, it is important to note the following. First, all of the above cases dealt with public secondary schools. The rulings may not apply to post-secondary schools in light of the age differences. When looking at the First Amendment Establishment Clause, courts have often looked at the age of the students involved. The older the student, the less risk the religious practice will be perceived as establishing a religion. Second, the case involving prayers before a public high school football game, and the prayer composed and led by a basketball coach, are similar in nature to the 1962 and 1963 Supreme Court rulings in *Engel* and *Schempp*. The high school basketball coach composed the prayer just like the State of New York did in the 1962 *Engel* case. Third, none of the above cases dealt with a moment of silence. Moments of silence most likely would be considered constitutional by the United States Supreme Court. Finally, if students were leading the prayer at these athletic events in conjunction with other student-initiated nonreligious speech, then to prohibit the students from the religious speech may well violate their First Amendment free speech rights. In other words, if students were allowed to speak

---

[29]*Id.* at 164.

[30]*Collins v. Chandler Unified School District*, 644 F.2d 759 (9th Cir. 1981), *cert. denied*, 454 U.S. 863 (1981).

at the athletic events or other assemblies, and if part of the content of the program were handed over to the guidance and direction of students, then presumably a student would be able to pray within this context. To prevent student speech because it is religious while allowing student secular speech may well violate the student's First Amendment right to free speech and show hostility toward religion.

Graduation Prayers

We have already addressed prayers at public school graduations in another chapter. Briefly, prayers at public school graduations have been somewhat restricted since 1992. However, prayer at graduation is not completely prohibited. The Supreme Court in *Lee v. Weisman*[31] was concerned that school officials were actively involved in (1) placing prayer on the agenda, (2) inviting a religious clergyman to speak for the purpose of prayer, and (3) giving the clergyman specific guidelines for saying nonsectarian prayers. Prayer can still be conducted at public school graduations if school officials use secular criteria to invite the speaker, and once there, the speaker voluntarily prays. A valedictorian, salutatorian, or class officer can also voluntarily pray as part of the ceremony. The student body can elect a class chaplain or elect a class representative for the specific purpose of prayer. Part of the school program can be given over to the students and therefore be student-led and student-initiated. A parent and/or student committee can create and conduct part of the ceremony and, therefore, avoid state involvement. The ceremony can be conducted off the school premises by private individuals and therefore no state involvement would occur. The school may also adopt a free speech policy which allows the senior class an opportunity to devote a few minutes of the ceremony to uncensored student speech. The student speech can be secular or sacred. Finally, private individuals can sponsor public school graduations on or off the public campus.[32]

The restrictions on prayer during graduation at a public

---

[31]112 S. Ct. 2649 (1992).

[32]*See Jones v. Clear Creek Independent School District*, 977 F.2d 963 (5th Cir. 1992), *cert. denied*, 113 S. Ct. 2950 (1993). For a more detailed discussion see the chapter on Graduation Prayer in Public Schools.

secondary school are not applicable to the post-secondary level, such as a college or university.[33] Courts have stated that the maturity level of students is in part the reason for removing some of the restrictions on graduation prayer. Courts have reasoned that students in post-secondary school are less impressionable, more mature, and can better understand that the prayer offered by a student or an outside clergy does not necessarily represent the school.

Court Prayers

A North Carolina state court judge regularly opened his court saying: "Let us pause for a moment of prayer." The judge would then bow his head and recite aloud the following prayer:

> Oh Lord, our God, our Father in heaven, we pray this morning that You will place Your divine guiding hand on this courtroom and that with Your mighty outreached arm You will protect the innocent, give justice to those who have been harmed and mercy to us all. Let truth be heard and wisdom be reflected in the light of Your presence with us here today. Amen.[34]

The American Civil Liberties Union brought suit against this state court judge, and a federal court of appeals agreed that the judge violated the First Amendment Establishment Clause. The court reasoned that the prayer's primary purpose was religious, and it advanced and endorsed religion under the auspices of the state.[35]

In Alabama, the ACLU brought suit against Judge Roy Moore who regularly opened his court day by allowing citizen volunteers to offer a brief prayer. Another Alabama state judge sided with the ACLU, stating that the practice of opening court every day with

---

[33]*Tanford v. Brand*, 104 F.3d 982 (7th Cir. 1997); *Chaudhuri v. Tennessee*, 886 F. Supp. 1374 (M.D. Tenn. 1995).

[34]*North Carolina Civil Liberties Union Legal Foundation v. Constangy*, 947 F.2d 1145 (4th Cir. 1991), *cert. denied*, 112 S. Ct. 3027 (1992).

[35]*Id.* at 1149-1152.

prayer offered by voluntary citizens was unconstitutional.[36]

Both of these cases addressing prayers offered in courtrooms seem to be misplaced. Prayers in the courtroom should be analyzed like prayers offered in legislative chambers. The United States Supreme Court has already ruled that prayer offered by a legislative chaplain is constitutional.[37] In fact, the Supreme Court observed the following:

> The opening of sessions of legislative and other deliberative public bodies with prayer is deeply embedded in the history and tradition of this country. From colonial times to the founding of the Republic and ever since, the practice of legislative prayer has coexisted with the principals of disestablishment and religious freedom. In the very courtroom in which the United States District Judge and later three Circuit Judges heard and decided this case, the proceedings opened with an announcement and concluded "God save the United States and this Honorable Court." *This same invocation occurs at all sessions of this Court.*[38]

The Supreme Court of the United States itself acknowledged that every day when it opens the Court, a paid official offers an "invocation," stating "God save the United States and this Honorable Court." If the Supreme Court of the United States acknowledges that every day it opens its sessions with an invocation, then surely a lower state court or federal court should be able to open its day with prayer. In fact, the Supreme Court not only acknowledged daily invocations within the Supreme Court building, it also acknowledged that these daily invocations occurred in federal, district and appellate courtrooms.

---

[36] *Alabama v. American Civil Liberties Union of Alabama*, CV95-919-PR (Mont. Cty. Cir. Ct.) (1997). The same court also ruled that the posting of the Ten Commandments in Judge Moore's courtroom was unconstitutional. Responding to this case, Governor Fob James of Alabama indicated that he will call out the National Guard if anyone attempted to remove the Ten Commandments from the courtroom.

[37] *Marsh v. Chambers*, 463 U.S. 783 (1983).

[38] *Id.* at 786 (emphasis added).

Legislative Prayers

The issue of legislative prayers came before the United States Supreme Court in 1983 in its landmark decision of *Marsh v. Chambers.*[39] This case dealt with a challenge to the Nebraska legislature opening up its sessions with prayer offered by a paid chaplain chosen by the Legislative Counsel. In finding the practice constitutional, the Court did not use its previous three-part test from the case of *Lemon v. Kurtzman.*[40] The so-called *Lemon* test requires that for a statute to be found constitutional and not a violation of the First Amendment Establishment Clause it (1) must have a secular purpose, (2) must not have a primary purpose of promoting religion, and (3) must not foster excessive governmental entanglement with religion. This test has caused great confusion among the federal courts.[41] Instead of using this often criticized

---

[39]463 U.S. 783 (1983).

[40]403 U.S. 602 (1971).

[41]Justices Scalia and Thomas have been very critical of the Supreme Court's use of the so-called *Lemon* test. The two joined in a stinging critique of the Court as follows:

> Like some ghoul in a late-night horror movie that repeatedly sits up in its grave and shuffles abroad, after being repeatedly killed and buried, *Lemon* stalks our Establishment Clause jurisprudence once again, frightening the little children and school attorneys. . . . Its most recent burial, only last Term [in *Lee v. Weisman*] was, to be sure, not fully six-feet under. . . . Over the years, however, no fewer than five of the currently sitting Justices have, in their own opinions, personally driven pencils through the creature's heart. . . .

> The secret of the *Lemon* test's survival, I think, is that it is so easy to kill. It is there to scare us (and our audience) when we wish it to do so, but we can command it to return to the tomb at will. . . . When we wish to strike down a practice it forbids, we invoke it. . . . Sometimes we take a middle ground of course, calling its three prongs "no more than helpful signposts." Such a docile and useful monster is worth keeping around, at least in a somnolent state; one never knows when one might need him.

Lamb's Chapel v. Center Moriches Union Free School District, 113 S. Ct. 2141, 2150 (1993). A number of Supreme Court Justices have criticized the *Lemon* test. *See Lee v. Weisman,* 112 S. Ct.2649 (1992) (Scalia, J., joined by, *inter ailios*, White, J., and Thomas, J., dissenting); *Allegheny County v. American Civil Liberties Union*, 492 U.S. 573, 655-57 (1989) (Kennedy, J., concurring in judgment in part and dissenting in part); *Corporation of the Presiding Bishop of the Church of Jesus Christ of Latter-Day Saints v. Amos*, 483 U.S. 327, 346-349 (1987) (O'Connor, J., concurring); *Wallace v. Jaffree*, 472 U.S. 38, 107-113 (1985) (Rehnquist, J., dissenting); *Id.* at 90-91 (White, J., dissenting); *School District of*

Lemon test, the Court looked at the original intent of the First Amendment by overviewing history.

The Court began by stating the "opening of sessions of legislative and other deliberative public bodies with prayer is deeply imbedded in the history and tradition of this country."[42] Indeed, judicial proceedings are always begun by the announcement: "God save the United States and this Honorable Court."[43] In 1774, the Continental Congress adopted the tradition of opening its sessions with prayer offered by a paid chaplain.[44] As one of its first items of business, the First Congress "adopted the policy of selecting a chaplain to open each session with prayer."[45] In 1789, the same year that the First Amendment was drafted, the Senate appointed a committee to consider the manner of electing chaplains and a similar committee was appointed in the House of Representatives. The first chaplain was elected in the Senate on April 25, 1789, and in the House on May 1, 1789.[46] On September 25, 1789, three days after Congress authorized the appointment of paid chaplains, a final agreement had been reached on the language of the Bill of Rights including the First Amendment. The Court gleaned from this early history that "the men who wrote the First Amendment Religion Clauses did not view paid legislative chaplains in opening prayers as a violation of that Amendment, for the practice of opening sessions with prayer has continued without interruption ever since that early session of Congress."[47]

In reviewing the history of legislative prayers, the Court went to the heart of the First Amendment's intent by stating the following:

[H]istorical evidence sheds light not only on what the

Grand Rapids v. Ball, 473 U.S. 373, 400 (1985) (White, J., dissenting); *Widmar v. Vincent*, 454 U.S. 263, 282 (1981) (White, J., dissenting); *New York v. Cathedral Academy*, 434 U.S. 125, 134-135 (1977) (White, J., dissenting); *Roemer v. Maryland Board of Public Works*, 426 U.S. 736, 768 (1976) (White, J., concurring in judgment); *Committee for Public Education & Religious Liberty v. Nyquist*, 413 U.S. 756, 820 (1973) (White, J., dissenting).

[42]*Marsh*, 463 U.S. at 786.
[43]*Id.*
[44]*Id.* at 787.
[45]*Id.* at 787-88.
[46]*Id.*
[47]*Id.* at 788.

draftsmen intended the Establishment Clause to mean, but also on how they thought that Clause applied to the practice authorized by the First Congress -- their actions reveal their intent.[48]

The Supreme Court concluded "that legislative prayer presents no more potential for establishment then the provision of school transportation, beneficial grounds for higher education, or tax exemptions for religious organizations."[49] After reviewing the more than two hundred years of unbroken history, the Court noted:

[T]here can be no doubt that the practice of opening legislative sessions with prayer has become part of the fabric of our society. To invoke Divine guidance on a public body entrusted with making the laws is not, in these circumstances, an "establishment" of religion or a step toward establishment; it is simply a tolerable acknowledgment of beliefs widely held among the people of this country. As Justice Douglas observed, "[w]e are a religious people whose institutions presuppose a Supreme Being."[50]

The Supreme Court also observed the following:

Clearly the men who wrote the First Amendment Religion Clauses did not view paid legislative chaplains and opening prayers as a violation of that Amendment, for the

---

[48]*Id.* at 790.

[49]*Id.* at 791, (citing *Everson v. Board of Education*, 330 U.S. 1 (1947)). *See also Tilton v. Richardson*, 403 U.S. 672 (1971); *Walz v. Tax Commission*, 397 U.S. 664 (1970).

[50]*Marsh*, 463 U.S. at 792 (citing *Zorach v. Clauson*, 343 U.S. 306, 313 (1952)). A California appeals court ruled that a presidential proclamation for a national day of thanksgiving was constitutional. In an interesting turn of events, President Bush declared April 5-7, 1991, as National Days of Thanksgiving following the conclusion of the Persian Gulf War. In the state of California, the educational code required community colleges to close on every day appointed by the President as a public fast, thanksgiving, or holiday. Certain school employees requested the three days off as paid holidays, but the Governing Board refused, claiming that the presidential proclamation was unconstitutional. The California appeals court ruled that the presidential proclamation was consistent with the First Amendment. *California School Employees Ass'n. v. Marin Community College District*, 15 Cal. App. 4th 273 (Cal. Ct. App. 1993).

practice of opening sessions with prayer has continued without interruption ever since that early session of Congress.[51]

The Supreme Court's analysis makes sense. Obviously those who drafted the First Amendment saw no conflict between that Amendment and the offering of a prayer at a public setting.

Board Meetings

Prayers are frequently said at county, municipal and school board meetings, as well as other meetings of public officials. In many respects, these prayers are very similar to prayers preceding legislative sessions.

A federal court of appeals ruled that a resolution of the County Board of St. Louis County in Minnesota providing for an invocation at its public meetings was not a violation of the First Amendment Establishment Clause.[52] Under this policy, a board of commissioners invited local clergymen to offer prayers prior to the commencement of each board meeting. The chairman of the board would generally announce the following: "As is our practice, the Reverend John Doe will now give a prayer." The Court found that this practice was consistent with the First Amendment because the prayer had a "secular legislative purpose of setting a solemn tone for the transaction of governmental business" and assisted "the maintenance of order and decorum."[53] The practice of opening these board meetings with prayers was not "an establishment of religion proscribed by the establishment clause of the First Amendment in any pragmatic, meaningful and realistic sense of that clause."[54] Similarly, the state Supreme Court of New Hampshire ruled that inviting local ministers to open town meetings with an invocation was not prohibited by the First Amendment

---

[51]*Marsh*, 463 U.S. at 788.
[52]*Bogen v. Doty*, 598 F.2d 1110 (8th Cir. 1979).
[53]*Id.* at 1114-115.
[54]*Id.* at 1115.

Establishment Clause.[55]

A federal court has also ruled that prayer offered to open a school board meeting is constitutional.[56] The Cleveland school board traditionally opened its deliberative session with prayer. Historically the school board invited representatives of the protestant, Roman Catholic, Jewish and Muslim faiths. On occasion when the person scheduled to offer the prayer was not in attendance, the meeting was opened with a moment of silence followed by the board president saying, "Amen." In analyzing the situation, the court noted that there was "an unbroken history of official acknowledgment by all three branches of government of the role of religion in American life from at least 1789."[57] The court stated that the inquiry must first consider the understanding of the framers of the First Amendment. The court noted that the very first week Congress approved the Bill of Rights, it also enacted legislation providing for paid chaplains for the House and Senate.[58] The First Congress "was a Congress whose constitutional decisions have always been regarded, as they should be regarded, as of the greatest weight in the interpretation of that fundamental instrument."[59] Similar to the Supreme Court's historical analysis, this federal court also looked at the historical support for religion in public life, stating that there were "countless examples of government deference to religion in our history," including paid chaplains for the military, state legislative chaplains, Thanksgiving and Christmas as national holidays, the Pledge of Allegiance with the language "one nation under God," our national motto "In God We Trust," the invocation to open courts, "God save the United States and this Honorable Court," and the long-standing tradition of

---

[55]*Lincoln v. Page*, 109 N.H. 30, 241 A.2d 799 (N.H. 1968). Other courts have similarly ruled that prayer offered at the outset of public assemblies are constitutional. *See, e.g., Marsa v. Wernik*, 430 A.2d 888 (N.J.) *app. dismissed and cert. denied*, 454 U.S. 958 (1981) (Prayer at the outset of borough council meeting constitutional); *Lincoln v. Page*, 341 A.2d 799 (N.H. 1968) (Invocation at town meeting constitutional); *Colo v. Treasurer and Receiver General*, 392 N.E.2d 1195 (Mass. 1979) (Salaries for legislative chaplains constitutional); *Snyder v. Murray City Corp.*, 902 F. Supp. 1444 (D. Utah 1995) (Statements by a minister at outset of council meeting constitutional).

[56]*Coles v. Cleveland Board of Education*, 950 F. Supp. 1337 (N.D. Ohio 1996).

[57]*Id.* at 1341, *quoting Lynch v. Donnelly*, 465 U.S. 668, 674 (1984).

[58]*Coles*, 950 F. Supp. at 1342.

[59]*Id., quoting Myers v. United States*, 272 U.S. 52, 174-75 (1926).

our country accommodating faith and religious expression.[60]

The court noted that the prayer of a public deliberative body occurred in a fundamentally adult atmosphere, rather than in a student or school oriented atmosphere, and consequently was constitutional.[61]

---

[60]*Coles*, 950 F. Supp. at 1342.
[61]*Id.* at 1347.

12

RELIGIOUS SYMBOLS
ON PUBLIC PROPERTY

The relationship between religion and the United States Constitution is often misunderstood. Some have assumed that the Constitution requires total separation of church and state. However, according to the United States Supreme Court, "[t]otal separation is not possible in the absolute sense. Some relationship between government and religious organizations is inevitable."[1]

Though some have argued that there must be a "wall of separation between church and state,"[2] the Supreme Court has stated that this so-called "wall" metaphor is not an "accurate description" of the relationship between church and state.[3] Accordingly, the Supreme Court has stated that it "has never been thought either possible or desirable to enforce a regime of total separation. . . ."[4] The Constitution does not "require complete separation of church and state; it affirmatively mandates accommodation, not merely tolerance, of all religions, and forbids

---

[1] *Lemon v. Kurtzman*, 403 U.S. 602, 614 (1971).

[2] The so-called "wall of separation between church and state" is not in the Constitution. This phrase came from a letter written by Thomas Jefferson to a group of Danbury Baptists. President Jefferson assured the religious group that he had no intention of creating a national religious holiday wherein he would require the individual states to adhere to a sectarian doctrine. In this sense, President Jefferson is correct. The First Amendment did prohibit the federal government from establishing a national church, or requiring sectarian policy to be imposed on the individual states. However, the "wall" metaphor has been used out of context. Thomas Jefferson was not involved in drafting the First Amendment. At the time the First Amendment was drafted, he was in France. Moreover, Thomas Jefferson did not take the extreme separation view today as promoted by some organizations. As founder of the University of Virginia and Chairman of the District of Columbia School Board, he saw no conflict having the Bible and the Watts Hymnals as primary textbooks. He also declared that to exclude religious instruction from the public schools would create a great chasm in the public education system. While the First Amendment prohibits government from controlling religion and prohibits government from requiring sectarian support, it was never intended to prohibit people of faith from influencing government or from expressing their religious convictions in the public square or through public policy.

[3] *Lynch v. Donnelly*, 465 U.S. 668, 673 (1984).

[4] *Committee for Public Education & Religious Liberty v. Nyquist*, 413 U.S. 756, 760 (1973).

hostility toward any."[5] Anything less than mandating affirmative accommodation of religion would require "callous indifference," which the Constitution never intended.[6]

Total separation of church and state would actually result in hostility toward religion and would bring this country into "war with our national tradition as embodied in the First Amendment's guarantee of the free exercise of religion."[7]

A correct interpretation of the First Amendment must be in accord "with what history reveals was the contemporaneous understanding of its guarantees."[8] The Supreme Court recognizes "that religion has been closely identified with our history and our government."[9] The history of this country "is inseparable from the history of religion."[10] American history clearly indicates that "[w]e are a religious people whose institutions presuppose a Supreme Being."[11]

Clearly, the First Amendment requires that the state affirmatively accommodate religion and prevents the state from showing hostility toward any religion. Examples of accommodation of religion throughout history include legislation providing paid chaplains for the House and Senate, adopted by the First Congress in 1789 when the First Amendment was framed;[12] national days of thanksgiving;[13] Executive Orders proclaiming Christmas and Thanksgiving as national holidays,[14] the national motto "In God We Trust;"[15] the term "one nation under God" as part of the Pledge of Allegiance;[16] art galleries supported by public revenues displaying religious paintings of the 15th and 16th centuries, including the National Gallery in Washington maintained by

---

[5]*Lynch,* 465 U.S. at 673. *See, e.g., Zorach v. Clauson,* 343 U.S. 306, 314 (1952); *Illinois ex rel. McCullom v. Board of Education,* 333 U.S. 203, 211 (1948).

[6]*Zorach,* 343 U.S. at 314; *Lynch,* 465 U.S. at 673.

[7]*McCullom,* 333 U.S. at 211-212.

[8]*Lynch,* 465 U.S. at 673.

[9]*School District of Abington Township v. Schempp,* 374 U.S. 203, 212 (1963).

[10]*Engel v. Vitale,* 370 U.S. 421, 434 (1962).

[11]*Zorach,* 343 U.S. at 313.

[12]*Lynch,* 465 U.S. at 674.

[13]*Id.* at 675.

[14]*Id.* at 676.

[15]36 U.S.C. § 186. The national motto was also mandated for currency. 31 U.S.C. § 5112(d)(1).

[16]*Lynch,* 465 U.S. at 676.

government support exhibiting masterpieces with religious messages such as the Last Supper and paintings depicting the Birth of Christ, the Crucifixion, and the Resurrection, along with many other explicit Christian themes,[17] and the inscription of Moses with the Ten Commandments etched in stone in the Supreme Court of the United States of America.[18] These are just a few of many examples. Clearly, "our history is pervaded by expressions of religious beliefs."[19] Consequently, government would do well to "respect the religious nature of our people."[20]

The Judeo-Christian history of this country is evident when considering religious symbols on public property. These symbols include crosses perched atop water towers, crosses within city seals, the Ten Commandments on public buildings, scripture verses etched in stone, nativity scenes, and many other symbols. One cannot walk through our nation's capitol without realizing the Judeo-Christian impact on this country. Indeed, in the United States Supreme Court, inscribed directly above the Chief Justice, is Moses with the Ten Commandments. The centrality of the Ten Commandments within the United States Supreme Court is meant to symbolize that all other laws throughout history are based upon and derived from the Ten Commandments. Each day the court is in session, the justices sit below the Ten Commandments purportedly to apply its principles.

Religious symbols within the public sector have come under attack. The battle over nativity scenes greatly contributed to pushing my career from ministry to law. Every year as I read about one nativity scene falling after another, I became frustrated. After entering law school, I began to realize that nativity scenes are still constitutional when displayed in the proper context.

Nativity scenes on public property and religious Christmas carols in the public schools are rapidly disappearing from American culture. The loss of religious consensus and the "separation of church and state" myth have contributed toward the demise of America's Christian heritage.

---

[17]*Id.* at 677. The National Gallery regularly exhibits more than 200 similar religious paintings. *Id.* at 677 n.4.

[18]*Id.* at 677.

[19]*Id.*

[20]*Zorach,* 343 U.S. at 314; *Lynch,* 465 U.S. at 678.

In the 1970s the American Civil Liberties Union (hereafter "ACLU") was initially successful in removing nativity scenes from public property. However, the United States Supreme Court has now dealt with the issue of nativity scenes.[21] The Supreme Court has never ruled that all nativity scenes on public property are unconstitutional. To the contrary, nativity scenes are constitutional if properly displayed. Unfortunately, the ACLU has used smoke and mirrors to intimidate public officials into removing nativity scenes and Christmas carols from the public square. More unfortunate is the fact that many public leaders cower to these threats without ever considering whether the ACLU is right.

Publicly and Privately Sponsored Symbols

The display of nativity scenes and religious symbols takes on two forms: publicly sponsored and privately sponsored, both of which can be displayed on public property. A publicly sponsored scene is one that is erected and maintained by public officials. A privately sponsored scene is one that is erected and maintained by private citizens. Both are constitutional, and both can be displayed on public property. The main difference is that a publicly sponsored scene should have some form of secular display in the same context, while a privately sponsored scene need not have any secular symbols. The private display should probably have a sign indicating the display is privately sponsored.

Publicly Sponsored Symbols

An example of a publicly sponsored scene is one that is erected and maintained by city officials on public property. The key to the constitutionality of a publicly sponsored scene is that it must have a secular symbol within the context of the scene. The display of a publicly sponsored religious scene standing by itself would be considered unconstitutional.[22] However, if secular symbols are displayed within the context of the religious scene, the Supreme

---

[21]*Lemon v. Kurtzman*, 403 U.S. 602 (1971); *County of Allegheny v. American Civil Liberties Union*, 492 U.S. 573 (1989).
[22]*Id.*

Court would consider it constitutional. Therefore, in a publicly sponsored scene, there should also be a secular symbol.

The proximity of the secular symbols to the religious display is also important. The secular and religious symbols should be within the same parameter of view. In other words, when viewing the scene, one should also be able to view the secular displays in close proximity to the religious display. For example, a nativity scene could be displayed with Mary and Joseph looking into the manger at Baby Jesus, and Santa Claus could be standing near the manger; his reindeer could be parked somewhere nearby, and a Christmas tree could also be located nearby.

The main point to consider in a publicly sponsored scene is that there must be a combination of both secular and religious symbols of the holiday. A publicly sponsored display of religious symbols standing alone is unconstitutional. According to the United States Supreme Court, adding secular symbols to a publicly sponsored religious display magically makes the display constitutional.

Privately Sponsored Symbols

A privately sponsored religious scene can also be displayed on public property. The main difference is that the display is erected and maintained by private citizens instead of public officials. Privately sponsored scenes are more common in public parks where citizens are allowed to engage in expressive activity.[23] In most public parks, citizens are allowed to hold gatherings and erect displays. To prohibit religious expression in a public park where other expressive activity is permitted violates the Constitution. Public officials cannot show hostility toward religion by allowing secular expression but prohibiting religious expression.

In a privately sponsored scene, there is no need for secular symbols to be displayed within the same context of the religious symbols. A privately sponsored scene can stand alone without secular symbols. However, in order to clearly designate that the display is privately sponsored, a sign should be erected, similar to

---

[23]See *Capitol Square Review and Advisory Board v. Pinette*, 115 S. Ct. 2440 (1995); *Doe v. Small*, 964 F.2d 611 (7th Cir. 1992) (en banc).

the following example: "This display is privately sponsored by ABC."[24]

Nativity Scenes And Other Holiday Symbols

Publicly Sponsored

Some have the mistaken idea that publicly sponsored nativity scenes on public property, maintained by public entities, are unconstitutional. This is clearly not the law as stated by the United States Supreme Court. In the famous case of *Lynch v. Donnelly*,[25] the United States Supreme Court ruled that the city of Pawtucket, Rhode Island, could continue to display its nativity scene, which it had done for the previous forty years.

When considering the constitutionality of the nativity scene, the Court addressed the following three questions: (a) whether the display had a secular purpose, (b) whether the display had the primary effect of advancing religion, and (c) whether the display fostered excessive governmental entanglement.

Whether There Is A Secular Purpose

In addressing this first question, the Court stated that the focus must be on the entire Christmas display, not simply on the nativity scene (creche) as separated from the context of the Christmas display. Also, it is important to note that there must only be *a* secular purpose. There certainly may be a religious purpose in parts of the display, but when looking at the display in its entirety, if at least some secular aspect exists, then there is a secular purpose. Thus, a nativity scene by itself may only have a religious purpose, but when placed in the context of the Christmas holiday season, and in the context of other secular symbols of Christmas such as Santa Claus, a Christmas tree, or reindeer, the entire display may be said to have at least *a* secular purpose. In fact, the Supreme Court has declared that a nativity scene sponsored by the government, on

---

[24]A disclaimer on a privately sponsored religious scene on public property is not necessary but may be helpful to alert the public that the display is in fact privately sponsored.
[25]465 U.S. 668 (1984).

government property, accompanied by other secular symbols, serves "legitimate secular purposes."[26]

Whether The Primary Effect Is To Advance Religion

In looking at this question, the issue is whether the *primary* effect is to advance religion by the entire context of the display. To answer this question, the entire context should be viewed as a whole, not in isolation. If one were to focus solely on the nativity scene in isolation from the Christmas tree, then the impression might be that the primary effect is to advance religion. However, the Supreme Court has indicated that the display as a whole must be considered simultaneously.[27] Though the nativity scene by itself may be said to advance religion, when viewed in the entire context of the surrounding secular symbols, it cannot be said that the *primary* purpose is to advance religion. In making this decision, the *Lynch* Court cited other examples of governmental aid to religion which did not have the primary effect of advancing religion, namely expenditures of large sums of public money for textbooks supplied throughout the country to students attending church-sponsored schools,[28] expenditure of public funds for transportation of students to church-sponsored schools,[29] federal grants for college buildings of church-sponsored institutions of higher education combining secular and religious education,[30] noncategorical grants to church-sponsored colleges and universities,[31] tax-exemptions for

---

[26]*Lynch*, 465 U.S. at 681.

[27]Similarly, if an outsider walked into a public school auditorium to hear a Christmas program, and the first song heard was "Silent Night, Holy Night," the impression this person might receive is that the school is promoting the Christian religion. However, if this same person stayed for the entire program and later heard secular songs, such as "Here Comes Santa Claus," this person would then understand the school was acknowledging both the sacred and secular aspects of the holiday. Courts refers to this person as a "reasonable observer," meaning the person is informed of the context including the history surrounding the event. Such a person is informed of what went on before and what will take place later. If this were not the standard, then every religious display would be called into question by an "Ignoramus veto." *See Capitol Square Review and Advisory Board*, 115 S. Ct. 2440 (1995); *Chabad-Lubavitch of Georgia v. Miller*, 5 F.3d 1383 (11th Cir. 1993) (en banc).

[28]*Board of Education v. Allen*, 392 U.S. 236, 244 (1968).

[29]*Everson v. Board of Education*, 330 U.S. 1, 17 (1947).

[30]*Tilton v. Richardson*, 403 U.S. 672 (1971).

[31]*Roemer v. Maryland Board of Public Works*, 426 U.S. 736 (1976).

church properties,[32] Sunday Closing Laws,[33] release time programs for religious training during public school hours,[34] and legislative prayers.[35] Since the Supreme Court has in the past found all of these activities to be consistent with the Constitution, the mere display of a nativity scene within a Christmas display provides no greater aid to religion and clearly would not violate the Constitution. In fact, the Court noted that not every law which confers an indirect, remote, or incidental benefit upon religion is, for that reason alone, constitutionally invalid.[36]

The Supreme Court in *Lynch* specifically noted that the "display of the creche is no more an advancement or endorsement of religion than the Congressional and Executive recognition of the origins of the Holiday as 'Christ's Mass,' or the exhibition of literally hundreds of religious paintings in governmentally-sponsored museums."[37]

Whether There Is Excessive Governmental Entanglement

The Supreme Court in *Lynch* found that there was no excessive governmental entanglement when a public entity displays a nativity scene during Christmas because there is no excessive administrative entanglement between the state and church concerning the content, the design of the exhibit, or upkeep. The monetary expense is also minimal. In fact, the display required far less ongoing, day-to-day interaction between church and state than religious paintings in public galleries.[38]

As the above shows, the context of the nativity scene is most important. In one case, the United States Supreme Court ruled that a nativity scene was unconstitutional while a Jewish menorah was constitutional.[39] In the *County of Allegheny* case, the Supreme Court considered two recurring holiday displays located on public

---

[32]*Walz v. Tax Commissioner*, 397 U.S. 664 (1970).

[33]*McGowan v. Maryland*, 366 U.S. 420 (1961).

[34]*Zorach*, 343 U.S. at 306.

[35]*Marsh v. Chambers*, 463 U.S. 783 (1983).

[36]*Lynch*, 465 U.S. at 683 (citing *Nyquist*, 413 U.S. at 771).

[37]*Lynch*, 465 U.S. at 683.

[38]*Id.* at 684.

[39]*County of Allegheny v. American Civil Liberties Union*, 492 U.S. 573 (1989).

property in downtown Pittsburgh. The first was a creche depicting the Christian nativity scene which was placed on the Grand Staircase of the Allegheny County courthouse. This was the main, and apparently, the most beautiful and most public part of the courthouse. The creche was donated by the Holy Name Society, a Roman Catholic group, and bore a sign to that effect. The second holiday display was an eighteen-foot Hanukkah menorah, or candelabrum, which was placed just outside the city-county building next to the city's forty-five foot decorated Christmas tree. The menorah was owned by Chabad, a Jewish group, but was stored and erected by the city each year.

Splitting hairs in this case, the Supreme Court ruled that the nativity scene violated the First Amendment Establishment Clause, but the menorah did not. They reasoned that the nativity scene was at the prime entrance to the courthouse and was not surrounded by any secular symbols of Christmas. However, the menorah was not at the prime entrance and was in fact surrounded by secular symbols of Christmas, such as the Christmas tree. Presumably, the nativity scene would have been constitutional had the menorah and the Christmas tree been at the same entrance, or had the nativity scene been at the same location as the menorah and the Christmas tree. However, because the nativity scene did not have any corresponding secular symbols of Christmas, the Court ruled that the nativity display was unconstitutional and had the primary effect of endorsing religion.

The main teaching to be gleaned from the *County of Allegheny* case is that for a nativity scene to be constitutional it must be within close proximity to some other secular symbol of Christmas, such as a Christmas tree, Santa Claus or reindeer. This seems to be splitting hairs and is clearly not the original intent of the First Amendment. Nevertheless, using this analysis today a publicly sponsored nativity scene can still be displayed on any public property. Unfortunately, some city officials have become frustrated or confused. Some have jettisoned the whole idea of nativity scenes. Such drastic measures are not required by the Supreme Court's interpretation of the Constitution.

Privately Sponsored

The main difference between a publicly sponsored versus a privately sponsored religious symbol, aside from the sponsorship, is that while the former must have a secular symbol mixed in the context, the latter does not. A publicly sponsored nativity scene must have a secular symbol of the holiday, but a privately sponsored nativity scene displayed on public property can exclude other secular symbols and erect only the nativity scene.

The Supreme Court has unquestionably ruled that the private display of a religious symbol in a public park is constitutional.[40] In an unusual case, the Ku Klux Klan sought to erect a Latin (christian) cross during the Christmas season in the State house plaza in Columbus, Ohio. To use the public square to temporarily erect unattended symbols, all groups were required to fill out an application form. Historically, the City of Columbus allowed a broad range of speakers and events in what was known as Capitol Square. In the past the City permitted a variety of unattended displays including a State-sponsored Christmas tree, a privately-sponsored menorah, and a display showing the progress of a United Way fundraising campaign. Booths, exhibits, and art festivals were periodically on the public grounds. However, when the Ku Klux Klan sought to erect the Latin cross, Columbus officials who opposed the message of hate and bigotry promoted by the KKK, declined the request. After the KKK filed suit, the City of Columbus took the position that the Constitution required the City to censor religious displays because the casual observer would probably assume that the religious display was endorsed by the City. City officials took the position that to allow the display to remain on public property would violate the Constitution.

The Supreme Court rejected arguments put forth by the City of Columbus. First, the Supreme Court found that the KKK's Latin cross was private expression. The Court stated that prior "precedent establishes that private religious speech, far from being a First Amendment orphan, is as fully protected under the Free Speech Clause as secular private expression."[41] "Indeed, in Anglo-

[40]*Capitol Square Review and Advisory Board v. Pinette*, 115 S. Ct. 2440 (1995).
[41]*Id.* at 2446 (citations omitted).

American history, at least, government suppression of speech has so commonly been directed precisely at religious speech that a free-speech clause without religion would be Hamlet without the prince."[42] The Court stated that its prior cases "have not excluded from free-speech protections religious proselytizing, . . . even acts of worship."[43] The Court also reasoned that there was no Establishment Clause problem because the Latin cross was private, rather than public speech. The Court also rejected arguments put forth by the City that the Latin cross should be excluded because it may produce the perception that the cross bears the state's approval in that it was in close proximity to the seat of government. The Court noted the following:

> We find it peculiar to say that government "promotes" or "favors" a religious display by giving it the same access to a public forum that all other displays enjoy. And as a matter of Establishment Clause jurisprudence, we have consistently held that it is no violation for government to enact neutral policies that happen to benefit religion.[44]

In finding the private display of the cross in a public park constitutional, the Court poignantly noted the following:

> It will be a sad day when this Court casts piety in with pornography, and finds the First Amendment more hospitable to private expletives, . . . than to private prayers. This would be merely bizarre were religious speech simply as protected by the Constitution as other forms of private speech; but it is outright perverse when one considers that private religious expression receives preferential treatment under the Free Exercise Clause. It is no answer to say that the Establishment Clause tempers religious speech. By its terms that Clause applies only to the words and acts of government. It was never meant, and has never been read by this Court, to serve as an

---

[42]Id.
[43]Id. (citations omitted).
[44]Id. at 2447.

impediment to purely private religious speech connected to the State only through its occurrence in a public forum.[45]

The Court concluded by summing up its opinion as follows: "Religious expression cannot violate the Establishment Clause where it (1) is purely private, and (2) occurs in a traditional or designated public forum, publicly announced and open to all on equal terms."[46]

Similarly, an Illinois federal appeals court ruled that privately displayed nativity pictures in a public park were constitutional. In 1956, the Ottawa Retail Merchants Association, a private organization, commissioned the painting of sixteen canvases depicting scenes from the life of Christ in an effort to "put Christ back in Christmas."[47] These paintings were displayed in Washington Park located in the center of the city of Ottawa, Illinois, during the Christmas season from 1957 to 1969. These paintings were again displayed from 1980 through 1988. Except for the years 1964 through 1967, when the city arranged for the erection of the paintings, the display had been exhibited by private parties. However, these paintings were not displayed during the 1970s but were stored in an old grandstand structure and apparently forgotten. A newspaper article in 1980 discussed the paintings, upon which a local chapter of the Junior Chamber of Commerce (Jaycees), a national service-oriented organization, contacted the city and volunteered to take charge of the paintings.

When these private paintings were displayed in the city park, they occupied less than one-half of the west side of Washington Park. These paintings were accompanied by a sign that stated: "This Display Has Been Erected And Maintained Solely By The Ottawa Jaycees, A Private Organization, Without The Use Of Public Funds."[48] In considering this situation, the court of appeals found that the park was a traditional public forum, and it was therefore obviously open to the public. This public park had been open to the

---

[45]Id. at 2449 (citations omitted).

[46]Id. at 2450.

[47]Doe v. Small, 964 F.2d 611, 612 (7th Cir. 1992) (en banc).

[48]Id. at 612.

public and space had always been allocated on a first-come, first-served basis. Since this was a public park, and the displays were owned and maintained privately with a disclaimer indicating private ownership, the federal court ruled that it was constitutionally permissible to display these paintings. To remove these paintings would violate the First Amendment Free Speech Clause. The First Amendment prohibits government from censoring speech or expression solely based on content. Since this display was privately sponsored on public property, the court need not even consider the Establishment Clause. The Establishment Clause does not apply to private speech. It only applies to government. Just because the display occurs on public property does not transform private speech into government speech.

Similar to the Seventh Circuit Court of Appeals, the Sixth, Ninth and Eleventh Circuit Courts of Appeals have ruled that the private display of a Jewish menorah in a public park during Hanukkah is constitutionally permissible under the First Amendment Free Speech Clause.[49] The city of Grand Rapids had since 1964

---

[49]*Kreisner v. City of San Diego*, 1 F.3d 775 (9th Cir. 1993) (the private sponsorship in a public park of a display of life-size statuaries depicting biblical scenes from the life of Christ having a disclaimer sign indicating that the display was privately sponsored is constitutional and is protected free expression); *Americans United for Separation of Church and State v. City of Grand Rapids*, 980 F.2d 1538 (6th Cir. 1992) (en banc). In another case, the City of Cincinnati enacted an ordinance which stated "The proposed use including presence of any display, exhibit, or structure, will not occur in Fountain Square between the hours of 10:00 p.m. and 6:00 a.m." However, this limitation on the use of the public square exempted "agencies, political subdivisions and instrumentalities of governments of the United States, the State of Ohio, the County of Hamilton, the City of Cincinnati, and the Board of Education of the City of Cincinnati." The Congregation Lubavitch wished to display its eighteen-foot high menorah during Hanukkah. It had displayed this menorah in the past. The assembly and disassembly of this structure took approximately six hours. The new city ordinance requiring that no use of Fountain Square could occur between 10:00 p.m. and 6:00 a.m. would have required the dismantling of this menorah everyday. Congregation Lubavitch sued the city of Cincinnati, claiming that the ordinance was not content-neutral because, as applied to them, it violated their First Amendment right to free speech. Unlike other outside organizations, Congregation Lubavitch would not be able to adequately use Fountain Square with this limitation. A federal court of appeals agreed stating that the ordinance was not content-neutral and therefore violated the Constitution. *Congregation Lubavitch v. City of Cincinnati*, 997 F.2d 1160 (6th Cir. 1993). *See also Chabad-Lubavitch of Georgia v. Miller*, 5 F.3d 1383 (11th Cir. 1993) (en banc) (ruling that a state could not deny permission to a private Jewish organization to display in a designated or limited public forum its fifteen foot tall menorah in the State Capitol Rotunda because not being accompanied by other secular symbols and without a disclaimer of private sponsorship the display would violate the First

granted Chabad House of Western Michigan a permit to display a twenty foot high steel menorah during the eight days of the Jewish holiday of Hanukkah. The menorah was purchased entirely with private funds and was owned by Chabad House, a private organization. The city of Grand Rapids had no role in the planning, erecting, removal, maintenance, or storage of the menorah. All the display costs were privately funded, except for a small cost for providing electricity.

The display was located in Calder Plaza in the center of downtown Grand Rapids and was the principal public plaza in the area. The city required that the menorah be accompanied by two signs measuring two feet by three feet, which were illuminated at night. The signs read as follows:

HAPPY CHANUKAH TO ALL
This Menorah display has been erected by Chabad House, a
private organization. Its presence does not constitute
an endorsement by the City of Grand Rapids of
the organization or the display.[50]

The city of Grand Rapids had made the plaza available to the public for all forms of speech and assembly and clearly this was a traditional public forum. Since this was a traditional public forum, and since other members of the public had access to the public forum for expressive activities, the appeals court ruled that the Jewish organization had a right to display the menorah, and that to prohibit display of the menorah would be content-based censorship and violative of the First Amendment Free Speech Clause.

The Eleventh Circuit Court of Appeals also found that the private display of a Jewish menorah in a public park was constitutional.[51] This case is very significant because it was decided by the entire panel of the Eleventh Circuit Court, rather than the usual three judge panel. The court found that the public entity allowed secular speech and therefore had created a limited public forum. Consequently, the public entity could not exclude

---

Amendment Establishment Clause).
[50]*City of Grand Rapids*, 980 F.2d at 1540.
[51]*Chabad-Lubavitch of Georgia v. Miller*, 5 F.3d 1383 (11th Cir. 1993) (en banc).

religious speech from this forum. The court stated that private speech in a public forum does not violate the Establishment Clause. "The speech that takes place in a public forum belongs and can be attributed to the private speaker only; neither approbation nor condemnation of the private speaker's message may be imputed to the State."[52] "Any perceived endorsement of religion is simply misperception; the Establishment Clause is not, in fact, violated."[53] The court concluded as follows:

> Giving full effect to the public forum doctrine does not elevate the Free Speech Clause above the Establishment Clause. . . . [I]n the public forum, . . . the speech of private parties does not enjoy the State's imprimatur. There is no Establishment Clause violation in the first instance to weigh against . . . the Free Speech Clause. Courts that have found otherwise, . . . simply misunderstood the principals they sought to apply.[54]

In a case involving the private distribution of literature by public school students on campus, another federal court observed similarly:

> The Establishment Clause is a limitation on the power of government: it is not a restriction on the rights of individuals acting in their private lives. The threshold question in any Establishment Clause is whether there is sufficient governmental action to invoke the prohibition. . . It is clear that the mere fact that [private] speech occurs [public] property fails to make it government supported.[55]

When private speech occurs on public property, "the Establishment Clause simply is inapplicable."[56] Public officials cannot argue that religious speech must be censored because it may

---

[52]*Id.* at 1392.
[53]*Id.* at 1393.
[54]*Id.* at 1393-94 n.17.
[55]*Rivera v. Board of Regents*, 721 F. Supp. 1189, 1195 (D. Col. 1989).
[56]*Id.*

be divisive or offensive. One federal court of appeals was right on when it observed:

> The potency of religious speech is not a constitutional infirmity; the most fervently devotional and blatantly sectarian speech is protected when it is private speech in a public forum. Zealots have First Amendment rights too.[57]

In summary, publicly sponsored religious scenes are constitutional so long as within the context of the religious display there are other secular symbols. Privately sponsored religious scenes are also constitutional. There is no requirement that secular symbols be within the same context of the display. However, a disclaimer should probably be posted indicating that the display is privately sponsored.

Unfortunately some public officials mistakenly believe that censoring religion from the public square is the safest approach. City officials have removed nativity scenes under the mistaken belief that the display of religious symbols is unconstitutional. School principals have prohibited the singing of religious carols under the same misguided belief. However, rather than avoiding a constitutional violation by removing religion, these officials actually create a constitutional violation by censoring religion. Indeed, the display of religious symbols on public property and the singing of religious Christmas carols in public schools are protected by the constitutional guarantee to freedom of speech and freedom of religion. Censoring religion violates the core of our constitutional freedoms.

Other Symbols

There has been a great deal of litigation regarding the display of crosses on public property. Many crosses have been removed from water towers and from city seals.

In the city of St. Cloud, Florida, the city owned and maintained

---

[57]*Capitol Square Review and Advisory Board v. Pinette*, 30 F.3d 675, 680 (6th Cir. 1994), *aff'd*, 115 S. Ct. 2440 (1995).

a water tower on top of which was a lighted cross. This cross was not surrounded by any other object and was plainly visible throughout the entire city. A federal court ruled that this display of a Latin cross on top of a city water tower was unconstitutional.[58] Similarly, a federal court ruled that a Latin cross in a county seal was unconstitutional.[59]

In the state of California, the city of La Mesa and the city of San Diego were sued for the display of crosses. The Mt. Helix cross was erected as a memorial to a private citizen and was originally on privately-owned land on one of the highest hills in San Diego County. It was visible from a substantial distance. In 1929, the owner of this private land conveyed the property to San Diego County and the conveyance obligated the county to maintain the cross. A cross was also placed atop Mt. Soledad by private citizens on a piece of land owned by the city of San Diego. This land was dedicated as a public park in 1916.

Relying upon the California Constitution rather than the federal Constitution, the federal court ruled that both of these crosses were unconstitutional under the state's constitution. The factors considered were the religious significance of the display, the size and visibility of the display, the inclusion of other religious symbols, and the historical background of the display, as well as the proximity of the display to government buildings or religious facilities. Interestingly, after the filing of the federal lawsuit, the city of San Diego voted to authorize the sale of a fifteen square foot portion of land underneath the Mt. Soledad cross to the Mt. Soledad Memorial Association. San Diego County similarly voted to give the San Diego Historical Society the Mt. Helix cross and a thirty foot diameter partial of land beneath the cross. The effect of these transfers to private citizens meant that the crosses would no longer be on publicly-owned land, and as such, there would be no constitutional violation because constitutional limitations do not apply to individuals but only to governmental entities.

Two Illinois towns, the cities of Zion and Rolling Hills, both displayed Latin crosses in their city seals. The Illinois federal court

---

[58]*Mendelsohn v. City of St. Cloud*, 719 F. Supp. 1065 (M.D. Fla. 1989).

[59]*Friedman v. Board of County Commissioners of Beralillo County*, 781 F.2d 777 (10th Cir. 1985).

of appeals ruled that the display of these Latin crosses in the city seals violated the First Amendment Establishment Clause.[60] However, in response to this court's ruling, the city of Zion removed the Latin cross and replaced the cross with the national motto, "In God We Trust." The city seal, therefore, carried the words of the national motto. The Society of Separationists which sued the city to remove the Latin cross again sued the city to remove the national motto. However, this time the federal court ruled that the national motto, "In God We Trust," was constitutional.[61] Indeed, there are more than sixty federal cases that suggest that the national motto is constitutional.[62]

---

[60]*Harris v. City of Zion*, 927 F.2d 1401 (7th Cir. 1991).

[61]*Harris v. City of Zion*, No. 87-C-7204, slip op. (N.D. Ill. 1992).

[62]*County of Allegheny v. American Civil Liberties Union*, 492 U.S. 573 (1989); *Regan v. Time, Inc.*, 468 U.S. 641 (1984); *Lynch v. Donnelly*, 465 U.S. 668 (1984); *Marsh v. Chambers*, 463 U.S. 783 (1983); *Stone v. Graham*, 449 U.S. 39 (1980); *Wooley v. Maynard*, 430 U.S. 705 (1977); *School District of Abington Township v. Schempp*, 374 U.S. 203 (1963); *Engel v. Vitale*, 370 U.S. 421 (1962); *Sherman v. Community Consolidated School District*, 980 F.2d 437 (7th Cir. 1992), *cert. denied*, 113 S. Ct. 2439 (1993); *Americans United for Separation of Church and State v. City of Grand Rapids*, 980 F.2d 1538, (6th Cir. 1992)(en banc); *Murray v. City of Austin*, 947 F.2d 147 (5th Cir. 1991), *cert. denied*, 112 S. Ct. 3028 (1992); *North Carolina Civil Liberties Union Legal Foundation v. Constangy*, 947 F.2d 1145 (4th Cir. 1991), *cert. denied*, 112 S. Ct. 3027 (1992); *Society of Separationists, Inc. v. Herman*, 939 F.2d 1207 (5th Cir. 1991), *on rehearing*, 959 F.2d 1283 (5th Cir. 1992) (en banc), *cert. denied*, 113 S. Ct. 191 (1992); *Jones v. Clear Creek Independent School District*, 930 F.2d 416 (5th Cir. 1991), *on rehearing*, 977 F.2d 963 (5th Cir. 1992), *cert. denied*, 113 S. Ct. 2950 (1993); *Harris v. City of Zion*, 927 F.2d 1401 (7th Cir. 1991); *Doe v. Village of Crestwood*, 917 F.2d 1476 (7th Cir. 1990); *Mather v. Village of Mundelein*, 864 F.2d 1291 (7th Cir. 1989); *Jager v. Douglas County School District*, 862 F.2d 824 (11th Cir. 1989) *cert. denied*, 490 U.S. 1090 (1989); *American Jewish Congress v. City of Chicago*, 827 F.2d 120 (7th Cir. 1987); *Stein v. Plainwell Community Schools*, 822 F.2d 1406 (6th Cir. 1987); *American Civil Liberties Union v. City of Birmingham*, 791 F.2d 1561 (6th Cir. 1986); *American Civil Liberties Union of Illinois v. City of St. Charles*, 794 F.2d 265 (7th Cir. 1986); *United States v. Covelli*, 738 F.2d 847 (7th Cir. 1984), *cert. denied*, 469 U.S. 867 (1984); *Chambers v. Marsh*, 675 F.2d 228 (8th Cir. 1982); *Hall v. Bradshaw*, 630 F.2d 1018 (4th Cir. 1980), *cert. denied*, 450 U.S. 965 (1981); *Florey v. Sioux Falls School District 49-5*, 619 F.2d 1311 (8th Cir. 1980), *cert. denied*, 449 U.S. 987 (1980); *O'Hair v. Murray*, 588 F.2d 1144 (5th Cir. 1979), *cert. denied, O'Hair v. Blumenthal*, 442 U.S. 930 (1979); *United States v. Nabrit*, 554 F.2d 247 (5th Cir. 1977); *Tollett v. United States*, 485 F.2d 1087 (8th Cir. 1973); *Aronow v. United States*, 432 F.2d 242 (9th Cir. 1970); *Stevens v. Summerfield*, 257 F.2d 205 (D.C. Cir. 1958); *Doe v. Louisiana Supreme Court*, 1992 WL 373566 (E.D. La. 1992); *Carpenter v. City and County of San Francisco*, 803 F. Supp. 337 (N.D. Cal. 1992); *Sherman v. Community Consolidated School District 21 of Wheeling Township*, 758 F. Supp. 1244 (N.D. Ill. 1991); *North Carolina Civil Liberties Union v. Constangy*, 751 F. Supp. 552 (W.D.N.C. 1990); *Memorandum Opinion and Standing Rule for Courtroom of*

The issue of whether Latin crosses will remain on public property has not yet been finally decided. A federal appeals court in Texas ruled that the display of a Latin cross within a city seal was constitutional.[63] In Austin, Texas, the home of atheist Madalyn Murray O'Hair, Jon Murray, her son, brought suit against the city of Austin claiming that the Latin cross within the city seal was unconstitutional. However, the federal court ruled that the display of the Latin cross within the context of that particular city

---

William M. Acker, Jr., 1990 WL 126265 (N.D. Ala. 1990); *Allen v. Consolidated City of Jacksonville*, 719 F. Supp. 1532 (M.D. Fla. 1989), *aff'd*, 880 F.2d 420 (11th Cir. 1989); *Sherman v. Community Consolidated School District*, 714 F. Supp. 932 (N.D. Ill. 1989); *Horn & Hardart Co. v. Pillsbury Co.*, 703 F. Supp. 1062 (S.D.N.Y. 1989), *judgment aff'd*, 888 F.2d 8 (2nd Cir. 1989); *Smith v. Lindstrom*, 699 F. Supp. 549 (W.D. Va. 1988); *Jewish War Veterans of United States v. United States*, 695 F. Supp. 3 (D.D.C. 1988); *Berlin by Berlin v. Okaloosa County School District*, 1988 WL 85937 (N.D. Fla. 1988); *Shomon v. Pott*, 1988 WL 4960 (N.D. Ill. 1988); *benMiriam v. Office of Personnel Management*, 647 F. Supp. 84 (M.D.N.C. 1986); *American Jewish Congress v. City of Chicago*, 1986 WL 20750 (N.D. Ill. 1986); *Libin v. Town of Greenwich*, 625 F. Supp. 393 (D. Conn. 1985); *Greater Houston Chapter of American Civil Liberties Union v. Eckels*, 589 F. Supp. 222 (S.D. Tex. 1984); *Time, Inc. v. Regan*, 539 F. Supp. 1371 (S.D.N.Y. 1982), *aff'd in part, rev'd in part*, 468 U.S. 641 (1984); *Citizens Concerned for Separation of Church and State v. City and County of Denver*, 526 F. Supp. 1310 (D. Colo. 1981), *cert. denied*, 452 U.S. 963 (1981); *Voswinkel v. City of Charlotte*, 495 F. Supp. 588 (W.D.N.C. 1980); *McRae v. Califano*, 491 F. Supp. 630 (E.D.N.Y. 1980), *rev'd, Harris v. McRae*, 448 U.S. 297 (1980); *Citizens Concerned for Separation of Church and State v. City and County of Denver*, 481 F. Supp. 522 (D. Colo. 1979); *Gavin v. Peoples Natural Gas Co.*, 464 F. Supp. 622 (W.D. Pa. 1979), *vacated*, 613 F.2d 482 (3rd Cir. 1980); *O'Hair v. Blumenthal*, 462 F. Supp. 19 (W.D. Tex. 1978); *United States v. Handler*, 383 F. Supp. 1267 (D. Md. 1974); *Reed v. Van Hoven*, 237 F. Supp. 48 (W.D. Mich. 1965); *Crown Kosher Super Market of Mass., Inc. v. Gallagher*, 176 F. Supp. 466 (D. Mass. 1959), *rev'd*, 366 U.S. 617 (1961); *Stevens v. Summerfield*, 151 F. Supp. 343 (D.D.C. 1957); *Petition of Plywacki*, 107 F. Supp. 593 (D. Haw. 1952), *rev'd, Plywacki v. United States*, 205 F.2d 423 (9th Cir. 1953).

[63]The Supreme Court recently recognized that this issue had not yet been settled despite the fact that some of the circuit appellate courts have disagreed on the constitutionality of crosses or religious symbols within city seals. In the *City of Edmond* case, the City lost its battle to maintain its religious symbol. The City petitioned the United States Supreme Court to review the case. Though the Supreme Court refused to review the case, Justices Rehnquist, Scalia and Thomas, filed a dissent, stating that the Court should have accepted the case for review to resolve the split within the circuit courts. *City of Edmond v. Robinson*, 116 S. Ct. 1702 (1996). The Court pointed out that the case in *City of Edmond v. Robinson*, 68 F.3d 1226 (10th Cir. 1995) and the case of *Harris v. City of Zion*, 927 F.2d 1401 (7th Cir. 1991) conflicted with *Murray v. City of Austin*, 947 F.2d 147 (5th Cir. 1991). Thus, the Court pointed out that while the Seventh and Tenth Circuit Courts of Appeal found the display of religious symbols in a public seal unconstitutional, the Fifth Circuit found such a display constitutional.

seal did not violate the First Amendment Establishment Clause.[64]

The United States Supreme Court has ruled that the Ten Commandments standing alone may not be placed on a classroom bulletin board,[65] but the Ten Commandments may still be displayed on public property so long as within the same context is displayed other depictions of secular lawgivers. Commenting on the religious and secular mix, one Supreme Court Justice stated the following:

> [A] carving of Moses holding the Ten Commandments, if that is the only adornment on a courtroom wall, conveys an equivocal message, perhaps of respect for Judaism, for religion in general, or for law. The addition of carvings depicting Confucius and Mohammed may honor religion, or particular religions, to an extent that the First Amendment does not tolerate any more than it does "the permanent erection of a large Latin cross on the roof of city hall." Placement of secular figures such as Caesar Augustus, William Blackstone, Napoleon Bonaparte, and John Marshall alongside these three religious figures, however, signals respect not for great proselytizers but for great lawgivers. It would be absurd to exclude such a fitting message from a courtroom, as it would to exclude religious paintings by Italian Renaissance masters from a public museum.[66]

Thus, like a nativity scene, the display of the Ten Commandments would be permissible under current law if placed in the context of other secular laws or lawgivers. The constitutionality of any publicly sponsored religious symbol in large part depends upon the context. If within the context of the religious symbol there are other secular symbols, then the religious symbol

---

[64]*Murray v. City of Austin*, 947 F.2d 147 (5th Cir. 1991), *cert. denied*, 112 S. Ct. 3028 (1992).

[65]*Stone v. Graham*, 449 U.S. 39 (1980).

[66]*County of Allegheny*, 492 U.S. at 652 (Stevens, J., concurring in part and dissenting in part) (citations and footnote omitted).

is constitutional.[67]

In summary, the courts are presently split on whether Latin crosses on public property are constitutional. As noted under the section dealing with nativity scenes and in this section dealing with crosses, there are other ways to display religious symbols within a public setting. One way might be for governmental officials to convey parts of public land to private entities. However, another way is to display privately-owned symbols within a public forum such as a park. However, the most common and time tested approach is to place secular symbols in the context of the religious symbols.

---

[67]It is likely that the portrait of Jesus hanging in the public school hallway in Bloomingdale, Michigan would have been considered constitutional had there been other portraits of secular leaders hanging in the same hallway. A federal court found the portrait of Jesus standing alone unconstitutional. *Washegesic v. Bloomingdale Public Schools*, 33 F.3d 679 (6th Cir. 1994). The Supreme Court would consider such a situation similar to how the Ten Commandments in the United States Supreme Court would be viewed since, though the Ten Commandments occupy the prominent location in the Supreme Court building, Moses with the Ten Commandments is surrounded by other secular lawgivers.

USE OF PUBLIC FACILITIES

The use of public facilities is an important aspect of religious liberty. Use of such facilities is significant because of the number of people who gather in public areas. Unfortunately, oftentimes those charged with oversight have the mistaken idea that religious persons must be prohibited from conducting expressive activity because to allow religious expression might somehow violate the so-called separation of church and state. Sometimes this misunderstanding occurs from ignorance, and sometimes it occurs from blatant hostility or bigotry toward religion. No matter the motive, this understanding is wrong and outright unconstitutional.

Traditional Public Forums

Parks, Streets, and Sidewalks

Regarding free speech in general, and religious speech in particular, public parks, streets, and sidewalks are critical areas for the discussion of public debate. According to the United States Supreme Court, public parks, streets, and sidewalks "have immemorially been held in trust for use of the public . . . and are properly considered traditional public fora."[1] The Court has also noted that the "purpose of the public forum doctrine is to give effect to the broad command of the First Amendment to protect speech from governmental interference."[2]

Unlike a limited or designated public forum, a traditional public forum such as a park, street, or sidewalk is always open to the public and cannot be permanently closed to public use.[3] A speaker can be prohibited from using a traditional public forum only

---

[1] *Frisby v. Schultz*, 487 U.S. 474, 481 (1988). *See also Perry Education Ass'n. v. Perry Local Educators' Ass'n.*, 460 U.S. 37 (1983).

[2] *ISKCON v. Lee*, 112 S. Ct. 2711, 2717 (1992).

[3] In an interesting case, a federal court of appeals ruled that the Naturist Society, which advocated "clothing optional" lifestyles and educated the public through writings, lectures, and public demonstrations could use a Florida park near a public beach to distribute literature, circulate petitions, and display a sign because the park was a public forum. *Naturist Society, Inc. v. Fillyaw*, 958 F.2d 1515 (11th Cir. 1992).

if the government has a compelling interest and has used the least restrictive means in order to achieve that compelling interest. Reasonable content neutral[4] restrictions may be placed upon the use of a public forum such as time, place, and manner restrictions. For example, so long as the restriction has nothing to do with the content of the message, the government may allow use of a street for a parade only at certain hours so as not to interfere with rush hour traffic. However, the government cannot flatly prohibit parades.

One case which was brought to Liberty Counsel's attention dealt with a public park in Texas. The park allowed use of its facilities by the general public. However, churches were required to sign a waiver that they would not offer prayer in the public park or perform baptisms. This is clearly unconstitutional. Once brought to the attention of Liberty Counsel, the policy was quickly changed. Public parks can be used by religious groups for evangelization, drama, skits, speaking, congregating, or distributing religious literature. Streets may also be used by religious speakers for parades.

Palm Beach County in Florida learned the hard way that political and religious speech cannot be excluded from public parks. The County adopted a policy that required permission from government officials prior to engaging in political or religious speech in public parks. The ordinance also prohibited the distribution of political or religious literature. In the fall of 1994 on Labor Day weekend, Ken Connor, who was running for governor of the State of Florida, took his campaign trip through Palm Beach County. When he stopped at a public park with the intention of greeting people and passing out "Connor for Governor" literature, he was met by a police officer who told him that he could not enter the park without written permission. He was also informed that park policy prohibited the distribution of political or religious literature. Mr. Connor was an experienced trial attorney, but nothing in his career had prepared him for such a shock when he was threatened with arrest simply for distributing political literature in a public

---

[4]Content-neutral regulations are those that are "justified without reference to the content of the regulated speech." *Virginia State Board of Pharmacy v. Virginia Citizens Consumer Council*, 425 U.S. 748, 771 (1976).

park. On behalf of Mr. Connor, Liberty Counsel filed suit against Palm Beach County. The federal court ruled that the park policy was unconstitutional. First, the court ruled that public parks are traditional public forums. Second, the court stated that political and religious speech could not be excluded from a public park. Finally, the court ruled that requiring prior permission before engaging in political or religious speech in a public park is unconstitutional. The court also pointed out that had this policy been around during the time of Abraham Lincoln, Mr. Lincoln himself would apparently have been prohibited from standing on a nearby stump to talk about the political and social issues of his day.[5] Obviously, government may not prohibit political or religious speech in public parks.

Public sidewalks are traditional public forums that may be used by religious speakers. While the use of sound magnification devices may be restricted to certain levels,[6] and blocking ingress or egress is not permissible, peaceful picketing on a public sidewalk is clearly protected First Amendment activity. Simply because the government disagrees with the content of the protesters' message does not allow the government to restrict speech in a traditional public forum. Indeed, the government "may not prohibit the expression of an idea simply because society finds the idea itself offensive or disagreeable."[7] The Supreme Court has also noted that its prior cases have "consistently stressed that we are often captives outside the sanctuary of the home and subject to objectionable speech."[8] Restricting speech within a public forum based upon the content of the speech is repugnant to the Constitution. Stressing its disdain for content-based restrictions on speech, the United States Supreme Court has stated:

[A]bove all else, the First Amendment means that the

---

[5]*Connor v. Palm Beach County*, 1996 WL 438779 (May 29, 1996 S.D. FL).

[6]*Saia v. New York*, 334 U.S. 558 (1948); *Kovacs v. Cooper*, 336 U.S. 77 (1949) (anti-noise ordinances must meet the strict tests of vagueness and overbreadth); *U.S. Labor Party v. Pomerlau*, 557 F.2d 410 (4th Cir. 1977).

[7]*Simon & Schuster v. New York Crime Victims Board*, 112 S. Ct. 501, 509 (1991). *See also Cohen v. California*, 403 U.S. 15 (1971) (overturning a criminal conviction based on a breach of the peace charge for wearing a t-shirt in a public forum with the words "F— the Draft").

[8]*Cohen*, 403 U.S. at 21.

government has no power to restrict expression because of
its message, its ideas, its subject matter or its content. . .
. The essence of this forbidden censorship is content
control. Any restriction on expressive activity because of
its content would completely undercut the "profound
national commitment to the principles that debate on
public issues should be uninhibited, robust and wide
open."[9]

Sidewalks within residential neighborhoods are also considered
traditional public forums. Picketing within a residential
neighborhood is a constitutionally protected First Amendment right.
The United States Supreme Court has ruled that a person can picket
within a residential neighborhood so long as the picketing is not
targeted toward a specific residence.[10] In other words, so long as
the picketer moves about within the residential neighborhood on the
public sidewalk and does not localize the picketing activities in
front of one specific residence, the picketing is permissible speech
activity. Picketers should, therefore, continually move on the public
sidewalk within the residential neighborhood and not constantly
stand in front of the same residential address.

Limited or Designated Public Forums

Facilities such as public schools, libraries, public housing,
public arenas, or any other public facility other than parks, streets,
or sidewalks, are considered limited or designated public forums. As
mentioned earlier, parks, streets, and sidewalks are considered
traditional public forums. As such, parks, streets, and sidewalks are
always open to the public. On the other hand, limited or designated
public forums such as schools, libraries, housing facilities, or other
public facilities are governed according to the limited or designated

---

[9]*Police Department of Chicago v. Mosley*, 408 U.S. 92, 95-96 (1972) (quoting *New York Times Co. v. Sullivan*, 376 U.S. 254, 270 (1963)).

[10]*Frisby v. Schultz*, 487 U.S. 474 (1988). *See also Madsen v. Women's Health Center, Inc.*, 114 S. Ct. 2516 (1994); *Carey v. Brown*, 447 U.S. 455 (1980); *Vittitow v. City of Upper Arlington*, 830 F. Supp. 1077 (S.D. Ohio 1993) (picketing near the home of a physician who performs abortions is permissible so long as the protestors move about the neighborhood and do not solely target one residence).

public forum analysis. To be a limited or designated public forum, the public facility must intentionally open use of that facility to the general public. This is an important key to the use of these public facilities. Thus, if a public school allows use of its facilities to outside guests after school hours as a meeting place for a Rotary club or a Tupperware party, then the school is deemed to have opened its facilities for use by the general public. The same holds true for a library, which frequently opens its facilities to use by the public for meeting. Public housing facilities frequently open use of the facilities either to the residents for meeting places, and as such it would be open to residents on a general basis, or to nonresidents for outside meetings, and in such cases it would be open on a general basis to outside organizations.

In order to determine whether a public facility is a limited or designated public forum, one must consider who and what type of organizations use the facility. Once it is clear that outside persons or groups use the facilities, then it is also clear that the public facility must not discriminate against other outside organizations even if the organizations are religious in nature. Once open for use by the general public, the same analysis as is found in parks, streets, or sidewalks should be used. However, unlike in the public forum setting, the government is not required to keep the facility open to the public and can therefore close the forum so long as it closes it to all outside use. While it is open to use for the public, a speaker can be excluded only when such exclusion is necessary to serve a compelling state interest and the exclusion is narrowly drawn to achieve that interest. Of course, use of these facilities can be restricted in terms of time, place, and manner so long as the restriction has nothing to do with the content of the message and ample alternative channels of communications are available. In other words, a public school could require that use of its facilities by outside organizations occur after 4:00 p.m., or use of its facilities only includes the cafeteria, the gym, or the public school classrooms. This type of restriction is permissible so long as the same restriction is applicable to all organizations and is not applied to certain groups based on the content of a particular organization's message.

Public Schools

The landmark decision governing use of public schools by outside organizations is the United States Supreme Court's opinion in *Lamb's Chapel v. Center Moriches Union Free School District*.[11] In *Lamb's Chapel*, New York law authorized local school boards to adopt reasonable regulations permitting the after-hours use of school property for ten specified purposes. Religious purposes were not one of the ten specified. In fact, the school district, while allowing use of its facilities to secular organizations, specifically prohibited use to any group for religious purposes. A pastor of an evangelical church requested to use the school facilities in order to show a six-part film series containing lectures by Dr. James Dobson. The content of this film included traditional Christian family values. Because the content was religious, the school district denied the request.

Since the school offered use of its facilities to outside secular organizations, the United States Supreme Court agreed that the school had become a limited or designated public forum. The school argued that it was offering use of its facilities to religious groups in a nondiscriminatory manner, namely that it did not allow any religious group to use its facilities. Indeed, the principle that had already previously emerged from Supreme Court opinions was that "the First Amendment forbids the government to regulate speech in ways that favor some viewpoints or ideas at the expense of others."[12]

The school also argued that to allow use of its facilities by religious organizations would violate the First Amendment Establishment Clause because of the appearance that the school was endorsing religion. However, the United States Supreme Court rejected this argument stating that because the school offered use of its facilities to other secular organizations, "there would have been no realistic danger that the community would think that the District was endorsing religion or any particular creed, and any benefit to religion or to the Church would have been no more than

---

[11]113 S. Ct. 2141 (1993).

[12]*City Council of Los Angeles v. Taxpayers for Vincent*, 466 U.S. 789, 804 (1984).

incidental."[13] In short, the school violated the First Amendment when it offered use of its facilities to secular organizations but denied use of the same facilities to a religious organization.

The principle is clear that if a school opens its facilities to the "community for meetings and discussions during nonschool hours, then it becomes a public forum for the community" which cannot exclude religious groups.[14] Clearly, a high school cannot legally prohibit a religious group from using its auditorium when the auditorium is made available to nonreligious groups.[15] Moreover, if a school is a limited or designated public forum for outside use purposes, religious organizations such as churches may request use of the school facility to conduct, for example, a public school graduation ceremony.[16] On one occasion, a federal court ruled that the Arizona Board of Regents did not violate the First Amendment Establishment Clause when it rented the Sun Devil Stadium to an evangelist in order to conduct an evangelistic service.[17]

The Supreme Court of Delaware found that the University of Delaware's absolute ban on use of its common facilities by students for religious activities was unconstitutional.[18] The court stated that

the University cannot support its absolute ban of all religious worship on the theory that, without such a ban, University policy allowing all student groups, including religious groups, free access to dormitory common areas would necessarily violate the Establishment Clause. The Establishment cases decided by the United States Supreme Court indicate that neutrality is the safe harbor in which

---

[13]*Lamb's Chapel v. Center Moriches Union Free School District*, 113 S. Ct. 2141, 2148 (1993).

[14]*Country Hills Christian Church v. Unified School District*, 560 F. Supp. 1207 (D. Kan. 1983).

[15]*Gregoire v. Centennial School District*, 674 F. Supp. 172 (E.D. Pa. 1987); *See also Gregoire v. Centennial School District*, 907 F.2d 1366 (3rd Cir. 1990) *cert. denied*, 498 U.S. 899 (1990).

[16]*Verbena United Methodist Church v. Chilton County Board of Education*, 765 F. Supp. 704 (M.D. Ala. 1991). *See also Shumway v. Albany County School District #1*, 826 F. Supp. 1320 (D. Wyo. 1993).

[17]*Pratt v. Arizona Board of Regents*, 110 Ariz. 466, 520 P.2d 514, (Ariz. 1974).

[18]*Keegan v. University of Delaware*, 349 A.2d 14 (Del. 1975), *cert. denied*, 424 U.S. 934 (1976).

to avoid First Amendment violations: 'neutral
accommodation' of religion is permitted, while
'promotion' and 'advancement' of religion are not.
University policy without the worship ban could be
neutral towards religion and could have the primary effect
of advancing education by allowing students to meet
together in the common room of their dormitory to
exchange ideas and share mutual interests. If any religious
group or religion is accommodated or benefited thereby,
such accommodation or benefit is purely incidental, and
would not, in our judgment, violate the Establishment
Clause.[19]

One school allowed use of its facilities including a public
auditorium to outside groups for secular use but denied equal access
to a Christian group because the group might engage in religious
worship. Fortunately the Christian group understood that such
discrimination is not permissible under the Constitution. The federal
court sided with the Christian organization, and required the school
to allow use of its public auditorium for the outside Christian
organization, and further stated that the public school cannot
prohibit the Christian organization from worshipping or having
other religious activities in the public school auditorium.[20] The
basic lesson is that once public facilities are opened up to use for
secular organizations, the same facilities must also allow access to
religious organizations. The public facility cannot limit the religious
use to only innocuous speech but must also allow worship. To draw
the line between where worship begins and ends is impossible. To
permit such line drawing is itself unconstitutional.

Some schools have charged rental fees for use of their facilities
by religious organizations. Additionally, some schools have allowed
churches to use their facilities as places of worship only if the
church has a building permit or is actively seeking another site with
the intention of moving from the public school. In *Fairfax Covenant*

---

[19]*Id.* at 16 (citations omitted).
[20]*Gregorire v. Centennial School Dist.*, 907 F.2d 1366 (3rd Cir. 1990).

Church v. Fairfax County School Board,[21] the school board allowed a church to use its facilities as a place of worship. In addition to allowing the church to use its facilities for Sunday worship, an array of other community groups were also allowed to rent the facilities during weeknights and weekends. However, the regulation governing use of the school facilities stated that "church/religious groups may be authorized usage after five years of use at increasing rental values until the full commercial rates become effective in the ninth year of use." Thus, for the first five rental years, churches were permitted to rent school facilities at the same rate as all other groups. However, after five years only churches were required to pay the higher rate. Moreover, the school policy required churches to provide "satisfactory evidence of progress towards the construction or acquisition of a church site."[22] No other rental group was required to make such a showing.

The school board argued that it must treat religious groups differently from secular groups, especially when religious groups use the facilities on a long term basis, because to do otherwise would violate the First Amendment Establishment Clause. The court reasoned that since the school facilities were open to other community groups, the school had created a limited or designated public forum. The court noted that "religious speech cannot be barred from a limited public forum simply because it is religious speech."[23] Indeed, a limited or designated public forum "does not confer any imprimatur of state approval on religious sects or practices."[24] The court stated that "by creating a forum generally open for use by various groups, the Fairfax County School Board does not thereby endorse or promote any of the particular ideas aired there."[25] The court further noted that "First Covenant Church cannot be treated differently from other groups that use the forum simply because of the content of its speech."[26] The court warned that to single out a religious organization as opposed to a secular

[21]*Fairfax Covenant Church v. Fairfax County School Board,* 811 F. Supp. 1137 (E.D. Va. 1993).
[22]*Id.* at 1138.
[23]*Id.* at 1139.
[24]*Widmar v. Vincent,* 454 U.S. 263, 274 (1981).
[25]*Fairfax Covenant Church,* 811 F. Supp. at 1139.
[26]*Id.*

organization would not only violate the Free Speech Clause but would also violate the Free Exercise Clause of the First Amendment.[27] Certainly "the government may not impose special disabilities on the basis of religious views or religious status."[28] Courts must "strictly scrutinize governmental classifications based on religion."[29] Finally, the court rejected the school's argument that it must exclude the religious organization in order to not violate the First Amendment Establishment Clause. Since the school offered use of its facilities to other secular groups, offering such use to a religious group does not in any way violate the First Amendment Establishment Clause or raise any church/state problems. The court further rejected the idea that it was providing a monetary benefit to the school. The court noted that "the Supreme Court has also ruled that it does not violate the Establishment Clause for religious groups to partake of governmental financial benefits that are available for everyone."[30] The result of the *Fairfax Covenant Church* case was that the policy requiring increased rent and evidence of progress toward the construction or acquisition of a church site was ruled unconstitutional. Since the school had overcharged the church $235,000.00, the court ordered that the money be refunded.

The Gideons have had a long tradition of coming on public school campuses to distribute Bibles to students. Though students clearly have the right to distribute Bibles to others students, Gideons may or may not have that right depending upon the circumstances.

---

[27]*Id.* (relying on *Employment Division v. Smith*, 494 U.S. 872 (1990)).

[28]*Smith*, 494 U.S. at 877.

[29]*Id.* at 886, n.3.

[30]*Fairfax Covenant Church*, 811 F. Supp. at 1141 (citing *Mueller v. Allen*, 463 U.S. 388 (1983)) (upholding the Minnesota tax deduction for student expenses at all schools including parochial schools); *Witters v. Washington Department of Services for the Blind*, 474 U.S. 481 (1986) (rejecting a claim by the State of Washington that it was required to ban a blind person from a state program funding the college educations of blind people because he wanted to go to a Bible college); *Bowen v. Kendrick*, 487 U.S. 589 (1988) (upholding a federal program to teach sexual chastity to teenagers that funded many secular as well as religious groups to promote that goal); *Walz v. Tax Commission*, 397 U.S. 664 (1970). Another case which could be cited, but which was not because it was not decided until after *Fairfax Covenant Church*, is the United States Supreme Court decision in *Zobrest v. Catalina Foothills School District*, 113 S. Ct. 2462 (1993) (providing government funds for the services of an interpreter to a student attending a religious school does not violate the Establishment Clause).

Students have the right to distribute literature including Bibles because students are rightfully on campus, and in fact commanded to be there. However, when considering the use of public school facilities by outside persons or organizations, there is no absolute right to be on campus. However, the same analysis used in a limited or designated public forum must be considered with respect to Gideon distribution of Bibles. For example, if a school allows use of its facilities after school hours to any secular organization, it must also allow use of that facility to a religious organization. The difference with Gideon distribution of Bibles is that it usually occurs during school hours, rather than after school hours. The unique aspect here is that the Gideons actually distribute the Bibles to the students. Though some courts have ruled that Gideon distribution of Bibles is unconstitutional,[31] others have ruled that Gideons may distribute Bibles to public school students.[32] To determine whether Gideons distributing Bibles to public school students is constitutional, three factors must be considered. First, if the school allows other outside organizations to come on campus to distribute information to public school students, then the school has probably created a limited or designated public forum and therefore cannot prohibit religious persons or groups from coming on campus to distribute their literature. Second, the place of distribution is probably also important. It is probably better to distribute the material in the hallways from a table so that willing students may approach and those who are not interested may pass. Distributing the Bibles to all of the school students in class may be considered by some courts unconstitutional. It is probably better to make the Bibles available from a stationary table. In this manner an announcement could be made indicating that the literature is available but that no student is required or compelled to accept the material. Finally, the time of the distribution may also be important.

---

[31]See e.g., Berger v. Rensselaer Central School Corp., 982 F.2d 1160 (7th Cir.), cert. denied, 113 S. Ct. 2344 (1993); Bacon v. Bradley-Bourbonnais High School Dist. No. 307, 707 F. Supp. 1005 (C.D. Ill. 1989); Goodwin v. Cross County School Dist. No. 7, 394 F. Supp. 417 (E.D. Ark. 1973).

[32]Meltzer v. Board of Public Instruction of Orange County, 548 F.2d 559 (5th Cir. 1977) and 577 F.2d 311 (5th Cir. 1978) (en banc); Peck v. Upshur County Board of Educ., 941 F. Supp. 1465 (N.D. W.Va. 1996); Schanou v. Lancaster County School Dist. No. 160, 863 F. Supp. 1048 (D. Neb. 1994).

The timing should probably be just before or just after the official school day begins or ends. In this manner students coming to class or leaving class may voluntarily pick up material from a designated table.

In summary, if a school allows other outside organizations to come on campus to distribute material to the public school students, then the school has opened a forum for the distribution of material by other religious persons or organizations. The distribution should probably occur outside of the classroom and probably is best done before or after the official school day begins. The materials should be put on a designated table so that individuals would not be coerced into accepting the literature. In this manner one student can voluntarily approach the table while another student can continue on their intended course.

Public Libraries

Public libraries are governed by the same analysis used above for public schools. Both are public facilities. Whenever a public library opens its facilities for use by the general public, it creates a designated or limited public forum. When this occurs, religious organizations must receive equal treatment. Unfortunately, many libraries retain unconstitutional policies that specifically prohibit use of facilities by political or religious organizations. These policies violate the First Amendment.

Concerned Women for America, came face to face with one of these discriminatory policies in Mississippi. The library had created a limited or designated public forum. A library policy allowed outside persons to use its facilities for meetings of a "civic, cultural or educational character." However, the library policy specifically excluded use of its facilities by religious groups. The federal court rightfully found that this was a violation of the First Amendment.[33]

Public Housing Facilities

Almost every city or county contains some form of public

---

[33]*Concerned Women for America v. Lafayette County and*, 883 F.2d 32, 34 (5th Cir. 1989).

housing facilities. Often these facilities have general meeting rooms. These general meeting rooms are used by the residents, and frequently these meeting places are made available to the general public.

Sometimes religious tenants or outside religious groups have been discriminated against when attempting to use these type of public facilities. The analysis in a public housing facility is basically the same as for schools and libraries. The only difference is whether the person requesting the meeting is a tenant or a nontenant. For example, a public housing facility can allow use of its facilities by tenants only and thereby exclude all nontenants. That would be permissible under the First Amendment because it seems reasonable to accommodate the tenants over and above the nontenants. It would probably be unreasonable to allow use of the facilities by nontenants while excluding the tenants.

If use of the facilities is allowed for tenants, then there must be no discrimination based upon the content of the tenant's speech. Tenants who use such a facility for religious Bible studies or religious purposes should be allowed the same use of the facility as tenants who use it for secular purposes. Likewise, if use of the facilities is offered to nontenants, a nontenant speaker should be treated equally even if the content of the speech is religious.

A tenant living in a public housing facility in Atlanta wanted to use the facility to conduct a Bible study. Though the housing authority allowed use of its facilities by tenants for secular purposes, it tried to discriminate against this tenant. Part of the reasoning was that the use of the facilities by tenants should benefit all tenants rather than just a few. After several requests, a representative of the housing authority agreed to allow use of the facilities for a Bible study on Friday evenings. However, since many of the tenants were elderly, the Friday evening time was not convenient in that most were in their homes at that time. Over the objection of the tenant, the housing authority would not change its position. Consequently, the tenant conducted the Bible study anyway during the day at another time. The housing authority called the police and had the tenant arrested for conducting a Bible study. The federal court of appeals ruled that the housing authority violated the First Amendment by limiting the time for the Bible study to a Friday night when it did not equally apply this time limitation to other secular usages.[34] If the housing authority allows use of its facilities by tenants or nontenants for secular purposes, it must offer its facilities on an equal basis to tenants or nontenants who seek to conduct religious meetings.

In one case a Tallahassee housing authority allowed use of its facilities by tenants and nontenants for secular meetings. One day when a Christian organization was conducting a meeting, the director of the facility noted that the leader of the group was reading from the Bible. He interrupted the meeting and later told the leader that he did not want any "Jesus stuff" in his facility. Liberty Counsel worked for several months with the organization to no avail. After filing a federal lawsuit, the Tallahassee Housing Authority agreed to allow the tenants and non-tenants equal access to its facilities. In a similar case, a nursing home in Albuquerque, New Mexico, refused to allow a showing of the film *Jesus*. This film was prepared by Campus Crusade for Christ and has been translated in more languages than any other film in history. The *Jesus* film has been shown throughout the United States and the world. Amazingly, a residential facility refused to allow the film on the basis that it would violate the "separation of church and state." A federal court of appeals ruled that the public facility violated the Constitution by discriminating against the film solely because of its Christian content.[35]

Shopping Malls

The issue of shopping malls has proved to be difficult for the United States Supreme Court. If the shopping mall is owned by a governmental entity, then the first consideration is whether the government has opened use of the shopping mall to outside persons for expressive activity. If so, those desiring access to the government-owned facility cannot be turned away simply because the content of their speech is religious.

However, most shopping malls are privately owned. As such,

---

[34]*Crowder v. Housing Authority of the City of Atlanta*, 990 F.2d 586 (11th Cir. 1993).

[35]*Church on the Rock v. City of Albuquerque*, 84 F.3d 1273 (10th Cir. 1996). Even after the public facility lost its battle at the federal court of appeals level, it took an emergency petition to the United States Supreme Court in a final attempt to block the film. The Supreme Court rejected their request to hear the case. Later the film *Jesus* was shown without incident.

there is no government action in the purest sense and, therefore, no application of the First Amendment. Notwithstanding, the issue has not been clear from its inception.

The United States Supreme Court developed a doctrine known as the "public function doctrine" which is distinguished from the public forum doctrine. One authority describes it as follows:

> It is now clear that constitutional limitations on state activities restrict the manner in which governmental functions are conducted. If private persons are engaged in the exercise of governmental functions their activities are subject to similar constitutional restrictions. The state cannot free itself from the limitations of the Constitution in the operations of its governmental functions merely by delegating certain functions to otherwise private individuals. If private actors assume the role of the state by engaging in these governmental functions then they subject themselves to the same limitations on their freedom of action as would be imposed upon the state itself.[36]

The fact that a private person engages in activity that could be performed by a governmental entity does not transform the activity into a public function. Only "those activities or functions which are traditionally associated with sovereign governments, and which are operated almost exclusively by governmental entities . . . will be deemed public functions."[37]

In 1946, the United States Supreme Court considered a case involving a "company town" which was a privately-owned area including residential and commercial districts. The Golf Shipbuilding Corporation owned and governed the area but had no direct connections with governmental authorities. Jehovah's Witnesses wished to distribute religious literature in the area but were prohibited from doing so. The Supreme Court stated that this prohibition against literature distribution violated the First

---

[36]Nowak, Rotunda, and Young, 5th Ed. *Constitutional Law* 477-78 (1995).
[37]*Id.*

Amendment.[38] The Court reasoned that the state allowed private ownership of land and property to such a degree as to allow the private corporation to replace all the functions and activities which would normally belong to a city. Since the area served as an equivalent of a community shopping district in a city, the First Amendment applied.

The Court considered a similar issue in 1968. The Logan Valley Plaza was a privately-owned shopping center where striking laborers attempted to picket a store during a labor dispute. The Supreme Court ruled that the shopping center was the functional equivalent of a company town and therefore the picketers were protected by the First Amendment.[39] The Supreme Court in *Lloyd Corporation* altered its opinion in 1972 when confronted with a group of anti-war demonstrators who desired to enter a private shopping mall to distribute literature. The Supreme Court attempted to distinguish this case from the two previous cases on the basis that in *Logan Valley Plaza* the labor picketing was directly related to the shopping mall, but here the anti-war literature distribution was not related to the shopping center's purpose, and consequently, the private mall could prohibit the literature distribution.[40]

Finally, in 1976, the Supreme Court ruled in *Hudgens* that the First Amendment does not apply to privately-owned shopping centers. Unfortunately, the members of the Court could not agree on how they reached that decision. A majority agreed that the result in denying the application of the First Amendment to a private shopping mall was permissible in this particular case.[41] Justice Stevens did not take part in the decision. Two Justices wrote opinions concurring in the result but specifically mentioned that the prior Supreme Court decision in *Logan Valley Plaza* was not overruled while two other Justices dissented relying upon the prior decision in *Logan Valley Plaza*.

One other case is relevant to this inquiry. In 1980, the United States Supreme Court in *Pruneyard Shopping Center* considered a case involving provisions of the California state constitution which

---

[38]*Marsh v. Alabama*, 326 U.S. 501 (1946).
[39]*Amalgamated Food Employees Union v. Logan Valley Plaza*, 391 U.S. 308 (1968).
[40]*Lloyd Corp. v. Tanner*, 407 U.S. 551 (1972).
[41]*Hudgens v. National Labor Relations Board*, 424 U.S. 507 (1976).

specifically granted access for free speech purposes to privately-owned property. The private property owners argued that this state constitutional provision violated their Due Process rights under the federal constitution. The Supreme Court ruled that the state constitutional provision did not violate Due Process or the unlawful taking of property.[42] The Supreme Court noted that its 1976 ruling in *Hudgens* did not preclude a state from granting free speech protection in privately-owned shopping centers.

As is clear from the analysis above, the private shopping center issue is far from settled. Clearly, if a shopping center is a governmentally-owned institution, the First Amendment is applicable, and presumably literature could be distributed at such malls. Verbal discussion should clearly be permitted at such malls. If the shopping center is privately-owned, the United States Supreme Court's position is somewhat murky. If the shopping mall is performing a public function, presumably the First Amendment would apply. However, if the shopping mall is solely private in nature, the most recent Supreme Court opinion holds that the First Amendment would not be applicable. The Supreme Court also has ruled, however, that states may grant protection to free speech and association at privately-owned shopping malls. Several states currently grant free speech access to privately-owned facilities.

While the federal constitution may not afford a general right to free speech in privately-owned shopping centers, at least six states have found such a constitutional right under their state constitutions. These states include California,[43] Colorado,[44] Massachusetts,[45] New Jersey,[46] Oregon,[47] and Washington.[48] However, several

---

[42]*Pruneyard Shopping Center v. Robins*, 447 U.S. 74 (1980) (California's State Constitution prohibited the use of trespass laws by shopping center owners to exclude peaceful distribution of literature and petitions in the mall area of the shopping center).

[43]*Robins v. PruneYard Shopping Center*, 592 P.2d 341, 347 (Cal. 1979) *aff'd*, 447 U.S. 74 (1980).

[44]*Bock v. Westminster Mall Co.*, 819 P.2d 55 (Colo. 1991).

[45]*Batchelder v. Allied Stores International*, 445 N.E.2d 590, 593 (Mass. 1983).

[46]*New Jersey Coalition Against War in the Middle East v. J.M.B. Realty Corp.*, 650 A.2d 757 (N.J. 1994); *State v. Schmid*, 423 A.2d 615 (N.J. 1980), *appeal dismissed sub. nom. Princeton University v. Schmid*, 455 U.S. 100 (1982).

[47]*Lloyd Corp. v. Whiffen*, 849 P.2d 446, 453-54 (Or. 1993).

[48]*Alderwood Associates v. Washington Environmental Council*, 635 P.2d 108 (Wash. 1981).

other states that have considered this matter found no state constitutional basis for allowing expressive activity on private property. These states include Arizona,[49] Connecticut,[50] Georgia,[51] Michigan,[52] New York,[53] North Carolina,[54] Ohio,[55] Pennsylvania,[56] South Carolina,[57] and Wisconsin.[58] Most of the state courts that found no constitutional right to engage in expressive activity on private property analyzed their state constitutions.[59] However, some relied primarily on federal constitutional doctrine without independently analyzing their own state constitutions.[60]

California,[61] Colorado,[62] Massachusetts,[63] New Jersey,[64] Oregon,[65] and Washington[66] have held that their citizens have a constitutional right to engage in certain types of expressive conduct at privately-owned malls. Of these six, only California and New Jersey found that their state constitutional right to free speech protects citizens from private action as well as state action and grants issue-oriented free speech rights at regional shopping centers. The other four states have granted limited access to private shopping centers for expressive activity. For example, Massachusetts only permits political speech in private shopping centers on the basis that its state constitution places high priority on free elections and the right of its citizens to elect officers to public

---

[49]*Fiesta Mall Venture v. Mecham Recall Committee*, 767 P.2d 719 (Ariz. Ct. App. 1989).
[50]*Cologne v. Westfarms Associates*, 469 A.2d 1201 (Conn. 1984).
[51]*Citizens for Ethical Government v. Gwinnett Place Association*, 392 S.E.2d 8 (Ga. 1990).
[52]*Woodland v. Michigan Citizens Lobby*, 378 N.W.2d 337 (Mich. 1995).
[53]*SHAD Alliance v. Smith Haven Mall*, 488 N.E.2d 1211 (N.Y. 1985).
[54]*State v. Felmet*, 273 S.E.2d 708 (N.C. 1981).
[55]*Eastwood Mall v. Slanco*, 626 N.E.2d 59 (Ohio 1994).
[56]*Western Pennsylvania Socialist Workers 1982 Campaign v. Connecticut Gen. Life Ins. Co.*, 515 A.2d 1331 (Pa. 1986).
[57]*Charleston Joint Venture v. McPherson*, 417 S.E.2d 544 (S.C. 1992).
[58]*Jacobs v. Major*, 407 N.W.2d 832 (Wis. 1987).
[59]*E.g., SHAD Alliance*, 488 N.E.2d at 1211; *Eastwood Mall*, 626 N.E.2d at 59.
[60]*E.g., Citizens for Ethical Government*, 392 S.E.2d at 8; *Felmet*, 273 S.E.2d at 708.
[61]*Robins*, 592 P.2d at 347.
[62]*Bock*, 819 P.2d at 55.
[63]*Batchelder*, 445 N.E.2d at 590.
[64]*New Jersey Coalition*, 650 A.2d at 757.
[65]*Lloyd Corp.*, 849 P.2d at 446.
[66]*Alderwood Associates*, 635 P.2d at 108.

office.[67] The Massachusetts Supreme Court did not base its ruling on the state's constitutional free speech provision, but instead focused on another state constitutional provision which guarantees free elections and the right to be elected. The political activity in the Massachusetts case involved a person's attempt to solicit signatures for his nomination as a congressional candidate. The Massachusetts court ruled that shopping centers must permit solicitation of signatures for ballot access because of its fundamental importance to the state's form of government. The court ruling is so far limited to that narrow issue. The court also stated that shopping centers may impose reasonable regulations as to time, place and manner with respect to the solicitation of signatures.

Like Massachusetts, Oregon also relied on state constitutional provisions other than free speech. The specific provision the Oregon court relied upon was the state constitution's "free-and-equal elections" provision[68] and the initiative and referendum provision.[69] Like Massachusetts, Oregon so far appears to limit distribution of literature or solicitation of signatures in private shopping centers to political issues. Colorado relied upon its state constitution's free speech provision when finding that a political activist had a constitutional right to distribute literature at a privately-owned mall.[70] Like the United States Supreme Court, the state of Washington has vacillated on this issue. However, it still appears that the Washington state constitution provides some right to distribute literature or solicit signatures at private shopping malls.[71]

---

[67]*Batchelder*, 445 N.E.2d at 590.

[68]*Id.* at 593.

[69]*Lloyd Corp.*, 849 P.2d at 453-54.

[70]*Bock*, 819 P.2d at 55.

[71]In *Alderwood Associates*, 635 P.2d at 108, a majority of the Washington Supreme Court ruled that it was improper to issue a court order against a group seeking to collect signatures at a private shopping mall. However, a four-justice plurality, rather than a majority, concluded that the state's constitutional free speech clause did not require state action. In other words, the state's free speech provision not only applied to government actors, but to private shopping centers, thereby prohibiting private shopping centers from excluding free speech. Later in the case of *Southcenter Joint Venture v. National Democratic Policy Committee*, 780 P.2d 1282 (Wash. 1989), the Washington Supreme Court, in a deeply divided decision, rejected the four-justice plurality position in *Alderwood*, and instead held that the state's free speech provision does not protect speech on private property. Interestingly, the opinion in *Southcenter* did not disturb or reverse the remainder of the holding in *Alderwood*

Some courts have ruled that a shopping center "now performs a traditional public function by providing the functional equivalent of a town center or community business block."[72] In 1950 there were fewer than 100 privately-owned shopping centers throughout the country.[73] The number of larger regional shopping malls grew to 105 by 1967. This number continued to grow to 199 in 1972 and 333 in 1978.[74] Shopping centers continued to expand to at least 1,835 by the year 1992.[75] During the 20-year time period from 1972 to 1992, the number of regional shopping centers grew by approximately 800%. A New Jersey court remarked that "malls are where the people can be found today."[76] The shopping center industry frequently refers to large shopping malls as "the new downtowns."[77]

One industry expert observed the following:

> The suburban victory in the regional retail war was epitomized by the enclosed regional mall. . . . [Regional malls] serve as the new "main streets" of the region -- the dominant form of general merchandise retailing.[78]

Associates -- that in fact there is a right to solicit signatures on private property under the state constitution's initiative provision. In other words, while it appears that there is no right under Washington state's free speech provision to solicit signatures in a private shopping mall, there still remains a right to solicit signatures under the state constitution's initiative provision. At present it appears that the Washington Supreme Court's position is that the state constitution's free speech clause does not grant a right to solicit signatures or distribute literature at private shopping malls, but the state constitution does provide a right to solicit signatures for certain political issues under the state constitution's initiative provision. Thus, the right to distribute literature or solicit signatures in private shopping malls in Washington appears to be limited to ballot initiatives.

[72]*Alderwood Associates*, 635 P.2d at 117. *But see Southcenter Joint Venture*, 780 P.2d at 1282.

[73]Steven J. Eagle, *Shopping Center Control: The Developer Besieged*, 51 J. URB. L. 585, 586 (1974).

[74]Thomas Muller, *Regional Malls and Central City Retail Sales: An Overview*, SHOPPING CENTERS: USA 180, 189 (1991).

[75]*Shopping Center World/NRB 1992 Shopping Center Census*, SHOPPING CENTER WORLD, Mar. 1993, at 38 n.8.

[76]*New Jersey Coalition Against War in the Middle East v. J.M.B. Realty Corp.*, 650 A.2d 757, 765 (N.J. 1994).

[77]Note, *Private Abridgment of Speech in the State Constitutions*, 90 YALE L.J. 165, 168 n.19 (1980) (citation omitted).

[78]James W. Hughes and George Sternlieb, 3 *Rutgers Regional Report*, RETAILING IN REGIONAL MALLS 71 (1991).

Another expert has pointed out that shopping centers have "evolved beyond the strictly retail stage to become a public square where people gather" and such malls provide "a place for exhibitions that no other space can offer."[79]

Several legal commentators have written that today's shopping malls are the functional equivalent of yesterday's downtown business districts. One commentator stated that "privately-owned shopping centers are supplanting those traditional public business districts where free speech once flourished."[80] Indeed, the "privately held shopping center now serves as the public trading area for much of metropolitan America."[81] While it seems obvious that today's privately-owned regional shopping malls perform the functional equivalent of yesterday's downtown business districts, not all courts agree. In fact, one court specifically noted that shopping malls "are not the functional equivalent of towns."[82] Though in reality privately-owned regional shopping malls have supplanted yesterday's town forums, courts have been reluctant to extend free speech rights to these facilities primarily because of their privately-owned nature. There is an inherent tension between the shrinking of the town forum with its reemergence in privately-owned shopping malls, and government intrusion into privately-owned businesses.

In summary, six states allow some free speech activity in private shopping centers. In California and New Jersey there is a state constitutional free speech right to distribute political and non-political literature in private shopping malls. Colorado provides a state constitutional free speech right to distribute political literature in private malls. It is possible that Colorado courts might extend this right to non-political literature. Massachusetts, Oregon and Washington offer a state constitutional right to distribute literature and solicit signatures regarding political elections and ballot access. This right is not based on free speech and has not yet been extended to political issues in general, or to non-political issues.

---

[79]*Specialty Malls Return to the Public Square Image*, SHOPPING CENTER WORLD, Nov. 1995, at 104.

[80]James M. McCauley, *Transforming the Privately-Owned Shopping Center Into a Public Forum: PruneYard Shopping Center v. Robin*, 15 U. RICH. L. REV. 699, 721 (1981).

[81]Note, *Private Abridgment of Speech and the State Constitutions*, 90 YALE L.J. at 168.

[82]*Fiesta Mall Venture*, 767 P.2d at 724.

The Supreme Court seems to be confused on this matter in general.

Public Arenas

Public arenas may be considered designated or limited public forums if the facilities are opened to certain expressive activities. If these facilities are not open to any expressive activities, they may be analyzed under a nonpublic forum analysis outlined below. Many public stadiums allow private citizens to hang banners in the seating area. We've all seen these banners during Monday night football supporting or opposing a particular team.

In the city of Cincinnati a baseball fan whose religious sign was confiscated by stadium security officials during a World Series game filed a lawsuit challenging the constitutionality of the team's banner policy. The banner policy permitted fans to hang signs only if they were in "good taste." A federal court found this policy was unconstitutionally vague and overbroad and therefore ruled in favor of the religious banner.[83]

A football fan who regularly attended RFK Stadium to watch the Washington Redskins claimed that his constitutional rights were violated when stadium officials removed his banner.[84] This football fan hung the banner with the scripture verse "John 3:16" in the end zone area so that it would be clearly visible on television. Stadium officials removed the banner because of its religious content. Since stadium officials did allow other secular banners to be placed within the stadium by private fans, the stadium was prohibited from restricting the banner solely because of its religious message.

In Fargo, North Dakota, Martin Wishnatsky sought to distribute small pamphlet Bibles to people entering the 30,000-seat Fargodome. Mr. Wishnatsky wanted to distribute these pamphlet Bibles on a public area located at the entrance to the Fargodome. The Fargodome attracts people from three surrounding states. People come for rock concerts, Christian concerts, football games, and other public events. Fargo officials threatened to arrest Mr. Wishnatsky if he did not cease distributing his Bibles. Liberty

---

[83] *Aubrey v. City of Cincinnati*, 815 F. Supp. 1100 (S.D. Ohio 1993).
[84] *Stewart v. District of Columbia Armory Board*, 863 F.2d 1013 (D.C. Cir. 1988).

Counsel filed suit against the Fargodome Authority and the City of Fargo, claiming that Mr. Wishnatsky had a constitutional right to distribute the Bibles. After the lawsuit was filed, city officials cooperated with Liberty Counsel to draft a new policy. The first month after the policy was put into place, Martin distributed 1,000 Bibles. In the second and third months after the policy was adopted, he distributed another 1,000 Bibles each month for a total of 3,000 Bibles over a period of three months. Martin continually goes to the Fargodome since the policy was adopted and distributes these Bibles to thousands of people who attend the public events within the Fargodome.

Public arenas may be analyzed under a traditional public forum, a designated or limited public forum, or nonpublic forum analysis. The analysis under a traditional public forum would occur on the public sidewalk area or entrance ways surrounding the arena. A limited or designated forum analysis would occur if there are certain places that do not fall within the traditional public forum context (streets, sidewalks or parks), but which the facility has opened for use to the general public. A nonpublic forum analysis would generally only occur if the distribution took place inside the facility at a location that is not generally open to expressive activities. At any rate, public forums provide a unique opportunity for expressive activity.

Other Public Facilities

Other public facilities which do not fall into the category of parks, streets, or sidewalks, or which are not specifically mentioned above, can also be considered limited or designated public forums. Such facilities can be any public place that allows use by the community. This applies to buildings or nonbuildings. For example, a court ruled that a rotunda in a state capitol was a limited or designated public forum if expressive activities such as political, religious, or other varieties of symbolic speech had been permitted in the past.[85] A public fair may also be an ideal location for

---

[85]*Chabad-Lubavitch of Georgia v. Miller*, 5 F.3d 1383 (11th Cir. 1993) (en banc).

evangelization.[86]

Nonpublic Forums

Airports, Metros, Rails and Bus Stations

Airports, metros, rail stations, and bus stations are ideal places for First Amendment expressive activity. Millions of people traverse through these public transportation facilities every year, many of them from around the country, and many from around the world. Such places are ideal locations for distributing religious literature.

An airport does not fall into the category of a traditional public forum such as a public park, street, or sidewalk. Consequently, its facilities are not automatically deemed to be open to the public. Moreover, airports, like the other forms of public transportation facilities, generally do not intentionally open their facilities for expressive activity by outside organizations and therefore are not considered limited or designated public forums. The third type of a public forum is known as a nonpublic forum. In nonpublic forums, the government regulation "need only be reasonable, as long as the regulation is not an effort to suppress the speaker's activity due to disagreement with the speaker's view."[87]

A restriction on speech in a nonpublic forum is reasonable when it is consistent with the government's legitimate interest in preserving the property for the use to which it is lawfully dedicated.[88] With respect to the regulation of the distribution of literature at airport facilities or other transportation facilities, "the reasonableness inquiry is not whether the restrictions on speech are consistent with preserving the property for air travel, but whether they are reasonably related to maintaining the multi-purpose that the authority has deliberately created."[89]

The Los Angeles International Airport formerly had a policy

---

[86]*Heffron v. ISKCON*, 452 U.S. 640 (1981). This case involved a state fair which designated a specific location for the distribution or sales of literature for both secular and religious groups. The Krishna group wanted to be in a different location, but the court upheld the place regulation because it was applied evenly to secular and religious groups.

[87]*ISKCON v. Lee*, 112 S. Ct. 2711, 2705 (1992).

[88]*Id.* at 2712.

[89]*Id.* at 2713.

that prohibited all First Amendment activities within any of the airport facilities. When Jews for Jesus wanted to distribute religious literature, they were unable to do so because of this restriction. The United States Supreme Court ruled that this restriction on free speech was unreasonable and consequently violated the First Amendment.[90]

In a case involving the International Society for Krishna Consciousness, the United States Supreme Court ruled that the New York Airport Authority could prohibit solicitation of funds at the airport facilities, but could not prohibit the distribution of literature, because to do so would violate the First Amendment. The court noted that

> Leafletting does not entail the same kinds of problems presented by face-to-face solicitation. Specifically, "[o]ne need not ponder the contents of a leaflet or pamphlet in order to mechanically take it out of someone's hand. . . . 'The distribution of literature does not require that the recipient stop in order to receive the message the speaker wishes to convey; instead the recipient is free to read the message at a later time.'" With the possible exception of avoiding litter, it is difficult to point to any problems intrinsic to the act of leafletting that would make it naturally incompatible with a large, multipurpose forum such as those at issue here.[91]

In ruling that airports cannot prohibit the distribution of religious literature, the Supreme Court looked at the nature and character of the airport. Airports are often, in a sense, like small cities. Many airports have restaurants, banking facilities, retail facilities, newspapers, and some even have hotel accommodations. These airports look, act, and sound like small cities. However, the Court did not classify modern airports as traditional public forums simply because they have not been around as long as traditional public parks, streets, or sidewalks. Yet the nature and character of

---

[90]*Board of Airport Commissioners of Los Angeles v. Jews for Jesus*, 482 U.S. 569 (1987).
[91]*ISKCON v. Lee*, 112 S. Ct. at 2713-2714 (citing *United States v. Kokinda*, 497 U.S. 720, 734 (1990)).

these airports are very similar to traditional public forums. They provide a place for many people to meet, conduct business, and make transactions. They have sidewalks around the facilities and hallways for congregating. They have benches, restroom facilities, and for all practical purposes, operate like traditional public forums.

In one case which came to the attention of Liberty Counsel, the Orlando International Airport allowed literature distribution with certain strict and unreasonable requirements. The airport required that anyone seeking to distribute literature must fill out a lengthy application form and must wait at least three days prior to approval. The application form also required that the person distributing literature obtain $500,000.00 in liability insurance naming the City of Orlando and the Greater Orlando Aviation Authority as additional insureds, and wear a name badge identifying their name, home address, height, age, weight, eye color, hair color, principal occupation, and organization affiliation, if applicable. During an international conference by the Gideon Bible Society, one particular Gideon was unable to obtain the $500,000.00 liability insurance policy. After correspondence between Liberty Counsel and the airport, the liability insurance policy was dropped from $500,000.00 to $100,000.00. However, other individuals seeking to distribute literature could not obtain this policy. On behalf of Tom and Shirley Snyder, Liberty Counsel then filed suit against the Orlando International Airport. After the filing of the suit, the airport dropped these restrictive requirements. In one year, Orlando International Airport transports through its facilities approximately twenty-four million people. Many of these visitors to Orlando are from foreign countries visiting the entertainment facilities in central Florida. In order to understand the magnitude of twenty-four million, compare that to the total population of the state of Florida which is over thirteen million. In other words, almost two times the population of the state of Florida traverses through the Orlando International Airport every year. Religious literature given to these individuals literally goes around the entire world. The same can be true for other airports and other major locations for public transportation. By the way, the Snyders still go to the airport at least once per month to distribute gospel tracts.

The same analysis applied to airports can be applied to metro or subway systems, railway systems, and bus stations. These facilities are very similar to airport facilities. In fact, one court ruled that literature distribution cannot be prohibited by the Massachusetts Bay Transportation Authority within the subway system.[92] The Authority prohibited the distribution of any printed materials for political or nonprofit purposes, prohibiting all noncommercial expressive activities from the paid areas of the subway stations and from the free areas of at least twelve stations. Within the free areas of the remaining stations, the Authority required prior authorization to engage in noncommercial speech. For many years, Jews for Jesus had distributed religious literature throughout the paid areas of the transit system. The new policy prohibited distribution in these particular areas, whereupon Jews for Jesus filed suit. The Authority argued that the ban on literature distribution was necessary for the public safety. The Authority argued that leafletting threatened public safety by disrupting passenger flow and creating litter. Litter, in turn, could cause accidents and fires or other disruptions, especially if paper clogged the switching devices on the tracks. The court remarked that the "Authority thus bears a heavy burden in justifying its absolute ban on leafletting, an activity that long has enjoyed the full protection of the First Amendment."[93] Noting that the Supreme Court had previously dismissed the danger to traffic congestion as a justification to ban leafletting, the court ruled that this flat ban in the subway area was unconstitutional.[94]

In summary, nonpublic forums such as airports, metros, rail or subway systems, and bus stations are areas where First Amendment activity can occur. These are ideal areas for distributing religious literature because of the enormous amount of people passing through these transportation facilities.

---

[92]*Jews for Jesus v. Massachusetts Bay Transportation Authority*, 984 F.2d 1319 (1st Cir. 1993).

[93]*Id.* at 1324 (citing *Lovell v. City of Griffin*, 303 U.S. 444, 450-52 (1938)).

[94]*Id.* at 1324-25.

14

THE RIGHT TO PICKET, DEMONSTRATE AND PARADE

The ability of citizens to peacefully gather and demonstrate for a particular cause is an important aspect of maintaining liberty. The First Amendment prohibits the government from "abridging the freedom of speech" and from prohibiting "the right of the people peacefully to assemble." The Supreme Court has noted that

> [p]ublic places are of necessity the locus for discussion of public issues, as well as protest against arbitrary government action. At the heart of our jurisprudence lies the principle that in a free nation citizens must have the right to gather and speak with other persons in public places.[1]

Picketing is expressive activity protected by the First Amendment Free Speech Clause. The right to picket or demonstrate is, in part, dependent upon the location. Picketing in traditional public forums such as parks, streets, and sidewalks is clearly protected speech. Picketing may also occur outside of these areas in limited or designated public forums and may also occur in nonpublic forums.[2] When considering picketing, it is also important to determine whether the property site is privately or publicly owned. There may be certain noise level restrictions on picketing. Some courts have placed buffer zones around areas frequented by picketers to protect private business interests. Some pickets have turned violent, and courts have attempted to restrain this violence. The media is fond of showing pro-life demonstrators being dragged off to jail, and based upon this display, many people have a misconception that picketing may be prohibited activity. However, picketing and demonstrating pre-date the Constitution and are clearly protected by the First Amendment.

The act of picketing may encompass several factors, including

---

[1]*ISKCON v. Lee*, 112 S. Ct. 2711, 2716-17 (1992).
[2]See Chapter Eleven regarding definitions of public forums.

carrying picket signs, wearing inscribed messages on clothing, speaking, distributing literature, or merely congregating. The Supreme Court has noted that direct one-on-one communication is probably "the most effective, fundamental, and perhaps economical avenue of political discourse."[3] The First Amendment protects the speakers' right "not only to advocate their cause but also to select what they believe to be the most effective means for doing so."[4]

The First Amendment limits the government's ability to restrict picketing because of the content of the speech. The Supreme Court stated:

> [T]he First Amendment means that the government has no power to restrict expression because of its message, its ideas, its subject matter, or its content. . . . Any restriction on expressive activity because of its content would completely undercut the "profound national commitment to the principle that debate on public issues should be uninhibited, robust, and wide-open."[5]

Indeed, "[r]egulations which permit the government to discriminate on the basis of the content of the message cannot be tolerated under the First Amendment."[6] Any "content-based restriction on political speech in a public forum . . . must be subjected to the most exacting scrutiny."[7] Restricting picketing or demonstrating based upon the content of the speech constitutes "censorship in a most odious form" which violates the First Amendment.[8] Rather than restricting speech, the government should continue to offer other avenues of speech. Speech should be combated with speech rather than censorship. Education is the proper and preferable alternative.[9]

A correlative of individual picketing and demonstration is the

---

[3]*Meyer v. Grant*, 486 U.S. 414, 424 (1988).

[4]*Id.*

[5]*Police Department of Chicago v. Mosley*, 408 U.S. 92, 95-96 (1972) (quoting *New York Times Co. v. Sullivan*, 376 U.S. 254, 270 (1963)).

[6]*Simon & Schuster v. New York Crime Victims Board.*, 112 S. Ct. 501, 508 (1991).

[7]*Boos v. Barry*, 485 U.S. 312, 321 (1988).

[8]*Cox v. Louisiana*, 379 U.S. 536, 581 (1965).

[9]*Whitney v. California*, 274 U.S. 357 (1927).

constitutional right to engage in such activity with others of similar beliefs. The "freedom to associate applies to the beliefs we share, and to those we consider reprehensible. It tends to produce the diversity of opinion that oils the machinery of democratic government and insures peaceful, orderly change."[10] Though freedom of association is not specifically set out in the First Amendment, "it has long been held to be implicit in the freedoms of speech, assembly, and petition."[11] The Supreme Court has declared that the

> freedom to speak, to worship, and to petition the Government for the redress of grievances could not be vigorously protected from interference by the State [if] a correlative freedom to engage in group effort toward those ends were not also guaranteed.[12]

Whether picketing is done individually or in a group, there would be "no conceivable government interest" that would justify a complete ban on this protected First Amendment activity.[13] Although some courts have attempted to restrict peaceful literature distribution, "a complete ban on handbilling would be substantially broader" than any necessary government interest.[14] Indeed, peaceful literature distribution cannot be prohibited under the concern that to allow such might block the flow of traffic on a public sidewalk, because one "need not ponder the contents of a leaflet or pamphlet in order to mechanically take it out of someone's hand."[15]

Collective First Amendment expression may take the form of a picket or a parade. While it may be reasonable to require a parade permit, it is not reasonable to require a permit to picket. Parades are fundamentally different from pickets. Generally pickets occur on

---

[10]*Gilmore v. City of Montgomery,* 417 U.S. 556, 575 (1974).

[11]*Healy v. James,* 408 U.S. 169, 181 (1972).

[12]*Roberts v. United States Jaycees,* 468 U.S. 609, 622 (1984).

[13]*Board of Airport Commissioners of Los Angeles v. Jews for Jesus,* 482 U.S. 569, 575 (1987).

[14]*Ward v. Rock Against Racism,* 491 U.S. 781, 799 n.7. (1989).

[15]*ISKCON v. Lee,* 112 S. Ct. at 2713-14 (citing *United States v. Kokinda,* 497 U.S. 720, 734 (1990)).

public sidewalks or public property, but not on public roads.
Parades are generally conducted on public roads or right-of-ways.
Obviously a parade cannot be conducted in the midst of traffic.
Therefore, it is reasonable to require a parade permit which places
time, place, and manner restrictions on the parade. Such a
restriction would designate a time, place, and route of the parade.
So long as the permit does not regulate the content of speech, and
so long as the permit has specific, neutral guidelines which provides
for a quick resolution of the parade application, a parade permit will
be upheld.

Since a parade is a collective expressive activity, it is protected
by the First Amendment. If a public entity were to put on a parade,
it could not restrict from the parade a participant based upon
disagreement with the participant's message. However, if private
citizens organize their own parade, the private group can exclude
participants with which the group disagrees.

City officials in Boston attempted to force the South Boston
Allied War Veterans Council to allow a homosexual activist group
in its privately organized parade. When the Veterans Council
excluded the homosexual group, the City of Boston refused to grant
the parade permit. The Veterans Council sued and the United States
Supreme Court issued a unanimous opinion, finding that a privately
organized parade may restrict participants which may dilute or
confuse the purpose of the private parade.[16] The Court noted the
following:

> Since all speech inherently involves choices of what to
> say and what to leave unsaid, one important manifestation
> of the principle of free speech is that one who chooses to
> speak may also decide what not to say. Although the State
> may at times prescribe what shall be orthodox in
> commercial advertising by requiring the dissemination of
> purely factual and uncontroversial information, outside
> that context it may not compel affirmance of a belief with
> which the speaker disagrees. Indeed this general rule, that
> the speaker has the right to tailor the speech, applies not

---

[16]*Hurley v. Irish-American Gay, Lesbian and Bisexual Group of Boston*, 115 S. Ct. 2338
(1995).

only to expressions of value, opinion, or endorsement, but equally to statements of fact the speaker would rather avoid, subject, perhaps, to the permissive law of defamation. Nor is the rule's benefit restricted to the press, being enjoyed by business corporations generally and by ordinary people engaged in unsophisticated expression as well as by professional publishers. Its point is simply the point of all speech protection, which is to shield just those choices of content that in someone's eyes are misguided, or even hurtful.[17]

In fact, the Supreme Court has noted that a private organizer of a parade is "like a composer" selecting "the expressive units of the parade from potential participants."[18]

Inherent in the right to free speech is the right to choose what not to say. The Supreme Court could not be more clear when it declared the following:

Disapproval of a private speaker's statement does not legitimize use of the [State's] power to compel the speaker to alter the message by including one more acceptable to others.[19]

While the government may not exclude participants from a government-sponsored parade based upon disagreement with the content of the participant's message, a private group organizing a privately sponsored parade may discriminate on the content of speech. The remedy for being excluded from a privately-sponsored parade is simply to go out and organize another parade espousing the desired message. There is no constitutional harm in not being invited to another person's party.

Some governmental entities have required picketers or demonstrators to notify public officials prior to the conducted activity. While this may be reasonable for a parade in terms of logistics and traffic control, it is not reasonable for a peaceful

---

[17]*Id.* at 2347-2348 (quotations and citations omitted).
[18]*Id.* at 2348.
[19]*Id.* at 2351.

demonstration on a public sidewalk. The requirement of giving advance notice to the government of one's intent to speak inherently inhibits free speech.[20] The Supreme Court has indicated that prior notification is "quite incompatible with the requirements of the First Amendment."[21] The "simple knowledge that one must inform the government of his desire to speak and must fill out appropriate forms and comply with applicable regulations discourages citizens from speaking freely."[22] The "delay inherent in advance notice requirements inhibits free speech by outlawing spontaneous expression."[23] It is clear that when "an event occurs, it is often necessary to have one's voice heard promptly, if it is to be considered at all."[24]

In addition to prior notice requirements, some governmental authorities have attempted to place financial burdens on free speech. Certainly the government may impose minimal financial burdens on the exercise of free speech such as permit fees, but these burdens are permitted only when the amount involved is reasonable and directly related to the accomplishment of legitimate governmental purposes.[25] A parade permit probably would be permissible, but a permit to picket on a sidewalk is unreasonable. However, the government cannot make the requirements for the financial cost of obtaining a parade permit so unreasonable as to restrict free speech activities. One federal court struck down an ordinance requiring groups to obtain a liability insurance policy in the amount of at least $300,000 and property damage insurance in the amount of at least $50,000. The court ruled that these requirements were unconstitutional since the activity involved free speech.[26] If a parade permit is necessary to picket or demonstrate on a public street, the cost should be minimal and the standards for requiring

---

[20]*NAACP v. City of Richmond,* 743 F.2d 1346 (9th Cir. 1984).

[21]*Thomas v. Collins,* 323 U.S. 516, 540 (1945).

[22]*NAACP v. City of Richmond,* 743 F.2d at 1455 (citing *Rosen v. Port of Portland,* 641 F.2d 1243 (9th Cir. 1981)).

[23]*NAACP v. City of Richmond,* 743 F.2d at 1355.

[24]*Shuttlesworth v. City of Birmingham,* 394 U.S. 147, 163 (1969).

[25]*Collin v. Smith,* 447 F. Supp. 676, 684 (N.D. Ill. 1978), *cert. denied,* 439 U.S. 916 (1978). *See also Cox v. New Hampshire,* 312 U.S. 569, 575-77 (1941); *Lubin v. Panish,* 415 U.S. 709 (1974); *Bullock v. Carter,* 405 U.S. 134 (1972); *United States Labor Party v. Codd,* 527 F.2d 118 (2d Cir. 1975).

[26]*Collin,* 447 F. Supp. at 676.

the permit must be objective and applied equally.[27] In the context of literature distribution, Liberty Counsel filed suit against the Orlando International Airport's requirement of obtaining $100,000 of liability insurance prior to the distribution of literature. After filing suit, the airport eliminated the financial requirement.

While some government entities have attempted to limit picketing and demonstrating activities by restricting the distribution of literature or by requiring the picketer to be publicly identified, courts have routinely struck down these restrictions. A regulation banning literature distribution while picketing would actually suppress "a great quantity of speech that does not cause the evils that it seeks to eliminate, whether they be fraud, crime, litter, traffic congestion or noise."[28] Neither the picketer nor the organization represented need be identified in the material used during the picket. The Supreme Court has consistently stated that "anonymous pamphlets, leaflets, brochures and even books have played an important role in the progress of mankind."[29] The right to remain anonymous is an important First Amendment right.[30]

The use of anonymity when expressing ideas has a long and respectable history in America and Great Britain. The Supreme Court resoundingly upheld this tradition in the context of distribution of political literature.[31] The Supreme Court noted that authors such as Benjamin Franklin, Charles Dickens and Samuel Clemmons (Mark Twain) shielded their identities when publishing.[32] The tradition of anonymity extends beyond literature to political advocacy: "Persecuted groups and sects from time to time throughout history have been able to criticize oppressive practices and laws either anonymously or not at all."[33] Even the *Federalists Papers* were published under fictitious names.[34] The Court recognized that "an advocate may believe her ideas will be more persuasive if her readers are unaware of her identity.

---

[27] *Forsyth County v. Nationalist Movement*, 112 S. Ct. 2395 (1992).

[28] *Ward*, 491 U.S. at 799 n.7. (citation omitted).

[29] *Talley v. California*, 362 U.S. 60, 64 (1960).

[30] *McIntyre v. Ohio Elections Commission*, 115 S. Ct. 1511 (1995).

[31] *McIntyre*, 115 S. Ct. at 1511.

[32] *Id.* at 1516 n.4.

[33] *Id.* at 1516 (*quoting Talley v. California*, 362 U.S. 60, 64 (1960)).

[34] *McIntyre*, 115 S. Ct. at 1517.

Anonymity thereby provides a way for a writer who may be personally unpopular to ensure that readers will not prejudice her message simply because they do not like its proponent."[35] The occasional need for anonymity goes to the very heart of Free Speech:

> Anonymity is a shield from the tyranny of the majority. . . . and thus exemplifies the purpose behind the Bill of Rights, and of the First Amendment in particular; to protect unpopular individuals from retaliation -- and their ideas from suppression -- at the hand of an intolerant society.[36]

Moreover, the government may not compel members of groups involved in picketing to be publicly identified.[37] Any identification requirement "would tend to restrict freedom to distribute information and thereby freedom of expression."[38] Public identification is repugnant to the Constitution. The Supreme Court declared the following:

> Persecuted groups and sects from time to time throughout history have been able to criticize oppressive practices and laws either anonymously or not at all. The obnoxious press licensing law of England, which was also enforced on the Colonies was due in part to the knowledge that exposure of the names of printers, writers and distributors would lessen the circulation of literature critical of the government. The old seditious libel cases in England show the lengths to which government had to go to find out who was responsible for books that were obnoxious to the rulers. . . . Before the Revolutionary War colonial patriots frequently had to conceal their authorship or distribution of literature that easily could have brought down on them prosecutions. . . . Even the Federalist Papers, written in

---

[35]*Id.*

[36]*Id.* at 1524.

[37]*Bates v. City of Little Rock*, 361 U.S. 412 (1960); *NAACP v. Alabama* ex. re. Patterson, 357 U.S. 449 (1957).

[38]*Talley*, 362 U.S. at 64.

favor of adoption of our Constitution, were published under fictitious names. It is plain that anonymity has sometimes been assumed for the most constructive purposes. . . . [I]dentification and [its concomitant] fear of reprisal might deter perfectly peaceful discussions of public matters of importance.[39]

In the past, some states have attempted to obtain membership lists of organizations that are actively engaged in picketing or protest activities. This has often been done in an effort to restrict free speech, but it is clearly unconstitutional. Requiring organizations to identify their members may cause fear in those members and thus prevent them from continuing association with the organization. Consequently, anonymity of those engaged in First Amendment speech and those associated with groups participating in such activities is constitutionally protected.[40]

The government cannot prohibit speech or expressive conduct "because of disapproval of the ideas expressed."[41] Courts cannot restrict picketing or demonstrating "simply because society finds the idea itself offensive or disagreeable."[42] Indeed, "the mere presumed presence of unwitting listeners or viewers does not serve automatically to justify curtailing all speech capable of giving offense."[43] The Supreme Court has noted that "[w]e are often captives outside the sanctuary of the home and subject to objectionable speech."[44] Merely because the speech is unwelcome

---

[39]*Id.* at 64-65.

[40]In *Bates*, the Court noted the chilling effect that would result from identification and disclosure requirements. "For example, a witness testified: 'Well, the people are afraid to join, afraid to join because the people—they don't want their names exposed and they are afraid their names will be exposed. . . . They will be intimidated and they are afraid to join.'" *Bates*, 361 U.S. at 416 n.6. The Court also highlighted the following testimony: "Well, I have—we were not able to rest at night or day for quite awhile. We had to have our phone number changed because they called at day and night. . . . I would tell them who is talking and they have throwed [sic] stones at my home. They wrote me—I got a—I received a letter threatening my life and they threatened my life over the telephone." *Id.* at 416 n.7.

[41]*R.A.V. v. City of St. Paul*, 112 S. Ct. 2538, 2542 (1992).

[42]*Simon & Schuster*, 112 S. Ct. at 509. *See also Cohen v. California*, 403 U.S. 15 (1971).

[43]*Cohen*, 403 U.S. at 21.

[44]*Id.*

"does not deprive it of protection."[45]

Picketing and demonstrating often create confrontation of opposing views. However, even hostile audience reactions cannot justify the suppression of speech.[46] One federal court struck down a ban on "persisting in talking to or communicating in any manner with" a person or persons "against his, her or their will" in order to persuade that person to quit or refrain from seeking certain employment.[47] The First Amendment was meant to permit disputatious speech, speech that "may start an argument or cause a disturbance."[48] The Supreme Court has noted that

> free speech is not a right that is given only to be so circumscribed that it exists in principle but not in fact. Freedom of expression would not truly exist if the right could be exercised only in an area that a benevolent government has provided as a safe haven for crackpots.[49]

The First Amendment which requires that government may not abridge the right to free speech "means what it says."[50] Like it or not, the First Amendment is strong medicine to those who attempt to suppress speech because the content is offensive. The Supreme Court declared:

> [T]he fact that society may find speech offensive is not a sufficient reason for suppressing it. Indeed, if it is the speaker's opinion that gives offense, that consequence is a reason for according it constitutional protection.[51]

---

[45] *United Food and Commercial Workers International Union v. I.B.P., Inc.*, 857 F.2d 422, 432 (8th Cir. 1988) (and cases cited).

[46] *Forsyth County*, 112 S. Ct. at 2404 (and cases cited).

[47] *United Food*, 857 F.2d at 425 n.4, 435.

[48] *Tinker v. Des Moines Independent School District*, 393 U.S. 503, 508 (1969).

[49] *Id.* at 513.

[50] *Id.*

[51] *FCC v. Pacifica Foundation*, 438 U.S. 726, 745 (1978), *quoted in Hustler Magazine, Inc. v. Falwell*, 485 U.S. 46, 55 (1988).

Private Versus Public Property

The site of the picket or demonstration activity is important to determining its constitutionality. As stated in a previous chapter, the First Amendment protects individuals against government action seeking to restrict free speech. The First Amendment consequently restrains only government action, not private action. Therefore, a private individual has no First Amendment right to picket on private property since the First Amendment does not restrain the private property owner. However, since the First Amendment restrains government activity, a citizen does have the right to picket within a traditional public forum or possibly within a designated, limited, or nonpublic forum.

Traditional public forums include parks, streets, and sidewalks. Access to traditional public forums or other similar public places "for the purpose of exercising First Amendment rights cannot constitutionally be denied broadly."[52] Public parks, streets, and sidewalks "have immemorially been held in trust for the use of the public."[53] "In [these] quintessential public forums, the government may not prohibit all communicative activity."[54]

Some protesters at abortion clinics have been arrested for trespassing on private property. These arrests generally arise out of situations involving picketers blocking ingress to or egress from an abortion clinic, or physically being on private rather than public property. Sometimes pro-life demonstrators have used what is known as the "necessity defense" to justify breaking the trespass laws. The so-called necessity defense was defined in the early 1900s. The defense involves the necessity of one person trespassing on the private property of another person in order to either avoid serious personal harm or to save the life of another. This defense grew out of a case known as *Ploof v. Putnam*,[55] which involved a boat dock on Lake Champlain. While sailing, a violent tempest

---

[52]*Grayned v. City of Rockford*, 408 U.S. 104, 117 (1972).

[53]*Frisby v. Schultz*, 487 U.S. 474, 481 (1988), (quoting *Hague v. CIO*, 307 U.S. 496, 515 (1939)). *See also Perry Education Ass'n. v. Perry Local Educators' Ass'n*, 460 U.S. 37 (1983).

[54]*Frisby*, 487 U.S. at 481 (quoting *Perry Education Ass'n*, 460 U.S. at 45 (1983)). *See also Heffron v. ISKCON*, 452 U.S. 640 (1981).

[55]71 A. 188 (Vt. 1908).

arose. In order to avoid personal injury and property damage to the sailing vessel, the owner of the vessel moored the sloop to a private dock. When the dock owner noticed the sloop moored to his dock, he untied the sloop and it was destroyed in the storm. The court ruled that the defense of necessity applied with special force to the preservation of human life and that one may sacrifice the personal property of another in order to save either his life or those lives around him. In another case known as *Vincent v. Lake Erie Transportation Company*,[56] a state court ruled that, because of necessity, it was lawful for a ship to maintain its tie to a dock even though the waves forcing the ship up and down destroyed the dock, but also indicated that the ship owner was responsible for repairing the dock.

Based on the defense of necessity, pro-life picketers have argued that it is permissible to break the law of trespass in order to save the life of an unborn child by blocking access to, or trespassing upon, the private property of an abortion clinic. So far this defense has met with very little success in relieving picketers from trespass laws.[57]

Residential picketing involves both public and private issues. Residences are certainly privately-owned, but the sidewalks in front of residential areas are public sidewalks and therefore traditional public forums. As stated in a previous chapter, the Supreme Court has ruled that peaceful picketing within a residential area is constitutionally protected so long as the picketing activities move throughout the neighborhood on the sidewalk and are not directly localized at one particular residential address.[58] Picketing in a residential area is permissible so long as the protesters move about on public sidewalks within the neighborhood. For example, courts have ruled that pro-life demonstrators may picket in a residential neighborhood where a physician who performs abortions resides so long as the protesters move about in the neighborhood and do not

---

[56]124 N.W. 221 (Minn. 1910).

[57]*City of Wichita v. Tilson*, 855 P.2d 911 (Kan. 1993) (ruling that when the objective sought is to prevent by criminal activity a lawful, constitutional right of abortion, the defense of necessity is inapplicable and evidence of when life begins is irrelevant and should not be admitted at trial).

[58]*Frisby*, 487 U.S. at 479. See Chapter 15, Door-to-Door Witnessing.

solely target one residential address.[59]

Buffer Zones

A buffer zone is a parameter set by either a court or legislative body around a particular facility where pickets frequently take place. These buffer zones have restricted the amount of picketers and the activity of picketing within a certain parameter. In light of the escalating activity around abortion clinics, some courts have placed buffer zones around clinics. Legislative attempts to create buffer zones around abortion clinics and other medical facilities have also occurred. These buffer zones are clearly a threat to free speech activities.

Polling Places

The concept of buffer zones may be traced back to voter intimidation around polling booths. The United States Supreme Court ruled that the state of Tennessee may place a 100-foot buffer zone around a polling place within which no literature distribution or display of campaign posters, signs, or other campaign material may occur on the day of elections.[60] In reaching this conclusion, the Supreme Court recognized that the First Amendment "'has its fullest and most urgent application' to speech uttered during a campaign for political office."[61] The Court also noted that First Amendment expression around the polling place in question occurred in a public forum where people were invited to be present. The Court further noted that the specific regulation on speech was content-based because only political speech was prohibited whereas other speech was not. Consequently, the Court ruled that such a buffer zone must be subjected to "exacting scrutiny" and could only survive constitutional challenge if a state had a "compelling interest" for the buffer zone.

To reach its conclusion, the Court reviewed extensive history.

---

[59]*Vittitow v. City of Arlington*, 830 F. Supp. 1077 (S.D. Ohio 1993). *See Madsen v. Women's Health Center, Inc.*, 114 S. Ct. 2516, 2529-30 (1994).

[60]*Burson v. Freeman*, 112 S. Ct. 1846 (1992).

[61]*Id.* at 1850, (quoting *UEU v. San Francisco Democratic Commission*, 489 U.S. 214, 223 (1989)).

States clearly have a compelling interest to protect the rights of citizens to vote freely in an election conducted with integrity and reliability.[62] Indeed, the Court noted the following:

> No right is more precious in a free country than that of having a voice in the election of those who make the laws under which, as good citizens, we must live. Other rights, even the most basic, are illusory if the right to vote is undermined.[63]

Though a content-based regulation of speech in a public forum "rarely survives such scrutiny," based on the history involved, the buffer zone was constitutional.[64] This history dates back to the colonial period, when many government officials were elected *viva voce* or by the showing of hands. Voting was not a private affair, but, in fact, "an open, public decision witnessed by all and improperly influenced by some."[65] Approximately twenty years after the formation of the Union, most states had incorporated a paper ballot in the electoral process. The various political parties wishing to gain influence then began producing their own paper ballots in flamboyant colors. Persons taking these paper ballots to polling places were frequently met by "ticket peddlers" who tried to convince individuals to vote for a particular party ticket. These discussions often became heated and influenced the outcome of votes. This situation was not a "pleasant spectacle."[66]

Australia adopted an official ballot encompassing all candidates of all parties on the same ticket. The Australian system then incorporated the erection of polling booths. This system appeared to be a vast improvement and was eventually adopted in England in 1872. The polling booth concept failed after several attempts but eventually began in Louisville, Kentucky, and then moved to Massachusetts and the state of New York in 1888. The city of

---

[62]*Burson*, 112 S. Ct. at 1851. The Court noted that the "right to vote freely for the candidate of one's choice is the essence of a democratic society." *Reynolds v. Sims*, 377 U.S. 533, 555 (1964).

[63]*Wesberry v. Sanders*, 376 U.S. 1, 17 (1964).

[64]*Burson*, 112 S. Ct. at 1852.

[65]*Id.*

[66]*Id.* at 1852-53.

Louisville "prohibited all but voters, candidates or their agents, and electors from coming within fifty feet of the voting room enclosure."[67] The Massachusetts and New York laws placed a guard rail around the booths and excluded the general public from mingling within the guard rail areas. New York eventually adopted a 100-foot buffer zone around any polling place, and consequently, much of the intimidation and fraud encountered in earlier years had been cured. One commentator remarked, "We have secured secrecy; and intimidation by employers, party bosses, police officers, saloon keepers and others has come to an end."[68]

Today all fifty states limit access to areas in and around polling places. Even the National Labor Relations Board limits activities at or near its polling places during union elections. After reviewing this history, the Court concluded by stating the following:

> In sum, an examination of the history of election regulation in this country reveals a persistent battle against two evils: voter intimidation and election fraud. After an unsuccessful experiment with an unofficial ballot system, all 50 States, together with numerous other Western democracies, settled on the same solution: a secret ballot secured in part by a restricted zone around the voting compartments. We find that this wide-spread and time-tested consensus demonstrates that some restricted zone is necessary in order to serve the States' compelling interest in preventing voter intimidation and election fraud.[69]

Although buffer zones originally arose out of elections and polling booths, the significant history is important. It is improper to take buffer zones arising out of elections processes and, in turn, place buffer zones around other facilities. Buffer zones will rarely survive the First Amendment. The only reason buffer zones in the election process survived a First Amendment analysis is because of the fundamental right to vote which is one of the most important

---

[67]*Id.* at 1854.
[68]*Id.*
[69]*Id.* at 1855.

right of an American citizen. Moreover, buffer zone restrictions around polling places are deeply imbedded in American history.

Churches

Though somewhat unanticipated, one city in the state of Kansas passed an ordinance creating a type of buffer zone around churches. An individual sought to picket around the church carrying a pro-life sign. Even though he was aware of the no picketing buffer zone ordinance around the church, he picketed anyway and was arrested. The Supreme Court of Kansas ruled that the picketer did not violate the buffer zone because the ordinance was read as prohibiting only targeted picketing of churches.[70]

Public Schools

An ordinance placing a 150-foot buffer zone around public schools but exempting from this buffer zone labor dispute picketing was found by the United States Supreme Court to be unconstitutional.[71] The Court primarily found this buffer zone unconstitutional because it treated different forms of speech unequally. No speech was allowed within the 150-foot buffer zone except labor picketing disputes, and based on that unequal treatment, the buffer zone was struck down.

Abortion Clinics

Abortion clinics have been the primary areas of controversy for an increasing number of decisions regarding buffer zones.[72] One

---

[70]*City of Prairie Village v. Hogan*, 855 P.2d 949 (Kan. 1993).

[71]*Grayned*, 408 U.S. at 104; *Mosley*, 408 U.S. at 92.

[72]Though not a buffer zone case, the United States Supreme Court ruled in *Bray v. Alexandria Women's Health Clinic*, 113 S. Ct. 753 (1993), that 42 U.S.C. § 1985(3), the so-called Ku Klux Klan Act, could not be used to restrict picketing of abortion clinics. The Court ruled that abortion does not qualify as an individiously discriminatory animus directed toward women in general, that the incidental effect of abortion clinic demonstrations on some women's right to interstate travel was not sufficient to show a conspiracy to deprive those women of their protected interstate travel right, and that the deprivation of the right to an abortion could not serve as the basis for a purely private conspiracy. Though the Supreme Court ruled that the first part of section 1985(3), known as the "deprivation" clause, does not

court noted that pro-life advocates must "be permitted to articulate their belief that abortion should not be permitted because it involves the taking of human life."[73] One court correctly recognized that "although the words 'killings' or 'murder' are certainly emotionally charged, it is difficult to conceive of a forceful presentation of the anti-abortion viewpoint which would not assert that abortion is the taking of human life."[74] Abortion speech is certainly political speech and therefore should receive the highest protection under the First Amendment. "Indeed, abortion may be the political issue of the last twenty years."[75]

Some have reasoned that buffer zones are permissible because they do not prohibit all free speech and pro-life demonstrators may exercise their right to speak in another locale. However, the Supreme Court stated that one "is not to have the exercise of his liberty of expression in appropriate places abridged on the plea that it may be exercised in some other place."[76] The mere fact that pro-life demonstrators "remain free to employ other means to disseminate their ideas does not take their speech . . . outside the bounds of First Amendment protection."[77] Though some buffer zones restricting the blocking of access to and from an abortion clinic and limiting the amount of picketers present at a given time have been upheld by some state and federal courts, other courts have struck down such bans.[78] In the absence of illegal conduct,

---

provide a federal cause of action against persons obstructing access to abortion clinics, the same Supreme Court left open the possibility that the second part of section 1985(3), known as the "hindrance" clause, may provide a federal cause of action. The Tenth Circuit Court of Appeals has picked up on this idea and suggested that the "hindrance" clause may be used against abortion protestors. *National Abortion Federation v. Operation Rescue*, 8 F.3d 680 (9th Cir. 1993). *See also* Nina Pillard, "Litigating § 1985(3) Claims After *Bray v. Alexandria Women's Health Clinic*," *Civil Rights Litigation and Attorney Fees Annual Handbook*, ed. Steve Saltzman and Barbara M. Wolvovitz, Vol. 9, (1993), p. 325.

[73]*Planned Parenthood Shasta-Diablo v. Williams*, 16 Cal. Rptr. 2d 540, 549 (Cal. 1st DCA 1993).

[74]*Cannon v. City and County of Denver*, 998 F.2d 867 (10th Cir. 1993).

[75]*Planned Parenthood Shasta-Diablo*, 16 Cal. Rptr. at 549.

[76]*Schneider v. New Jersey*, 308 U.S. 147, 163 (1939).

[77]*Meyer v. Grant*, 468 U.S. at 424.

[78]*Cheffer v. McGregor*, 6 F.3d 705 (11th Cir. 1993), *vacated and remanded*, 41 F.3d 1422 (11th Cir. 1994) (a 36-foot and 300-foot buffer zone and a ban on images violates free speech); *Cannon v. City and County of Denver*, 998 F.2d 867 (10th Cir. 1993) (ruling that arrest of abortion protestors violated the constitutional right to picket on a public sidewalk in front of an abortion clinic and further ruling that words such as "murder" or "The Killing

Place" were not fighting words and could not be proscribed); *Mississippi Women's Medical Clinic v. McMillan*, 866 F.2d 788 (5th Cir. 1989) (ruling a 500-foot buffer zone around an abortion clinic unconstitutional); *United Food*, 857 F.2d at 430-32 (same); *Howard Gault Company v. Texas Rural Legal Aid, Inc.*, 848 F.2d 544, 548-61 (5th Cir. 1988) (ruling unconstitutional a ban on more than two picketers within 50 feet of one another); *Davis v. Francois*, 395 F.2d 730 (5th Cir. 1968) (ban on more than two picketers at a building "patently unconstitutional"); *Town of West Hartford v. Operation Rescue*, 792 F. Supp. 161 (D. Conn. 1992) (order upheld prohibiting blocking of clinic but not prohibiting other free speech or association activities), *vacated in part*, 991 F.2d 1039 (2d Cir. 1993); *Jackson v. City of Markham*, 773 F. Supp. 105 (N.D. Ill. 1991) (granting an injunction to protect the right to picket on a sidewalk outside of a roller rink); *Thomason v. Jernigan*, 770 F. Supp. 1195 (E.D. Mich. 1991) (ruling it unconstitutional to prohibit pro-life individuals in a public right of way); *Northeast Women's Center, Inc. v. McMonagle*, 939 F.2d 57 (3rd Cir. 1991) (a buffer zone allowing six protestors within a buffer zone was permissible but a 500-foot buffer zone in a residential area was unconstitutional); *Southwestern Medical Clinics, Inc. v. Operation Rescue*, 744 F. Supp. 230 (D. Nev. 1989) (order prohibiting blockading of clinic but allowing other free speech or free association activities upheld); *National Organization for Women v. Operation Rescue*, 726 F. Supp. 1483 (E.D. Va. 1989) (a restriction on activities tending to intimidate, harass or disturb patients by expression of views on the issue of abortion was ruled unconstitutionally overbroad), *aff'd*, 914 F.2d 582 (4th Cir. 1990), *rev'd in part, vacated in part, Bray v. Alexandria Women's Health Clinic*, 113 S. Ct. 753 (1993); *National Organization for Women v. Operation Rescue*, 726 F. Supp. 300 (D.C. District 1989) (upholding an order blockading a clinic but not prohibiting or restricting other free speech activities); *Fargo Women's Health Organization, Inc. v. Lambs of Christ*, 488 N.W.2d 401 (N.D. 1992) (a buffer zone allowing only two protestors within 100 feet and prohibiting literature distribution and prohibiting speaking to abortion clinic staff was unconstitutional but the noise restriction was upheld); *Hirsch v. City of Atlanta*, 401 S.E.2d 530 (Ga. 1991), *cert. denied*, 112 S. Ct. 75 (1991) (upholding a restriction allowing only 20 protestors to use a sidewalk at any one given time within a 50-foot buffer zone); *Planned Parenthood v. Maki*, 478 N.W.2d 637 (Iowa 1991) (a prohibition against one individual from blocking entrance to and trespassing upon clinic property upheld because no other protestor's right to free speech was restricted); *Dayton Women's Health Center v. Enix*, 68 Ohio App. 3d 579, 589 N.E.2d 121 (Ohio App. 2d. 1991); *Planned Parenthood v. Project Jericho*, 52 Ohio St. 3d 56, 556 N.E.2d 157 (Ohio 1990) (a buffer zone permitting picketing and literature distribution within reasonable limits for the purpose of expression of opinion upheld); *Planned Parenthood v. Operation Rescue*, 550 N.E.2d 1361 (Mass. 1990) (upholding a restriction blocking a clinic while allowing the right to pray, sing, and peacefully picket on public sidewalks); *Cousins v. Terry*, 721 F. Supp. 426 (N.D.N.Y. 1989) (prohibiting blocking access to an abortion clinic); *Zimmerman v. D.C.A. at Welleby, Inc.*, 505 So. 2d 1371 (Fla. 4th DCA 1987) (overturning an injunction against peaceful picketing at sales office of condominium project); *Bering v. Share*, 106 Wash. 2d 212, 721 P.2d 918 (Wash. 1986), *cert dismissed*, 479 U.S. 1060 (1987) (upholding a buffer zone restriction which did not prohibit picketing on a public sidewalk); *Planned Parenthood v. Cannizzaro*, 204 N.J. Super. 531, 499 A.2d 535 (N.J. Super. Ch. 1985) (a restriction allowing picketing in sidewalks or streets abutting the clinic but requiring five feet distance between picketers upheld); *Parkmed Company v. Pro-Life Counseling, Inc.*, 442 N.Y.S. 396 (N.Y. App. Div. 1981) (injunction on demonstrating in public areas outside and abortion business unconstitutional).

a flat ban on all peaceful picketing within a traditional public forum such as a park, street, or sidewalk, is patently unconstitutional. To prohibit all peaceful picketing having no history of violence in a traditional public forum, such as a sidewalk outside of an abortion clinic, is unconstitutional.[79]

In one case interesting case, the District of Columbia prohibited the "display [of] any flag, banner, or device designed or adapted to bring into public notice any party, organization, or movement" in the United States Supreme Court building or on its grounds, which were defined to include the public sidewalks constituting the outer boundaries of the grounds.[80] A picketer was threatened with arrest when he distributed leaflets on the sidewalk in front of the courthouse regarding the removal of unfit judges from the bench. In addressing this situation, the United States Supreme Court indicated there was "no doubt that as a general matter peaceful picketing and leafletting are expressive activities involving 'speech' protected by the First Amendment."[81] The Court further noted that places such as streets, sidewalks and parks, without more, are considered public forums.[82] The Court went on to state the following:

> In such places, the government's ability to permissively restrict expressive conduct is very limited; the government may enforce reasonable time, place, and manner regulations as long as the restrictions "are content neutral, or narrowly tailored to serve a significant government interest, and leave open ample alternative channels of communication.". . . Additional restrictions such as an absolute prohibition on a particular type of expression will be upheld only if narrowly drawn to accomplish a

---

[79]*Madsen v. Women's Health Center, Inc.*, 114 S. Ct. 2516 (1994). *Cf. Thornhill v. Alabama*, 310 U.S. 88 (1940).

[80]40 U.S.C. § 13K.

[81]*United States v. Grace*, 461 U.S. 169, 176 (1983). *See also Carey v. Brown*, 447 U.S. 455, 460 (1980); *Gregory v. Chicago*, 394 U.S. 111, 112 (1969); *Jamison v. Texas*, 318 U.S. 413 (1943); *Thornhill v. Alabama*, 310 U.S. 88 (1940); *Schneider v. New Jersey*, 308 U.S. 147 (1939).

[82]*Grace*, 461 U.S. at 177.

compelling governmental interest.[83]

There might be rights of other persons to consider in picketing cases, but "the Supreme Court's First Amendment jurisprudence tilts the scale assessing threatened harm decisively in favor of the protesters."[84] Certainly the "First Amendment retains a primacy in our jurisprudence because it represents the foundation of a democracy — informed public discourse."[85]

Sometimes state courts enter injunctions creating their own buffer zones. In one case a state court during the civil rights movement entered a 300-foot buffer zone around white-owned businesses due to civil rights protesting activities. A federal court was requested to block enforcement of the state court injunction, and ruled that the 300-foot buffer zone was an unconstitutional violation of free speech.[86]

The leading case on buffer zones around abortion clinics is the landmark decision in *Madsen v. Women's Health Center, Inc.*[87] This case arose in Melbourne, Florida, when a state court judge entered an injunction placing a 36-foot buffer zone around three sides of an abortion clinic. Within this zone was a public highway and a public sidewalk. The injunction also contained a noise restriction and prohibited the display of any "images observable" from within the clinic. Additionally, a 300-foot buffer zone was placed around the clinic and around the private residential homes of any owner, employee, staff member, or agent of the clinic. Pro-life speech could occur within the 300-foot buffer zone only upon the consent of the listener. Violations of these buffer zones resulted in criminal prosecution. In addition to those named in the state court injunction, the buffer zone restriction applied to anyone "acting in concert with" those named in the injunction. After the injunction was entered on April 8, 1993, numerous pro-life picketers were arrested merely for being present on a public sidewalk. Many were

---

[83]*Id.* (quoting *Perry Education Ass'n*, 460 U.S. at 45). *See also Hudgens v. NLRB*, 424 U.S. 507, 515 (1976); *Hague v. CIO*, 307 U.S. 496, 515 (1939).

[84]*McMillan*, 866 F.2d at 795.

[85]*Id.* at 796.

[86]*Machesky v. Bizzell*, 414 F.2d 283 (5th Cir. 1969).

[87]114 S. Ct. 2516 (1994). *See also Schenck v. Pro-Choice Network of Western New York*, 117 S. Ct. 855 (1997) (moving bubble zones are unconstitutional).

arrested after kneeling down to pray on this sidewalk. However, pro-choice demonstrators were not arrested. Myrna Cheffer was not named in the state court injunction. She desired to peacefully picket at the clinic but feared arrest. On her behalf, Liberty Counsel filed suit in federal court against the state court judge who entered the buffer zone restriction. The federal court of appeals first noted that the buffer zone was content-based and pointed out the following:

> That the speech restrictions at issue are viewpoint-based cannot seriously be doubted. The order enjoins Operation Rescue, Operation Rescue America, [O]peration Goliath, their officers, agents, members, employees and servants, and Ed Martin, Bruce Cadle, Pat Mahoney, Randall Terry, Judy Madsen, and Shirley Hobbs, and all persons acting in concert or participation with them or on their behalf. . . . Such a restriction is no more viewpoint-neutral than one restricting the speech of "the Republican Party, the state Republican Party, George Bush, Bob Dole, Jack Kemp and all persons acting in concert or participation with them or on their behalf." The practical effect of this section of the injunction was to assure that while pro-life speakers would be arrested, pro-choice demonstrators would not.[88]

The federal court of appeals went on to state the following:

> A viewpoint-specific restriction in a traditional public forum is unconstitutional unless (1) it is necessary to serve a compelling state interest and (2) it is narrowly drawn to achieve that end. . . . The state court injunction does not seem to be either.[89]

The federal court in *Cheffer* proclaimed: "We protect much that offends in the name of free speech—we cannot refuse such

---

[88]*Cheffer v. McGregor*, 6 F.3d 705 (11th Cir. 1993), *vacated and remanded*, 41 F.3d 1422 (11th Cir. 1994).
[89]*Id.* (citation omitted).

protection to those who find abortion morally reprehensible."[90] The court ruled the buffer zone unconstitutional.

At the same time Liberty Counsel was representing Myrna Cheffer in a federal lawsuit against the judge who entered the buffer zone injunction, Liberty Counsel also appealed the judge's decision through the state courts on behalf of three pro-life sidewalk counselors who were named on the injunction. Eight days after the *Cheffer* opinion, the Florida Supreme Court ruled that the entire injunction was constitutional.[91] The case was appealed to the United States Supreme Court which rendered its decision in the case known as *Madsen v. Women's Health Center, Inc.*[92] Stating that an injunction may not "burden more speech than necessary," the court ruled that the 300-foot zone around residential property violated the First Amendment right to free speech.[93] The Court also ruled that the 300-foot buffer zone around the clinic was unconstitutional. The Court also stated that the injunction's requirement that pro-life picketers receive consent from those persons seeking access to the clinic was unconstitutional. The Court further struck down the ban on all images observable and two sides of the 36-foot speech buffer around the clinic. The *Madsen* Court upheld a ban on excessive noise which could be heard within the clinic and part of the 36-foot zone near the entrance and driveway to the clinic.

Under *Madsen*, before any injunction may be sought, there must be a showing that (1) the picketers have violated, or imminently will violate, some provision of statutory or common law, and (2) there is a cognizable danger of recurrent violation.[94] Moreover, before a speech restrictive buffer zone can be instituted, a less restrictive injunction must first be tried. For example, if the two aforementioned prerequisites are met, an injunction may prevent blocking access to the clinic. If the protester violates that injunction, a more restrictive injunction may be applied against the

---

[90] *Id.* at 7. The *Cheffer* case recognizes that a nonparty may file suit in federal court against the state court judge who entered the injunction requesting the federal courts to intervene and block the state court proceeding.

[91] *Operation Rescue v. Women's Health Center, Inc.*, 626 So. 2d 664 (Fla. 1993).

[92] *Madsen*, 114 S. Ct. 2516.

[93] *Id.* at 2525.

[94] *Id.* at n.3.

individual protester, thus limiting the protester's free speech.[95]
The *Madsen* test can be summarized as follows:

> Injunctive relief affecting speech is permissible only upon
> a showing that: (1) the defendant has violated, or
> imminently will violate, some provision of statutory or
> common law;[96] (2) there is a cognizable danger of
> recurrent violation;[97] (3) a nonspeech-restrictive
> injunction preventing the repeated illegal conduct has
> proven ineffective to protect the significant government
> interests because the defendant has repeatedly violated the
> injunction;[98] and (4) a subsequent speech-restrictive
> injunction may not burden more speech than necessary to
> serve a significant government interest.[99]

The first two prongs of the above test are applicable to any
injunction since injunctive relief is an equitable remedy.[100] Thus,
prongs one and two must be met before the entry of any injunction,
whether the injunction restricts speech or conduct. After prongs one
and two are met, a court may restore law and order by a
nonspeech-restrictive injunction, and once that injunction proves to
be ineffective, a subsequent speech-restrictive injunction may be
issued, but that injunction may not burden more speech than
necessary to serve a significant government interest.[101] As a result

---

[95]Mathew D. Staver, *Injunctive Relief and the* Madsen *Test* 14:2 ST. LOUIS U. PUB. L.
REV. 456-494 (1995).

[96]*Madsen*, 114 S. Ct. at 2524 n.3.

[97]*Id.*

[98]*Id.* at 2527.

[99]*Id.* at 2525-26. But see, *Schenck*, 117 S. Ct. at 864.

[100]*Madsen*, 114 S. Ct. at 2524 n.3.

[101]The *Madsen* Court relied heavily on the assumption that the pro-life protestors
repeatedly violated a nonspeech-restrictive injunction, and it is based on this reliance that the
Court upheld a portion of the 36-foot buffer zone involving the speech-restrictive section of
the second injunction. The *Madsen* Court suggested that individuals may have restrictions
placed on their right to free speech if they repeatedly engage in illegal conduct. *See National
Society of Professional Engineers v. United States,* 435 U.S. 679, 697-98 (1978). Though it
is apparent from reading the *Madsen* that the Court followed the above-noted four step
analysis, the Supreme Court later noted that the third step in this analysis may not be
mandatory in all cases. However, it is at least a strong consideration. *See Schenck v. Pro-
Choice Network of Western New York,* 117 S. Ct. 855, 869 (1997). Step 1 and 2 of the

of the *Madsen* decision, most buffer zones around abortion clinics will be considered unconstitutional.[102] Relying on the *Madsen* case that was enunciated in 1994, the Supreme Court of 1997 ruled that a floating bubble zone was

---

Madsen analysis is mandatory in any case. Step 1 requires that the defendant has violated, or eminently will violate, some provision of statutory or common law. Step 2 requires that there is a cognizable danger of recurrent violation. Once these two mandatory steps have been proven, then a court may enter an injunction. In *Madsen* the Supreme Court recognized that the trial court entered a nonspeech-restrictive injunction which allegedly failed to prevent illegal conduct. The Court took this action into consideration when it upheld a portion of a subsequent speech-restrictive injunction that imposed a 36 foot buffer zone at the clinic entrance and driveway. However, in the subsequent case following *Madsen*, the *Schenck* court noted that the trial court's first injunction included a speech-restrictive provision, but that alone did not mean that the subsequent injunction was automatically invalid. *Schenck*, 117 S. Ct. at 869. The record in *Schenck* indicated an extensive past history of conduct that attempted to interfere with access to an abortion clinic.

[102]*See, e.g., Schenck*, 117 S. Ct. at 855.

Below is a diagram of the clinic and surrounding geography which was part of the record before the United States Supreme Court:

In upholding the portion of the 36-foot zone at the clinic entrance and driveway, the Court focused on two factors: (1) an assumption that the protestors had violated a prior nonspeech-restrictive injunction which was ineffective in maintaining free ingress and egress; and (2) the narrow confines of the clinic which included a strip of sidewalk approximately four feet wide and 37-feet long that connected the two parking lots. The road directly in front of the clinic, Dixie Way, was only 21 feet, four inches wide. Other than the narrow strip of sidewalk directly in front of the clinic, no other sidewalks existed in the residential area along Dixie Way or U.S. Highway 1. Clearly, if the first factor was absent, the Court would not have upheld the 36-foot zone at the clinic entrance and driveway. Additionally, if the second factor was absent, the Court may not have upheld this portion of the zone. In other words, if the confines of the clinic were not so narrow, leaving little other alternative but the imposition of the 36-foot zone, the Court more than likely would have stricken this portion of the injunction like it struck the majority of the injunction.

unconstitutional. In *Schenck* the trial court issued an injunction that created a 15 foot floating bubble zone that moved with people and vehicles entering and leaving an abortion clinic. These floating bubble zones would move with the person or vehicle. As a person seeking access to the clinic moved closer, the pro-life speaker would have to retreat. The Court found that these floating buffer zones burdened more speech than necessary.[103] The Court found that a floating bubble zone would prohibit communicating a message from a normal conversational distance and would also prohibit handing leaflets to people entering or leaving the clinic.[104] The Court then pointed out the following:

> Leafletting and commenting on matters of public concern are classic forms of speech that lie at the heart of the First Amendment, and speech in public areas is at its most protected [sic] on public sidewalks, a prototypical example of a traditional public forum.[105]

Picketing on matters of public concern, including picketing in and around abortion clinics, must be a highly guarded right under the First Amendment. The Supreme Court acknowledged this much when it stated:

> [W]e have indicated that in public debate our own citizens must tolerate insulting, and even outrageous, speech in order to provide adequate breathing space to the freedoms protected by the First Amendment.[106]

Certainly "[t]here is no right to be free of unwelcome speech on the public streets while seeking entrance to or exit from abortion clinics."[107]

It should be pointed out that in reference to abortion clinics there is an important difference between an injunction and an

---

[103]*Schenck*, 117 S. Ct. at 866-67.

[104]*Id.* at 867.

[105]*Id.*

[106]*Schenck*, 117 S. Ct. at 870, (quoting *Madsen*, 114 S. Ct. at 2529, (quoting *Boos v. Barry*, 485 U.S. 312, 322 (1988))).

[107]*Schenck*, 117 S. Ct. at 871 (Scalia, J. dissenting).

ordinance. An injunction is a court ordered remedy addressed to specific people based upon specific conduct. An ordinance is a law passed by a deliberative body designed to address general public concerns. Unlike an injunction, an ordinance cannot target specific people but must neutrally apply to the public as a whole. The Supreme Court reasoned in *Madsen* and *Schenck* that a small buffer zone around an abortion clinic's entrance or driveway may be upheld if it is designed to address a specific problem against certain individuals with a history of attempting to block access. Even against that specific history, *Madsen* demands that certain standards must be followed in order to protect free speech. However, an ordinance by design cannot be addressed to a specific individual with specific past history. While the concern may have arisen from a specific individual, the ordinance applies to more than the original perpetrator. Though someone who repeatedly breaks the law may have certain constitutional rights withdrawn or restricted, that same restriction would be unconstitutional against someone who had no past illegal conduct. Consequently, it is generally impermissible to impose a buffer zone through legislation.[108]

In 1994 Congress passed the Freedom of Access to Clinic Entrances Act (hereafter FACE).[109] FACE applies to reproductive health services (a euphemism for abortion clinics)[110] and places of religious worship.[111] FACE prohibits anyone who "by force or a threat of force or by physical obstruction, intentionally injures, intimidates, or interferes" with (1) another person obtaining or providing reproductive health services or (2) a person lawfully exercising or seeking to exercise their First Amendment right of religious freedom at a place of religious worship. FACE also applies to anyone who intentionally damages or destroys the property of any facility that provides "reproductive health services" or the property of a place of religious worship.[112] Though a few courts have found FACE unconstitutional on the basis that Congress

---

[108]*Sabelko v. City of Phoenix*, 68 F.3d 1169 (9th Cir. 1995), *vacated*, 117 S. Ct. 1077 (1997).
[109]18 U.S.C. § 248.
[110]18 U.S.C. § 248(a)(1).
[111]18 U.S.C. § 248(a)(2).
[112]18 U.S.C. § 248(a)(3).

lacked authority to regulate private activity around abortion clinics,[113] a majority of courts have upheld FACE against constitutional challenges.[114] One federal court correctly recognized that FACE is only applicable against acts of "physical" force.[115] FACE does not, and cannot, restrict peaceful, nonviolent speech no matter how offensive so long as acts of physical force are not used to convey the message.

Noise Levels

Noise levels, with or without sound amplification, have often become an issue in picketing or demonstrating activities. Noise ordinances must be precise and sometimes have been ruled unconstitutional either because they are vague or overbroad. Indeed,

> an enactment is void for vagueness if its prohibitions are not clearly defined. Vague laws offend several important values. First, because we assume that man is free to steer between lawful and unlawful conduct, we insist that laws give the person of ordinary intelligence a reasonable opportunity to know what is prohibited, so that he may act accordingly. Vague laws may trap the innocent by not providing fair warning. Second, if arbitrary and

---

[113]*Hoffman v. Hunt*, 23 F. Supp. 791 (W.D. N.C. 1996), *rev'd*, 126 F.3d 575 (4th Cir. 1997); *U.S. v. Wilson*, 880 F. Supp. 621 (E.D. Wis. 1995), *rev'd* 73 F.3d. 675 (7th Cir. 1995).

[114]*U.S. v. Bird*, 124 F.3d 667 (5th Cir. 1997); *Terry v. Reno*, 101 F.3d 1412 (D.C. Cir. 1996); *U.S. v. Unterberger*, 97 F.3d 1413 (11th Cir. 1996); *U.S. v. Soderna*, 82 F.3d 1370 (7th Cir. Wis. 1996); *Cook v. Reno*, 74 F.3d 97 (5th Cir. 1996); *U.S. v. Dinwiddie*, 76 F.3d 913 (8th Cir. 1996); *U.S. v. Wilson*, 73 F.3d 675 (7th Cir. 1995); *Cheffer v. Reno*, 55 F.3d 1517 (11th Cir. 1995); *American Life League, Inc. v. Reno*, 47 F.3d 642 (4th Cir. 1995); *U.S. v. Weslin*, 964 F. Supp. 83 (W.D. N.Y. 1997); *U.S. v. Scott*, 958 F. Supp. 761 (D. Conn 1997); *Planned Parenthood Ass'n of Southeastern Pennsylvania, Inc. v. Walton*, 949 F. Supp. 290 (E.D. Penn. 1996); *U.S. v. Roach*, 947 F. Supp. 872 (E.D. Penn. 1996); *Planned Parenthood of Columbia/Williamette, Inc. v. American Coalition of Life Activists*, 945 F. Supp. 1355 (D. Or. 1996); *U.S. v. McMillan*, 946 F. Supp. 1254 (S.D. Miss. 1995); *U.S. v. Scott*, 919 F. Supp. 76 (D. Conn 1996); *U.S. v. White*, 893 F. Supp. 1423 (C.D. Cal. 1995); *U.S. v. Lucero*, 895 F. Supp. 1421 (Dist. Kan. 1995); *U.S. v. Lindgren*, 883 F. Supp. 1321 (D.N.D. 1995); *U. S. v. Hill*, 893 F. Supp. 1034 (N.D. Fla. 1994); *U.S. v. Brock*, 863 F. Supp. 851 (E.D. Wis. 1994); *Riely v. Reno*, 860 F. Supp. 693 (D. Ariz. 1994); *Council for Life v. Reno*, 856 F. Supp. 1422 (S.D. Cal. 1994).

[115]*Cheffer*, 55 F.3d at 1517.

discriminatory enforcement is to be prevented, laws must provide explicit standards for those who apply them. A vague law impermissibly delegates basic policy matters . . . for resolution on an *ad hoc* and subjective basis, with the attendant dangers of arbitrary and discriminatory application. Third, but related, where a vague statute "abut[s] upon sensitive areas of basic First Amendment freedoms," it "operates to inhibit the free exercise of those freedoms."[116]

A noise ordinance would be unconstitutional if it "either forbids or requires the doing of an act in terms so vague that men of common intelligence must necessarily guess at its meaning and differ as to its application."[117] Certainly those expected to obey a noise ordinance must "be informed as to what the state commands or forbids."[118]

Sometimes noise ordinances are so broad that there is no clearly identifiable noise level which, when reached, would result in violating the ordinance. Ordinances which retain decibel levels are more specific than ordinances which simply prohibit loud noises. Oftentimes noise ordinances which do not have decibel levels require specific case-by-case evaluation to determine the facts and whether the protester willfully created a noise level incompatible with the area.[119] For example, in the city of Beaufort, South Carolina, city officials enacted a noise ordinance that prohibited any person from willfully disturbing any neighborhood or business in the city or making or continuing loud and unseemly noises. This ordinance was passed as a result of several years of street preaching on Saturdays in front of business establishments while standing on the sidewalk or in the bed of pickup trucks. The noise levels of these preachers were obviously loud, and their preaching was found to be in violation of the ordinance. The South Carolina Supreme Court ruled that the language was not vague and that adequate notice had been given to

[116]*Grayned*, 408 U.S. at 108-109 (citations omitted).
[117]*Connally v. General Construction Co.*, 269 U.S. 385, 391 (1926).
[118]*Lanzetta v. New Jersey*, 306 U.S. 451, 453 (1939).
[119]*Kovacs v. Cooper*, 336 U.S. 77 (1949).

the preachers by the police authorities.[120]

Violent Mixed With Nonviolent Activity

Many of the recent attempted restrictions, including buffer zones, on picketing activity in the context of abortion protests have arisen because of escalating violent activity. While courts do have a right to restrict violent activity, which is not protected by the First Amendment, any restriction on picketing or protesting must be precise so as to separate the violent from the nonviolent activity. Indeed, a "free society prefers to punish the few who abuse rights of speech *after* they break the law than to throttle them and all others beforehand."[121]

The classic case involving violent activity mixed with nonviolent activity is *NAACP v. Claiborne Hardware*.[122] The facts of *Claiborne Hardware* are quite interesting. In March of 1966, several hundred black demonstrators implemented a boycott of white merchants following racial abuses in Claiborne County, Mississippi. The business merchants sued for an injunction against the demonstrators and Charles Evers, a leader of the movement who "sought to persuade others to join the boycott through pressure and the 'threat' of social ostracism."[123] Mr. Evers and other active participants of the boycott furthered their cause by seeking to embarrass nonparticipants and "coerce them into action" and conformity.[124]

Some of the demonstrators, acting for all others, became involved in "acts of physical force and violence" against potential customers and used "[i]ntimidation, threats, social ostracism, vilification, and traduction" in order to achieve their desired results.[125] "Enforcers" known as "black hats" were stationed in the vicinity of the white-owned business to record the names of the boycott violators and those violators were later disclosed in a pamphlet entitled the *Black Times*, which was published by the

---

[120]*City of Beaufort v. Baker*, 432 S.E.2d 470 (S.C. 1993).
[121]*Southeastern Promotions, Ltd. v. Conrad*, 420 U.S. 546, 559 (1975).
[122]458 U.S. 886 (1982).
[123]*Id.* at 909-10.
[124]*Id.* at 910.
[125]*Id.* at 894.

organization.[126] "In two cases, shots were fired at a house; in a third, a brick was thrown through a windshield; . . . and a group of young blacks apparently pulled down the overalls of an elderly black mason known as 'Preacher White' and spanked him for not observing the boycott."[127] Momentum was added to the boycott following the assassination of Dr. Martin Luther King, Jr., on April 4, 1968, and "[t]ension in the community neared a breaking point." On April 18, 1969, a local civil rights leader was shot and killed.[128] Mr. Evers was quoted as saying: "If we catch any of you going into any of them racist stores, we're going to break your damn neck."[129] Nevertheless, coinciding with the escalation in activities was the continuous "uniformly peaceful and orderly" picketing of the white-owned businesses which often involved small children and occurred "primarily on weekends."[130]

After hearing all of the above evidence, the Mississippi Supreme Court entered a permanent injunction restricting the demonstrators from stationing "store watches" at the merchants' business premises, from "persuading" any person to withhold his patronage from the merchants, and from "using demeaning and obscene language to or about any person," and finally, from "picketing or patrolling" the premises of any of the merchants.[131] However, the United States Supreme Court overruled the Mississippi Supreme Court decision, stating that every element of the boycott was "a form of speech or conduct that is ordinarily entitled to protection under the First and Fourteenth Amendments."[132] The Supreme Court also stated that when restricting free speech activities, there must be "precision of regulation" when "conduct occurs in the context of constitutionally protected activity."[133] The Court further noted that "only unlawful conduct and the persons responsible for conduct of that character"

---

[126]*Id.* at 904-05.
[127]*Id.* at 904-05.
[128]*Id.* at 901-02.
[129]*Id.* at 902.
[130]*Id.* at 903.
[131]*Id.* at 893.
[132]*Id.* at 907.
[133]*Id.* at 916.

may be restrained.[134]

In another case, a court ruled that it is improper to lump together protected peaceful activity with violent unprotected activity and to prohibit both forms of activity because one is unlawful.[135] In a similar but unrelated situation, the United States Supreme Court ruled that a university could not prohibit the presence of a student group simply because its parent or national affiliate organization had displayed violent and disruptive behavior.[136] It is, therefore, impermissible to use violent activities to justify prohibiting peaceful picketing activities around abortion clinics or any other facility. There must be a distinction made between the violent and nonviolent activities. While violent activities can be prohibited as not being protected by the Free Speech Clause, legitimate peaceful demonstration cannot be restrained under the guise that someone else became violent. Moreover, simply because an individual is a member of an organization known for its violent activities is not sufficient to restrict that individual's free speech activities. Only if the individual has demonstrated violent disruptive activities can that individual be restricted.

It is unconstitutional for one person to lose his or her First Amendment free speech rights because someone else acted unseemly. Indeed, the "right to associate does not lose all constitutional protection merely because some members of the group may have participated in conduct or advocated doctrine that itself is not protected."[137] The Supreme Court has firmly held that "peaceful assembly for lawful discussion cannot be made a crime."[138] If "absolute assurance of tranquillity is required, we

---

[134]*Id.* at 927 n.67.

[135]*Machesky*, 414 F.2d at 283.

[136]*Healy*, 408 U.S. at 169.

[137]*Claiborne Hardware*, 458 U.S. at 908. *See also Citizens Against Rent Control/Coalition for Fair Housing v. City of Berkeley*, 454 U.S. 290, 294 (1981) (the "practice of persons sharing common views banning together to achieve a common end is deeply embedded in the American political process"); *Scales v. United States*, 367 U.S. 203, 229 (1961) (a "'blanket prohibition of association with a group having both legal and illegal aims' would present 'a real danger that legitimate political expression or association would be impaired'"); *NAACP v. Alabama ex. rel. Patterson*, 357 U.S. 449, 460 (1958) ("Effective advocacy of both public and private points of view, particularly controversial ones, is undeniably enhanced by group association.").

[138]*De Jonge v. Oregon*, 299 U.S. 353, 365 (1937).

may as well forget about speech."[139] While dissidents elsewhere face legal sanctions for every stripe, in the United States the right to free speech belongs to the politically correct and incorrect, the disaffected as well as the loyal, the obnoxious as well as the sensitive, the vociferous as well as the meek.[140]

---

[139]*City of Houston v. Hill,* 482 U.S. 451, 462 n.11 (1987) (quoting *Spence v. Washington,* 418 U.S. 405, 416 (1974) (editing remarks and citations omitted)).

[140]*See e.g., Forsyth County v. Nationalist Movement,* 112 S. Ct. 2395 (1992) (racist march); *Texas v. Johnson,* 491 U.S. 397 (1989) (flag burning); *Hustler Magazine, Inc. v. Falwell,* 485 U.S. 46 (1988) (lewd parody); *NAACP v. Claiborne Hardware Co.,* 458 U.S. 886 (1982) (aggressive boycott enforced with threats of ostracism).

15

DOOR-TO-DOOR WITNESSING

The right to witness in private residential neighborhoods going door-to-door is an important right protected by the Constitution. Most of the door-to-door witnessing cases have dealt with Jehovah's Witnesses. In one case, a city attempted to impose a licensing scheme essentially banning Jehovah's Witnesses from witnessing door-to-door in predominantly Roman Catholic neighborhoods. The Jehovah's Witnesses played records attacking the Roman Catholic church as an "enemy" and stating that the church was of the devil. This licensing scheme attempted to prohibit the door-to-door witnessing activities of the Jehovah's Witnesses, but the United States Supreme Court ruled that this was unconstitutional.[1] The *Cantwell* opinion was the landmark opinion first ruling that the Free Exercise Clause of the First Amendment was applicable to the states. The regulation at issue allowed the city officials to determine who would be permitted to engage in solicitation or distribution of literature based upon the content of the message.

The United States Supreme Court has also ruled unconstitutional a municipal "license tax" that was imposed upon door-to-door solicitation and witnessing by Jehovah's Witnesses. The Court noted the following:

Those who can tax the privilege of engaging in this form of missionary evangelism can close its doors to all those who do not have a full purse. Spreading religious beliefs in this ancient and honorable manner would thus be denied the needy. Those who can deprive religious groups of their colporteurs can take from them a part of the vital power of the press which has survived from the Reformation.[2]

In one case, the Supreme Court considered the constitutionality of a city ordinance that made it unlawful for any person distributing

[1]*Cantwell v. Connecticut*, 310 U.S. 296 (1940); *Church of Scientology Flag Service Organization, Inc. v. City of Clearwater*, 2 F.3d 1514 (11th Cir. 1993).
[2]*Murdock v. Pennsylvania*, 319 U.S. 105, 112 (1943).

literature "to ring the doorbell, sound the door knocker, or otherwise summon the inmate or inmates of any residence to the door for the purpose of receiving" such literature. The United State Supreme Court ruled that this type of ordinance was unconstitutional and stated the following:

> Freedom to distribute information to every citizen wherever he desires to receive it is so clearly vital to the preservation of a free society that, putting aside reasonable police and health regulations of time and manner of distribution, it must be fully preserved.[3]

The right to distribute literature door-to-door is an important First Amendment right. Oftentimes other forms of communication are too costly. The Supreme Court has recognized that "[d]oor to door distribution of circulars is essential to the poorly financed causes of little people."[4]

A federal district court in New York ruled that an ordinance requiring the consent of a householder before approaching the home was unconstitutional. Interestingly named, the *Town of Babylon* court ruled that to require "consent of householders before approaching their homes constitutes, in effect, an indirect unconstitutional imposition of a licensing fee; it generates costs which burden the exercise of first amendment rights in direct proportion to the number of persons the speaker wants to reach."[5]

In addition to the above, many other federal courts have ruled that cities may not flatly and unreasonably prohibit door-to-door witnessing.[6]

In the City of Ocoee, Florida, Pamela Jones and Marcia Muller sought to distribute political and religious literature in residential neighborhoods. However, the City of Ocoee had a policy stating

---

[3]*Martin v. City of Struthers*, 319 U.S. 141, 146-67 (1943).

[4]*Id.*

[5]*Troyer v. Town of Babylon*, 483 F. Supp. 1135 (E.D.N.Y. 1980), *aff'd* 628 F.2d 1346 (2nd Cir. 1980), *aff'd*, 449 U.S. 998 (1980).

[6]*See eg. Largent v. Texas*, 318 U.S. 418 (1943); *Jamison v. Texas*, 318 U.S. 413 (1943); *Weissman v. City of Alamogordo*, 472 F. Supp. 425 (D.N.M. 1979); *McMurdie v. Doutt*, 468 F. Supp. 766 (N.D. Ohio 1979); *Levers v. City of Tullahoma*, 446 F. Supp. 884 (E.D. Tenn. 1978); *Murdock v. City of Jacksonville*, 361 F. Supp. 1083 (M.D. Fla. 1973).

that a permit was necessary prior to distributing any literature. This permit had to be filled out on a specified form which was then reviewed by the Chief of Police. The applicant was required to identify various physical features including any scars or markings on their body. Prior to the issuance of the permit, the Chief of Police was required to determine that the applicant was a person of "good moral character." After Liberty Counsel filed suit, the city changed the policy. No longer does the City of Ocoee require prior permission to distribute literature door to door.

Reviewing an attempt by a municipality to regulate neighborhood activities like canvassing and soliciting, the United States Supreme Court stated that any regulation in this area must be such so "as not to intrude upon the rights of free speech and free assembly."[7] Courts have recognized the value in literature distribution.

> From the time of the founding of our nation, the distribution of written material has been an essential weapon in the defense of liberty. Throughout the years, the leaflet has retained its vitality as an effective and inexpensive means of disseminating religious and political thought. Today when selective access to the channels of mass communication limits the expression of diverse opinion, the handbill remains important to the promise of full and free discussion of public issues. For those of moderate means, but deep conviction, freedom to circulate flyers implicates fundamental liberties.[8]

Indeed, the freedom to speak and circulate flyers, especially in your neighborhood, implicates fundamental constitutional liberties.

> Because of their vital role for people who lack access to more elaborate (and more costly) channels of communication, certain public places have special status under the First Amendment. . . . The doctrine of the public forum achieves a central purpose of the freedom of

---

[7]*Thomas v. Collins*, 323 U.S. 516, 540-41 (1945).
[8]*Paulsen v. County of Nassau*, 925 F.2d 65, 66 (2nd Cir. 1991).

the speech -- the role of equality of communicative opportunities -- by opening avenues of expression for the "poorly financed causes of little people.". . . As our court has articulated the theme of the public forum cases, regulation of free expression in the public areas. . . affects most frequently those who advocate unpopular causes. It is those who seek to change the status quo who have historically taken to the streets or other public places to promote their causes. Those who are satisfied with our society as it is, normally use other forums.[9]

Most people don't have access to major media outlets. It is therefore important to maintain an avenue of expression for the "poorly financed causes of little people."[10] The Supreme Court ruled unconstitutional a city ordinance that made it a crime for a solicitor or canvasser to knock on the front door of a resident's home and ring the doorbell.[11] The Supreme Court noted that the ordinance was too broad and impinged upon constitutional freedoms by substituting "the judgment of the community for the judgment of the individual householder."[12] The Supreme Court has invalidated an ordinance that prohibited the distribution of "literature of any kind . . . without first obtaining written permission from the city manager."[13] The Supreme Court has also ruled unconstitutional a city policy that required persons to obtain a permit, which would not be issued if the Chief of Police decided that the "canvasser is not of good character or is canvassing for a project not free from fraud."[14] The Court found the ordinance unconstitutional because the canvasser's "liberty to communicate with residents of the town at their homes depends upon the exercise of the officer's discretion."[15] In another case, the Supreme Court ruled unconstitutional a municipal ordinance, which required that

---

[9]*Carreras v. City of Anaheim*, 758 F.2d 1039, 1043 (9th Cir. 1985) *quoting Martin v. City of Struthers*, 319 U.S. 141, 146 (1943) (citations omitted).

[10]*Martin*, 319 U.S. at 146.

[11]*Martin*, 319 U.S. at 141. *See also Staub v. City of Baxley*, 355 U.S. 313 (1958).

[12]*Id.* at 144.

[13]*Lovell v. Griffin*, 303 U.S. 444, 447 (1938).

[14]*Schneider v. New Jersey*, 308 U.S. 147 (1939).

[15]*Id.* at 158.

advanced written notice be given to the local police department by any person desiring to canvas, solicit or call from house to house for a recognized charitable cause, or for a federal, state, county, or municipal political campaign or cause.[16] The problem presented by any policy that requires prior permission before engaging in speech is that it acts as a prior restraint on speech. "A prior restraint on the exercise of First Amendment rights comes to [the Supreme] Court bearing a heavy presumption against its constitutional validity."[17] The heavy presumption is justified because "prior restraints on speech . . . are the most serious and the least tolerable infringements on First Amendment rights."[18] Any prior restraint bears a "heavy presumption" against its constitutional validity.[19] The state must bear a "heavy burden" to impose a prior restraint on speech. The presumption against prior restraints is heavier, and the degree of protection broader, than that against limits on expression imposed by criminal statutes. This is so because society "prefers to punish the few who abuse rights of speech *after* they break the law rather than throttle them and all others beforehand."[20]

"In determining the extent of the constitutional protection, it has been generally, if not universally, considered that it is the chief purpose of the [First Amendment] to prevent previous restraints. . . ."[21] The Supreme Court has repeatedly reaffirmed that "the prevention of [prior restraints] was a leading purpose in the adoption of the [First Amendment]."[22] "Prior restraint upon speech suppresses the precise freedom which the First Amendment sought to protect against abridgement."[23]

In the context of an international airport, a federal court ruled that a one day permit application process was unconstitutional because it created an unreasonable delay on the expression of speech. The court stated:

---

[16]*Hynes v. Maro Oradell*, 425 U.S. 610 (1976).

[17]*Vance v. Universal Amusement Co., Inc.*, 445 U.S. 308, 317 (1980).

[18]*Nebraska Press Ass'n v. Stuart*, 427 U.S. 539, 559 (1975).

[19]*See Bantam Books, Inc. v. Sullivan*, 372 U.S. 58, 70 (1963).

[20]*Southeastern Promotions, Ltd. v. Conrad*, 420 U.S. 526, 559-60 (1975) (emphasis in original).

[21]*Near v. Minnesota*, 283 U.S. 697, 713 (1931).

[22]*Lovell v. Griffin*, 303 U.S. 444, 451 (1938).

[23]*Carroll v. Presidents and Commissioners of Princess Anne*, 393 U.S. 175, 181 (1968).

We find the requirement of advanced registration as a condition to peaceful pamphleteering, picketing, or communicating with the public to be unconstitutional. The United States Supreme Court has held more than thirty-five years ago that persons desiring to exercise their free speech rights may not be required to give advanced notice to the state.[24]

Another court struck down a permit policy as an unconstitutional prior restraint on free speech and free assembly stating that the prior delay constituted a prior restraint and was therefore unconstitutional.[25]

Any prior permission policy creates unreasonable delays on the expression of free speech. "The delay adherent in advanced notice requirements inhibits free speech by outlawing spontaneous expression."[26] "When an event occurs, it is often necessary to have one's voice heard promptly, if it is to be considered at all."[27] Indeed, the Supreme Court has indicated that a prior notification requirement is "quite incompatible with the requirements of the First Amendment."[28] "The simple knowledge that one must inform the government of his desire to speak and must fill out appropriate forms and comply with applicable regulation discourages citizens from speaking freely."[29] The Supreme Court has traditionally condemned licensing schemes as prior restraints without regard to content restrictions.[30]

In addition to the inherent delay in a prior permit policy, prior licensing schemes are generally unconstitutionally vague and vest excessive authority in administrative officials which may use that

---

[24]*Rosen v. Port of Portland*, 641 F.2d 1243, 1247 (9th Cir. 1981) (citing *Thomas*, 323 U.S. at 523).

[25]*Grossman v. City of Portland*, 33 F.3d 1200 (9th Cir. 1994).

[26]*NAACP v. City of Richmond*, 743 F.2d 1346 (9th Cir. 1984).

[27]*Shuttlesworth v. City of Birmingham*, 394 U.S. 147, 163 (1969).

[28]*Thomas*, 323 U.S. at 540.

[29]*City of Richmond*, 743 F.2d at 1455.

[30]*See Forsyth County v. The Nationalist Movement*, 112 S. Ct. 2395 (1992) (Parade permits); *Shuttlesworth v. City of Birmingham*, 394 U.S. 147 (1969) (*Shuttlesworth II*) (Public demonstration permits); *Lovell*, 303 U.S. at 444 (Literature distribution permit).

authority to censor unwanted speech.[31] Discretionary licenses to suppress speech violate the core of the First Amendment. "It is not merely the sporadic abuse of power by the censor but the pervasive threat inherent in its very existence that constitutes a danger to freedom of discussion."[32] One court pointed out the following in this regard:

> Vesting [government authorities] with this discretion permits the government to control the viewpoints that will be expressed. Whether the city council or the police exercise this power, we believe that it runs afoul of the basic principle that "forbids the government from regulating speech in ways that favor some viewpoints or ideas at the expense of others."[33]

As pointed out above, prior licensing schemes are frequently ruled unconstitutional because a prior restraint inhibits speech and often vests too much discretionary authority in the licensing official to suppress speech. Sometimes this vesting authority is in part because there are no time limits set for granting or denying the permit, and therefore the government official may censor speech simply through inaction or delay. However, another reason why a prior licensing scheme is not consistent with the First Amendment is because sometimes it is unconstitutionally vague. As a matter of due process, "[n]o one may be required at peril of life, liberty or property to speculate as to the meaning of penal statutes. All are entitled to be informed as to what the State commands or forbids."[34] The general test for vagueness applies with particular force in review of laws dealing with speech. "[S]tricter standards of permissible statutory vagueness may be applied to a statute having a potentially inhibiting effect on speech; a man may the less be required to act at his peril here, because the free dissemination of

---

[31]*Forsyth County*, 112 S. Ct. at 2395. *See also Lakewood v. Plain Dealer Publishing Co.*, 486 U.S. 750 (1988).

[32]*Thornhill v. Alabama*, 310 U.S. 88, 97 (1940).

[33]*Ass'n of Community Org. v. Mun of Golden, Colorado*, 744 F.2d 739, 747 (10th Cir. 1984) (quoting *City Council of Los Angeles v. Taxpayers for Vincent*, 466 U.S. 789, 804 (1984)).

[34]*Lanzetta v. New Jersey*, 306 U.S. 451, 453 (1939).

ideas may be the loser."[35] A regulation is considered unconstitutionally vague if it "either forbids or requires the doing of an act in terms so vague that [persons] of common intelligence must necessarily guess at its meaning and differ as to its application."[36] The prohibition against overly vague laws protects citizens from having to voluntarily curtail their First Amendment activities because of fear that those activities could be characterized as illegal.[37] "Precision of regulation" is the touchstone of First and Fourteenth Amendments.[38]

Vague laws "may trap the innocent by not providing fair warning," "provide for arbitrary and discriminatory enforcement," impermissibly delegate policy matters to enforcement officials on an "*ad hoc* and subjective basis," and consequently chill free expression.[39] Promises put forth by government officials not to unconstitutionally apply a vague law does not save its unconstitutionality. "Well-intentioned prosecutors and judicial safeguards do not neutralize the vice of a vague law."[40] The Supreme Court has noted that it must apply strict scrutiny to any policy infringing on speech if it is vague because such a policy has an "inhibiting effect on speech."[41] When free speech is at stake, "precision of drafting and clarity of purpose are essential."[42]

The right to freedom of speech is a precious liberty. It is important that this liberty be vigilantly guarded within residential neighborhoods because it is important to allow free communication in these areas. Whether the issue is door-to-door canvassing, picketing on a public sidewalk, or carrying on expressive activity in a public park, any policy that contains a prior licensing scheme is

---

[35]*Smith v. California*, 361 U.S. 147, 151 (1959). *See also Buckley v. Valeo*, 424 U.S. 1, 76-82 (1976); *Broadrick v. Oklahoma*, 413 U.S. 601, 611-12 (1973).

[36]*Connally v. General Construction Co.*, 269 U.S. 385, 391 (1926).

[37]*See Grayned v. City of Rockford*, 408 U.S. 104, 109 (1972).

[38]*NAACP v. Button*, 371 U.S. 415, 435 (1963). Vague laws violate both free speech and due process. *Cf. Grayned*, 408 U.S. at 108-09 (Noise ordinance); *Papachristou v. City of Jacksonville*, 405 U.S. 156 (1972) (Loitering law); and *Coates v. City of Cincinnati*, 402 U.S. 611 (1971) (Ordinance prohibiting three or more persons from assembling in an annoying manner void for vagueness).

[39]*Grayned*, 408 U.S. at 108-09; *see also Baggett v. Bullitt*, 377 U.S. 360, 374 (1964).

[40]*Baggett*, 377 U.S. at 374.

[41]*Hynes*, 425 U.S. at 620; *see also Smith v. California*, 361 U.S. 147, 151 (1959).

[42]*Erznoznik v. City of Jacksonville*, 422 U.S. 205, 212-13 (1975).

automatically constitutionally suspect. Generally the government has no business monitoring the speech activities of its citizens. An individual resident can protect their dwelling by placing a sign which indicates that solicitors, canvassers, or leafletters are not welcome. However, this decision is best left to the individual resident and not to the government.

Picketing in residential neighborhoods is also constitutionally protected. Most residential neighborhoods have public sidewalks and these public sidewalks are considered traditional public forums.[43] As the Supreme Court has noted, public sidewalks "have immemorially been held in trust for the use of the public."[44] Notwithstanding the fact that the public sidewalks are in residential neighborhoods, they still are classified as traditional public forums and therefore are open to expressive activity by the public.

One difference between residential and business areas containing public sidewalks is the fact that in residential areas, the government has an interest in protecting "the well-being, tranquility, and privacy of the home."[45] In this regard, the Supreme Court has stated that the home is the "last citadel of the tired, the weary, and the sick."[46] In order to protect residential privacy, a city may pass an ordinance that restricts targeted picketing of a single residential address. Focused "picketing taking place solely in front of a particular residence" may be prohibited, but the government may not ban the general "marching through residential neighborhoods, or even walking around in front of an entire block of houses."[47] In other words, while the government may prohibit picketing targeted at a single residential address, it may not prohibit general picketing throughout a neighborhood. Individuals may protest a particular residence, but must do so by marching on the public sidewalk throughout the neighborhood. Congregating solely in front of a single residential home can be restricted, but marching generally throughout the neighborhood protesting an individual location is

[43]*Frisby v. Schultz*, 487 U.S. 474, 481 (1988). *See also Perry Education Ass'n v. Perry Local Educators' Ass'n*, 460 U.S. 37 (1983); *Hague v. CIO*, 307 U.S. 496, 515 (1939).
[44]*Frisby*, 487 U.S. at 481 (quoting *Hague*, 307 U.S. at 515).
[45]*Frisby*, 487 U.S. at 484.
[46]*Id.*
[47]*Frisby*, 487 U.S. at 477, 483. *See also Madsen v. Women's Health Center, Inc.*, 114 S. Ct. 2516, 2529-30 (1994).

constitutionally protected.

16

THE RIGHT TO
DISPLAY RELIGIOUS SIGNS
ON PRIVATE PROPERTY

The display of religious signs is another area of religious liberty that has come under attack. In a Wisconsin case, Liberty Counsel worked with an individual who wanted to display 4,000 crosses on his private property. Local city officials argued that the display of crosses was not permitted by the sign ordinance and was, therefore, unlawful. This allegation was clearly incorrect.

In another case brought to Liberty Counsel's attention, a person erected a sign on his private property with a pro-life message. One day he noticed that the sign was gone. He then erected another sign at the same location. To his surprise, he saw a crew of people dismantling the sign, and when he approached, he realized they were city officials. Though other commercial signs were allowed in the area, city officials attempted to remove his sign because it had a pro-life message.

Another instance brought to Liberty Counsel's attention involved a church sign. This sign included crosses on the church property in memorial to those unborn children who lost their lives through abortion. In the middle of the crosses, the church erected a sign explaining the meaning of the crosses as a memorial. City officials interpreted the crosses to meet the requirements of the sign ordinance but wanted to remove the sign in the midst of the crosses. The church argued that without the sign in the midst of the crosses, passersby would not know the meaning of the multiple crosses. In response, city officials determined that in order to prohibit the display of the religious sign, the city would pass an ordinance prohibiting the display of all religious signs. Liberty Counsel attorneys attended a city council meeting on this issue and warned that if the city chose this route, it would face a federal lawsuit. The city then requested the assistance of Liberty Counsel to draft a new sign ordinance.

The above examples illustrate the many conflicts that have arisen over signs. When considering whether government can restrict the display of a religious or pro-life sign, several factors must be considered including the location of the display, the size of the display, and whether the government allows other commercial signs such as advertising or real estate signs to be displayed.

The Supreme Court has stated that noncommercial speech receives higher First Amendment protection than commercial speech.[1] An ordinance allowing commercial signs, such as those involving advertising or real estate, but disallowing religious or pro-life signs, would clearly be a content-based regulation and therefore presumptively invalid.[2] It is impermissible to restrict signs simply because of the content of the speech. Therefore, it is impermissible to allow commercial signs while disallowing noncommercial signs.[3] Courts have ruled that an ordinance permitting commercial and other signs, but banning political or issue-related messages, violates the First Amendment.[4]

Based upon the above, it is evident that a city cannot allow commercial billboards while restricting the use of noncommercial billboards.[5] The Supreme Court has noted the following in this regard:

> The fact that the city may value commercial messages relating to on-site goods and services more than it values commercial messages relating to off-site goods and services does not justify prohibiting an occupant from displaying its own ideas or those of others. . . . Insofar as the city tolerates [signs] at all, it cannot choose to limit their contents to commercial messages; the city may not conclude that the communication of commercial information concerning goods and services connected with a particular site is of greater value than the

---

[1]*Metromedia, Inc. v. City of San Diego*, 453 U.S. 490 (1981); *Matthews v. Town of Needham*, 596 F. Supp. 932, 934 (D. Mass. 1984) ("Noncommercial speech is afforded more protection than commercial speech."). In *City of Cincinnati v. Discovery Network, Inc.*, 113 S. Ct. 1505 (1993), the Supreme Court seems to have narrowed the distinction between commercial and noncommercial speech.

[2]*R.A.V. v. City of St. Paul*, 112 S. Ct. 2538, 2542 (1992).

[3]*Runyon v. Fasi*, 762 F. Supp. 280, 284 (D. Haw. 1991).

[4]*City of Ladue v. Gilleo*, 114 S. Ct. 2038 (1994); *Tauber v. Town of Longmeadow*, 695 F. Supp. 1358, 1362 (D. Mass. 1988) (city bylaws banning posting of political signs but allowing others constituted impermissible content-based restriction on speech).

[5]*Messer v. City of Douglasville*, 975 F.2d 1505 (11th Cir. 1992).

communication of noncommercial messages.[6]

Since the Supreme Court has noted that noncommercial speech retains greater First Amendment protection than commercial speech, a government entity cannot award more protection to commercial signs than is afforded noncommercial signs.

Certainly government entities can regulate signs in the interest of aesthetics and traffic safety.[7] However, "aesthetic judgments are necessarily subjective, defying objective evaluation, and for that reason must be carefully scrutinized to determine if they are only a public rationalization of an impermissible purpose."[8] Moreover, aesthetic interests are never "sufficiently compelling to justify a content-based restriction on . . . freedom of expression."[9] In other words, in the interest of aesthetics, a government entity may not place differing restrictions on noncommercial versus commercial signs. Restrictions on the basis of aesthetics must be equally applied to religious as well as to secular speech. However, simply because there is equal treatment between religious and secular speech does not necessarily mean that all aesthetic restrictions are constitutional. Government may not, under the guise of aesthetics, prohibit free speech.

Another interest that a government entity may have in regulating signs deals with traffic safety. Sometimes aesthetics and traffic safety may combine in terms of limiting the size of signs. However, when considering "the universe of distractions that face motorists" on city streets, noncommercial signs "are not sufficiently significant to justify so serious a restriction upon expression."[10]

It is an important principle that the Constitution protects the display of noncommercial religious, pro-life, and political signs. If individuals were not allowed to display signs, then they may not be

---

[6]*Metromedia*, 453 U.S. at 513. *See also John Donnelly & Sons v. Campbell*, 639 F.2d 6 (1st Cir. 1980).

[7]*Messer*, 975 F.2d at 1505; *Citizens United for Free Speech II v. Long Beach Township Board of Commissioners*, 802 F. Supp. 1223 (D.N.J. 1992).

[8]*Metromedia*, 453 U.S. at 510.

[9]*Loftus v. Township of Lawrence Park*, 764 F. Supp. 354 (W.D. Pa. 1991). *See also Signs, Inc. v. Orange County*, 592 F. Supp. 693, 697 (M.D. Fla. 1983).

[10]*Arlington County Republican Committee v. Arlington County*, 790 F. Supp. 618, 624 (E.D. Va. 1992), *aff'd in part, rev'd in part, vacated in part*, 983 F.2d 587 (4th Cir. 1993).

able to speak at all to the general public. One court noted that other options of speaking through television and radio "involve substantially more cost and less autonomy and reach a significant number of nonlocal persons who [may] likely not have the interest or inclination to receive or act on such information."[11] Indeed, many citizens cannot afford to spend large sums of money to exercise their First Amendment rights.[12] In this regard, one court noted:

> [M]any messages advocating religious, social, or political views are greatly restricted from dissemination if they must primarily or solely rely upon costly print and electronic means for exposure; the expense and ineffectiveness in using either of these two forms of communication is often prohibitive, and signage remains an important alternative.[13]

Indeed, a long standing principle of constitutional law is that "one is not to have the exercise of his liberty of expression in appropriate places abridged on the plea that it may be exercised in some other place."[14] Therefore, it is insufficient to restrict the usage of signs simply because there might be alternative means of disseminating the message.

Though not often encountered, it is clearly impermissible to require the daily removal of signs or displays because such a requirement would result in the denial of free speech. In one such case, the city of Cincinnati passed an ordinance prohibiting the presence of any display, exhibit, or structure in Fountain Square between the hours of 10:00 p.m. and 6:00 p.m. Though not strictly a sign ordinance, the case involved the Congregation of Lubavitch which had regularly displayed an eighteen-foot menorah in Fountain Square in preceding years. The requirement of having no displays between certain specified hours appeared to be content-neutral, but

---

[11]*Burkhart Advertising, Inc. v. City of Auburn*, 786 F. Supp. 721, 733 (N.D. Ind. 1991).

[12]*Arlington County Republican Committee*, 790 F. Supp. at 627 (citing *Martin v. City of Struthers*, 319 U.S. 141 (1943) ("Door-to-door distribution of circulars is essential to the poorly financed causes of little people.")).

[13]*Burkhart Advertising*, 786 F. Supp. at 733.

[14]*Schneider v. New Jersey*, 308 U.S. 147, 163 (1939).

in reality, it would have required the Jewish organization to dismantle its menorah every single day. It took approximately six hours to assemble and disassemble the structure. This unreasonable burden would have prohibited the display of the menorah. In this context, a federal appeals court rightfully struck down the ordinance because of its unconstitutionality.[15] Since "communication by signs and posters is virtually pure speech,"[16] the government may not easily restrict this form of expression.

In summary, the display of religious, political, and pro-life signs is constitutionally protected speech. Clearly, if a governmental entity allows commercial signs, then it may not restrict the presence of noncommercial signs. Most residential neighborhoods allow commercial signs in the form of real estate signs. As such, religious, political, and pro-life speech may be displayed on signs in such neighborhoods. Commercial signs are found throughout many business districts, and consequently, governmental entities may not restrict the presence of noncommercial signs. Certain restrictions may be placed on the display of signs for aesthetic purposes or traffic control. These restrictions primarily involve regulations pertaining to the distance in which the sign may be displayed in proximity to the street or the size of the display. However, simply because an aesthetic or traffic display restriction applies to both commercial and noncommercial speech does not necessarily mean the restriction is constitutional. The regulation may not be so restrictive as to essentially prohibit First Amendment activity.

---

[15]*Congregation Lubavitch v. City of Cincinnati*, 997 F.2d 1160 (6th Cir. 1993).

[16]*Baldwin v. Redwood*, 540 F.2d 1360, 1366 (9th Cir. 1976), *cert. denied sub nom.*, *Leipzig v. Baldwin*, 431 U.S. 913 (1977).

17

RELIGIOUS DISCRIMINATION IN EMPLOYMENT

The Civil Rights Act of 1964 is a fairly broad-reaching civil rights law. Title II applies to discrimination in places of public accommodation based on race or religion. Titles III and IV ban racial and religious segregation in public facilities and in public education. Title VI requires that federal assistance recipients not be discriminated against on the basis of race, and Title VII, the subject of this chapter, applies to nondiscrimination in employment.

The wording applicable to religious discrimination in employment states as follows:

(a) It shall be an unlawful employment practice for an employer

(1) to fail or refuse to hire or to discharge any individual, or otherwise to discriminate against any individual with respect to his compensation, terms, conditions, or privileges of employment, because of such individual's race, color, religion, sex, or national origin; or

(2) to limit, segregate, or classify his employees or applicants for employment in any way which would deprive or tend to deprive any individual of employment opportunities or otherwise adversely affect his status as an employee, because of such individual's race, color, religion, sex, or national origin.[1]

This ban on discrimination applies to all employers, including religious organizations, which engage in any industry or activity

---

[1]42 U.S.C. § 2000e-2(a).

"affecting commerce" and which employ fifteen or more employees for each working day in each of the twenty or more calendar weeks in the current or preceding calendar year.[2] Part-time employees can be counted in computing an organization's total number of employees.[3] Courts are without authority to consider employment discrimination suits against employers under Title VII if the employer has fewer than fifteen employees.[4]

In addition to having the prerequisite fifteen employees for the specified time period, the employer must be engaged in an industry or activity "affecting commerce." In general, churches which are not engaged in commercial enterprises would have few interstate business transactions and may not be considered to affect commerce even if the fifteen requisite employees have been employed for the requisite time period. However, even minimal interstate activity may be enough to affect commerce. For example, the sale of cassette tapes across state lines, or the broadcasting of church services across state lines, could be considered "affecting commerce."

There are several important exemptions to Title VII. Religious educational institutions are exempt under Title VII as follows:

> [I]t shall not be an unlawful employment practice for a school, college, university, or other educational institution or institution of learning to hire and employ employees of a particular religion if such school, college, university, or other educational institution or institution of learning is, in whole or in substantial part, owned, supported, controlled, or managed by a particular religion or by a particular religious corporation, association, or society, or if the curriculum of such school, college, university, or other educational institution or institution of learning is directed toward the propagation of a particular religion.[5]

It should be noted that the exemption for religious educational

---

[2] 42 U.S.C. § 2000e-2.
[3] *Pedreyra v. Cornell Prescription Pharmacies, Inc.*, 465 F. Supp. 936 (D. Colo. 1979).
[4] *Bonomo v. National Duck Pin Bowling Congress, Inc.*, 469 F. Supp. 467 (D. Md. 1979).
[5] 42 U.S.C. § 2000e-2(e)(2).

institutions is an exemption from *religious* discrimination, not from the other forms of discrimination. Another exemption is the "bona fide occupational qualification." This exemption is as follows:

> Notwithstanding any other provision of this subchapter . . . it shall not be an unlawful employment practice for an employer to hire and employ employees . . . on the basis of his religion, sex, or national origin in those certain instances where religion, sex, or national origin is a bona fide occupational qualification reasonably necessary to the normal operation of that particular business or enterprise. . . .[6]

This exemption applies to religion, sex, or national origin. For example, the Moroccan Pavilion at EPCOT Center may hire only those of Moroccan descent because of the necessity to create a Moroccan atmosphere. Finally, religious organizations are exempt from the religious discrimination requirement as follows:

> This subchapter shall not apply to . . . a religious corporation, association, educational institution, or society with respect to the employment of individuals of a particular religion to perform work connected with the carrying on by such corporation, association, educational institution, or society of its activities.[7]

In 1972, Congress amended Title VII to enable religious organizations to discriminate on the basis of religion in all employment decisions. Therefore, a Baptist church may hire all Baptists and a Catholic church may hire all Catholics.[8]

For other employers who are covered by Title VII, the employer is restricted from discriminating on the basis of religion. The employee must first have a sincerely held religious belief that is negatively impacted or burdened by a particular employment

---

[6]42 U.S.C. § 2000e-2(e).

[7]42 U.S.C. § 2000e-1.

[8]*Corporation of the Presiding Bishop of the Church of Jesus Christ of Latter-day Saints v. Amos*, 483 U.S. 327 (1987).

practice. The employee then has the obligation to notify the employer of the belief and of the negative impact on that belief. The burden then shifts to the employer to provide reasonable accommodation to that belief unless doing so would result in an undue hardship to the employer. Take an example that was brought to the attention of Liberty Counsel. A Seventh-day Adventist had a sincerely held religious belief that Saturday is the seventh day Sabbath upon which no work should be conducted. This employee was a salesperson who had worked for the same employer for some time. During the week, the employer required a sales meeting to be conducted. For an unexplained reason, the employer then required the sales meeting to be conducted on Saturday. In this case, the employer already knew of the salesperson's religious belief. The employee brought his belief to the attention of the employer again and requested that the sales meeting be held on some other day or possibly even Sunday. The employer did not accommodate this religious belief even though accommodation was clearly possible. In this situation, the employer discriminated on the basis of religion.

The Equal Employment Opportunity Commission (hereafter EEOC) brought suit in federal court against Dillard Department Stores because of its so-called "no excuses" policy.[9] This national department chain apparently had a policy wherein it would accept no excuse from any employee for not working at least one Sunday per month. One employee objected to working on Sunday because of sincerely held religious beliefs, but the store would not accept the excuse and therefore terminated the employee. The employee then filed a complaint with the EEOC and after the EEOC reviewed the case, the EEOC itself filed suit against the department store. This policy has now been changed. This was a blatant violation of federal law prohibiting discrimination based on religion. By federal law, an employer is mandated to at least attempt accommodation of the employee's sincerely held religious belief, but this department store refused to accept any excuses. Their policy has now been changed.

In one case a professor at the University of Detroit refused to pay his labor union agency fees. He offered to pay an amount equal to his entire agency fee to a charity or to remit that portion of his

---

[9]*EEOC v. Dillard Department Stores*, 1994 WL 738971 (E.D. Mo.).

fee which was allocated solely to the union's local responsibilities and to pay the balance to a charitable organization.[10] The reason he refused to pay the agency fees to the union was because of the union's support of abortion related causes. This teacher declared: "Since I believe that abortion is absolutely wrong I must choose the course that minimizes the support of it. The gravity of this issue is so great that I must consider my job expendable."[11] However, the University informed the professor that he was being terminated for failure to pay the agency fees. The court stated that in order "to invoke the employer's duty to offer a reasonable accommodation, it is sufficient that the employee establishes that he holds a sincere religious belief that conflicts with an employment requirement."[12] The court also pointed out that "one reasonable accommodation may be for [the teacher] to pay all of the agency fee, including the amount normally forwarded to the EMA and the NEA, to the union to be used solely for local collective bargaining purposes."[13] The court ruled against the University because it did not attempt to reasonably accommodate the teacher's sincerely held religious belief. The court pointed out that there were alternative ways that the University could have at least attempted to accommodate these beliefs, and they must do so.

When discrimination does occur after following the above steps, the employee should contact the EEOC and should also contact the state human rights commission. Contact with these commissions is extremely important because of short time limits. Failure to contact these commissions may result in the inability to use either the state discrimination law or the federal Title VII law as a basis for a discriminatory claim. The employee should document in writing a request to the employer stating the religious belief, noting the adverse impact on that belief, and requesting an accommodation of the belief. The employer should attempt to accommodate this religious belief, unless to do so results in an undue hardship.

---

[10]*EEOC v. University of Detroit*, 904 F.2d 331 (6th Cir. 1990).
[11]*Id.* at 333.
[12]*Id.* at 335.
[13]*Id.* at 335.

18

UNION MEMBERSHIP
AND ITS
CONSTITUTIONAL IMPLICATIONS

Union membership unquestionably implicates the First Amendment. The First Amendment protects the right to free speech, the right to free association, and the right to religious freedom. A correlative of the right to free speech is the right not to speak at all. Often times unions engage in activities which are not directly related to negotiating labor agreements. Unions publish their views, lobby, litigate, and undertake public relations campaigns on political, moral, and religious issues not directly related to negotiating the labor contract. Whenever unions engage in these peripheral activities, the First Amendment is implicated. To require a member to pay for activities to which the member is either politically or religiously opposed may violate constitutional freedoms. To better understand the First Amendment right of employees in the union context, it is important to briefly overview certain federal laws affecting labor unions.

Background

In the early twentieth century two major labor federations emerged to address concerns regarding the labor market: the American Federation of Labor (hereafter "AFL") and the Congress of Industrial Organizations (hereafter "CIO"). The AFL organized workers by crafts which meant that one company might have multiple small-craft unions working in the same factory. The CIO organized labor on an industry-wide basis. Rather than dealing with the individual crafts within a single employer, the CIO treated multiple employers as one unit. One example of this structure is the United Auto Workers.

The AFL eventually adopted an industry-wide union concept similar to the CIO, but when the CIO became infiltrated by communist influences and began losing membership, the two federations merged in 1955 under the leadership of George Meany to form what is now known as the AFL-CIO.

National Labor Relations Act

In 1935 Congress passed the National Labor Relations Act (hereafter "NLRA").[1] Originally certain unions had what was known as a Closed Shop. A Closed Shop involved a contract between labor and management whereby management agreed not to hire employees who were not already members of the union. A Closed Shop essentially made the union the hiring agent. In order to work for the employer, the worker had to be a member of the union. In 1947 Congress passed the Taft-Hartley Act in response to criticisms of unfair labor practices carried on by organized labor following the passage of the NLRA. The Taft-Hartley Act, also known as the Labor-Management Relations Act (hereafter "LMRA")[2] instituted several major changes to labor unions.[3] Though President Lyndon B. Johnson attempted to repeal the act in 1965, that attempt failed and it is still a part of the NLRA. The following summarizes some of the significant areas of labor law that affect religious liberty.

Closed, Agency and Union Shops

The Closed Shop concept was abolished by the passage of the LMRA in 1947. No longer is it lawful for a contract to be entered into between labor and management whereby management agrees not to hire employees who are not already members of the union. Unions may set up what is known as an Agency Shop whereby the union acts as the agent for the employee even though the employee is not a member of the union. There is typically a security clause that requires all Agency Shop employees to pay a service fee to the union which is usually equal to the union dues. An Agency Shop is

---

[1] 29 U.S.C. § 151 et seq.

[2] 29 U.S.C. § 141 et seq.

[3] The Labor Management Reporting and Disclosure Act (hereinafter "LMRDA"), also known as the Landrum-Griffin Act, was passed by Congress in 1949. This law further amended the NLRA by creating what was known as the union members' "Bill of Rights." The LMRDA defines certain unfair labor practices with respect to secondary boycotts and picketing. For example, a union having a grievance with a certain employer may not picket another employer not having direct relationship with the employer against whom the grievance is alleged.

most often found in the public employment sector. In addition to the Agency Shop, the Union Shop replaced the Closed Shop after the passage of the LMRA. Under the Union Shop, after a brief period on the job, employees may be required to pay initiation fees and dues to the union. The requirement to "join" has been modified by court challenges so that the payment of the fees may be all that the union is allowed to require.[4] In practice, the Union Shop is now similar to an Agency Shop.[5]

Right to Work

Under the LMRA passed by Congress in 1947, the NLRA was revised to allow state exemption from the Union Shop provision by adopting right-to-work laws under section 14(b) of the NLRA.[6] Many states have adopted such right-to-work laws, and in those states unions have less power. In such a state, it is unlawful to require someone to join a union in order to work with a specific

---

[4]"Under a union-shop agreement, an employee must become a member of the union within a specified period of time after hire, and must as a member pay whatever union dues and fees are uniformly required." *Abood v. Detroit Board of Education*, 431 U.S. 207, 217 n.10 (1977). Under both the National Labor Relations Act and the Railway Labor Act, "[i]t is permissible to condition employment upon membership, but membership, insofar as it has significance to employment rights, may in turn be conditioned only upon payment of fees and dues." *NLRB v. General Motors*, 373 U.S. 734, 732 (1963). In the absence of a union security provision, Congress recognized that many employees who share in the fruits of union benefits true collective bargaining would refuse to pay their share of the union costs. *Id.* at 740-41. After the abolition of the closed shop, Congress enacted legislation allowing "employers to enter into agreements requiring all the employees in a given bargaining unit to become members 30 days after being hired as long as such membership is available to all workers on a nondiscriminatory basis," so long as employers were prohibited from mandatory discharge of an employee expelled from the unit for any reason other than failure to pay initiation fees or dues. *Communication Workers' of America v. Beck*, 487 U.S. 735, 749 (1988). The "legislative history clearly indicates that Congress intended to prevent utilization of Union security agreements for any purpose other than to compel payment of union dues and fees." *Id.* Though employees may not be required to join a union or participate in union activity, employees may be required to pay the union dues or fees. 29 U.S.C. § 158(a)(3). *See also Beck*, 487 U.S. at 749.

[5]Although "a union shop denies an employee the option of not formally becoming a union member, under federal law it is the single 'practical equivalent' of an agency shop." *General Motors*, 373 U.S. at 373. *See also Lathrop v. Donohue*, 367 U.S. 820, 828 (1961).

[6]"Unlike section 14(b) of the National Labor Relations Act, 29 U.S.C. § 164(b), the Railway Labor Act preempts any attempt by the State to prohibit a union-shop agreement." *Abood*, 431 U.S. at 118 n.12.

employer. Additionally, in right-to-work states, employees may not be forced to pay initiation fees or dues to the union. As noted above, the Union Shop replaced the Closed Shop. Under the Union Shop concept, employees may be forced to pay fees and dues to the union. However, in right-to-work states, employees are not required to pay union dues or initiation fees.

Freedom Of Speech And Association

The United States Supreme Court has recognized that compulsory union membership implicates important First Amendment rights.

To compel employees financially to support their collective bargaining representative has an impact on their First Amendment interests. An employee may very well have ideological objections to a wide variety of activities undertaken by the union in its role as exclusive representative. His moral or religious views about the desirability of abortion may not square with the union's policy in negotiating the medical benefits plan. One individual might disagree with the union policy of negotiating limits on the right to strike, believing that to be the road to serfdom for the working class, while another might have economic or political objections to unionism itself. An employee might object to the union's wage policy because it violates guidelines designed to limit inflation or might object to the union's seeking a clause in the collective bargaining agreement proscribing racial discrimination. The examples could be multiplied. To be required to help finance the union as a collective bargaining agent might well be thought, therefore, to interfere in some way with an employee's freedom to associate for the advancement of ideas, or to refrain from doing so, as he sees fit.[7]

Indeed, the "right of freedom of thought protected by the First

---

[7]*Abood*, 431 U.S. at 222.

Amendment against state action includes both the right to speak freely and the right to refrain from speaking at all."[8] Clearly, membership in a union implicates First Amendment freedoms. However, the United States Supreme Court has allowed some interference with First Amendment freedoms in the context of union membership because of the "governmental interest in industrial peace."[9]

In both the private[10] and public[11] sector outside of a right-to-work state, union dues may be required of an objecting employee but no part of that employee's dues or assessment may be used for activities not germane or directly related to the union's duties as the collective bargaining representative.

The forced payment of union dues for public employment presents constitutional concerns under the First Amendment. Surely "government may not require an individual to relinquish rights guaranteed him by the First Amendment as a condition of public employment."[12] "For at the heart of the First Amendment is the notion that an individual should be free to believe as he will, and that in a free society one's belief should be shaped by his mind and his conscience rather than coerced by the State."[13]

A union may "spend funds for the expression of political views, on behalf of political candidates, or toward the advancement of other ideological causes" which are germane to its duties as a collective bargaining representative.[14] However, the Constitution requires that such expenditures not germane to the union's duties as a collective bargaining representative be financed from charges, dues, or assessments paid by employees who do not object to advancing those ideas and who are not coerced into doing so against their will by threat of loss of employment.[15] According to the Supreme Court, any expenditures by the union must (1) be

---

[8]*Wooley v. Maynard*, 430 U.S. 705, 714 (1977).

[9]*Ellis v. Railway Clerks*, 466 U.S. 435, 455-56 (1984). *See also Abood*, 431 U.S. at 222-23.

[10]*Lehnert v. Ferris Faculty Association*, 111 S. Ct. 1950, 1957 (1991).

[11]*See e.g., Chicago Teachers Union, Local No. 1 v. Hudson*, 475 U.S. 292 (1986); *Abood*, 431 U.S. at 207; *Lehnert*, 111 S. Ct. at 1950.

[12]*Abood*, 431 U.S. at 234. *See also Elrod v. Burns*, 427 U.S. 347 (1976).

[13]*Abood*, 431 U.S at 234.

[14]*Id.*

[15]*Id.* at 236.

"germane" to collective bargaining activity; (2) be justified by the government's vital policy interest in labor peace in avoiding "free riders"; and (3) not significantly add to the burden of free speech that is inherent in the allowance of an agency or union shop.[16] It is not an adequate remedy to limit the use of the actual dollars collected from dissenting employees to collective bargaining purposes.[17] A union may not exact dues from an objecting employee and then later rebate a portion of the dues. The difficulty in a rebate system whereby the employee first pays membership, objects to portions of the dues being used for advocacy unrelated to the collective bargaining representative's duty, and then obtains a refund means that the employee is actually advancing an interest-free loan to the union. The union "should not be permitted to exact a service fee from nonmembers without first establishing a procedure which will avoid the risk that their funds will be used, even temporarily, to finance ideological activities unrelated to collective bargaining."[18]

Once an employee objects to funds being used by the union, the burden rests on the union to present information documenting expenditures, and in some cases, showing the percentages of the expenses used toward the objectionable activities.[19] The burden of the objecting employee is simply to make the objection known.[20] Once the objection is made, the union must identify the expenditures for collective bargaining and contract administration as well as those expenditures used for purposes that do not benefit the dissenting nonmember.[21]

The Supreme Court has indicated that the Railway Labor

---

[16]*Lehnert*, 111 S. Ct. at 1959.

[17]*Abood*, 431 U.S. at 237 n.35.

[18]*Hudson*, 475 U.S. at 305, *quoting Abood*, 431 U.S. at 244.

[19]*Hudson*, 475 U.S. at 306. "Since the unions possess the facts and records from which the portion of political to total union expenditures can reasonably be calculated, basic considerations of fairness compel that they, not the individual employees, bear the burden of proving such proportion." *Abood*, 431 U.S. at 239-40 n.40 (quoting *Railway Clerks v. Allen*, 373 U.S. 113, 122 (1963)).

[20]*Machinists v. Street*, 367 U.S. 740, 774 (1961).

[21]Although public sector unions are not subject to the disclosure requirements of the Labor Management Reporting and Disclosure Act located at 29 U.S.C. § 402(e), "the fact that private sector unions have a duty of disclosure suggests that a limited notice requirement does not impose an undue burden on the union." *Hudson* 475 U.S. at 306 n.17.

Act[22] does not permit a union, over the objection of nonmembers, to expend compelled agency fees on political causes.[23] The Supreme Court has also ruled that employees governed by the National Labor Relations Act[24] are not required to fund objectionable political causes of the authorized union.[25] Indeed, NLRA and the RLA "authorizes the exaction of only those fees and dues necessary to 'performing the duties of an exclusive representative of the employee in dealing with the employer on labor-management issues.'"[26]

In light of the above, the First Amendment requires that: (1) unions may not exact a service fee from nonmembers without first establishing a procedure which will avoid the risk that their funds will be used, even temporarily, to finance ideological or political activities unrelated to collective bargaining; (2) unions have the burden to provide adequate justification for the advance reduction of dues by detailing the amount of dues used for administrative activity directly related to the collective bargaining representative; and (3) unions must offer a reasonably prompt decision by an impartial decision maker to resolve the objections raised by the employee. While unions are not required to put 100% of the funds into escrow pending final resolution, a union may, at the minimum, be required to put a sufficient amount of the funds into an interest-bearing escrow account until the objection has been resolved.[27]

Unions may constitutionally subsidize lobbying and other political activities with fees from the objecting employee so long as those activities are pertinent to the duties of the union as a bargaining representative.[28] However, when lobbying activities do not relate to the ratification or implementation of an objecting employee's collective bargaining agreement, but rather relate to the financial support of the employee's profession or of public employees generally, the connection to the union's function as a bargaining representative is too attenuated to justify compelled

---

[22]45 U.S.C. § 151.

[23]*Machinists v. Street*, 367 U.S. 740 (1961).

[24]29 U.S.C. § 158(a)(3).

[25]*Beck*, 487 U.S. at 761-63.

[26]*Id.* (quoting *Ellis v. Railway Clerks*, 466 U.S. 435, 448 (1984)).

[27]*Hudson*, 475 U.S. at 310.

[28]*Lehnert*, 111 S. Ct. at 1959.

support by objecting employees.[29] In other words, an employee may not be compelled "to subsidize legislative lobbying or other political union activities outside the limited context of contract ratification or implementation."[30] In the public sector context, "a local bargaining representative may charge objecting employees for their pro rata share of the costs associated with otherwise chargeable activities of its state and national affiliates, even if those activities were not performed for the direct benefit of the objecting employees' bargaining unit."[31] However, the union may not charge objecting employees for a direct donation or interest-free loan to an unrelated bargaining unit for the purpose of promoting employee rights or unionism generally. A "contribution by a local union to its parent that is not part of the local's responsibility as an affiliate but is in the nature of a charitable donation would not be chargeable to dissenters."[32]

A union may use an objecting member's dues to help defray the cost of conventions.[33] While social activities are not central to bargaining, they may be charged to an objecting employee.[34] Union publications directly related to the union's collective bargaining duties may be chargeable to an objecting employee but publications that promote political causes that are not directly related to the collective bargaining duties may not be charged to an objecting employee.[35] Funds expended to organize the union to increase membership or make the union stronger may not be charged to an objecting employee.[36] The expenses of litigation incident to negotiating and administering the contract or to settling grievances and disputes arising in the bargaining unit are chargeable to an objecting employee, but expenses of litigation having no such connection with the bargaining unit are not chargeable to the

---

[29]Id. at 1959-1960. In *Lehnert* the Court ruled that a state teachers education union may not use fees from an objecting employee to lobby state government to finance education because that activity is not directly related to the collective bargaining agreement.

[30]Id. at 1960-1961.

[31]Id. at 1961.

[32]Id.

[33]*Ellis v. Brotherhood of Railway, Airline and Steamship Clerks*, 104 S. Ct. 1883, 1892-1893 (1984).

[34]Id. at 1893.

[35]Id. at 1893-1894.

[36]Id. at 1894.

objecting employee.[37] As noted above, funds may not be used in the public employment context to lobby governmental branches in order to secure funds for public employees.[38] Similarly, public relations campaigns designed to enhance the reputation of the teaching profession or any other profession associated with the union may not be chargeable to an objecting employee.[39] Finally, money expended toward an illegal strike may not be chargeable to an objecting employee.[40]

All of the monies which may not be chargeable to an objecting employee must be deducted pro rata from the employee's dues or fees. To not allow such a deduction violates not only the First Amendment right to freedom of speech but also the right to free association.

Religious Freedom

Conscience Clause

On December 24, 1980, President Jimmy Carter signed into law section 19 of the NLRA, which is sometimes referred to as the "Conscience Clause." Section 19 provides in pertinent part:

> Any employee who is a member of and adheres to established and traditional tenets or teachings of a bona fide religion, body, or sect which has historically held conscientious objections to joining or financially supporting labor organizations shall not be required to join or financially support any labor organization as a condition of employment; except that such employee may be required...to pay sums equal to such dues and initiation fees to a nonreligious, nonlabor charitable fund.[41]

---

[37]*Id.* at 1895. Since such nonrelated litigation expenses may not be chargeable to the objecting employee, writing about such litigation in a union publication may not be charged to an objecting employee. *Id.* at 1894.

[38]*Lehnert*, 111 S. Ct. at 1963.

[39]*Id.* at 1964.

[40]*Id.* at 1965.

[41]29 U.S.C. § 169.

Under the Conscience Clause, employees with sincerely held religious convictions against joining or financially supporting labor unions may, instead of paying their dues and initiation fees to the union, pay the equivalent amount to a nonreligious, nonunion charity recognized as a 501(c)(3) organization by the Internal Revenue Service. This is a significant provision that preserves religious liberty. Many Americans have sincerely held religious beliefs that prohibit them from financially supporting certain labor union practices. Some labor unions, like the National Education Association, have become very political and take controversial positions adverse to religious liberty. To force an employee to financially contribute to a union contrary to their sincerely held religious convictions would violate constitutional protections. When confronted with such a situation, an employee can take the equivalent of the union dues and initiation fees required by the union and pay those fees to any nonreligious, nonunion charitable organization that is recognized as a nonprofit, tax-exempt organization under 501(c)(3) of the Internal Revenue Code.

Many unions don't like this provision because it takes away union dues which they would otherwise receive. Unions have attempted to bring legal challenges against the Conscience Clause but none of these challenges have been successful. Some unions give a list of charitable organizations to which the opting-out employee may contribute to, but a union may not force an employee to give to only their selected list. An employee can opt out and give to any organization that meets the above-mentioned criteria.

In right-to-work states, employees may not be forced to pay the union initiation fees or union dues. In those states without right-to-work laws, employees may be forced to pay initiation fees and union dues. However, if the employee has a sincerely held religious conviction against union membership or support, the employee may utilize the Conscience Clause to pay the equivalent of the initiation fees and union dues to a nonreligious charitable organization.

Section 19 of the NLRA is somewhat limited in scope.[42] It

---

[42]In *Wilson v. NLRB*, 920 F.2d 1282 (6th Cir. 1990), a federal appeals court found that section 19 of the NLRA violated the Establishment Clause of the First Amendment precisely because it is limited only to members of a bona fide religious organization having a long

applies only to those employees who are members of and adhere to "established and traditional tenets or teachings of a bona fide religion, body, or sect which has historically held conscientious objections to joining or financially supporting labor organizations.[43] If an employee is not a member of a church or a religious body that has long established traditional tenets opposed to union membership, then the employee may not use the so-called Conscience Clause. However, the employee may rely upon other federal and constitutional law as noted below.[44]

Free Exercise of Religion

An employee who does not fit within the confines of section 19 of the NLRA may raise an objection based upon freedom of religion protected under federal antidiscrimination laws and the First Amendment.[45] The federal law known as Title VII restricts employment discrimination based on religion and defines religion as "all aspects of religious observance and practice, as well as belief."[46] An employee who has a sincerely held religious belief "opposing unions could be relieved from paying dues under Title VII, even if he or she was not a member of an organized religious

---

history opposing union membership. In other words, the court found that section 19 of the NLRA actually discriminates among religions. An employee who has a sincerely held religious belief opposing union membership but who does not belong to a church having a long history or tradition in opposition to unions may not utilize section 19. However, an employee with the same religious belief who happens to be a member of such a church having historical beliefs in opposition to union membership may utilize section 19. Consequently, the application of section 19 gives preferential treatment to some denominations but not others.

[43]29 U.S.C. § 169.

[44]It is important to note that for those governed by the Railway Labor Act, 45 U.S.C. §151 et seq. (hereafter "RLA"), passed by Congress in 1926, upheld by the United States Supreme Court in 1930, and amended in 1935, there is no similar Conscience Clause. The RLA is completely separate from the NLRA and provides the framework for collective bargaining by the railroad and airline industry. The Conscience Clause in the NLRA does not apply to workers who are governed by the RLA. However, an employee governed by the RLA may still utilize Title VII which prohibits discrimination in the work place based upon religion or may alternatively utilize the Free Exercise Clause of the First Amendment.

[45]An employee may rely upon the federal law known as Title VII since Title VII defines religion as "all aspects of religious observance and practice, as well as belief." 42 U.S.C. § 2000e(j).

[46]42 U.S.C. § 2000e(j).

group that opposes unions."[47]

In one case a Roman Catholic professor was employed at the University of Detroit. Based upon his pro-life beliefs, he objected to joining the local and state education association because the National Education Association and the Michigan Education Association had campaigned to promote abortion rights. These actions of the state and National Education Association were contrary to the professor's religious beliefs. Because the professor would not join the union, the University terminated his contract. A federal appeals court ruled that in order to invoke the employer's duty to offer a reasonable accommodation, "it is sufficient that the employee establishes that he holds a sincere religious belief that conflicts with an employment requirement."[48] The court ruled that one reasonable accommodation would be to pay the agency fee, including the amount normally forwarded to the Michigan Education Association and the National Education Association, "to the local union to be used solely for local collective bargaining purposes."[49]

In addition to Title VII involving federal employment discrimination, an employee may utilize the First Amendment Free Exercise Clause.[50] Under the First Amendment, an employee who

---

[47]*International Association of Machinists v. Boeing Co.*, 833 F.2d 165, 169 (9th Cir. 1987). *See also* 29 C.F.R. § 1605(1). Title VII was designed to supplement, rather than supplant, existing laws and institutions relating to employment discrimination. *Alexander v. Gardner-Denver Co.*, 415 U.S. 36 (1974). "Congress did not intend section 19 of the NLRA to supersede section 701(j) of Title VII. The House report accompanying H.R. 4774 expressly stated that '[t]he bill would accommodate the religious beliefs of these persons and thereby *reconcile the National Labor Relations Act with section 701(j) of the Equal Employment Opportunity Act.'" International Association of Machinists*, 833 F.2d at 17, *quoting* H.R. Rep. No. 496, 96th Cong. 1st Sess., 2 (1980)(emphasis added), U.S. Cod. Cong. Admin. News 1980, pp. 7158-59.

[48]*Equal Employment Opportunity Commission v. University of Detroit*, 904 F.2d 331, 335 (6th Cir. 1990).

[49]*Id.*

[50]An employee may raise a free exercise objection under the First Amendment to the United States Constitution and combine this claim with a free speech or free association claim under the First Amendment. Combining both constitutional rights would result in the so-called hybrid claim recognized under *Employment Division v. Smith*, 494 U.S. 872 (1990). In other words, when combining a free exercise claim with some other recognized constitutional right (in this case free speech or free association) the employee may argue that the rule or regulation must meet a compelling interest test. If the employee can show (1) a sincerely held religious belief, that (2) is burdened by some government rule or regulation

has a sincerely held religious belief must apprise the employer of that belief and point out what employment practice impinges on that belief. Certainly, an employment arrangement that requires an employee to pay union dues may impinge upon a sincerely held religious belief. The employer must attempt to accommodate that belief. Accommodation may require that a portion of the union dues be deducted so as not to support objectionable activities, or that the dues are used only for local collective bargaining arrangements, or that the employee be allowed to pay the equivalent of the dues to a nonreligious, nonunion charitable organization recognized as a nonprofit, tax-exempt organization under 501(c)(3) of the Internal Revenue Code.

In summary, union membership clearly implicates federal and constitutional rights. For those employees having no religious objections to union membership, union membership may still implicate the First Amendment right of free speech and freedom of association. For those employees having religious objections, union membership may implicate both the free exercise of religion guaranteed by the First Amendment to the United States Constitution and employment discrimination under Title VII.

The First Amendment right to freedom of speech includes the right not to speak at all. Union membership, whereby an employee

---

or government backed rule or regulation as would be the case under NLRA or RLA, then (3) the government must show that it has a compelling governmental interest in the rule or regulation and that it has achieved it interest in the least restrictive means. Pursuant to the analysis in *Smith*, combining free exercise of religion with some other federally recognized individual right such as free speech brings the standard of protection to its highest level. *Id.* at 1601. *Hobbie v. Unemployment Appeals Commission of Florida*, 480 U.S. 136 (1987) (unemployment benefits); *Thomas v. Review Board, Indiana Employment Security Div.*, 450 U.S. 707 (1981) (unemployment benefits); *Wooley v. Maynard*, 430 U.S. 705 (1977) (invalidating compelled display of a license plate slogan that offended individual religious beliefs); *Wisconsin v. Yoder*, 406 U.S. 205, (1972) (invalidating compulsory school attendance laws as applied to Amish parents who refused on religious grounds to send their children to public school); *Sherbert v. Verner*, 375 U.S. 398 (1963) (unemployment benefits); *Follett v. McCormick*, 321 U.S. 573 (1944) (same); *Murdock v. Pennsylvania*, 319 U.S. 105 (1943) (invalidating a flat tax on solicitation as applied to the dissemination of religious ideas); *West Virginia Board of Education v. Barnette*, 319 U.S. 624 (1943) (invalidating compulsory flag salute statue challenged by religious objectors); *Cantwell v. Connecticut*, 310 U.S. 296 (1940) (invalidating a licensing system for religious and charitable solicitations under which the administrator had discretion to deny a license to any cause he deemed nonreligious); *Pierce v. Society of Sisters*, 268 U.S. 510 (1925) (directing the education of children).

is forced to pay dues or initiation fees which in turn finance a union's ideological causes to which the employee is opposed, may violate cherished constitutional freedoms. Union membership in the public sector context clearly collides with First Amendment protections because the government may not require an individual to relinquish rights guaranteed by the First Amendment as a condition of public employment. An employee who has an objection to union membership or union expenditures, should make the objection known to the union. The union then has the burden of presenting information justifying and itemizing the expense. The union may not take dues from an objecting member only to rebate them later. While a union in a state with no right-to-work laws[51] may take a small portion of the dues that would cover expenditures for collective bargaining and contract administration, the union at a minimum is required to put the remainder of the dues in an interest-bearing escrow account, detail the amount of dues used for administrative activity directly related to the collective bargaining agreement, and offer a reasonably prompt decision by an impartial decision maker. An objecting employee may not be required to pay for union activities that are not germane or directly related to the union's role as a collective bargaining representative.

In addition to utilizing the right to free speech and free association guaranteed by the First Amendment, an employee may also rely upon the Conscience Clause under section 19 of the NLRA. However, the scope of the Conscience Clause is limited to those employees who are members of and adhere to established and traditional tenets of a bona fide religion, body, or sect which has historically held conscientious objections to joining or financially supporting labor organizations. If an employee is not a member of a church or religious body having long established traditional tenets opposed to union membership, then the employee may not use the so-called Conscience Clause. Such an employee can continue to use the First Amendment right to freedom of speech and free association and also may use other federal and constitutional laws protecting religious liberty.

---

[51]Unions are generally less powerful in states which have right-to-work laws. In a right-to-work state, employees may not be required to join the union or pay union dues or initiation fees.

An employee who does not fit within the confines of section 19 of the NLRA may rely upon federal antidiscrimination laws found in Title VII. Title VII defines religion much broader than the Conscience Clause. Under Title VII an employee who has a sincerely held religious belief opposing unions could be relieved of paying union dues even if not a member of an organized religious group that opposes unions.

Finally, an employee may also rely upon the First Amendment right to free exercise of religion. Under the Constitution, an employee who has a sincerely held religious belief must first apprise the employer of that belief and point out what employment or union practice impinges on that belief. The employer is then required to accommodate the employee's sincerely held religious belief unless doing so would result in an undue hardship to the employer. Some remedies designed to protect the religious beliefs of the employee might include withholding union dues from the state or national affiliate and applying those dues only to the local affiliate which does not engage in objectionable activities, or allowing an employee a pro rata deduction of union dues that do not support objectionable activities, or allowing the employee to pay the equivalent of the dues to a nonreligious, nonunion charitable organization recognized as a nonprofit, tax-exempt organization under 501(c)(3) of the Internal Revenue Code.

19

POLITICAL ACTIVITY
OF NONPROFIT ORGANIZATIONS

The extent to which churches and nonprofit organizations may engage in lobbying and political campaigns is illusive and often misunderstood.[1] Pastors and leaders of nonprofit corporations are frequently leery about becoming too vocal on political matters for fear of jeopardizing the organization's nonprofit status. Paralyzed by this fear, many leaders refuse to address political issues. It is important to know the parameters imposed on nonprofit corporations. Only when these parameters are known can the organization truly be free to communicate without jeopardizing its tax structure.

The information presented below can be summarized as follows: (a) a 501(c)(3) nonprofit organization and a church are permitted to engage in lobbying activities so long as no substantial part of their overall activities are directed toward lobbying, but these organizations are strictly prohibited from endorsing or opposing a candidate for public office; (b) a 501(c)(4) organization is permitted to engage in lobbying activities without any limitation, but is prohibited from endorsing or opposing a political candidate for public office; (c) a 501(h) organization is permitted to engage in lobbying activities without limitation if the activities are performed by volunteer services or with certain specified monetary limitations if expenditures are directed toward lobbying activities, but this type of an organization is prohibited from endorsing or opposing a candidate for public office; (d) a political action committee may engage in lobbying activities without limitation and may endorse or oppose a candidate for public office with the only limitation being that which is imposed by state or federal law pertaining to the amount of contributions permissible per candidate; and (e) as long as a pastor or representative is not purporting to speak for the church or 501(c)(3) organization, but is, instead, expressing views as an individual citizen, there are no lobbying

---

[1]Since churches are exempt from federal income tax, they are treated as nonprofit organizations exempt from income tax under the Internal Revenue Code § 501(c)(3).

limitations on the pastor or representative, and the only political limitations would be the amount of money allowed by state or federal law to contribute to a political candidate.

Prior to 1934, there were no lobbying limitations imposed upon nonprofit organizations by the Internal Revenue Code. However, without benefit of Congressional hearings, an amendment was added to the Revenue Act of 1934, which was designed to prohibit tax exemption for organizations that attempt to influence legislation.[2] In 1954, then Senator Lyndon B. Johnson proposed an amendment to what later became the Internal Revenue Code of 1954. This amendment specifically prohibited nonprofit organizations from endorsing or opposing a candidate for public office.[3] Senator Johnson, who later became President Johnson, apparently proposed this amendment to counteract a nonprofit organization which opposed his candidacy for senator.

To determine the extent of political activity of a nonprofit organization, an important distinction must be made between (1) legislative or lobbying activities, and (2) intervention in a political campaign. Nonprofit organizations are permitted to engage in legislative or lobbying activities, but are strictly prohibited from endorsing or opposing a candidate for public office. An organization will be regarded as attempting to influence legislation if the organization (a) contacts, or urges the public to contact, members of the legislative body for the purpose of proposing, supporting, or opposing legislation; or (b) advocates the adoption or rejection of legislation.[4] The term "legislation" includes any action by Congress, any state legislature, any local council or similar governing body, or by the public in a referendum, initiative, constitutional amendment, or similar procedure. However, *a 501(c)(3) tax-exempt organization may attempt to influence legislation so long as it devotes only an insubstantial part of its activities to the adoption or rejection of such legislation.* A 501(c)(4) organization can engage in lobbying without any limitation. However, neither organization may endorse or oppose a

---

[2]Bruce Hopkins, *The Law of Tax-Exempt Organizations,* 1991 Cum. Supp. pp. 14-15; Douglas Kirk, *Cases and Materials on Nonprofit Tax-exempt Organizations,* 1992 § 5-10.

[3]Bruce Hopkins, *The Law of Tax-Exempt Organizations,* 281 (5th Edition 1987).

[4]Treas. Reg. § 1.501(c)(3)-1(c)(3)(ii).

candidate for office. However, supporting or opposing a person to an appointed office is not considered to be supporting or opposing a candidate. Therefore, nonprofit organizations may support or oppose cabinet or judicial nominees. Consistent with this distinction, the following guideline will be divided between legislative activity and political campaigns.[5] The ban against engaging in a political campaign on behalf of any candidate for public office "is an absolute prohibition. There is no requirement that political campaigning be substantial."[6]

Organizational Structures

501(c)(3) Organizations

A nonprofit organization that elects 501(c)(3) status under the Internal Revenue Code is afforded (1) federal tax-exempt status and (2) tax deductibility on behalf of the donors who contribute to the organization. One of the main advantages of a 501(c)(3) is that the donors under § 170 of the Internal Revenue Code can claim a federal tax deduction on their contributions.

Churches organized exclusively for religious or charitable purposes are automatically exempt from federal taxes. A church may apply for exemption but is not required to do so. However, other nonprofit organizations seeking federal tax-exempt status must apply for exemption, utilizing Form 1023. The advantage of being recognized as a 501(c)(3) organization is obvious, but there are some restrictions. A 501(c)(3) organization is described as one in

---

[5]*Id.* at § 1.501(c)(3)-1(c)(3)(ii)(b). An organization cannot be tax-exempt if it has the following characteristics: (a) its main or primary objective(s) (as distinguished from its incidental or secondary objectives), may be obtained only by legislation or a defeat of proposed legislation; and (b) it advocates, or campaigns for, the obtainment of such main or primary objective(s) as distinguished from engaging in a nonpartisan analysis, study, or research, and making the results thereof available to the public. *Id.* at § 1.501(c)(3)-1(c)(3)(iii). *See also Cammarano v. United States,* 358 U.S. 498 (1959); *Christian Echoes National Ministry, Inc. v. United States,* 470 F.2d 849 (10th Cir. 1972), *cert. denied,* 414 U.S. 864 (1973).

[6]*Internal Revenue Manual § 3(10)1. See also United States v. Dykema,* 666 F.2d 1096, 1101 (7th Cir. 1981), *cert. denied,* 456 U.S. 983 (1982); 696 F.2d 757 (10th Cir. 1982); *Hutchinson Baseball Enterprises, Inc. v. Commissioner,* 696 F.2d 757,760 (10th Cir. 1982); *Association of the Bar of the City of New York v. Commissioner,* 858 F.2d 876 (2d Cir. 1988).

which "no substantial part of the activities . . . is carrying on propaganda, or otherwise attempting, to influence legislation . . . and which does not participate in or intervene in (including the publishing or distributing of statements), any political campaign on behalf of any candidate for public office."[7]

The "substantial part" wording was enacted by Congress in 1934. The Internal Revenue Service (hereafter "IRS") has stated that an organization will be regarded as attempting to influence legislation if the organization: (1) contacts or urges the public to contact members of the legislative body for the purpose of proposing, supporting, or opposing legislation; or (2) advocates the adoption or rejection of legislation.[8]

The IRS has further noted that an organization may not be considered exempt if: (1) its primary objective may be obtained only by legislation or defeat of proposed legislation; and (2) it advocates or campaigns for the attainment of such main or primary objective as distinguished from engaging in nonpartisan analysis, study, or research, and making the results thereof available to the public.[9] Furthermore, the IRS has stated that attempts to influence legislation are not limited to direct appeals to members of the legislature but may include indirect appeals to legislators through the electorate or the general public.[10]

The *Internal Revenue Manual*[11] recognizes that "there is no simple rule" as to what constitutes a "substantial" portion of the total activities of the organization, and has further recognized that the determination is a "factual one."[12]

In one case, a court found that legislative activity is not substantial if it does not exceed five percent of the organization's total activities. This so-called five percent rule was originally taken from the case of *Seasongood v. Commissioner*.[13] Since the so-called substantial part test looks at the organization's overall

---

[7]I.R.C. § 501(c)(3).
[8]Treas. Reg. § 1.501(c)(3)-1(c)(3)(ii).
[9]*Id.* at § 1.503(c)(3)-1(c)(3)(iii).
[10]*Internal Revenue Manual* §§ 392-394 (1989).
[11]*Id.*
[12]*Id.*
[13]*Seasongood v. Commissioner*, 227 F.2d 907 (6th Cir. 1955) (The organization in this case was neither a church nor a religious organization.)

activities, one federal court of appeals indicated that in addition to time spent "writing, telegraphing, or telephoning" legislators and testifying before legislative committees, the time spent within the organization "formulating, discussing and agreeing upon the positions" which are to be advocated must be taken into account in order to determine substantiality.[14] While the so-called five percent test is still used by some as the benchmark, the IRS has rejected that test and instead indicated that the determination is a factual one and is "more often one of characterizing the various activities as attempts to influence legislation."[15]

Generally speaking, a 501(c)(3) organization may: (1) educate on social issues which have political ramifications; (2) urge the general public to become involved in the democratic political process, so long as it is nonpartisan; (3) publish neutral voting records of political candidates so long as there is no endorsement; (4) provide education about the political process; (5) lobby, if the legislation directly affects the tax-exempt status of the organization or directly impacts the operation of the organization; and (6) influence legislation so long as such activity does not constitute more than a "substantial" part of the organization's total activities.

A 501(c)(3) organization may lose its tax-exempt status if its legislative activities exceed more than a "substantial" part of its total activities. Moreover, a 501(c)(3) organization is prohibited from engaging in any political campaign on behalf of any candidate for public office. This is an absolute prohibition, and thus a 501(c)(3) organization is prohibited from directly endorsing or opposing a candidate for public office. Having said this, it should be noted that only a few organizations have ever lost their tax-exempt status for engaging in political activity, none of which have been churches.

501(h) Organizations

In 1976, Congress provided a new option for 501(c)(3)

---

[14]*Kuper v. Commissioner*, 332 F.2d 562 (3rd Cir. 1964), *cert. denied*, 379 U.S. 920 (1964). *See also League of Women Voters of United States v. United States*, 180 F. Supp. 379 (Ct. Cl. D.C. 1960).

[15]*Internal Revenue Manual* §§ 392-394 (1989).

organizations that wish to engage in lobbying activity. The Internal Revenue Code created a 501(h) election for 501(c)(3) organizations; and instead of using the "substantial" part test of a 501(c)(3) organization, a 501(h) organization uses an "expenditure test." The 501(h) election is not available for all 501(c)(3) organizations. Churches, integrated auxiliaries of churches, conventions, and associations of churches may not elect 501(h) coverage.[16] Private foundations and government units are also prohibited from electing the 501(h) provision.

An eligible 501(c)(3) organization may, file IRS Form 5768 to elect 501(h) status. The election is made on Form 5768, known as "Elections/Revocation of Election by Eligible § 501(c)(3) Organization to Make Expenditures to Influence Legislation." In 1976, Congress enacted an alternative to the substantial part test. If an eligible organization elects the expenditure test of §§ 501(h) and 4911, specific statutory dollar limits on the organization's lobbying expenditures apply. "In contrast to the substantial part test, the expenditure test imposes no limit on lobbying activities that do not require expenditures, such as certain unreimbursed lobbying activities conducted by *bona fide* volunteers."[17]

Under the 501(h) election, the measuring factor is not the *activities* of the organization, but the *expenditures* of the organization directed toward lobbying. There are two types of lobbying: (1) grass roots expenditures, which include attempts to influence public attitudes or to encourage the public to contact their legislators regarding legislation; and (2) direct lobbying, which involves any attempt to influence legislation through communication with a member or employee of the legislative body or any government official or employee. A grass roots communication will be considered a lobbying communication only if it refers to a specific piece of legislation, advocates a view on such legislation, or encourages the recipient of the communication to take action on

---

[16]Several major denominations lobbied Congress not to permit churches the option to elect 501(h) status. The philosophical reasoning behind this unusual request was that the churches argued they should not be subject to any lobbying limitations at all. To concede that the churches needed a 501(h) status would be, in a sense, to concede that the lobbying limitations imposed in the first place were legitimate. Unfortunately, therefore, churches may not presently elect 501(h) status.

[17]Treas. Reg. § 1.501(h)-1 *et seq.*; § 56.4911-0 *et seq.*

the legislation. A direct lobbying communication will only be so considered if it refers to a specific piece of legislation and advocates a view on that legislation.

The limitation on direct lobbying expenditures is based on a sliding scale as follows: (1) twenty percent of the first $500,000 of the organization's exempt expenditures, plus (2) fifteen percent of the second $500,000, plus (3) ten percent of the third $500,000, plus (4) five percent of any additional exempt purpose expenditures. The expenditures may not exceed $1,000,000 for any one year period.

Grass roots lobbying expenditures may not exceed twenty-five percent of the above figures. For example, if an organization has $500,000 in exempt purpose expenditures, it may spend up to $100,000 in direct lobbying (20% of $500,000 = $100,000). The organization may spend either the entire $100,000 toward direct lobbying, or it may spend up to twenty-five percent of that figure for grass roots lobbying, resulting in $75,000 for direct lobbying and $25,000 for grass roots lobbying. A $17,000,000 organization may spend up to $1,000,000 on direct lobbying expenditures (20% of the first $500,000; 15% of the second $500,000; 15% of the third $500,000; and 5% of the remaining $15,500,000 of which $750,000 may go toward direct lobbying and $250,000 may go toward grass roots lobbying).

Volunteer activities are not considered expenditures if there are no funds expended on such activities. For a 501(c)(3) organization that has not made the 501(h) election, volunteer activities are considered part of the total activities of said organization, but a 501(h) organization is only concerned with actual money spent on lobbying activities.

If a 501(h) organization exceeds the expenditure limitation, there is a penalty excise tax imposed equal to twenty-five percent of the amount of the excess lobbying expenditures. If the organization's lobbying expenditures normally exceed the limits by fifty percent, then the organization will jeopardize its tax-exempt status, but this is based on a four year cycle. Thus, an organization may exceed its expenditure limit in one year by more than fifty percent, but the next year may not exceed the expenditure limit. However, if the average of the four years is more than fifty percent of the expenditure limits, the organization may have to pay an excise tax or may lose its tax-exempt status, but only for the years in which the limits were exceeded. Therefore, a 501(h) has more flexibility to engage in lobbying activities, but is still prohibited from directly endorsing or opposing a political candidate for public office.

501(c)(4) Organizations

The Internal Revenue Code also recognizes a third type of organization known as a 501(c)(4) organization, or sometimes referred to as a social welfare organization.

A 501(c)(4) organization is afforded tax-exempt status, but unlike a 501(c)(3) or 501(h), does not have the advantage of tax-deductible contributions. Because it does not allow donors to deduct contributions from federal income tax, 501(c)(4) organizations do not have the prohibition from engaging in efforts to influence legislation. In *Regan v. Taxation with Representation*,[18] the United States Supreme Court recognized that a 501(c)(3) organization could establish a separate organization under 501(c)(4) for the purpose of lobbying activities. The court noted that "the IRS apparently requires only that the two groups be separately incorporated and keep records adequate to show that tax deductible contributions are not used to pay for lobbying."[19]

A 501(c)(4) organization may therefore directly lobby, either by volunteer activity or by expenditures. However, a 501(c)(4) is still prohibited from directly opposing or supporting a political candidate for public office.

Summary of Organizations

In summary, a 501(c)(3) organization is tax-exempt, and contributions are tax- deductible. Such an organization is prohibited from expending more than a "substantial" part of its activities toward lobbying (which includes volunteer and expenditure activities). A 501(c)(3) organization which is not a church, integrated auxiliary of a church, association or convention of

---

[18]461 U.S. 540 (1983).
[19]*Id.* at 554 n.6.

churches, private foundation or government unit, is allowed to elect a 501(h) status and thus use an expenditure test. Under an expenditure test, only money spent toward lobbying is considered. A nonprofit organization may incorporate as a 501(c)(3) and separately incorporate as a 501(c)(4) organization. There are no lobbying limitations on 501(c)(4) organizations.

Neither a 501(c)(3), a 501(h) election, nor a 501(c)(4) may directly oppose or support a political candidate for public office. A 501(c)(4) organization can engage in lobbying without any limitation. However, neither organization may endorse or oppose a candidate for office. However, supporting or opposing a person to an appointed office is not considered to be supporting or opposing a candidate. Therefore, nonprofit organizations may support or oppose cabinet or judicial nominees. To directly oppose or support a candidate for public office, a state or federal political action committee (PAC) must be established. Though PACs are governed by the strict reporting requirements, the advantage is that PACs can directly support or oppose a candidate for public office. Contributions to a PAC are not tax-deductible.

Pastors And Representatives Of Nonprofit Organizations

In January of 1992, the IRS published a statement regarding Jimmy Swaggart Ministries. Jimmy Swaggart Ministries had apparently endorsed Pat Robertson for President in 1988. Jimmy Swaggart stated at a worship service that Pat Robertson would most probably announce his candidacy for President and that he would lend his support to Pat Robertson. Jimmy Swaggart then wrote an article entitled "From Me to You" in the church's official magazine known as *The Evangelist* in which he stated: "We are supporting Pat Robertson for the office of President of the United States" and "we are going to support him prayerfully and put forth every effort we can muster in his behalf." The magazine indicated on its masthead that it was "The voice of Jimmy Swaggart Ministries." According to the IRS, "when a minister of a religious organization endorses a candidate for public office at an official function of the organization, or when an official publication of a religious organization contains an endorsement of a candidate for public office by the organization's minister, the endorsement will be considered an endorsement of the organization since the acts and statements of a religious organization's minister at official functions of the organization and its official publications are the principal means by which a religious organization communicates its official views to its members and supporters."[20]

Though the publicized IRS statement may be an exaggeration and may not be supportable if challenged in court, it is nonetheless the IRS's view that when a minister speaks at an official church function, the expression of that minister will be considered the expression of the church. Prior to this news release, most assumed that a minister could appear in a pulpit during a worship service and state personal views so long as a disclaimer was made that the church was not endorsing or opposing those views. The IRS has apparently taken a different position on this matter. Presumably, a minister should be able to express personal views outside of an official church function so long as a disclaimer is made that the church is not endorsing or opposing a specific candidate for public office.

After the IRS finished with Jimmy Swaggart, it focused on Jerry Falwell. Rev. Jerry Falwell's "Old Time Gospel Hour" was ordered to pay the IRS $50,000 in back taxes for improperly engaging in political activities in 1986 and 1987. The settlement resulted in the IRS revoking Old Time Gospel Hour's tax-exempt status for both years. The IRS found that the Old Time Gospel Hour, which broadcasts Dr. Falwell's sermons, devoted both personal and other church assets to political fundraising efforts.[21]

Key To Abbreviations

Having outlined the general rules governing the various organizations, the following key will be used to designate each organization or entity in order to illustrate permissible political activity:

---

[20]Richard Hammar, ed., "Political Activities by Churches," *Church, Law and Tax Report*, Vol. VI, No. 5, September/October 1992, pp. 7-8.

[21]*Nonprofit Alert*, May 1993; Lynn Buzzard, ed., *Religious Freedom Reporter*, Vol. 13, No. 4, April 1993, p. 140.

Pastor   (or representative)
501(c)(3)   (or church; tax-exempt and tax-deductible)
501(h)   (tax-exempt and tax-deductible)
501(c)(4)   (tax-exempt but not tax-deductible)
PAC   (not tax-exempt and not tax-deductible)

Legislative Or Lobbying Activity

	Pastor	501(c)(3)	501(h)	501(c)(4)	PAC
1. Lobbying on issues unrelated to the organization's function or tax exempt status.	Y	Y*	Y**	Y	Y

*except that the lobbying activities cannot exceed a substantial part of the overall activities of the organization. **if the lobbying activity is done through volunteer services; otherwise, an expenditure test must be utilized.

	Pastor	501(c)(3)	501(h)	501(c)(4)	PAC
2. Lobbying on issues directly related to the existence, powers and duties, exempt status, or the deductibility of contributions to the organizations.	Y	Y	Y	Y	Y
3. Educating the members of the organization orally or through written communication regarding the status of legislation in a nonpartisan, objective manner without advocating a specific	Y	Y	Y	Y	Y

view on such legislation.[22]

4. Educating the members of the organization orally or through written communication regarding the status of legislation and advocating a specific view on such legislation.	Y[23]	Y*	Y**	Y	Y

*except that such activities cannot exceed a substantial part of the organization's overall activities.
**if done by volunteer services; otherwise the expenditure test must be unutilized.

5. Provide education regarding the political process and encourage members in a nonpartisan manner to become involved in the political process.	Y	Y	Y	Y	Y

6. Petition drives.	Y	Y*	Y**	Y	Y

*except that such activity should not exceed a substantial part of the organization's overall activities unless the petition drive directly relates to legislation affecting the function of the organization or the tax- exempt status of said organization.
**without limitation if performed by volunteer services; otherwise, the expenditure test should be utilized.

---

[22]The IRS has indicated that an organization which objectively studies legislation in a nonpartisan manner and which compiles this information for distribution to the general public but neither proposes specific legislation or advocates the passage or defeat of any pending legislation is not attempting to influence legislation. Rev. Rul. 64-195, 1964-2 C.B. 138.

[23]See above section on pastors and representatives of nonprofit organizations.

7. Rental of organization's mailing list.	N/A	Y*	Y*	Y*	Y

*if rented at fair market value. Said list could be loaned to a legislative group such as a 501(c)(4) organization since the Federal Election Campaign Act[24] applies only to political campaigns.

Political Campaign Activity

	Pastor	501(c)(3)	501(h)	501(c)(4)	PAC
1. Endorsement of political candidates.	Y[25]	N	N	N	Y
2. Contributions to political campaigns.	Y	N	N	N	Y
3. In-kind and independent expenditures for or against political candidates.	Y	N	N	N	Y
4. Fundraising for candidates.	Y[26]	N	N	N	Y
5. Introduction of political candidates at organization meetings.	Y[27]	Y*	Y*	Y*	Y

*but no endorsement

---

[24] 2 U.S.C. § 431.
[25] See above section on pastors and representatives of nonprofit organizations.
[26] *Id.*
[27] *Id.*

6. Political candidates to speak at organization functions.	N/A	Y[28]	Y[29]	Y[30]	Y
7. Nonpartisan voter registration.	Y	Y	Y	Y	Y
8. Distribution of candidate surveys and incumbent voting records which *do not* contain editorial opinions endorsing or opposing candidates.	Y	Y	Y	Y	Y

The following two situations, as proposed by the IRS, would be permissible distribution of voter guides by a 501(c)(3), 501(h) or 501(c)(4) organization:

Situation 1:

> Organization A has been recognized as exempt under section 501(c)(3) of the Code by the Internal Revenue Service. As one of its activities, the organization annually prepares and makes generally available to the public a compilation of voting records of all members of Congress on major legislative issues involving a wide range of subjects. The publication contains no editorial opinion, and

---

[28] A political candidate could speak at this organization so long as the candidate was speaking on issues that directly affected the organization and did not attempt to campaign at the organization. Based on Rev. Rul. 74-547, this type of an organization should be free to have political candidates address the members so long as (1) overt campaigning activities are avoided, (2) the same opportunity is afforded to other qualified candidates, and (3) the attendees are informed before or after the speech that the organization does not endorse any candidate for public office. However, a candidate could certainly preach at a church or address a nonprofit organization without the organization having to invite the candidate's opponent if no endorsements or campaigning activities occurred.

[29] *Id.*

[30] *Id.*

its contents and structure do not imply approval or disapproval of any members or their voting records.

The "voter education" activity of Organization A is not prohibited political activity within the meaning of section 501(c)(3) of the Code.

Situation 2:

Organization B has been recognized as exempt under section 501(c)(3) of the Code by the Internal Revenue Service. As one of its activities in election years, it sends a questionnaire to all candidates for governor in State M. The questionnaire solicits a brief statement of each candidate's position on a wide variety of issues. All responses are published in a voters' guide that it makes generally available to the public. The issues covered are selected by the organization solely on the basis of their importance and interest to the electorate as a whole. Neither the questionnaire nor the voters' guide, in content or structure, evidences a bias or preference with respect to the views of any candidate or group of candidates.

The "voter education" activity of Organization B is not prohibited political activity within the meaning of section 501(c)(3) of the Code.[31]

	Pastor	501(c)(3)	501(h)	501(c)(4)	PAC
9. Distribution of candidate surveys and incumbent voting records which *do* contain editorial opinions endorsing or opposing	Y	N	N	N	Y

---

[31]Rev. Rul. 78-248.

candidates.

The following two situations, as proposed by the IRS, would not be permissible voter guides by a 501(c)(3), 501(h) or 501(c)(4) organization:

Situation 3:

Organization C has been recognized as exempt under section 501(c)(3) of the Code by the Internal Revenue Service. Organization C undertakes a "voter education" activity patterned after that of Organization B in Situation 2. It sends a questionnaire to candidates for major public offices and uses the responses to prepare a voters' guide which is distributed during an election campaign. Some questions evidence a bias on certain issues. By using a questionnaire structured in this way, Organization C is participating in a political campaign in contravention of the provisions of section 501(c)(3) and is disqualified as exempt under that section.

Situation 4:

Organization D has been recognized as exempt under section 501(c)(3) of the Code. It is primarily concerned with land conservation matters. The organization publishes a voters' guide for its members and others concerned with land conservation issues. The guide is intended as a compilation of incumbents' voting records on selected land conservation issues of importance to the organization and is factual in nature. It contains no express statements in support of or in opposition to any candidate. The guide is widely distributed among the electorate during an election campaign.

While the guide may provide the voting

public with useful information, its emphasis on one area of concern indicates that its purpose is not nonpartisan voter education. By concentrating on a narrow range of issues in the voters' guide and widely distributing it among the electorate during an election campaign, Organization D is participating in a political campaign in contravention of the provisions of section 501(c)(3) and is disqualified as exempt under that section.[32]

	Pastor	501(c)(3)	501(h)	501(c)(4)	PAC
10. Maintaining a nonpartisan bulletin board regarding legislative and political campaign issues.	Y	Y*	Y*	Y*	Y

*if the organization allows all viewpoints to be presented in a nonpartisan manner without the organization's endorsement.

	Pastor	501(c)(3)	501(h)	501(c)(4)	PAC
11. Distribution of political statements and political endorsements in lobbies or parking lots.	Y	Y*	Y*	Y*	Y

*if the distribution is not controlled or organized by the organization and distribution is also permitted for opposing viewpoints.

	Pastor	501(c)(3)	501(h)	501(c)(4)	PAC
12. Use of the organization's facilities by political candidates.	N/A	Y*	Y*	Y*	Y

*if provided on a nonpartisan basis.[33]

---

[32]*Id.*
[33]See above under Political Campaign Activity, example 6.

13. Political forum where candidates are invited to discuss political viewpoints.	N/A	Y*	Y*	Y*	Y

*if done on a nonpartisan basis.[34]

14. Nonprofit radio or television media providing reasonable air time equally to all legally qualified candidates without endorsing a particular candidate.	N/A	Y[35]	Y	Y	Y

15. Supporting or opposing judicial appointments[36] to state or federal court or to the United States Supreme Court.	Y	Y*	Y*	Y*	Y

*because such an appointee is not involved in a political campaign, but such activity may be construed as lobbying.

Summary

It is important to note the difference between legislative activities and political campaigns. The IRS does not prohibit all involvement in lobbying or legislative activities, but this activity is somewhat restricted depending upon the nature of the organization. According to the United States Supreme Court, an organization

---

[34]*Id.*

[35]In 1974, the IRS stated that providing broadcasting facilities to "legally qualified candidates for elected public office furthers the education of the electorate by providing a public forum for the exchange of ideas and the debate of public issues which instructs them on subjects useful to the individual and beneficial to the community." The IRS stated that if the organization makes its facilities equally available to the candidates for public office, then this activity "does not make the expression of political views by the candidates the acts of the broadcasting station within the intendment of section 501(c)(3) of the Code." Rev. Rul. 74-574, 1974-2 C.B. 160.

[36]This only applies to *appointments*, not to *elective* judicial positions.

could divide its activities by incorporating as a 501(c)(3) tax-exempt and tax-deductible organization with certain lobbying limitations and by separately incorporating as a 501(c)(4) tax-exempt but not tax-deductible organization which has no lobbying limitations.[37]

There is no lobbying limit on a 501(c)(4) organization but there are lobbying limits on a 501(c)(3) and a 501(h) organization. It should be noted that since the amendments to the IRS Code in 1934 on lobbying activities and 1954 on political campaign activities, only a handful of organizations have ever lost their tax-exempt status for engaging in too much political activity. However, no church has ever lost its nonprofit status for engaging in political or lobbying activity.[38] One case challenging nonprofit status involved Christian Echoes National Ministry.[39] When the court looked at Christian Echoes Ministry, it found that it encouraged the public to: (1) write their Congressmen to influence political decisions; (2) work in politics at the precinct level; (3) support the Becker Amendment; (4) maintain the McCarrin Immigration Law; (5) contact their Congressmen to oppose interference with the freedom of speech; (6) purge the American press of its responsibility for misleading its readers; (7) inform congressmen that the House Committee on Un-American Activities must be retained; (8) oppose an Air Force Contract to disarm the United States; (9) dispel the mutual mistrust between North and South America; (10) demand an investigation of the biased reporting of major television networks; (11) support the Dirksen Amendment; (12) demand that Congress limit foreign aid spending; (13) discourage support for the World Court; (14) support the Connally Reservation; (15) cut off diplomatic relations with Communist Countries; (16) reduce the federal payroll by discharging needless job holders and balance the budget; (17) stop federal aid to education and socialized medicine as well as housing; (18) abolish the federal income tax; (19) end American diplomatic recognition of the Soviet Union; (20) withdraw from the United Nations; (21) outlaw the Communist Party in the United States; and (22) restore immigration laws. The

---

[37]*Regan v. Taxation With Representation,* 461 U.S. 540 (1983).

[38]Richard Hammer, ed., "Political Activities by Churches," *Church Law and Tax Report,* Vol. VI, No. 5, September/October 1992, p.2.

[39]*Christian Echoes National Ministry, Inc. v. United States,* 470 F.2d 849 (10th Cir. 1972), *cert. denied,* 414 U.S. 864 (1973).

organization also endorsed Senator Barry Goldwater. Since the organization's activities were *primarily* political, it lost its tax-exempt status.

Another nonprofit organization lost its tax-exempt status because of its campaign activities.[40] Nearly seventy-six percent of this particular organization's total budget was spent on legislative activities. Again, since its activities were *primarily* political, it lost its tax-exempt status. Only a few organizations have ever lost their tax-exempt status and clearly their overall activity excessively involved legislative and political activities, but again, no church has ever lost its tax-exempt status for engaging in too much political activity.

A 501(c)(3) organization is permitted to engage in certain lobbying activities so long as a substantial part of the organization's overall activities are not devoted to lobbying. A 501(c)(3) organization that makes a 501(h) election is permitted to engage in lobbying activities. The extent to which this type of organization may engage in lobbying activities is more clearly defined because an expenditure test is utilized. Volunteer services which are not reimbursed are not considered lobbying activities. There is no limit upon a 501(h) organization's lobbying activities if it used volunteers. A 501(c)(4) organization is specifically designed to engage in lobbying and there are no restrictions on its lobbying activities. The main tax difference between a 501(c)(4) as compared to a 501(c)(3) and a 501(h) is that the former is tax-exempt but contributions are not tax-deductible, while the latter are tax-exempt and contributions to these organizations are tax-deductible.

In terms of intervening in political campaigns, there is a strict prohibition against endorsing or opposing political candidates for public office. This strict prohibition applies to 501(c)(3), 501(c)(4), and 501(h) organizations. These organizations can still distribute literature designed to educate regarding candidate voting records or viewpoints. The main proviso is that these voter education guides should be nonpartisan and should not specifically endorse or oppose candidates. These cards should avoid indicating favorable or unfavorable ratings and be presented in an objective manner. A 501(c)(4) organization can engage in lobbying without any

---

[40]*IRS General Counsel Memorandum* 39811.

limitation. However, neither organization may endorse or oppose a candidate for office. However, supporting or opposing a person to an appointed office is not considered to be supporting or opposing a candidate. Therefore, nonprofit organizations may support or oppose cabinet or judicial nominees.

Since pastors and representatives of nonprofit organizations are individuals, there are no restrictions regarding the amount of activity they may engage in with regards to legislative or political campaign issues. When endorsing a political candidate, the pastor or representative should avoid the appearance that the organization is giving the endorsement.

Finally, Political Action Committees may engage in unrestricted legislative activities or political campaigns with the only limitation being state or federal reporting requirements.

Pastors, churches, and other nonprofit organizations can clearly be involved in the political process. It would be literally impossible for such organizations not to be involved in the political process because the viewpoints and issues advocated by churches and nonprofit organizations naturally have political consequences. To avoid the political process is to limit the effectiveness of churches and nonprofit organizations. The United States Supreme Court has recognized that "churches frequently take strong positions on public issues including . . . vigorous advocacy of legal or constitutional positions. Of course, churches as much as secular bodies and private citizens have that right."

20

SAME SEX MARRIAGE

The traditional family has never faced as great a threat as it does today. The radical homosexual movement hopes it can bury the traditional family and in its place create a new culture symbolized by same sex marriage. Though American culture has periodically adjusted the parameters of marriage in terms of legally sanctioned relationships, recognizing same sex marriage will not simply alter traditional marriage, it will destroy the sacred institution. Our society has shut the door to polygamy while opening the door to interracial marriage. However, these struggles are fundamentally different because they involve the same basic concept -- the union of male and female. Recognizing a legal union between two people of the same gender will precipitate a cultural revolution.

Accepting same sex marriage has nothing to do with tolerance. The terms "tolerance" and "homophobia" are terms used to silence critics of homosexuality. Make no mistake. The radical homosexual agenda is anything but tolerant. Tolerance is not the goal of the homosexual movement, nor is it the goal of same sex marriage. The homosexual movement is seeking to use the vehicle of marriage to force homosexuality on an unwilling population. The movement will destroy anything in its path that resists.[1]

The outspoken homosexual activist, Michelangelo Signorile,

---

[1] See Richard Duncan, *Homosexual Marriage and the Myth of Tolerance: Is Cardinal O'Conner a "Homophobe"?* 10 NOTRE DAME JOURNAL OF LAW, ETHICS & PUBLIC POLICY, 587, 602-607 (1996); Lynn Wardle, *A Critical Analysis of Constitutional Claims For Same-Sex Marriage*, 1996 B.Y.U.L. REV. 1, 18-24 (hereafter *"Critical Analysis"*); Richard Duncan, *Who Waits to Stop the Church: Homosexual Rights Legislation, Public Policy, and Religious Freedom*, 69 Notre Dame L. Rev., 393, 440-42 (1994); Ken Masters, *Here is "The Church;" Scenes from the Documentary PBS Yanked*, WASH. POST, Aug. 14, 1991 at C-1 (Discussing producer and director Robert Hilferty's film, *Stop the Church*, which was shown at the Berlin International Film Festival. This film won an award for the "Best Commentary" at the Ann Arbor Film Festival. Mr. Hilferty is a member of Act-Up, the AIDS Coalition To Unleash Power. This film is filled with epitaphs against the Roman Catholic Church because of its position on homosexuality. The church is described as hypocritical and filled with hate. One man on the film states that the "Catholic church is an archaic, anachronistic, futilist leftover which practices ritual sacrifice on the bodies of gay men, lesbians, women, and people of color.").

acknowledged that the goal of the homosexual movement is to "fight for same-sex marriage and its benefits and then, once granted, redefin[e] the institution of marriage completely, to demand the right to marry not as a way of adhering to society's moral codes but rather to debunk America and radically alter an archaic institution. . . ."[2]

Social Ramifications

Legally sanctioning same sex marriage will have far reaching social, moral, economic, and political ramifications. Certainly public education will be affected. Curriculum discussing human sexuality and family will by necessity redefine the definition of family to include anyone who associates with another in a "loving" relationship. Books like *Heather Has Two Mommies*[3] and *Daddy's Roommate*[4] will become standard textbooks. Already these two books have been recommended for first grade students as part of New York City's multicultural program.[5] One high school in Framingham, Massachusetts pushed the envelope in a class designed to promote tolerance, including tolerance of sexual preference. This class involved a "role reversal" exercise in which the students were given a handout that asked the following questions:

Is it possible that you are heterosexual because you fear the same sex? If you have never slept with someone of the same sex, how do you know you wouldn't prefer that?

---

[2]*Out*, December/January 1994, at 161.

[3]Leslie Newman, *Heather Has Two Mommies* (1989). This book is written for young children portraying a little girl by the name of Heather who has two lesbian parents, Mama Jane and Mama Kate. In the book Mama Jane and Mama Kate decided to have children and therefore visited a "special doctor" who "put some sperm into Jane's vagina." Heather is the result of this invitro fertilization. Heather eventually learns through day care that many other children have fathers. When Heather feels sad that she has no father, her teacher, Molly, assures her that she has two mommies and that's "pretty special."

[4]Michael Willhoite, *Daddy's Roommate* (1990). The main character in this picture book for children is a boy whose heterosexual parents divorce. However, soon after the divorce someone new came to Daddy's house. This new "roommate" by the name of Frank lives, works, eats and sleeps with Daddy. The book states that being "gay is just one more kind of love, and love is the best kind of happiness."

[5]*See* Midge Decter, *Homosexuality in the Schools*, COMMENTARY, March 1993, at 19-20.

Is it possible you merely need a good gay experience?[6]

If same sex marriage were legally sanctioned, public school textbooks would not only discuss homosexuality but would "legitimize" it as a normal and accepted part of family. Alongside Adam and Eve as the traditional mother and father will stand Adam and Steve. Sex education classes will instruct students in homosexual practices.

If accepting same sex marriage relies in part upon two consenting people having affection toward one another, then there will no longer be any legitimate basis to restrict marriage of any kind. If the criteria is two consenting people with affection for one another, then there is no reason why society should not legitimize polygamy, incestuous marriage, and pedophilia.

Private and public employers would have to provide "family" health benefits to homosexual couples. No doubt certain religious organizations would find themselves in a tremendous conflict. Presently there is no exemption for religious organizations against providing health benefits based upon religious objections. There will certainly be no exemption for religious organizations opposed to homosexuality. These organizations will be required to provide health benefits to homosexual partners in the same manner and terms provided to traditional family arrangements.

Children in a same sex marriage culture would be just as easily adopted by gay, lesbian and transsexual couples as by heterosexual couples. Accepting same sex marriage would radically redefine our cultural and moral values.

Political vs. Judicial

Liberal social engineers are fond of using the judicial system to shape public policy when there is not enough clout in the political arena to command a majority. One such example is evident

---

[6]THE WANDERER, Mar. 21, 1996, at 1. *See also* Mark Mueller, *Parents Rip Class on Gay Tolerance*, BOSTON HERALD, Mar. 1, 1996, at 1. In the case of *Brown v. Hot, Sexy and Safer Productions, Inc.*, 68 F.3d 525 (1st Cir. 1995), *cert. denied*, 116 S. Ct. 1044 (1996), a federal appeals court upheld the right of a public school to require students to attend a sex education program in which several monologues and skits were performed graphically discussing male and female genitals, excretory functions, anal sex, oral sex, masturbation, and homosexuality.

in the State of Hawaii. More than seventy percent of Hawaiians oppose same sex marriage. However, the Hawaii Supreme Court ruled that unless the State of Hawaii can show a compelling interest to deny a marriage license to couples of the same gender, the state statute is unconstitutional under the Equal Rights Amendment to the state constitution.[7]

Same sex marriage ought to be debated by the people in mass, not a few judges. "Vigorous, robust interchange on issues of public importance is one of the pillars of self-government. The full exchange of views not only informs ultimate decisions, but tempers and refines the character of the persons who participate in the debate."[8] Indeed, a "broad dissemination of principles, ideas, and factual information is crucial to the robust public debate and informed citizenry that are 'the essence of self-government.'"[9] "[F]ree and open debate is vital to informed decision-making by the

---

[7]*Baehr v. Lewin*, 852 P.2d 44 (Haw. 1993), *reconsideration granted in part*, 875 P.2d 225 (Haw. 1993). Interestingly, only two permanent members of the five-member Hawaii Supreme Court were present on the panel when this ruling was made. Acting Chief Justice Moon and Justice Levinson were the only permanent members. Justices Lum and Klein recused themselves and were replaced by Chief Judge Burns and Judge Heen of the Hawaii Intermediate Court of Appeals. The fifth seat was vacant at the time the case was argued. Retired Associate Justice Hayashi was temporarily assigned to fill the vacancy. However, by the time the court issued its opinion, the temporary vacancy had expired and therefore Judge Hayashi was not part of the final decision. Thus, Justice Hayashi's vote was not counted. The official case report noted that he would have joined in the dissent with Judge Heen. *Baehr*, 852 P.2d at 48. The vote was therefore 3 to 1. If Justice Hayashi's vote were counted it would be 3 to 2. Only Justice Moon and Justice Levinson voted in the majority with Judge Burns writing a concurring opinion. He concurred only in the result. He filed a much more narrow, separate opinion. The Equal Protection Clause in the Hawaii constitution provides as follows:

> No person shall be deprived of life, liberty or property without due process of law, nor be denied the equal protection of the laws, nor be denied the enjoyment of the person civil rights or be discriminated against in the exercise throughout because of race, religion, sex or ancestry.

HAW. CONST. art. I §5. Unlike the Fourteenth Amendment of the U.S. Constitution, the Hawaii state constitution expressly prohibits discrimination on the basis of sex. *Baehr*, 852 P.2d at 63, n.26.

[8]Wardle, *Critical Analysis*, 1996 B.Y.U.L. REV. at 23.

[9]*Harper & Row Publishers, Inc. v. National Enterprises*, 471 U.S. 539, 582 (1985) (Brennan, J., dissenting) (quoting *Garrison v. Louisiana*, 379 U.S. 64, 74-75 (1964)); *see also New York Times Co. v. Sullivan*, 376 U.S. 254, 270 (1964).

electorate."[10] "[R]obust debate of public issues" is of "essential First Amendment value"[11] and "essential to our democratic society."[12] Public debate permits "the continued building of our politics and culture,"[13] facilitates reforms through peaceful means,[14] and maintains a system of government that is "responsive to the will of the people."[15]

Recently Supreme Court Justice Antonin Scalia stated that it was "no business of the court (as opposed to the political branches) to take sides in this culture war."[16] Clearly, on an issue that is as socially important and radically redefining as same sex marriage, the people, not the courts, should have the final say. Marriage has been traditionally left to the legislative, not to the judicial branch of government. The debate on same sex marriage should be argued by the voters and debated from the political pulpits around America. This important issue should not be left to a few masters wearing black robes.

Political and Social Arguments Against Same Sex Marriage

Most cultures generally recognize three categories of social behavior. The first and least favorite category is prohibited conduct which includes activities and associations that are prohibited by law. The second category includes permitted behavior which includes activities and associations that are tolerated and condoned. The third category may be referred to as preferred conduct, which includes activities and associations that society singles out for "special approval, encouragement, and preference."[17] According to law professor, Lynn Wardle,

The boundary line between the first and second categories

---

[10]*Pickering v. Board of Education*, 391 U.S. 563, 571-72 (1968).

[11]*Dunn & Bradstreet, Inc. v. Greenmoss Builders, Inc.*, 472 U.S. 749, 757 n.4 (1985) (Brennan, J., dissenting).

[12]*Id.* at 775 n.1 (Brennan, J., dissenting).

[13]*Police Dept. of Chicago v. Mosley*, 408 U.S. 92, 95-96 (1972).

[14]*See Carey v. Brown*, 447 U.S. 455, 467 (1980).

[15]*Stromberg v. California*, 283 U.S. 359, 369 (1931).

[16]*Romer v. Evans*, 116 S. Ct. 1620, 1637 (1996) (Scalia, J., dissenting).

[17]Wardle, *Critical Analysis*, 1996 B.Y.U.L. REV. at 58.

is the line of tolerance. On one side the association of behavior is deemed socially intolerable (prohibited), but on the other side of the line it is tolerated (permitted). The boundary line between the second and third categories is the line of preference. Associations in the permitted category are deemed reasonably acceptable, but not uniquely important, while those in the preferred category are essential to the success of our society.[18]

Historically, homosexual conduct has been in the prohibited category. In 1986, the United States Supreme Court observed the following:

Proscriptions against [sodomy] has ancient roots. Sodomy was a criminal offense at common law and was forbidden by the laws of the original 13 States when they ratified the Bill of Rights. In 1868, when the Fourteenth Amendment was ratified, all but 5 of the 37 States in the Union had criminal sodomy laws. In fact, until 1961, all 50 States outlawed sodomy. . . .[19]

Removing homosexual conduct from what historically has been a prohibited category to a preferred category is a quantum leap. It is one thing to keep the government out of the bedroom, but it is quite another to require government to publicly endorse and promote a historically and overwhelmingly disfavored sexual practice. Same sex marriage is not about tolerance, the second category, but about preference. Same sex marriage is nothing less than a request for the state's imprimatur (stamp of approval) on aberrant sexual activity.

Legalizing same-sex marriage would ignore the distinction between tolerance and preference by extending the highest legal preferences to relationships which our society historically has condemned and which, even now, the

---

[18]*Id.; see also* Duncan, *Homosexual Marriage*, 10 NOTRE DAME JOURNAL OF LAW, ETHICS & PUBLIC POLICY at 593.

[19]*Bowers v. Hardwick*, 478 U.S. 186, 192-94 (1986) (citations and footnotes omitted).

most sympathetic states have chosen only to tolerate. The confusion comes when proponents of same-sex marriage assert that because homosexual relations are tolerated they are entitled to a state-endorsed preferred status. This blurs the distinction between the two categories contrary to the reality of all state law schemes -- states universally draw distinctions between tolerance and preference. [20]

Society has good reason to prefer heterosexual marriage. In the words of former Chief Justice Warren, traditional marriage is of critical importance because it is "fundamental to our very existence and survival." [21] Nature and common sense teaches us that male and female are biologically designed in such a way to propagate the human race. Without the male-female relationship the human race would cease to exist. Andrew Sullivan, the former editor of *New Republic* and outspoken homosexual activist, concedes that the "timeless, necessary, procreative unity of a man and a woman is inherently denied homosexuals." [22] Mr. Sullivan also concedes that "no two lesbians and no two homosexual men cannot be parents in the way that a heterosexual man and a heterosexual woman with a biological son or daughter can be." [23]

Homosexual activists have attempted to equate homosexuality with genetic predisposition along the lines of race. However, as General Colin Powell pointed out: "Skin color is a benign-behavioral characteristic. Sexual orientation is perhaps the most profound of human behavioral characteristics. Comparison of the two is a convenient but invalid argument." [24] Homosexuals have

---

[20]Wardle, *Critical Analysis*, 1996 B.Y.U.L. Rev. at 61 (citation omitted).

[21]*Loving v. Virginia*, 388 U.S. 1, 12 (1967).

[22]Andrew Sullivan, *Virtually Normal: An Argument About Homosexuality*, 196 (1995).

[23]*Id.*

[24]Letter from Gen. Colin Powell to R. Patricia Schroeder (May 8, 1992), *in* David F. Burrelli, *Homosexuals and U.S. Military Personnel Policy*, Jan. 14, 1993, at 25-26; *see also Assessment of the Plan to Lift the Ban on Homosexuals in the Military: Hearings Before the Military Forces and Personnel Subcommittee of the House Committee on Armed Services*, 103d Cong., 1st Sess. 31, 32 (1993) (statement of Gen. Colin Powell, Chairman, Joint Chiefs of Staff) ("[Homosexuality] is something quite different than the acceptance of benign characteristics such as color or race or background."). In 1971 Justice Peterson of the Minnesota Supreme Court stated in one of the first same-sex marriage cases: "[I]n common sense and in a constitutional sense, there is a clear distinction between a marital restriction based merely upon race and one based upon the fundamental difference of sex." *Baker v.*

attempted to point to certain "genetic" studies touting the idea that homosexuality is a genetically inherited characteristic. However, many of these studies are fraught with methodological flaws and have not been replicated by reputable scientists.[25] In contrast to these flawed methodological studies which will be discussed below, there are more than seventy years of therapeutic counseling and case studies that suggest homosexuality is a gender identification issue which is culturally influenced.[26] Homosexuals can choose their behavior and can change their orientation.[27] There are numerous examples of changed behavior and sexual orientation documented in many studies including the landmark research of Masters and Johnson.[28]

Homosexuals often point to so-called research attempting to "prove" that homosexuality is attributable solely to genetics. One such study was performed by Simon LeVay who attempted to trace homosexuality to brain structure based upon research on 41 postmortem brain samples.[29] LeVay reported that a particular part of the brain structure known as INAH3 was larger in the brains of heterosexual men than in the brains of homosexual men. However, LeVay's study is flawed. LeVay defined homosexuality as "sexual orientation," which he described as "the direction of sexual feelings or behavior toward members of one's own or the opposite sex."[30] LeVay included bisexuality with homosexuality. His definition

---

Nelson, 191 N.W.2d 185, 187 (Minn. 1971).

[25]*See* William Byne and Bruce Parsons, *Human Sexual Orientation: The Biological Theories Reprised*, 50 ARCHIVES OF GENERAL PSYCHIATRY 228-239 (Mar. 1993).

[26]*See* Elizabeth R. Moberly, *Psychogenesis: The Early Development of Gender Identity* (1983); Joseph Nicolosi, *Reparative Therapy of Male Homosexuality* (1991); and Charles W. Socarides, *Homosexuality: Freedom Too Far* (1995).

[27]E. Mansell Pattison and Myrna Loy Pattison, *Ex-Gays: Religiously Mediated Change in Homosexuals*, 137 AMERICAN JOURNAL OF PSYCHIATRY, 137:12 (Dec. 1980) ("All subjects manifested major before-after changes. Corollary evidence suggests that the phenomenon of substantiated change in sexual orientation without exclusive treatment and/or long term psychotherapy may be much more common than previously thought.").

[28]Mark F. Schwartz and William H. Masters, *The Masters and Johnson Treatment Program for Dissatisfied Homosexual Men*, 141 AMERICAN JOURNAL OF PSYCHIATRY 173-81 (1984). *See also* Starla Allen, *Uncovering the Real Me*, EXODUS INTERNATIONAL UPDATE, Feb. 1996.

[29]Simon LeVay, *A Difference in Hypothalamic Structure Between Heterosexual and Homosexual Men*, 253 SCIENCE 1034 (1991).

[30]*Id.*

failed "to require homosexual behavior and does not define which behaviors constitute homosexuality."[31] There is "still no universally accepted definition of homosexuality among clinicians and behavioral scientists."[32]

As Professor Lynn Wardle noted:

> Does merely thinking about having sexual relations with a person of the same sex make one homosexual, or is sexual behavior also required? If feeling is definitive, what level, amount, and intensity of feeling is required? If behavior is necessary, what kind of behavior is deemed defining? Is an isolated incident of sexual experimentation definitive? If not, what frequency is required? How recently must the activity have occurred? What if the subject engaged in both homosexual and heterosexual contact -- would he or she be defined as homosexual or heterosexual? What about "changers" -- for example, a man who was a practicing heterosexual for 15 years, but 2 months ago abandoned heterosexual for homosexual relations? Is the most recent behavior definitive or is it the historically predominant behavior? Does the motivation make any difference? For instance, if a happily married drug addict performed personally repugnant homosexual acts for money to pay for his drug fixes would he be classified as homosexual? No scientific study wishing to be taken seriously can avoid such fundamental definitional issues, but many of the high-profile biological-determinism studies gloss over them.[33]

---

[31]Wardle, *Critical Analysis*, 1996 B.Y.U.L. REV. at 65.

[32]William Byne, *The Biological Evidence Challenged*, SCIENTIFIC AMERICAN, May 1994, at 50-55; William Byne & Bruce Parsons, *Human Sexual Orientation: The Biologic Theory Reprised*, ARCHIVES GEN. PSYCHIATRY, Mar. 1993, at 228; Richard C. Freedman & Jennifer Downey, *Neurobiology and Sexual Orientation: Current Relationships*, 5 J. S. NEUROPSYCHIATRY 131 (1993); Stanton L. Jones & Don E. Workman, *Homosexuality: The Behavioral Sciences and the Church*, 17 (4) J. PSYCHOLOGY & THEOLOGY 213-25 (1989); Stanton L. Jones, *1993 Addendum to Jones & Workman*, in Homosexuality in the Church: A Reader and Study Guide (J. S. Sikered ed.), 1993.

[33]Wardle, *Critical Analysis*, 1996 B.Y.U.L. REV. at 63-64 (citations omitted).

LeVay gathered his information with regards to the past history from hospital records. If the records did not indicate the subject's past sexual history, he classified them as heterosexual since most males are heterosexual.[34] Relying only on past records is itself a significant flaw. Two of the patients' records indicated they had AIDS but did not engage in homosexual activity. LeVay therefore classified both of these subjects as heterosexual.[35]

All of the individuals classified as homosexual had died of AIDS. It is therefore a distinct possibility that the smaller brain size was either due to AIDS, or resulted from the medication the subject had taken to treat AIDS.[36] There was no data showing the size of the brain before and after medication or before and after contracting AIDS. The brains were not compared with the subject's parents or siblings. Moreover, there was no serious consideration given to the question of whether brain size causes homosexual orientation or whether the brain size was a consequence of the subject's sexual orientation.

Another study attempted to correlate homosexuality with genetic identity.[37] This study compared male identical twins, fraternal twins, nontwin brothers and adopted brothers. This study reported a coordinance rate among homosexuality for identical twins at fifty-two percent, for fraternal twins at twenty-two percent, for nonbiological brothers at nine percent and for adopted brothers at eleven percent. Since the coordinance rate was higher among identical twins, this study correlated homosexuality with genetics. This study was based upon self-classification as to sexual orientation, and when the second party was not available, the first party assumed what the sexual orientation was for the second. However, the study can also be cited against the genetic argument since the adopted brothers' coordinance rate was higher than the

---

[34]LeVay, *A Difference in Hypothalamic Structure Between Heterosexual and Homosexual Men*, 253 SCIENCE at 1034.

[35]*Id.* at 1036 n.7.

[36]Though LeVay acknowledges this possibility he found it not determinative. *Id.* at 1036. See Byne, *The Biological Evidence Challenged*, SCIENTIFIC AMERICAN, May 1994 at 53.

[37]J. Michael Bailey & Richard C. Pillard, *A Genetic Study of Male Sexual Orientation*, 48 ARCHIVES GEN. PSYCHIATRY 1089 (1991); *see also* J. Michael Bailey, et al., *Heritable Factors Influence Sexual Orientation in Women*, 50 ARCHIVES GEN. PSYCHIATRY 217 (1993) (female twins study).

nontwin biological brothers. There is no genetic link between adopted brothers. The only factor liking the two is environmental. Moreover, nontwin brothers share the same proportion of genes as fraternal twins, and "if homosexuality were genetically induced, the rates of homosexual coordinates should be the same for both groups rather then the reported less than half for the nontwin brothers than for the fraternal twins reported."[38]

Hormonal studies attempting to link homosexuality to genetics are also flawed. If homosexuality were only hormonal, then increasing or decreasing certain hormones should increase or decrease one's sexual orientation. However, "hormonal therapies have failed to influence sexual orientation in adults, and there is also no evidence that sexual orientation is shifted in adults as a consequence of [hormonal] changes."[39]

A study involving fruit flies tested reduction of serotonin supports environmental, rather than genetic, homosexuality. Though some male fruit flies with decreased serotonin levels attempted to mate with other males, the female fruit flies were not similarly affected. Moreover, after a two-hour exposure with the treated male fruit flies, some of the non-treated fruit flies mimicked the treated fruit flies and began engaging in male mating activity. On the other hand, when the treated male fruit flies were surrounded by a majority of non-treated fruit flies, there was little or no male mating activity. The "later findings contradicted [the] genetic-determinant theory and suggests that environment can induce 'homosexual' behavior in previously nonhomosexual fruit flies."[40]

There is no scientific basis to conclude homosexuality is an immutable characteristic trait caused solely by genetics. As it relates to same sex marriage, it is therefore permissible for a state to choose not to grant preferred status to same sex marriage. The presence or absence of immutability is not determinative as to whether a statute prohibiting a license to couples of the same gender is constitutional. For example, age and family relationship are immutable characteristics, meaning that these characteristics

---

[38]Wardle, *Critical Analysis*, 1996 B.Y.U.L. REV. at 69.
[39]Byne & Parsons, *Human Sexual Orientation: The Biologic Theories Reprised*, ARCHIVES GEN. PSYCHIATRY, Mar. 1993 at 230.
[40]Wardle, *Critical Analysis*, 1996 B.Y.U.L. REV. at 70.

cannot be changed. Yet, it is perfectly legitimate for a state to prohibit marriage to an unemancipated, non-pregnant minor and to likewise prohibit incestuous marriage.

Despite pleas and cries by homosexual activists, it appears that a law prohibiting same sex marriage will be considered constitutional if there is a rational or legitimate governmental reason for the restriction. Based on the long history of American tradition, there are certainly many rational and legitimate reasons for restricting marriage to those of the opposite gender. The first and obvious is the interest in procreation. Another is economic. Still another rational basis is protecting social mores, values, and health.

Defense of Marriage Act

In 1996, Congress passed federal legislation known as the Defense of Marriage Act (hereafter "DOMA"). DOMA states as follows:

> No state, territory, or possession of the United States, or Indian tribe, shall be required to give effect to any public act, record, or judicial proceeding of any other State, territory, possession, or tribe respecting a relationship between persons of the same sex that is treated as a marriage under laws of such other State, territory, possession, or tribe, or right or claim arising from such relationship.[41]

The intent of DOMA is to make sure that the battle over same sex marriage is fought out state by state. Some fear that if same sex marriage is legalized by any one state, homosexual couples may obtain a marriage license in that state and then return to their home state, arguing that the Full Faith and Credit Clause of the United States Constitution requires that the marriage be similarly recognized in the home state. The Full Faith and Credit Clause found in the United States Constitution states as follows:

> Full Faith and Credit shall be given in each State to the

---

[41]28 U.S.C. § 1738C.

public Acts, Records, and Judicial Proceedings of every other state. And the Congress may by general Laws prescribe the Manner in which such Acts, Records, and Proceedings shall be proved, and the Effect thereof.[42]

DOMA specifically traces the language of the Full Faith and Credit Clause, stating that no state or territory shall be required to recognize a marriage consummated in another state if that marriage is between two people of the same sex. While judgments are entitled to full faith and credit, marriages are not judgments and are not required to be recognized.[43]

Prior to the United States Supreme Court's ruling that statutes prohibiting marriage on the basis of race were unconstitutional, some states allowed miscegeneous (interracial) marriages while other states did not. Interracial couples who were validly married in one state found that after moving to other states their marriages were not legally recognized and their children were considered illegitimate.[44]

Similarly, while polygamy was recognized by one state, the same marriage was invalidated by another state.[45] Finally, an incestuous marriage recognized by one state has also been invalidated by another state.[46]

The basic rule relating to one state recognizing a marriage of another state is that "a marriage valid where celebrated is valid everywhere . . . [except] marriages deemed contrary to the laws of nature [and] marriages positively forbidden by statute because contrary to local public policy."[47] One reputable legal document regarding the conflict of laws between states recognized the following:

---

[42]U.S. Const. Art. IV, § 1. Congress passed federal legislation providing that "Such Act, Records and Judicial Proceedings or copies thereof . . . shall have the same full faith and credit in every court within the United States [that they have in the states] from which they are taken." 28 U.S.C. § 1738 (1988).

[43]See Haviv A. Balian, *Till Death Do Us Part: Granting Full Faith and Credit to Marital Status*, 68 S. CAL. L. REV. 397, 401, 406 (1995).

[44]See e.g., *Osoinach v. Watkins*, 180 So. 577 (Ala. 1938); *People v. Kay*, 252 N.Y.S. 518 (1931); *Pennegar v. State*, 10 S.W. 305 (Tenn. 1889).

[45]*People v. Kay*, 252 N.Y.S. 518 (1931).

[46]*Osoinach v. Watkins*, 180 So. 577 (Ala. 1938).

[47]*Toler v. Oakwood*, 4 S.E.2d 364, 366 (Va. 1939).

A marriage which satisfies the requirements of the state
where the marriage was contracted will everywhere be
recognized as valid unless it violates the strong public
policy of another state. . . .[48]

DOMA does not prohibit same sex marriage. It simply returns
the battle to the individual states. It is up to the individual states to
pass state legislation regarding same sex marriages. DOMA simply
states that if one state chooses not to recognize a marriage validated
in another state between two people of the same sex, then it will not
be forced to do so under the Full Faith and Credit Clause.

Proposed State Legislation

A number of states have taken steps to enact legislation
specifically prohibiting same sex marriage. While some states may
not have specific legislation prohibiting same sex marriage, the
wording of the legislation may already be enough to prohibit a
marriage license to couples of the same gender. However, it is
probably worthwhile to review each state's legislation to make sure
the language contained therein sufficiently addresses same sex
marriage. A sample piece of legislation may be drafted as follows:

A marriage licensed in any other country, state or
territory, if valid where licensed, is valid in this state
except that marriage between parties of the same gender
is not valid in this state because such marriage is contrary
to public policy.[49]

Judicial Arguments Against Same Sex Marriage

Though the right to marry may be a constitutionally recognized

---

[48]RESTATEMENT (SECOND) OF CONFLICT OF LAWS § 283(2)(1971).
[49]This sample legislation has been proposed by Liberty Counsel. *See* Mathew D. Staver,
Same Sex Marriages, THE LIBERATOR, Vol. 7, No. 5 (June/July 1996).

fundamental liberty interest,[50] there is no such fundamental right to same sex marriage. The United States Supreme Court has noted that a fundamental right depends, not on personal and private action, but on

> the "traditions and . . . conscience of our people" to determine whether a principle is "so rooted . . . as to be ranked as fundamental." The inquiry [is] whether a right involved "is of such a character that it cannot be denied without violating those 'fundamental principles of liberty and justice which lie at the base of all civil and political institutions.'"[51]

Therefore in order to classify a right as fundamental, the court must consider the following question: "[W]hether the practice or relationship is deeply rooted in the common law traditions of the American people or whether it is essential to the very concept of ordered liberty."[52]

The Supreme Court has recognized that upon marriage "society may be said to be built, and out of its fruit springs social relations and social obligations and duties, with which government is necessarily required to deal."[53] "Marriage and procreation are fundamental to the very existence and survival of the race."[54] The Supreme Court has described marriage as "the most important relation in life" and recognized that the marriage institution "has always been subject to the control of the legislature."[55] In 1967 the Supreme Court ruled unconstitutional a Virginia antimiscegenation (anti-interracial) statute that prohibited marriage between two people

---

[50]*See Zablocki v. Red Hail*, 434 U.S. 374 (1978); *Loving v. Virginia*, 388 U.S. 1 (1967); *see also Turner v. Safley*, 482 U.S. 78 (1987). Professor Wardle points out that the Supreme Court has not classified marriage as a "fundamental right" but instead has referred to marriage as a "fundamental interest" and described marriage as one of the "basic rights." Wardle, *Critical Analysis*, 1996 B.Y.U.L. REV. at 29 n.111.

[51]*Griswold v. Connecticut*, 381 U.S. 479, 486 (Goldberg, J., concurring) (citations omitted).

[52]Wardle, *Critical Analysis*, 1996 B.Y.U.L. REV. at 28.

[53]*Reynolds v. United States*, 98 U.S. 145, 165 (1878).

[54]*Skinner v. Oklahoma*, 316 U.S. 535, 541 (1942).

[55]*Maynard v. Hill*, 125 U.S. 190, 205 (1888).

of a different race.[56] Shortly thereafter the Supreme Court emphasized that "marriage involves interests of basic importance in our society."[57]

Clearly the right to homosexual marriage cannot be considered a fundamental right or a fundamental liberty interest. There is no longstanding history in this country, or for that matter around the world, to show societal support for same sex marriage. Moreover, in *Bowers v. Hardwick*,[58] the Supreme Court upheld the constitutionality of a Georgia sodomy statute that criminalized consensual sodomy. To "claim that a right to engage in . . . [homosexual behavior] is 'deeply rooted in this nation's history and tradition' or 'implicit in the concept of ordered liberty' is, at best, facetious."[59] The Supreme Court concluded that there was no "connection between family, marriage, or procreation on the one hand and homosexual activity on the other [hand]."[60] The recent Supreme Court decision in *Romer v. Evans*,[61] which struck down Colorado's Amendment 2, did not overrule *Bowers v. Hardwick* and is far from a Magna Carta for homosexuals. In *Romer v. Evans*,

[t]he Court did not reverse *Bowers v. Hardwick*. It did not find any new fundamental rights lurking in the penumbras of the written Constitution. It did not hold that homosexuals are a suspect or quasi-suspect class under the Equal Protection Clause. It did not hold that moral disapproval of homosexual conduct is invidious. It did not hold that it is illegitimate or irrational for government to make distinctions designed to discourage homosexuality. Most emphatically, it did not say anything that calls in question laws rejecting homosexual marriage. It *did* apply

---

[56]*Loving* , 388 U.S. at 1.

[57]*Boddie v. Connecticut*, 401 U.S. 371, 376 (1971). In 1977 the Supreme Court found unconstitutional a law that restricted the right of indigent fathers of children receiving public assistance. *Zablocki*, 434 U.S. 374 (1978). *See also Califano v. Jobst*, 434 U.S. 447 (1997).

[58]478 U.S. 186 (1986).

[59]*Id.* at 194.

[60]*Id.* at 191. The Supreme Court's recent decision in *Romer v. Evans*, 116 S. Ct. 1620 (1996), did not overrule its previous ruling in *Bowers*. *See* Richard F. Duncan, *Wigstock and the Kultur Kampf: Supreme Court Storytelling, the Culture War, and* Romer v. Evans, 72 NOTRE DAME L. REV. 345 (1997).

[61]116 S. Ct. at 1620.

the lowest level of scrutiny -- the rational basis test -- to laws disadvantaging homosexuals and explicitly held that such laws will be upheld so long as they are "narrow enough in scope and grounded in sufficient factual context" for the Court to ascertain that there exists "some relation between the classification and the purpose it served."[62]

Clearly the redefinition of family through the vehicle of same sex marriage is without question one of the most urgent social and moral dilemmas facing America. If same sex marriage is recognized, then ninety-five percent of the homosexual agenda will have been achieved. It will be just a matter of time before that agenda infiltrates every part of American culture. Certainly there is no constitutional basis for same sex marriage. There is no cultural mandate. The weight of history does not fall on the side of same sex marriage. The vast majority of Americans oppose same sex marriages. One may ask with the dumbfounded look of Detective Colombo: "With history, social mores, political, and judicial precedent opposing same sex marriage, how can we seriously consider the possibility that same sex marriage will come to be recognized?" The answer lies in Edmond Burke's oft quoted truism: "All that is necessary for evil to triumph is for good men to do nothing."[63]

---

[62]Duncan, *Wigstock and the Kultur Kampf,* 72 NOTRE DAME L. REV. at 248.

[63]Edmond Burke, *Letters on A Regicide Peace* (1797); William Federer, *America's God and Country* 83 (1994).

21

JUDICIAL TYRANNY

Aristotle once said that inherent in a free society is the ability of the people to debate the question: "How ought we to order our life together?"[1] Today we hear a lot of rhetoric that the Bill of Rights is designed to protect the liberties of the minority against the majority. However, our constitutional makeup does not give the minority veto rights over the majority. Certainly the majority cannot trample constitutional rights, but the major political and social questions of our day has by constitutional design been given to the majority through the legislative process. Continually taking away the right of the majority to shape their culture will ultimately result in rebellion. After all, the give and take of the political process provides that the majority voice have final say on major sociological issues. To take away the right of the people to debate the question leads to an oligarchy (government of the few) and results in tyranny.

Basis For Government

The signers of the Declaration of Independence clearly understood the purpose of government. They pinned the following poignant words:

> When in the course of human events, it becomes necessary for one people to dissolve the political bands which have connected them with another, and to assume among the Power of the earth, the separate and equal station to which the Laws of Nature and of Nature's God entitle them, decent respect to the opinions of mankind requires that they should declare the causes which impel them to the separation.

> We hold these truths to be self-evident, that all men are

---

[1] The Editors, *The End of Democracy? The Judicial Usurpation of Politics*, FIRST THINGS, November 1996, p. 18.

created equal, that they are endowed by their Creator with certain unalienable Rights, that among these are Life, Liberty, and the pursuit of Happiness.

That to secure these rights, Governments are instituted among Men, deriving their just powers from the consent of the governed.

That whenever any Form of Government becomes destructive of these ends, is the Right of the People to alter or to abolish it, to institute new Government, laying its foundation on such principles and organizing its powers in such form, as to them shall seem most likely to affect their Safety and Happiness. . . .But when a long train of abuses and usurpations, pursuing invariably the same Object, evinces a design to reduce them under absolute Despotism, it is their right, it is their duty, to throw off such Government, and to provide new Guards for the future security. . . .[2]

The founders clearly understood that government's purpose is to preserve life, liberty and the pursuit of happiness. These liberties are God-given. Such liberties predate government and are inalienable,[3] meaning that government cannot (at least should not) take away these liberties. The sole purpose of government is to make sure these liberties are protected. Whenever any form of government fails to protect, or in the worse case, affirmatively destroys, these liberties, then it is the right and duty of the people, to alter or abolish that system and to institute a new form of government.

Separation Of Powers

When contemplating a new form of government, the founders envisioned depositing governmental power into three separate

---

[2]Declaration of Independence, July 4, 1776, The Organic Laws of the United States of America.

[3]Or, as the signers of the Declaration said, "unalienable."

branches. The founders clearly feared that if one branch of government accumulated too much power, it would overcome the other two branches of government, thus leading to tyranny. The human experience was itself sufficient reason for separating the powers of government. The founders knew quite well that power corrupts, and absolute power corrupts absolutely. George Washington in his farewell address observed the following:

> A just estimate of that love of power, and proneness to abuse it which predominates in the human heart, is sufficient to satisfy us for the truth of this position. The necessity of reciprocal checks in the exercise of political power by dividing and distributing it into different depositories. . . has been [establish].[4]

Not only must government itself be checked and balanced, but government must also restrain human passion. When putting forth arguments to the people of New York as to why the colonies should adopt a constitution, Alexander Hamilton wrote: "Why has government been instituted at all? Because the passions of men will not conform to the dictates of reason and justice without constraint."[5]

The founders envisioned three separate branches of government which included the Executive, the Legislative and the Judiciary. The weakest branch of government was supposed to be the Judiciary, but today it has become the strongest branch. Indeed, not until 1935 did the United States Supreme Court find a permanent home in Washington, D.C. Prior to its present location, it met in the basement of the Senate. Alexander Hamilton described the three branches of government as follows:

> The executive not only dispenses the honors, but holds the sword of the community. The legislature not only commands the purse, but prescribes the rules by which the duties and rights of every citizen are to be regulated. The judiciary on the contrary has no influence over either the

---

[4]*Farewell Address of George Washington* 22 (1796).
[5]Alexander Hamilton, *The Federalist*, No. 15.

sword or the purse, no direction either of the strength or
of the wealth of the society, and can take no active
resolution whatsoever. It may truly be said to have neither
Force nor Will, but merely judgment; and must ultimately
depend upon the aid of the executive arm even for the
efficacy of its judgements.[6]

As Alexander Hamilton noted, the executive carries the sword,
the legislature holds the purse, and the judiciary merely exercises
judgment. However, the judiciary is ultimately dependent upon the
aid of the executive even for the efficacy of carrying out its
judgments. In other words, the judiciary can issue an opinion, but
that opinion has no power without the aid of the executive to
enforce that opinion.

As originally envisioned, the judiciary was not only the
weakest branch of government but was the least dangerous threat to
political liberty. Again, Alexander Hamilton pointed out the
following:

[T]he judiciary, from the nature of its functions, will
always be the least dangerous to the political rights of the
constitution; because it will least in capacity to annoy or
injure them. . . . [T]he judiciary is, beyond comparison,
the weakest of the three departments of power. . . . [T]he
general liberty of the people can never be endangered
from that quarter.[7]

Why did Alexander Hamilton believe the judiciary could never
threaten the liberties of the people? The judiciary was set up to
decide cases and controversies -- to solve disputes between parties.
The judiciary could not execute its judgments, it could simply
render them. The executive has the duty, and the discretion, to carry
out a judicial decree. As originally established, the judiciary was
only reactive, deciding cases and controversies that were brought to
its attention. These cases or controversies ultimately resolve the
disputes between the parties, and would not necessarily apply to the

---

[6]Alexander Hamilton, *The Federalist*, No. 78.
[7]*Id.*

populous in general. The judiciary could not levy taxes or create new law. The judiciary was charged with the task of applying existing law to resolve a case or controversy. Speaking of the Judiciary, Montesquieu stated that "of the three powers. . ., the Judiciary is next to nothing."[8]

James Madison understood how liberty could be undermined if too much power were exercised by the judiciary.

> It is necessary that the supreme judiciary should have the confidence of the people. This will soon be lost if they are employed in the task of remonstrating against [opposing and striking down] popular measures of the legislature.[9]

Today it has become common place for the judiciary to strike down "popular measures of the legislature." In 1996, the United States Supreme Court struck down Colorado's Amendment 2 which provided an amendment to the state constitution that would prohibit giving special rights to homosexuals.[10] In 1995 a federal court found unconstitutional a voter approved California initiative withholding welfare benefits from illegal aliens,[11] and in 1996 another federal court found unconstitutional another California voter approved initiative.[12] The latter voter initiative abolished affirmative action, and therefore in essence stated that instead of preference based on skin color, the state would now treat its citizens equally. Amazingly, a federal court found that a voter approved amendment requiring that all people be treated equally regardless of skin color violated Equal Protection under the United States Constitution. A later court reversed this decision.[13] In a desegregation case, a federal court ordered that property taxes be increased to fund a desegregation program.[14] Though the United

---

[8]Montesquieu, 1 *Spirit of Laws* 186.

[9]James Madison, 2 *The Papers of James Madison* 1161-1171, *quoting* Luther Morton at the Constitutional Convention on July 21, 1787.

[10]*Romer v. Evans*, 116 S. Ct. 1620 (1996).

[11]*League of United Latin American Citizens v. Wilson*, 908 F. Supp. 755 (C.D. Cal. 1995).

[12]*Coalition for Economic Equity v. California*, 946 F. Supp. 1480 (N.D. Cal. 1996).

[13]*Coalition for Economic Equity v. Wilson*, 110 F.3d 1431 (9th Cir. 1997), superseded, *California v. Coalition for Economic Equity*, 122 F.3d 692 (9th Cir. 1997).

[14]*Missouri v. Jenkins*, 672 F. Supp. 400 (W.D. Mo. 1987).

States Supreme Court later ruled that the federal court overstepped
its authority,[15] the mere fact that a court even thought of the
possibility of raising taxes is incomprehensible.

Some of the founders feared that the judicial branch contained
the potential root of tyranny. Thomas Jefferson once wrote:

> [T]he germ of disillusion of our federal government is in
> the [composition] of the federal judiciary. . . working like
> gravity by night and by day, gaining a little today and a
> little tomorrow, and advancing its noiseless step like a
> thief with a field of jurisdiction until all shall be
> usurped.[16]

Thomas Jefferson considered the three branches of government
to be coordinate. In other words, he did not assume that the
judiciary exercised the sole providence to interpret the Constitution
or to determine what laws are constitutional. In this respect he
observed the following:

> [T]he opinion that gives to the judges the right to decide
> what laws are constitutional and what not, not only for
> themselves in their own sphere of action but for the
> legislature and executive also in their spheres, would make
> the judiciary a despotic branch.[17]

> Indeed, "to consider the judges as the ultimate arbiters of
> all constitutional questions [is] a very dangerous doctrine
> indeed, and one which would place us under the
> despotism of an oligarchy. . . .The Constitution has
> erected no single tribunal."[18]

Thomas Jefferson felt that to protect liberty, the people in mass

---

[15]*Missouri v. Jenkins*, 110 S. Ct. 109 (1990).

[16]Albert Ellerybergh, ed., 14 *Writings of Thomas Jefferson*, 331-332. Thomas Jefferson
to Charles Hammond on August 18, 1821.

[17]11 *Writings of Thomas Jefferson* 50-51. Thomas Jefferson to Abigail Adams on
September 11, 1804.

[18]14 *Writings of Thomas Jefferson* 277. Thomas Jefferson to William Charles Jarvis on
September 28, 1820.

must have opportunity to decide the important question of the day. He observed:

> It should be considered an axiom of eternal truth in politics that whatever power in any government is independent is absolute . . . . Independence can be trusted no where but with the people in mass.[19]

James Madison, the architect of the Bill of Rights, feared that if one branch of government accumulated too much power, the result would be tyranny.

> The accumulation of all powers, legislative, executive, and judiciary in the same hands, whether of one, a few or many, and whether hereditary, self appointed, or elected, may justly be pronounced the very same definition of tyranny.[20]

The Problem

Interestingly, the United States Supreme Court once declared that the "Federal Constitution does not give this Court the power to overturn the State's choice under the guise of constitutional interpretation because the Justices of this Court believe that they can provide better rules."[21] However, that is exactly what the justices of the Supreme Court and judges of other courts do everyday. Therein lies the problem. In 1803 Supreme Court Justice John Marshall penned these now famous words: "It is, emphatically, the province and duty of the judicial department to say what the law is."[22] Sometime after the famous *Marbury v. Madison* decision, the

---

[19]14 *Writings of Thomas Jefferson* 213-214. Thomas Jefferson to Judge Spencer Roane on September 6, 1819.

[20]James Madison, *The Federalist* No. 47.

[21]*Labine v. Vincent*, 401 U.S. 532 (1971).

[22]*Marbury v. Madison*, 5 U.S. (1 Cranch) 137, 176 (1803). It should be pointed out that there were two views of the judiciary. One view was that the judiciary should be an extremely weak branch of government, but others viewed the judiciary as a stronger body, albeit not nearly as powerful as it is today. Supreme Court Justice Joseph Story who died in 1835, stated the following:

Supreme Court again resurrected John Marshall's words in the famous case of *Cooper v. Aaron*, where the Court stated that the *Marbury*

> decision declared the basic principle that the federal judiciary is supreme in the exposition of the law of the Constitution, and that principle has ever since been respected by this Court and the Country as a permanent and indispensable feature of our constitutional system.[23]

There are several problems inherent in the judicial branch. First, the federal judiciary is appointed, not elected. Once appointed, they are essentially appointed for life unless subsequently impeached. The federal judiciary is an unelected body precisely because it is supposed to be independent of, and not necessarily swayed by, popular political opinion. Generally this would work fine if the judiciary would exercise self restraint, and interpret, rather than create law. However, if the judicial branch has the ultimate responsibility of interpreting the meaning of the Constitution, then the judiciary will always have a trump card on the other two branches of government. If the branch which interprets the law has final word over the branch that creates the law, then the branch that creates the law is essentially irrelevant because no matter what is created, the judiciary can interpret it differently. Since the judiciary has evolved to this power platform

---

The decision then made, whether in favor or against the constitutionality of the act, by the State or by the national authority, by the legislature or by the executive, being capable, in its own nature, of being brought to the test of the Constitution, is subject to judicial revision. It is in such cases, as we conceive, that there is a final and common arbiter provided by the Constitution itself, to whose decisions all others are subordinate; and that arbiter is the supreme judicial authority of the courts of the Union.

Joseph Story, 2 *Commentaries on the Constitution of the United States* 266-67 (1833) (footnote omitted).

[23]*Cooper v. Aaron*, 358 U.S. 1, 18 (1958). *See also Baker v. Carr*, 369 U.S. 186, 210-11 (1962) (referring to the "responsibility of this Court as ultimate interpreter of the Constitution"); *Powell v. McCormack*, 395 U.S. 486, 549 (1969) ("[I]t is the responsibility of this Court to act as the ultimate interpreter of the Constitution"); *United States v. Nixon*, 418 U.S. 683, 704 (1974) (speaking of the "responsibility of this Court as ultimate interpreter of the Constitution").

over time, it has gradually taken away the opportunity from the people to debate the social issues of our day. All the major social and political questions of our time are now decided by the judiciary, not by the people in mass. For example, a single state court judge ruled that prohibiting same sex marriage is unconstitutional under the State of Hawaii's constitution.[24] The judge accepted testimony that there was no difference between homosexual and heterosexual marriage, and consequently there was no reason under Hawaii's equal protection clause of the state constitution to deny a marriage license to homosexuals.

As noted above, notwithstanding the fact that 53% of the Colorado voters adopted Amendment 2 which prohibited special treatment based upon sexual orientation, the United States Supreme Court found the state constitutional amendment to be contrary to the federal Constitution.[25] Justice Antonin Scalia in dissent criticized the Court for assuming a political role.

> Today's opinion has no foundation in American constitutional law, and barely pretends to. The people of Colorado have adopted an entirely reasonable provision which does not even disfavor homosexuals in any substantive sense, but merely denies them preferential treatment. Amendment 2 is designed to prevent piecemeal deterioration of the sexual morality favored by a majority of Coloradans, and is not only an appropriate means to that legitimate end, but a means that Americans have employed before. Striking it down is an act, not a judicial judgment, but of political will.[26]

Justice Scalia did not think it was any "business of the courts (as opposed to the political branches) to take sides in this culture war."[27] However, the Court did take sides.

---

[24]*Baehr v. Miike*, 65 U.S. L. Weekly 2399 (Cir. Ct. Hi. 1996).

[25]*Romer*, 116 S. Ct. at 1620. Though not specifically elevating sexual orientation to a class status such as sex or race status, the Supreme Court certainly elevated the status of homosexuals. As such, the Court planted the seed which may later develop into a recognition that homosexuals must be treated as a special class just like race or gender.

[26]*Romer*, 116 S. Ct. at 1637 (Scalia, J., dissenting).

[27]*Id.*

A federal court found unconstitutional a Washington statute that made it a felony to knowingly aid another person to commit suicide.[28] In dissent, one of the judges stated the following:

> The Supreme Court has never recognized a substantive due process right without first finding that there is a tradition of protecting a particular interest. Here, there is absolutely no tradition of protecting assisted suicide. Almost all states forbid assisted suicide and some states even permit the use of nondeadly force to thwart suicide attempts. No state has ever accepted consent of the victim as a defense to a charge of homicide. These are the political judgments made by the democratic process; if they are no longer "politically correct," let the legislatures act to change them, not life-tenured judges immune from the voters' reach.[29]

We have already noted how two federal courts in California struck down voter approved initiatives and how another court in Missouri attempted to impose property taxes. In one case a California state court found no constitutional right for a widow to refuse to rent to unmarried couples despite her religious convictions to the contrary.[30] After the widow lost her hearing before the Fair Employment and Housing Commission, she was required to put a poster on her rental property acknowledging her alleged "wrong." Essentially the State of California attempted to humiliate this widow for her sincerely held religious convictions.

In another case, a federal court found no constitutional right for parents to receive prior notification when their children were subjected to explicit sexual conduct.[31] The organization, Hot, Sexy and Safer, was invited to the school where students were directed to go to an auditorium. There the organization carried on extreme sexual vulgarities, most of which can not even be printed in this book. Some of the activities included placing lifesize condoms over

[28]Compassion in Dying v. Washington, 79 F.3d 790 (9th Cir. 1994). See also Quill v. Vacco, 80 F.3d 716 (2d Cir. 1996).
[29]Compassion in Dying v. Washington, 85 F.3d 1440, 1445 (9th Cir. 1996).
[30]Smith v. Fair Employment and Housing Commission, 913 P.2d 909 (Cal. 1996).
[31]Brown v. Hot, Sexy and Safer, 68 F.3d 525 (1st Cir. 1995).

a person's entire body and then licking the condom. The presenters brought certain students to the platform and commented on their clothing, their various sexual organs, and ways to arouse another person. Concerned parents sued over this mental rape, stating that they should be notified prior to their children being subjected to such sexually explicit behavior. However, a federal court found the parents did not have such a right and instead ruled in favor of the school.

Possible Remedies for Curing Judicial Tyranny

Congressional Limitation Of Jurisdiction

Some have suggested that the legislature should limit the jurisdictional power of the federal courts. Article III, Section 2, Clause 2 of the United States Constitution states:

> In all Cases affecting Ambassadors, other public Ministers and Consuls, and those in which a State shall have appellate Jurisdiction, both as to Law and Fact, with such exceptions, and under such Regulations as the Congress shall make.

Congress may impart as much or as little of judicial power as it deems appropriate, and the judiciary may not thereafter on its own motion refer to this article for additional jurisdiction.[32] Congress has the power to invest inferior federal courts[33] with all or any part of the federal judicial power and to withdraw at any time all or part of the jurisdiction which it has conferred upon them.[34] Congress need not establish any inferior federal courts and it might take all jurisdiction from them if it so desired.[35] The

---

[32]*Senate Select Committee on Presidential Campaign Activities v. Nixon*, 366 F. Supp. 51 (D.C.D.C. 1973).

[33]Inferior federal courts refers to federal district and appellate courts. The term does not refer to the United States Supreme Court.

[34]*Eldridge v. Richfield Oil Corp*, 247 F. Supp. 407 (D.C. Cal. 1965), *aff'd*, 364 F.2d 909 (9th Cir. 1966), *cert. denied*, 385 U.S. 1020 (1967).

[35]*McCann v. Paris*, 244 F. Supp. 870 (D.C. Va. 1965); *Harlan v. Pennsylvania R. Co.*, 180 F. Supp. 725 (D.C. PA. 1960).

inferior federal courts are creatures of Congress and can exercise only such jurisdiction as Congress confers on them, and Congress in its unfettered discretion may withhold or take away their jurisdiction.[36]

However, the exercise by Congress of its control over jurisdiction is subject to compliance with at least the requirements of the Fifth Amendment, which is to say that while Congress has undoubted power to give, withhold and restrict jurisdiction of courts other than the Supreme Court, it must not so exercise that power as to deprive any person of life, liberty or property without due process of law or take private property without just compensation.[37]

Everyone would agree that Congress has the authority to create new courts. If Congress can actually create a new federal court, then it can abolish the court. If it can abolish the court, then it can limit the court's jurisdiction. Some cases that have not been made federal questions, can be made federal questions through legislative enactment, and it is possible that other cases might be removed from federal jurisdiction. The big question to consider here is whether certain issues such as sexual orientation, abortion, and euthanasia could ultimately be removed from federal court jurisdiction. While it may be possible to limit jurisdiction of these subjects among inferior federal courts, Congress probably has less power to withdraw the Supreme Court's jurisdiction. Since Congress cannot take away the Supreme Court's power to decide constitutional questions, and since Congress has no authority over state courts, these constitutional questions would eventually reach the Supreme Court through the state court system. State courts are empowered to rule on federal constitutional questions, and the United States Supreme Court may review their decisions.[38]

---

[36]*Henderson v. Kimmel*, 47 F. Supp. 635 (D.C. Kan. 1942).

[37]*Battaglia v. General Motors Corp.*, 169 F.2d 254 (2d Cir. 1948), cert. denied 335 U.S. 887.

[38]Judge Robert Bork states that limiting federal court jurisdiction will accomplish little precisely because the same issues will still work their way to the Supreme Court through the state court system. Robert H. Bork, *Slouching Towards Gomorrah* 115-16 (1996).

Term Limits For Federal Judges

Another suggested remedy is to place term limits on judges much like term limits for the legislature. Article III, Section 1 of the United States Constitution states:

> The judicial Power of the United States, shall be vested in one supreme Court, and in such inferior Courts as the Congress may from time to time ordain and establish. The Judges, both of the supreme and inferior Courts, shall hold their Offices during good Behavior, and shall, as stated Times, receive for their Services, a Compensation, which shall not be diminished during their Continuance in Office.

Some scholars, such as Professor Sanford Levinson of the Boston University Law School, have advocated term limits for federal judges. Professor Levinson suggests a term of 18 years for Supreme Court justices and 12 to 14 years for district and appeals court judges.

Supermajority To Overturn Statutes

Professor Richard Duncan of the University of Nebraska College of Law has suggested amending the Constitution to require 7 votes of the Justices to declare state or federal legislation unconstitutional. His reasoning is that the will of the people should prevail unless there is a strong consensus on the Court that the Constitution has been violated. If a supermajority was required, Colorado's Amendment 2 would never have been ruled unconstitutional.

Impeachment

There are several constitutional provisions that directly or indirectly discuss impeachment. Included are the following:

> The Senate shall have power to try all impeachments. When sitting for that purpose, they shall be on oath or

affirmation. When the President of the United States is tried, the Chief-Justice shall preside; and no person shall be convicted without the concurrence of two-thirds of the members present. Judgement, in cases of impeachment, shall not extend further than to removal from office and disqualification to hold and enjoy any office of honor, trust, or profit under the United States. But the party convicted shall nevertheless be liable and subject to indictment, trial, judgment, and punishment, according to law.[39]

****

The president, vice-president, and all civil officers of the United States, shall be removed from office on impeachment for, and conviction of, treason, bribery, or other high crimes and misdemeanors.[40]

****

The trial of crimes, except in cases of impeachment, shall be by jury.[41]

****

[The president] shall have power to grant reprieves and pardons for offenses against the United States, except in cases of impeachment.[42]

****

The Judges, both of the Supreme and Inferior Courts, shall hold their office's during good behavior.[43]

---

[39]U.S. Const. Art. I, sec. 2, ¶5-7.
[40]U.S. Const. Art. II, sec. 4, ¶1.
[41]U.S. Const. Art. III, sec., 2, ¶3
[42]U.S. Const. Art. II, sec. 2, ¶1.
[43]U.S. Const. Art. III, sec. 1, ¶1.

To date, sixty-one judges have been investigated. Thirteen have been impeached. There have been three non-judicial impeachments.[44] When discussing impeachment, the question must be answered as to what is the basis to impeach a judge. Justice Joseph Story observed the following:

> [W]hat are to be deemed "high crimes and misdemeanors"?. . . [N]o one has yet been bold enough to assert that the power of impeachments is limited to offenses positively defined in the statute book of the Union as impeachable high crimes and misdemeanors.[45]

Justice Story penned the following regarding the ability of Congress to undertake impeachment activities:

> Congress has unhesitatingly adopted the conclusion that no previous statute is necessary to authorize an impeachment for any official misconduct. . . . In the few cases of impeachment that hitherto have been tried, not one of the charges has rested upon any statutable misdemeanors.[46]

Examples of impeachment include the following:

• In 1797, William Blount was impeached for seeking to violate American neutrality. According to Justice Story, the offense charged was not defined by any statute of the United States but was for an attempt to seduce United States' indian interpreters from their duty and to alienate the affections and confidence of the indians from the public officers residing among them.

• In 1803, Federal Judge John Pickering was impeached for issuing an order which contradicted an Act of Congress, for judicial high-handedness, drunkenness, and

---

[44]David Barton, *Impeachment!*
[45]Joseph Story, 2 *Commentaries on the Constitution* 263, 265 (1833).
[46]*Id.* at 267.

blasphemy.

• In 1804, Supreme Court Justice Pamela Chase was impeached for judicial high-handedness and for excluding evidence from a trial.

• In 1830, Federal Judge James H. Peck was also impeached for judicial high-handedness.

• In 1862, Federal Judge West H. Humphreys was impeached for supporting the secession movement.

• In 1868, President Andrew Johnson was impeached for removing and replacing the Secretary of War.

• In 1876, Secretary of War William W. Belknap was impeached for bribery.

• In 1904, Federal Judge Charles Swayne was impeached for financial improprieties and judicial high-handedness.

• In 1912, Federal Circuit Judge Robert W. Archibald was impeached for judicial high-handedness and misconduct.

• In 1926, Federal Judge George W. English was impeached for judicial high-handedness and for profanity.

• In 1933, Federal Judge Harold Lauderback was impeached for seeking to hide his assets during a personal divorce proceeding.

• In 1936, Federal Judge Halsted L. Ritter was impeached for corruption and income tax evasion.[47]

Today many people assume that impeachment is only for situations where a judge commits some heinous civil or criminal violation. However, then representative Gerald Ford, when

---

[47]David Barton, *Impeachment!* 23-25 (1996).

considering impeachment proceedings against Justice William Douglas, correctly observed that impeachment is not limited to a previously defined civil or criminal penalty.

> An impeachable offense is whatever the majority the House of Representatives considers it to be at a given moment in history; conviction results from whatever offense or offenses two-thirds of the other body considers to be sufficiently serious to require removal of the accused from office.[48]

Therefore, if Congress concluded that a judge overstepped judicial boundaries by attempting to become a superlegislator, that is an impeachable offense. Whatever Congress deems to be an impeachable offense is an impeachable offense regardless of whether the activity violates any civil or criminal statute.

Congressional Check On Supreme Court

In his recent book, Judge Robert Bork argues that the Supreme Court has become the agent of modern liberalism. Judge Bork observed the following:

> It will be extremely difficult to defend traditional values against intellectual class onslaught. Not only do the intellectuals occupy the commanding heights of the culture and the means by which values and ideas are created and transmitted, they control the most authoritarian institution of American government, federal and state judiciaries, headed by the Supreme Court of the United States. The courts have increasingly usurped the power to make our cultural decisions for us, and it is not apparent that we have any means of redress.[49]

---

[48]Robert A. Diamond, *Impeachment in the U.S. Congress*, ed. CONGRESSIONAL QUARTERLY, INC. 6-7 (1934) (quoting representative (later President) Gerald Ford when proposing the impeachment of Supreme Court Justice William Douglas).

[49]Robert H. Bork, *Slouching Towards Gomorrah* 95 (1996).

Judge Bork does not believe that limiting the jurisdiction of federal courts is a viable alternative. He reasons that even if all federal lower courts were abolished, the same kind of cases would still reach the United States Supreme Court on appeal from state courts.[50] Judge Bork concludes therefore that there is only one alternative:

> There appears to be only one means by which the federal courts, including the Supreme Court, can be brought back to constitutional legitimacy. That would be a constitutional amendment making any federal or state court decision subject to being over-ruled by a majority vote of each house of Congress. The mere suggestion of such a remedy is certain to bring down cries that this would endanger our freedoms. To the contrary, as already noted, it is the courts that are not merely endangering our freedoms but actually depriving us of them, particularly our most precious freedom, the freedom to govern ourselves democratically unless the Constitution actually says otherwise. The United Kingdom has developed freedoms without judicial review.[51]

Executive Refusal To Enforce Court Decisions

A final way to consider reigning in judicial power is for the executive branch not to enforce court decisions. This is also called the doctrine of nonacquiescence. It is precisely this issue that took place in Alabama where one state court ruled that state court Judge Roy Moore must remove the Ten Commandments from his courtroom wall. In defiance, Governor Fob James stated that he would call out the National Guard if anyone tried to remove the Ten Commandments. He is practicing the doctrine of nonacquiescence, and though it may seem radical today, it was not

[50]*Id.* at 115-16.
[51]*Id.* at 117.

so radical to our founding fathers.[52]

Several of the founding fathers believed in three coordinate branches of government. That is, these three branches of government each had an independent duty to interpret and uphold the Constitution. One branch of government did not have the sole authority to interpret the Constitution either for itself or for the other branch. Each branch was sworn to the duty to uphold the Constitution, although each branch had certain functions. To allow one branch the sole authority to interpret the Constitution for another would allow that branch to have autonomy over the opposing branch. In this regard, James Madison noted the following:

> [T]he people are the only legitimate fountain of power, and it is from them the constitutional charter, under which the several branches of government hold their power, is derived. . . . The several departments being perfectly co-ordinate by the terms of their common commission, neither of them, it is evident, can pretend to an exclusive or superior right of settling the boundaries between the respective powers.[53]

According to Professor Paulsen,

> The premise of coordinancy, as articulated by Madison, implies that no branch has final interpretive authority, but that each branch has interpretative authority within the sphere of its other constitutional powers; the resolution of disputed points depends on the pull-and-tug of the different branches, just as the Constitution's separation of powers in other respects works to preserve a system of checks and balances. The coordinancy principle thus implies that the executive branch -- that is the Presidency

---

[52]For a thorough discussion of this issue, see Michael Stokes Paulsen, *The Merryman Power and the Dilemma of Autonomous Executive Branch Interpretation*, 15 CARDOSO L. REV. 81 (1993) and Michael Stokes Paulsen, *The Most Dangerous Branch: Executive Power to Say What the Law Is*, 83 No. 2 GEORGETOWN L.J. 217 (1994). This section of the chapter is heavily indebted to the material compiled by Professor Paulsen.

[53]James Madison, *The Federalist* No. 49.

-- has completely independent interpretive authority within the sphere of its powers.[54]

The coordinancy concept can be illustrated when President Thomas Jefferson pardoned individuals convicted under the federalist-backed Sedition Act of 1798. This law forbade seditious libel against the government. A number of people were convicted under this Act. Notwithstanding the fact that Federalists judicial decisions upheld the constitutionality of the Sedition Act, President Jefferson pardoned those convicted under the Act on the basis that it was unconstitutional. John Adams had been President at the time that the Act was adopted and enforced, and out of respect, he wrote a letter to Abigail Adams justifying his pardons as follows:

> You seem to think that it devolved on the judges to decide on the validity of the sedition law. Nothing in the Constitution has given them a right to decide for the Executive, more than the Executive to decide for them. Both magistrates are equally independent in the sphere of action assigned to them. . . .[T]he opinion which gives to judges the right to decide what laws are constitutional, and what not, not only for themselves and their own sphere of action, but for the legislature and executive also in their spheres, would make the judiciary a despotic branch.[55]

In 1832, President Andrew Jackson vetoed legislation that attempted to recharter the Bank of the United States. Despite the fact that the United States Supreme Court rejected similar constitutional challenges on the question of whether Congress had power to create a national bank,[56] he nevertheless vetoed the bill on the basis of his own constitutional objections. In his veto message he penned the following:

> The Congress, the Executive and the Court must each for

---

[54]Paulsen, *The Merryman Power*, 15 CARDOSO L. REV. at 85 (footnote omitted).

[55]Thomas Jefferson, 11 *Writings of Thomas Jefferson* 50-51. Thomas Jefferson to Abigail Adams on September 11, 1804.

[56]*McCullouch v. Maryland*, 17 U.S. (4 Wheat.) 316 (1819).

itself be guided by its own opinion of the Constitution. Each public officer who takes an oath to support the Constitution swears that he will support it as he understands it, and not as it is understood by others. . . . The opinion of the judges has no more authority over Congress then the opinion of Congress has over the judges, and on that point the President is independent of both.[57]

While running as a candidate for the United States Senate in 1858, Abraham Lincoln declared his opposition to the infamous *Dred Scott* decision.[58] Lincoln boldly declared that he would not be bound by the *Dred Scott* decision if he were elected to the U.S. Senate:

We oppose the Dread Scott decision. . . as a political rule, which shall be binding on the voter. . . . We propose so resisting as to have it reversed if we can, and a new judicial rule established upon this subject.[59]

When Abraham Lincoln later became President, he was more forthright in his opposition to the *Dred Scott* decision during his First Inaugural address:

[T]he candid citizen must confess that if the policy of the government, upon vital questions, affecting the whole people, is to be irrevocably fixed by decisions of the Supreme Court, . . . the people will have ceased to be their own rulers, having, to that extent, practically resigned their government into the hands of that eminent tribunal.[60]

---

[57]Andrew Jackson, *Veto Message (July 10, 1832), reprinted in* 2 *A Compilation of the Messages and Papers of the Presidents, 1789-1897*, 582.

[58]*Dred Scott v. Sandford*, 19 How. 393 (1857) (declaring that blacks were not considered citizens under the United States Constitution).

[59]Abraham Lincoln, *Speech At Sixth Joint Debate with Stephen A. Douglas, Quincy, Ill.*, 3 (October 13, 1858), in *Collected Works of Abraham Lincoln*, 255.

[60]Abraham Lincoln, *First Inaugural Address* (March 4, 1861), *reprinted in* 4 *Collected Works of Abraham Lincoln*, 268.

President Lincoln then took active steps to oppose *Dred Scott*. He directed that patents and visas be given to black citizens.[61] This action by the President was in direct defiance of *Dred Scott*. The Supreme Court had previously ruled that blacks were not citizens under the Constitution, but President Lincoln treated blacks as though they were vested with full rights of citizenship. He therefore defied the Supreme Court's opinion on this matter.

President Lincoln's belief in the autonomy of the Executive did not stop with his opposition to *Dred Scott*. In the spring of 1861, in response to Lincoln's election, a number of southern states seceded from the Union. These secessionist activities became rampant around the State of Maryland. Washington, D.C. was surrounded by Confederates. Responding to increased secessionist violence in Maryland, Lincoln suspended the writ of habeas corpus.[62] Congress was apparently out of session at that time and therefore Lincoln took it upon himself to suspend the writ. Shortly thereafter a large number of suspected secessionists were arrested and imprisoned at Fort McHenry in Baltimore. One of those arrested was named John Merryman, a state legislator and lieutenant in a secessionist calvary. Merryman called upon Chief Judge Roger Taney, the author of the *Dred Scott* decision, to issue a writ of habeas corpus.[63] On May 26, 1861, Justice Taney issued a writ directed to the commanding officer at Fort McHenry. However, General George Cadwalader refused to produce Merryman, instead relying upon Lincoln's order. Taney then directed that an attachment be issued against General Cadwalader for contempt, but service of the writ was refused at the gate of Fort McHenry.

The following day, May 28, 1861, Judge Taney issued his ruling from the bench declaring that President Lincoln had no power to suspend the writ of habeas corpus as such power was implicitly vested in Congress by virtue of its location in Article I of the Constitution. He also ruled that John Merryman should be set free and that General Cadwalader was in contempt. He then noted that the U.S. Marshall had authority to summon the posse to aid him in seizing the General to bring him before the court, but

---

[61]Paulsen, *The Merryman Power*, 15 CARDOSO L. REV. at 88.
[62]Mark E. Neely, Jr., *The Fate of Liberty: Abraham Lincoln and Civil Liberties* 8 (1991).
[63]Paulsen, *The Merryman Power*, 15 CARDOSO L. REV. at 90.

because he reasoned that the posse would be met by a superior force authorized by President Lincoln, he felt that there was no point in proceeding. Judge Taney then concluded: "I have exercised all the power which the constitution and laws confer upon me, but that power has been resisted by a force too strong for me to overcome."[64]

Following the conflict between the Executive and the Judiciary over the arrest of John Merryman, Lincoln directed Attorney General Bates to develop a broader argument to defend the President's actions. Attorney General Bates issued an opinion on July 5, 1861, the day after President Lincoln's address, and developed an argument based upon the principles enunciated by James Madison. Bates wrote that the American people were "actuated by a special dread of the unity of power" and therefore adopted a system in which no one branch of government had "sovereignty."[65] Bates then penned the following:

> These departments are co-ordinate and coequal -- that is, neither being sovereign, each is independent in its sphere, and not subordinate to the others, either of them or both of them together. . . . [I]f we allow one of the three to determine the extent of its own powers, and also the extent of the powers of the other two, that one can control the whole government, and has in fact achieved the sovereignty.

****

> Our fathers, having divided the government into coordinate departments, did not even try (and if they had tried would probably have failed) to create an arbiter among them to adjudge their conflicts and keep them within their respective bounds. They were left . . . each independent and free, to act out its own granted powers, without any ordained or legal superior possessed in the power to revise and reverse its action. And this with the

---

[64]*Ex parte Merryman*, 17 F. Cas. 144, 147 (C.C.D. Md. 1861) (No. 9487).
[65]10 Op. Att'y A Gen. 74, 76 (1861).

hope that the three departments, mutually coequal and
independent, would keep each other within their proper
spheres by their mutual antagonism -- that is, by the
system of checks and balances, to which our fathers were
driven at the beginning by their fear of the unity of
power.[66]

In defying the Supreme Court, President Lincoln exercised
what might be termed coordinancy, or nonacquiescence. As James
Madison observed,

The several departments being perfectly co-ordinate by the
terms of their common commission, neither of them, it is
evident, can pretend to an exclusive or superior right of
settling the boundaries between their respective powers;
and how are the encroachments of the stronger to be
prevented, or the wrongs of the weaker to be redressed,
without an appeal to the people themselves; who, as the
granters of the commission, can alone declare its true
meaning and force its observance?[67]

Though Madison recognized that ordinarily the exposition of
the laws and the Constitution falls to the judiciary, he did not feel
this excluded independent interpretive power by the other two
branches.

I beg to know, upon what principle it can be contended,
that any one department draws from the Constitution
greater powers than another, in marking out the limits of
the powers of the several departments? . . . If the
Constitutional boundary of either be brought into question,
I do not see that any one of these independent
departments has more right than another to declare their
sentiments on that point. . . .[68]

---

[66]*Id.* at 76-77.
[67]James Madison, *The Federalist* No. 49.
[68]1 *Annals of Cong.* 500 (Joseph Gales ed., 1789).

In an unpublished letter, James Madison penned the following noteworthy commentary:

> As the Legislative, Executive, and Judicial departments of the United States are co-ordinate, and each equally bound to support the Constitution, it follows that each must, in the exercise in its functions, be guided by the text of the Constitution according to its own interpretation of it; and, consequently, that in the event of irreconcilable interpretations, the prevalence of the one or the other department must depend on the nature of the case, as receiving its final decision from the one or the other, and passing from that decision into effect, without involving the functions of any other.[69]

James Wilson once noted that "whoever would be obliged to obey a constitutional law is justified in refusing to obey an unconstitutional act of the legislature. . . . [W]hen a question, even of this delicate nature, occurs, everyone who is called to act, has a right to judge."[70]

The proposition of coordinancy, or nonacquiescence, may sound strange to modern jurisprudence. It certainly presents a give and take, or pull and tug concept. Under the coordinancy system, there may be times when the individual branches of government disagree on constitutional interpretation. Such disagreements occurred during the term of Thomas Jefferson, Abraham Lincoln, and Andrew Jackson. However, over time, the disagreements became agreements. Ultimately the courts agreed with Thomas Jefferson that the Sedition Act was unconstitutional. The Supreme Court also later agreed with Abraham Lincoln that its *Dred Scott* decision was erroneous. The dynamic of inherent tension at least allows the question to be debated. There may be a time when there is no resolution of the answer, but the fact that the question is being debated is more important than the answer to the question. It is

---

[69]James Madison, Unaddressed Letter of 1834, *In* 4 *Letters and Other Writings of James Madison* 349.

[70]1 *The Works of James Wilson* 168 (Robert Green McCloskey ed., 1967) (*taken from* LECTURES ON LAW, 1791).

certainly better than being ruled by an oligarchy living in a state of tyranny. When the liberties of the people are given one day and taken away the next by five unelected judges,[71] then our liberties are indeed fragile, depending more on the whim of a few individuals than upon immutable constitutional principles. Something must be done to prevent judicial tyranny. The judiciary must be thwarted in its effort to swallow up the other two branches of government. If the trend toward judicial supremacy over the other two branches continues, then there is no question that our Republican form of government has been exchanged for an oligarchy. The result is nothing less than tyranny.

---

[71]There are presently nine justices on the United States Supreme Court. The Court only needs five of the nine to make a majority.

22

RELIGION AND THE
FUTURE OF AMERICA

When the early pioneers of this country landed on the shores of what later became known as America, they brought with them a vision. Though certainly not all were Christian, a large portion of the pioneers operated under a Judeo-Christian worldview. This worldview taught them that history is not the monotonous repetitive cycle the Greeks once thought. History had a purpose. While certain events of history may repeat themselves, the Judeo-Christian worldview taught the pioneers that history was moving to a conclusion. These pioneers were part of this conclusion. The role that many of them played was to bring the gospel of Jesus Christ to a new land. In a real sense, these pioneers were missionaries to America.

It is no wonder that when these pioneers landed they erected crosses and staked out the land for Jesus Christ. It is also no wonder that when they framed their colonial documents, they expressed the view that their purpose in life was to spread the gospel, that laws should be consistent with the Bible, and, in reality, that they derived their laws from the Bible. In creating what is now known as the federal government, the founders drew from two primary sources. First, they were familiar with the monarchy from which they came and did not want to repeat the mistakes of their motherland. Second, they realized human frailty and the inevitable conclusion that power corrupts, and absolute power corrupts absolutely. In response, they formed a federal government with limited powers, having checks and balances between three branches of government. In setting up this government, many of the founders realized that if God did not build this house of America, those who labored did so in vain.

The founders recognized the importance of religion in their everyday lives. By and large, they did not schizophrenically separate their religious views from public life. Since the Judeo-Christian ethic was the primary worldview, public schools naturally taught students how to read using biblical verses, and biblical stories often taught points of morality. The average student who did not claim to be Christian probably knew more about the Bible than many of today's young people who regularly attend church. Many of the founders knew the original languages of the Bible. It was not unusual to study Greek and Latin. Today many students graduating from public schools do not even understand English.

Freedom and autonomy were important to the early founders. They established the federal government to be a government of certain limited and prescribed powers, primarily banding the colonies together for the purpose of national defense and security. The individual colonies did not want the federal government to intrude into matters of the states, particularly with matters of religion and education. The founders realized that with the increase of bureaucracy there was a concomitant decrease in liberties. As the federal government grew, freedom, and specifically religious freedom, would wane.

Many of the individual states took on characteristics different from one another primarily because they were inhabited by people of different religious faiths or unique ethnic heritage. The individual states were not afraid to take on peculiarities different from their neighbors, and yet, they all attempted to coexist and to assist one another in certain areas. As transportation increased, migration from one state to the next increased. The federal government continued to increase in size and power, and along with this increase, bureaucracy continued to mount. Uniformity became the rule of the day. Today, multiculturalism is in vogue and political correctness is the rule. Many people have merged into a melting pot with differing religious backgrounds or no religious backgrounds. Today, some have the goal of making this country totally secular.

There is a struggle going on for the heart and soul of America. This struggle involves the Judeo-Christian heritage of this country and religious freedom. A growing bureaucratic federal government is not necessarily compatible with freedom, particularly religious freedom. To some extent, this country mirrors the history of Egypt. In Egypt, the pharaohs believed that they were God. As God, the pharaohs etched their names on monuments throughout the land. Many Egyptian pharaohs chiseled off the previous pharaohs' names and inscribed their own as though they were the ones who had built the stone relics. Today, the same thing is taking place in America.

As bureaucracy continues to grow, and the trend toward secularism and political correctness continues to mount, there is an increasing clash between a secularistic mindset and Judeo-Christian worldview. As secularism triumphs, the god of the state eats away the religious symbols of yesteryear.

As the federal government continues to gain power, and as secularism continues to be the rule of the day, the symbols of our founders are being removed one-by-one. For many years, the city of St. Cloud, Florida, had erected a cross atop its water tower. Someone objected and filed suit. The cross is now gone. Only a bald water tower top remains. Corpus Christi, a city whose name means "the body of Christ," had for approximately four decades erected Latin crosses to commemorate Easter and the resurrection of Jesus Christ. Now it no longer does so. The crosses are gone. The city officials removed them out of fear of litigation, and the town became a victim of judicial terrorism.

The city of Zion chose the Star of David as part of its city seal. The star was synonymous with the city's name, but someone objected. The city was taken to court, and now the city's seal has been altered. The Star of David has been removed.

Another city, also named Zion, had a Latin cross in its city seal consisting of a seal draped with a ribbon that read "God Reigns." The seal was divided into four sections, one section containing a Latin cross, one with a dove carrying a branch, one with a scepter and one with a crown. This seal was designed in the early 1900s by the founder of Zion, the Reverend John Alexander Dowie, who was also the founder of the Christian Catholic Church. The city of Zion was established for "the purpose of the extension of the Kingdom of God upon earth." The city was taken to court and now the seal has been altered. The cross has been removed.

A painting of Jesus was donated to a Michigan school and placed in the school hallway. This painting had hung on the wall for many years, but one of the parents objected and took the school to court. Although it was like any other painting of a great leader, because Jesus was the founder of the Christian religion, the court stated that the painting must be removed. When you walk through this particular school today, the painting is gone. Another victim of judicial terrorism.

For many years a Latin cross stood on the memorial ground of a military cemetery. Someone was offended by this cross and took action in court. A court forced the removal of this historic Judeo-Christian symbol and now, on this military cemetery, the Latin cross is gone.

The Illinois town of Rolling Meadows had a city seal with a cross in one quadrant of the seal. After a school art assignment asking students to draw a potential city seal, one eighth-grade student designed a seal with a cross in one of the quadrants to depict the many churches in the area. In 1960, the city adopted the seal designed by the eighth-grade student. The seal actually consisted of a four leaf clover. Inside the clover were pictures of a school, industrial buildings, a church, a leaf, and a Latin cross. Someone objected to this cross and a federal court forced its removal. The city seal has now irrevocably been changed and the cross is gone.

In Wicker Memorial Park in Highland, Indiana, stood a twenty-foot crucifix erected by the Knights of Columbus in 1955 as a memorial to fallen World War II veterans. The figure of Jesus hung from this crucifix for thirty-eight years overlooking the public park. Five residents objected to the crucifix and brought suit in federal court claiming that the display violated the Constitution. After a very long legal battle, the appellate court ruled that the crucifix was unconstitutional. Bringing their cranes to the park, the city officials lowered the cross to the ground — a scene reminiscent of when the real cross and the real Jesus were lowered to the ground after His death. The crucifix is now gone, and the city of Highland became another victim of judicial terrorism.

When I attended public school, I remember each day was opened with a prayer and the Pledge of Allegiance. Opening class with prayer today is now foreign to all public school students. My public school used to have Christmas holidays, but now public school students have winter holidays. Whenever public schools had Christmas concerts, it was natural to sing religious Christmas carols. Now, school officials are jittery about putting religious Christmas carols in public school music. I remember the day President John F. Kennedy was assassinated. The teachers gathered all of our classes into a big auditorium, and we watched the news on television. We were led by our teachers to pray on behalf of our fallen president. Today, prayer probably would not have been part of that event which was so vividly impressed on my mind.

In 1990, I traveled to Moscow in the former Soviet Union. I was part of a delegation of attorneys traveling to Russia to participate in a constitutional conference between the USSR and the USA. The purpose of this interchange was to give ideas to the Soviet Union regarding the adoption and formation of a new constitutional form of government. While in the Kremlin, I was able to visit the church museums with their beautiful gold onion domes. Inside these beautiful structures the walls, including the ceilings and the enormous pillars, were painted with religious themes. Everywhere the eye could see were pictures of early New Testament events and other great Christian leaders throughout history. I was awed by these massive structures and also somewhat saddened. These churches had actually been thriving centers for religious worship in the very heart of the Kremlin. When the Soviet atheistic government took control, these churches lost their religious worship. Interestingly, the structures remained as relics to a bygone era and were used only as museums. I thought, had these church museums been in America through this transition, they may well have been ruled unconstitutional because of their religious heritage. In America, I wonder whether we will even have religious relics or whether we will continue to push all religious history and memory from existence.

During one of the meetings, a Soviet attorney sitting across the aisle stood up and announced to those that were assembled how thankful he was to be able to sit in a room with Americans. He expressed that in 1976, America celebrated its 200th anniversary of the Constitution, and he congratulated us. He hoped that the Soviet Union could do the same as it was moving through those days of transition. He stated he was so proud and privileged to be able to sit beside an American.

The words of this Soviet attorney have been etched forever in my mind. I am proud to be an American, but it is certainly a different America than what our founders envisioned. When Alexis de Tocqueville traveled this country in the 1830s, he stated that "the religious aspect of the country was the first thing that struck my attention."[1] If Alexis de Tocqueville returned to America today in the 20th century, I wonder what would impress him now? When he visited our public schools, would he be impressed by the religious influence? When the class began, would he hear a prayer? Would he look at an instructional book and see religious influences? When he talked to our representative leadership, on either a state or federal level, would he be impressed by their desire to serve this country out of a sense of mission? Or, instead, would he be impressed with the rising tide of teenage pregnancy, suicide, teenage abortion, juvenile crime, and indiscriminate killing? Would he feel safe when he entered our nation's capitol, one of the leading crime areas in the world? What would really impress Alexis de Tocqueville today? Would it be the religious aspect of this country, or would it be its secularistic trend? Would it be the fact that we are one of the most illiterate countries in the world, that we are in hopeless debt, that we are removing our nativity scenes from public property, or that we are erasing all of our religious heritage?

Yes the early founders did have a vision. This vision was inspired by their Judeo-Christian worldview. They came to this country for a purpose — to advance the gospel. Our country is slowly losing its religious vision, slowly losing the concept of its place in history. As the United States begins to melt into a one-world government, we lose our uniqueness which is our contribution to the world. Without a religious cohesiveness and religious worldview, what happened in Los Angeles after the Rodney King verdict is not unusual. After that verdict was handed down, it appeared that society had erupted and lost all its cohesive underpinnings. Having no Judeo-Christian worldview or no religious heritage, a society left with only secularism will disintegrate and destroy itself. Having to answer to no higher power and recognize no other world existence, society left with no absolutes will come unglued at the seams.

The struggle for this country is a real one. The contents of this book are not simply theoretical and are not just legal jargon. The issue of religious freedom in the public square is really the battle for the heart and soul of America. If we lose religious freedom in the public square, then we have lost America forever. As religion

---

[1] Alexis de Tocqueville, 1 *Democracy in America*, 319 (1945).

goes, so goes America. The early founders knew the importance of religion in society, and they were willing to forsake their homes, their comfort, their families and even sacrifice their lives for freedom.

Today we have grown complacent, having graciously inherited the freedom of our forefathers. If we do not catch the vision that they once held, if we let the flame of freedom that they carried die out, if we are not willing to sacrifice and put our lives on the line for freedom in whatever battle we face, then this country, as we now know it, will come to an end. Like an avalanche of snow tumbling down a mountain, it will crumble as surely as the world governments have crumbled in the past decades. I love this country too much to sit by and let that happen.

Appendix A

The Bill of Rights

AMENDMENT I

Congress shall make no law respecting an establishment of religion, or prohibiting the free exercise thereof; or abridging the freedom of speech, or of the press; or the right of the people peaceably to assemble; and to petition the Government for a redress of grievances.

AMENDMENT II

A well-regulated militia, being necessary to the security of a free State, the right of the people to keep and bear arms shall not be infringed.

AMENDMENT III

No soldier shall, in time of peace be quartered in any house, without the consent of the owner, nor in time of war, but in a manner to prescribed by law.

AMENDMENT IV

The right of the people to be secure in their persons, houses, papers, and effects, against unreasonable searches and seizures, shall not be violated, and no warrants shall issue, but upon probable cause, supported by oath or affirmation, and particularly describing the place to be searched, and the persons or things to be seized.

AMENDMENT V

No person shall be held to answer for a capital, or otherwise infamous crime, unless on a presentment or indictment of a Grand Jury, except in cases arising in the land or naval forces, or in the militia, when in actual service in time of war or public danger; not shall any person be subject for the same offense to be twice put in jeopardy of life or limb; nor shall be compelled in any criminal case to be a witness against himself, nor be deprived of life, liberty, or property, without due process of law; nor shall private property be taken for public use, without just compensation.

AMENDMENT VI

In all criminal prosecutions, the accused shall enjoy the right to a speedy and public trial, by an impartial jury of the State and district wherein the crime shall have been committed, which district shall have been previously ascertained by law, and to be informed of the nature and cause of the accusation; to be confronted with the witnesses against him; to have compulsory process for obtaining witnesses in his favor, and to have the assistance of counsel for his defense.

AMENDMENT VII

In suits at common law, where the value in controversy shall exceed twenty dollars, the right of trial by jury shall be preserved, and no fact tried by jury, shall be otherwise reexamined in any Court of the United States, than according to the rules of the common law.

AMENDMENT VIII

Excessive bail shall not be required, nor excessive fines imposed, nor cruel and unusual punishment inflicted.

AMENDMENT IX

The enumeration in the Constitution, of certain rights, shall not be construed to deny or disparage others retained by the people.

AMENDMENT X

The powers not delegated to the United States by the Constitution, nor prohibited by it to the States, are reserved to the States respectively, or to the people.

Appendix B

School Board Policy Regarding Religion

Symbols, Music, Art, Drama, and Literature

A.   It is the intent of this policy to promote tolerance and understanding among students, faculty and staff. It is further the intent of this policy to neither promote nor to denigrate religion or religious practices. Students and staff members should be excused from participating in practices which are contrary to their religious beliefs unless there are compelling reasons that would prevent excusal.

1.   The several holidays throughout the year which have a religious and secular basis may be observed in the public schools.

2.   The historical and contemporary values and the origin of religious holidays may be explained in an unbiased and objective manner without sectarian indoctrination.

3.   Music, art, drama, and literature having religious themes or bases are permitted as part of the curriculum for school-sponsored activities and programs if presented in a prudent and objective manner and as a traditional part of the cultural and religious heritage of the particular holiday.

4.   The use of religious symbols such as a cross, menorah, crescent, Star of David, crèche, symbols of Native American religions, or other symbols that are part of a religious holiday are permitted as a teaching aid or resource provided such symbols are displayed as an example of the cultural and religious heritage of the holiday and are temporary in nature. Among these holidays are included Christmas, Easter, Passover, Hanukkah, St. Valentine's Day,. St. Patrick's Day, Thanksgiving and Halloween.

5. The district's calendar should be prepared so as to minimize conflicts with religious holidays of all faiths.

B. Religious institutions and orientations are central to human experience, past and present. An education excluding such a significant aspect would be incomplete. It is essential that the teaching about and not of religion be conducted in a factual, objective and respectful manner.

1. The School Board supports the inclusion of religious literature, music, drama, and the arts in the curriculum and in school activities provided it is intrinsic to the learning experience in the various fields of study and is presented objectively. The Bible or other religious literature may be used as an appropriate study of history, civilization, ethics, or comparative religions so long as it is presented in an objective manner without promoting belief or nonbelief.

2. The emphasis on religious themes in the arts, literature and history should be only as extensive as necessary for a balanced and comprehensive study of these areas. Such studies should never foster any particular religious tenets or demean any religious beliefs.

3. Student-initiated expressions to questions or assignments which reflect their beliefs or non-beliefs about a religious theme shall be accommodated. Students are free to express religious belief or nonbelief in compositions, art forms, music, speech and debate.

Speech, Literature Distribution and Clothing

C. It is the intent of this policy to recognize the free

speech rights of students in public school. Students on public school campuses have the right to express their ideas verbally and through the distribution of literature so long as their speech does not disrupt the ordinary operation of the school.

1. Students may verbally express their ideas during class so long as their verbal expressions are consistent with the subject matter being taught.

2. Students may verbally express their ideas to other students during noninstructional time so long as their speech is not disruptive to the ordinary operation of the school and does not infringe on the rights of other students.

3. Students may distribute literature during noninstructional time so long as the distribution is not disruptive to the ordinary operation of the school and does not infringe on the rights of other students.

4. Students may wear symbols or articles of clothing which contain written or symbolic expressions so long as such symbols or clothing is not obscene and does not infringe on the rights of other students.

5. As used in this section, the term "noninstructional time" means before or after school hours, between classes, during lunch or recess times.

6. As used in this section, the term "does not disrupt the ordinary operation of the school" means that the speaker be the initiator and cause of disruption. It does not mean that other students must agree with the speaker. Disruption by other students in response to the student's expressions should not be construed to mean that the speaker is causing disruption. "Disruptive to the ordinary operation of the school" includes

littering, forcing other students to listen by shouting or preventing passage, and engaging in speech activities during instructional time which is not consistent with the subject matter being taught.

7. As used in this section, the term "infringe on the rights of other students" means defamatory expressions against another student.

Graduation Ceremonies

D. It is the intent of this policy to recognize the solemnity of graduation ceremonies. It is also the intent to recognize the delicate balance between free speech rights and establishment of religion concerns.

1. School officials shall not invite a clergyman for the specific purpose to pray at graduation, place the prayer on the agenda, and give the clergyman guidelines for saying the prayer.

2. School officials may use secular criteria to invite a speaker for the graduation ceremony, and if the speaker voluntarily chooses to pray, school officials should not prevent the prayer.

3. Schools may rent out their facilities to outside organizations to conduct graduation at which a clergyman or other person is invited to pray and where prayer is placed on the agenda so long as school officials do not organize, conduct, promote or prescribe the content of the graduation ceremony.

4. Schools may turn over part or all of the graduation ceremony to a parent and/or student committee to organize part or all of the ceremony at which the inclusion of prayer shall rest within the discretion of the

graduating senior class. The prayer, if used, shall be given by a student or other person who is not an employee of the school.

Alternative Section Regarding Graduation Ceremonies

1. The use of a brief opening and/or closing message, not to exceed two minutes, at high school graduation exercises shall rest within the discretion of the graduating senior class.
2. The opening and/or closing message shall be given by a student volunteer, in the graduating senior class, chosen by the graduating senior class as a whole.
3. If the graduating senior class chooses to use an opening and/or closing message, the content of that message shall be prepared by the student volunteer and shall not be monitored or otherwise reviewed by the school board, its officers, or employees.

Student Clubs

E. It is the intent of this policy to recognize noncurriculum-related student clubs as being a traditional and vital part of a student's educational process within the public school system. It is further the intent to provide nondiscriminatory guidelines for the continued operation of student-initiated clubs.

1. Any public secondary school which receives federal financial assistance and which has a limited open forum shall not deny equal access or a fair opportunity to, or discriminate against, any students who wish to conduct a meeting within that limited open forum on the basis of the religious, political, philosophical, or the content of the speech at such meetings.

2.   A public secondary school is a limited open forum whenever such school grants an offering to or opportunity for one or more noncurriculum-related student groups to meet on school premises during noninstructional time.

3.   Schools shall be deemed to offer a fair opportunity to students who wish to conduct a meeting within its limited open forum if such school uniformly provides that—

(a)   the meeting is voluntary and student-initiated;

(b)   there is no sponsorship of the meeting by the school, the government, or its agents or employees;

(c)   employees or agents of the school or government are present at religious meetings only in a nonparticipatory capacity;

(d)   the meeting does not materially and substantially interfere with the orderly conduct of educational activities within the school; and

(e)   nonschool persons may not direct, conduct, control, or regularly attend activities of student groups.

4.   Nothing in this section shall be construed to limit the authority of the school, its agents or employees, to maintain order and discipline on school premises, to protect the well-being of students and faculty, and to assure that attendance of students at meetings is voluntary.

5.   The term "sponsorship" includes the act of promoting, leading, or participating in a meeting. The assignment of a teacher, administrator, or other school employee to a meeting for custodial purposes does not

constitute sponsorship of the meeting.
6. The term "meeting" includes those activities of student groups which are permitted under a school's limited open forum and are not directly related to the school curriculum.
7. The term "noninstructional time" means time set aside by the school before actual classroom instruction begins or after actual classroom instruction ends.

Release Time

F. It is the intent of this policy to recognize that schools may offer a release time for students to leave the public school facilities for off-site instruction, including religious instruction.
1. Any school may provide a designated time during the school week for students to leave the public school facilities in order to obtain off-site instruction, which may include religious instruction.
2. Students shall not be required to attend off-site religious instruction, nor may students be required to leave the public school facilities during the designated time of this off-site instruction.
3. Any religious instruction that occurs during the release time shall not be on school premises, shall not be conducted by school personnel, and no academic credit shall be given for such instruction.

Use of School Facilities

G. It is the intent of this policy to recognize that school facilities are often made available for noncurriculum-related purposes to students as well as to nonstudents, and it is further the intent of this policy that such use shall be offered on an equal and nondiscriminatory basis.

1.   Any school which makes available use of its facilities to any nonstudent as a meeting place before or after the official school day shall offer use of the school facilities on an equal and nondiscriminatory basis without regard to the content of the requested meeting.

2.   Any school which offers use of its facilities to any nonstudent may charge a rental or use fee so long as such rental or use fee is required for any meeting requested by any nonstudent on an equal and nondiscriminatory basis without regard to the content of the requested meeting.

3.   Notwithstanding any use made available to any nonstudent, the school may prohibit continued use of the school as a meeting place to any nonstudent if there is particularized evidence to show that the nonstudent user has and will continue to cause disruption or violence to the ordinary operation of the school.

4.   In the request made by a student to use school facilities as a meeting place during school hours shall be governed by Section E of this policy relating to Student Clubs.

Severability

H.   If any provision of this policy or the application thereof to any person or circumstances is judicially determined to be invalid, the provisions of the remainder of the section and the application to other persons or circumstances shall not be affected thereby.

SIGNIFICANT CASES SUPPORTING SCHOOL BOARD POLICY REGARDING RELIGION

Symbols, Music, Art, Drama, and Literature

Sections A and B of the policy are taken verbatim from the Eighth Circuit Court of Appeals case of *Florey v. Sioux Falls School District 49-5,* 619 F.2d 1311 (8th Cir.), *cert. denied,* 449 U.S. 987 (1980). This Eighth Circuit Court of Appeals case found that the policy as outlined in Sections A and B was constitutional. The United States Supreme Court denied review and therefore this case establishes the most authoritative ruling on this policy regarding symbols, music, art, drama, and literature. Sections A and B are also supported by the United States Supreme Court decision in *School District of Abington Township v. Schempp,* 374 U.S. 203 (1963).

Speech, Literature Distribution, and Clothing

Section C is supported by several cases. Foremost is the United States Supreme Court decision in *Tinker v. Des Moines Independent School District,* 393 U.S. 503 (1969). This was the landmark decision regarding free speech rights on public school campuses. The test for limiting student free speech is taken almost verbatim from the *Tinker* case and is outlined in Section C2. As it relates to the distribution of religious literature, several federal court cases have been used to outline this portion of the policy. *Rivera v. East Otero School District R-1,* 721 F. Supp. 1189 (D. Colo. 1989) and *Burch v. Barker,* 861 F.2d 1149 (9th Cir. 1988).

Graduation Ceremonies

Section D pertaining to graduation ceremonies is based upon the United States Supreme Court ruling in *Lee v. Weisman,* 112 S. Ct. 2649 (1992). Section D1 essentially states the ruling of the *Lee* decision. The remainder of Section D is based upon the Fifth Circuit Court of Appeals decision in *Jones v. Clear Creek Independent Schools,* 977 F.2d 963 (5th Cir. 1992), *cert. denied,* 113 S. Ct. 2950 (1993). This case cites *Lee v. Weisman* and outlines an exception as it relates to student prayer. Section D also utilizes the case of *Verbena United Methodist Church v. Chilton County Board of Education,* 765 F. Supp. 704 (M.D. Ala. 1991). In this particular case involving the rental of school facilities to outside organization for the purpose of conducting graduation services, there would be no constitutional concerns as raised in *Lee v. Weisman.* To prohibit such activities could be construed as a violation of free speech rights. The alternative section regarding graduation ceremonies is based on the cases of *Harris v. Joint School District No. 241,* 821 Supp. 638 (D. Idaho 1993) and *Adler v. Duval County School Board,* 851 F. Supp. 446 (M.D. Fla. 1994).

Student Clubs

Section E deals with the federal law known as the Equal Access Act found at 20 U.S.C. §§ 4071-74. The Equal Access Act was upheld by the United States Supreme Court in *Board of Education v. Mergens,* 110 S. Ct. 2356 (1990).

Release Time

Section F pertaining to release time is governed by the United States Supreme Court decision in *Zorach v. Clauson,* 343 U.S. 306 (1952). Other cases used for this section include *Lanner v. Wimmer,* 662 F.2d 1349 (10th Cir. 1981), *Doe v. Shenandoah County School Board,* 737 F. Supp. 913 (W.D. Va. 1990), and *Minnesota Federation of Teachers v. Nelson,* 740 F. Supp. 694 (D. Minn. 1990).

Use of School Facilities

Section G pertaining to use of public school facilities is governed by the United States Supreme Court decision in *Lamb's Chapel v. Center Moriches Union Free School District,* 113 S. Ct. 2141 (1993). This is the landmark United States Supreme Court case holding that use of school facilities must be offered on a nondiscriminatory basis even if the requester is a religious organization. The section dealing with rental value is governed by *Fairfax Covenant Church v. Fairfax County School Board,* 811 F.

Supp. 1137 (E.D. Va. 1993), which ruled that a school may not require higher rent of a religious organization for use of its school facilities than as required of secular organizations.

Appendix C

The Equal Access Act

The Equal Access Act is a federal law that is applicable to all the states. The Act, passed by Congress and published at 20 U.S.C. §§ 4071-74, states as follows:

Sec. 4071.

(a)   It shall be unlawful for any public secondary school which receives federal financial assistance and which has a limited open forum to deny equal access or a fair opportunity to, or discriminate against, any students who wish to conduct a meeting within that limited open forum on the basis of the religious, political, philosophical, or the content of the speech at such meetings.

(b)   A public secondary school has a limited open forum whenever such school grants an offering to or opportunity for one or more noncurriculum-related student groups to meet on school premises during noninstructional time.

(c)   Schools shall be deemed to offer a fair opportunity to students who wish to conduct a meeting within its limited open forum if such school uniformly provides that—

    (1)   the meeting is voluntary and student-initiated;

    (2)   there is no sponsorship of the meeting by the school, the government, or its agents or employees;

    (3)   employees or agents of the school or government are present at religious meetings only in a nonparticipatory capacity;

    (4)   the meeting does not materially and substantially interfere with the orderly conduct of educational activities within the school; and

    (5)   nonschool persons may not direct, conduct, control, or regularly attend activities of student groups.

(d)   Nothing in this subchapter shall be construed to authorize the United States or any State or political subdivision thereof—

    (1)   to influence the form or content of any prayer or other religious activity;

    (2)   to require any person to participate in prayer or other religious activity;

(3)   to expend public funds beyond the incidental cost of providing the space for student-initiated meetings;

(4)   to compel any school agent or employee to attend a school meeting if the content of the speech at the meeting is contrary to the beliefs of the agent or employee;

(5)   to sanction meetings that are otherwise unlawful;

(6)   to limit the rights of groups of students which are not of a specified numerical size; or

(7)   to abridge the constitutional rights of any person.

(e,   Notwithstanding the availability of any other remedy under the Constitution or the laws of the United States, nothing in this subchapter shall be construed to authorize the United States to deny or withhold federal financial assistance to any school.

(f)   Nothing in this subchapter shall be construed to limit the authority of the school, its agents or employees, to maintain order and discipline on school premises, to protect the well-being of students and faculty, and to assure that attendance of students at meetings is voluntary.

Definitions of Common Terms

Sec. 4072. As used in this subchapter—

(1)   The term "secondary school" means a public school which provides secondary education as determined by State law.

(2)   The term "sponsorship" includes the act of promoting, leading, or participating in a meeting. The assignment of a teacher, administrator, or other school employee to a meeting for custodial purposes does not constitute sponsorship of the meeting.

(3)   The term "meeting" includes those activities of student groups which are permitted under a school's limited open forum and are not directly related to the school curriculum.

(4)   The term "noninstructional" time means time set aside by the school before actual classroom

instruction begins or after actual classroom instruction ends.

Severability

Sec. 4073. If any provision of this subchapter or the application thereof to any person or circumstances is judicially determined to be invalid, the provisions of the remainder of the subchapter and the application to other persons or circumstances shall not be affected thereby.

Construction

Sec. 4074. The provisions of this subchapter shall supersede all other provisions of federal law that are inconsistent with the provisions of this subchapter.

Appendix D

Student Club Constitution

[TEENS FOR LIFE][1] CONSTITUTION
Article I

The name of this club shall be known as [Teens for Life].[2]

Article II
General Purposes

The general purpose of [Teens for Life][3] is to provide an opportunity for students to meet together during noninstructional time to study and promote the [sanctity of human life from the moment of conception until natural death. Teens for Life is a pro-life, nondenominational student club which seeks to promote the following purposes:

1. To provide education opposing abortion and infanticide.
2. To provide education on abortion alternatives such as adoption.
3. To provide education on euthanasia.][4]

Article III
Membership

Any student desiring to participate in the study of [pro-life issues][5] may be a member of [Teens for Life].[6] However, only members professing to be [pro-life],[7] as that term may be defined from time-to-time by the officers of this organization, are entitled to vote. A quorum for voting purposes shall consist of not less than four students eligible to vote. If school policy requires a sponsor for

---

[1]Insert name of club.
[2]Insert name of club.
[3]Insert name of club.
[4]Insert description of purpose of club.
[5]Insert type of issues.
[6]Insert name of club.
[7]Insert profession.

each noncurricular organization, then the club sponsor shall not be entitled to vote and the appointment of said sponsor shall not be construed as a school endorsement of the club. The officers of the organization shall be as follows:

1.   President, Vice-President, Secretary and Treasurer.
2.   Secretary and Treasurer may be combined offices.
3.   Any student holding office must believe in and be committed to [pro-life][8] principles, as that term shall be defined by the preceding officers of this organization.

Article IV
Meetings and Election of Officers

Meetings shall be conducted weekly consistent with school policy for other noncurricular organizations and not inconsistent with state or federal law. There shall be at least one annual meeting for the purpose of electing officers to be held in [January][9] of each year unless otherwise agreed upon by a vote of the membership. One week before the annual meeting, nominations may be made by the membership for officers to be placed on the slate of membership the following week. Nomination of officers may also be made from the floor at the time of the annual meeting. All votes must be cast by secret ballot and the candidates receiving the most votes of those members eligible to vote shall be instated as officers which term shall take effect immediately. Any vacancy in any office occurring before the next annual meeting shall be filled within two weeks pursuant to the same procedures outlined herein.

Article V
Duties and Responsibilities

The duties and responsibilities of the officers shall be as follows:

Section I - President

---

[8]Insert type of principles.
[9]Insert month elections will be held.

The president or the president's designee shall preside at all meetings and shall insure that all meetings are conducted properly.

Section II - Vice President

The vice president shall assist the president. If at any time the president is unable to perform the duties of president by reason of illness, incompetence, absence, or resignation, the vice president shall temporarily act as president until such time as an election occurs to fill the vacancy of president.

Section III - Secretary

The secretary shall be responsible for posting any time or place of any meeting. The secretary or the secretary's designee shall also be responsible for counting ballots during the annual election. The secretary shall also be responsible for keeping any records or minutes.

Section IV - Treasurer

The treasurer shall be responsible for any monies under the direction, control or possession of the club.

Article VI
Adoption

This constitution shall be adopted by two-thirds majority vote of those members eligible to vote.

Article VII
Amendments

This constitution may be amended at any regular or annual meeting provided that the specific amendment is read or posted two consecutive weeks prior to the vote on the amendment. The amendment must be adopted by two-thirds majority vote of the membership entitled to vote. Any amendment shall take effect immediately unless a motion otherwise specifies a time certain.

Appendix E

Protection of Pupil Rights

20 U.S.C. § 1232h

(a) Inspection of instructional materials by parents or guardians

All instructional materials, including teacher's manuals, films, tapes, or other supplementary material which will be used in connection with any survey, analysis, or evaluation as part of any applicable program shall be available for inspection by the parents or guardians of the children.

(b) Limits on survey, analysis, or evaluations

No student shall be required, as part of any applicable program, to submit to a survey, analysis, or evaluation that reveals information concerning--

(1)   political affiliations;

(2)   mental and psychological problems potentially embarrassing to the student or his family;

(3)   sex behavior and attitudes;

(4)   illegal, anti-social, self-incriminating and demeaning behavior;

(5)   critical appraisals of other individuals with whom respondents have close family relationships;

(6)   legally recognized privileged or analogous relationships, such as those of lawyers, physicians, and ministers; or

(7)   income (other than that required by law to determine eligibility for participation in a program or for receiving financial assistance under such program), without the prior consent of the student (if the student is an adult or emancipated minor), or in the case of unemancipated minor, without the prior written consent of the parent.

(c) **Notice**

Educational agencies and institutions shall give parents and students effective notice of their rights under this section.

(d) **Enforcement**

The Secretary shall establish or designate an office and review board within the Department of Education to investigate, process, review, and adjudicate violations of the rights established under this section.

Appendix F

Title VII Employment Discrimination

42 U.S.C. § 2000e-1
FOREIGN AND RELIGIOUS EMPLOYMENT

(a)   Inapplicability of subchapter to certain aliens and employees of religious entitles

This subchapter shall not apply to an employer with respect to the employment of aliens outside any State, or to a religious corporation, association, educational institution or society with respect to the employment of individuals of a particular religion to perform work connected with the carrying on by such corporation, association, educational institution, or society of its activities.

42 U.S.C. § 2000e-2.
UNLAWFUL EMPLOYMENT PRACTICES

Employer practices

(a)   It shall be an unlawful employment practice for an employer—

     (1)   to fail or refuse to hire or to discharge any individual, or otherwise to discriminate against any individual with respect to his compensation, terms, conditions, or privileges of employment, because of such individual's race, color, religion, sex, or national origin; or

     (2)   to limit, segregate, or classify his employees or applicants for employment in any way which would deprive or tend to deprive any individual of employment opportunities or otherwise adversely affect his status as an employee, because of such individual's race, color, religion, sex, or national origin.

Employment agency practices

(b)   It shall be an unlawful employment practice for an employment agency to fail or refuse to refer for employment, or otherwise to discriminate against, any individual because of his race, color, religious, sex, or national origin, or to classify or refer for employment any individual on the basis of his race, color, religious, sex, or national origin.

Labor organization practices

(c)   It shall be an unlawful employment practice for a labor organization—

(1)   to exclude or to expel from its membership, or otherwise to discriminate against, any individual because of his race, color, religion, sex, or national origin;

(2)   to limit, segregate, or classify its membership or applicants for membership, or to classify or fail or refuse to refer for employment any individual, in any way which would deprive or tend to deprive any individual of employment opportunities, or would limit such employment opportunities or otherwise adversely affect his status as an employee or as an applicant for employment, because of such individual's race, color, religion, sex, or national origin; or

(3)   to cause or attempt to cause an employer to discriminate against an individual in violation of this section.

Training programs

(d)   It shall be an unlawful employment practice for any employer, labor organization, or joint labor-management committee controlling apprenticeship or other training or retraining, including on-the-job training programs to discriminate against any individual because of his race, color, religion, sex, or national origin in admission to, or employment in, any program established to proved apprenticeship or other training.

**Business or enterprises with personnel qualified on
basis of religion, sex, or national origin; educational
institutions with personnel of particular religion**

(e)   Notwithstanding any other provision of this subchapter—
          (1)   it shall not be an unlawful employment practice for
                   an employer to hire and employ employees, for an
                   employment agency to classify, or refer for
                   employment any individual, for a labor organization
                   to classify its membership or to classify or refer for
                   employment any individual, or for an employer,
                   labor organization, or joint labor-management
                   committee controlling apprenticeship or other
                   training or retraining programs to admit or employ
                   any individual in any such program, on the basis of
                   his religion, sex, or national origin is a bona fide
                   occupational qualification reasonably necessary to
                   the normal operation of that particular business or
                   enterprise; and
          (2)   it shall not be an unlawful employment practice for
                   a school, college, university, or other educational
                   institution or institution of learning to hire and
                   employ employees of a particular religion if such
                   school, college, university, or other educational
                   institution or institution of learning is, in whole or
                   in substantial part, owned, supported, controlled, or
                   managed by a particular religion or by a particular
                   religious corporation, association, or society, or if
                   the curriculum of such school, college, university,
                   or other educational institution or institution of
                   learning is directed toward the propagation of a
                   particular religion.

**Members of Communist Party or Communist-action
or Communist-front organizations**

(f)   As used in this subchapter, the phrase "unlawful
          employment practice" shall not be deemed to include any
          action or measure taken by an employer, labor organization,

joint labor-management committee, or employment agency with respect to an individual who is a member of the Communist Party of the United States or of any other organization required to register as a Communist-action or Communist-front organization by final order of the Subversive Activities Control Board pursuant to the Subversive Activities Control Act of 1950.

National security

(g)   Notwithstanding any other provision of this subchapter, it shall not be an unlawful employment practice for an employer to fail or refuse to hire and employ any individual for any position, for an employer to discharge any individual from any position, or for an employment agency to fail or refuse to refer any individual for employment in any position, or for a labor organization to fail or refuse to refer any individual for employment in any position, if—

    (1)   the occupancy of such position, or access to the premises in or upon which any part of the duties of such position is performed or is to be performed, is subject to any requirement imposed in the interest of the national security of the United States under any security program in effect pursuant to or administered under any statute of the United States or any Executive Order of the President; and

    (2)   such individual has not fulfilled or has ceased to fulfill that requirement.

Seniority or merit system; quantity or quality of production; ability test; compensation based on sex and authorized by minimum wage provisions

(h)   Notwithstanding any other provision of this subchapter, it shall not be an unlawful employment practice for an employer to apply different standards of compensation, or different terms, conditions, or privileges of employment pursuant to a bona fide seniority or merit system, or a system which measures earnings by quantity or quality of production or to employees who work in different locations, provided that such differences are not the result of an intention to discriminate because of race, color, religion, sex, or national origin, nor shall it be an unlawful employment practice for an employer to give and to act upon the results of any professionally developed ability test provided that such test, its administration or action upon the results is not designed, intended or used to discriminate because of race, color, religion, sex or national original. It shall not be an unlawful employment practice under this subchapter for any employer to differentiate upon the basis of sex in determining the amount of the wages or compensation paid or to be paid to employees of such employer if such differentiation is authorized by the provisions of section 206(d) of Title 29.

Businesses or enterprises extending preferential treatment to Indians

(i)   Nothing contained in this subchapter shall apply to any business or enterprise on or near an Indian reservation with respect to any publicly announced employment practice of such business or enterprise under which a preferential treatment is given to any individual because he is an Indian living on or near a reservation.

Preferential treatment not to be granted on account of existing number of percentage imbalance

(j)   Nothing contained in this subchapter shall be interpreted to require any employer, employment agency, labor organization, or joint labor-management committee subject to this subchapter to grant preferential treatment to any individual or to any group because of the race, color, religion, sex, or national origin of such individual or group on account of an imbalance which may exist with respect to the total number or percentage of persons of any race, color, religion, sex, or national origin employed by any employer, referred or classified for employment by any employment agency or labor organization, admitted to membership or classified by any labor organization, or admitted to, or employed in, any apprenticeship or other training program, in comparison with the total number or percentage of persons of such race, color, religion, sex, or national origin in any community, State, section, or other area, or in the available work force in any community, State, section, or other area.

Disparate impact as basis of practice

(k)   (1)   (A)   An unlawful employment practice based on disparate impact is established under this subchapter only if —

         (i)   a complaining party demonstrates that a respondent uses a particular employment practice that causes a disparate impact on the basis of race, color, religion, sex, or national origin and the respondent fails to demonstrate that the challenged practice is job related for the position in question and consistent with business necessity; or

         (ii)   the complaining party makes the demonstration described in subparagraph (C) with respect to an alternative employment practice and the respondent refuses to adopt such alternative employment practice.

   (B)   (i)   With respect to demonstrating that a particular employment practice causes a disparate impact as described in subparagraph (A)(i), the complaining party shall demonstrate that each particular challenged employment practice causes a disparate impact, except that if the complaining party can demonstrate to the court that the elements of a respondent's decision making process are not capable of separation for analysis, the decision making process may be analyzed as one employment practice.

(ii)   If the respondent demonstrates that a specific employment practice does not cause the disparate impact, the respondent shall not be required to demonstrate that such practice is required by business necessity.

(C)   The demonstration referred to by subparagraph (A)(ii) shall be in accordance with the law as it existed on June 4, 1989, with respect to the concept of "alternative employment practice."

(2)   A demonstration that an employment practice is required by business necessity may not be used as a defense against a claim of intentional discrimination under this subchapter.

(3)   Notwithstanding any other provision of this subchapter, a rule barring the employment of an individual who currently and knowingly uses or possesses a controlled substance, as defined in schedules I and II of section 102(6) of the Controlled Substances Act (21 U.S.C. § 802(6)), other than the use or possession of a drug taken under the supervision of a licensed health care professional, or any other use or possession authorized by the Controlled Substances Act or any other provision of Federal law, shall be considered an unlawful employment practice under this subchapter only if such rule is adopted or applied with an intent to discriminate because of race, color, religion, sex, or national origin.

Alteration of test results

(l)   It shall be an unlawful employment practice for a respondent, in connection with the selection or referral of applicants or candidate for employment or promotion, to adjust the scores of, use different cutoff scores for, or otherwise alter the results of, employment related tests on the basis of race, color, religion, sex, or national origin.

Motivation for practice

(m)   Except as otherwise provided in this subchapter, an unlawful employment practice is established when the complaining party demonstrates that race, color, religion, sex, or national origin was a motivating factor for any employment practice, even though other factors also motivated the practice.

Challenges to practices implementing litigated or consent judgments or orders

(n)   (1)   (A)   Notwithstanding any other provision of law, and except as provided in paragraph (2), an employment practice that implements and is within the scope of a litigated or consent judgment or order that resolves a claim of employment discrimination under the Constitution or Federal civil rights laws may not be challenged under the circumstances described in subparagraph (B).

         (B)   A practice described in subparagraph (A) may not be challenged in a claim under the Constitution or Federal civil rights laws—
                 (i)   by a person who, prior to the entry of the judgment or order described in subparagraph (a), had:
                         (I)   actual notice of the proposed judgment or order

sufficient to apprise such person that such judgment or order might adversely affect the interests and legal rights of such person and that an opportunity was available to present objections to such judgment or order by a future date certain; and

(II)   a reasonable opportunity to present objections to such judgment or order; or

(ii)   by a person whose interests were adequately represented by another person who had previously challenged the judgment or order on the same legal grounds and with a similar factual situation, unless there has been an intervening change in law or fact.

(2) Nothing in this subsection shall be construed to—

(A)   alter the standards for intervention under rule 24 of the Federal Rules of Civil Procedure or apply to the rights or parties who have successfully intervened pursuant to such rule in the proceeding in which the parties intervened;

(B)   apply to the rights of parties to the action in which a litigated or consent judgment or order was entered, or of members of a class represented or sought to be represented in such action, or of members of a group on whose behalf relief was sought in such action by the Federal Government;

(C)   prevent challenges to a litigated or consent judgment or order on the ground that such judgment or order was obtained through collusion or fraud, or is transparently invalid or was entered by a court lacking subject matter jurisdiction; or

(D)   authorize or permit the denial to any person of the due process of law required by the Constitution.

(3)   Any action not precluded under this subsection that challenges an employment consent judgment or order described in paragraph (1) shall be brought in the court, and if possible before the judge, that entered such judgment or order. Nothing in this subsection shall preclude a transfer of such action pursuant to section 1404 of Title 28.

Appendix G

Religious Freedom Restoration Act of 1993
42 U.S.C. § 2000bb

An Act

To protect the free exercise of religion.

Be it enacted by the Senate and House of Representatives of the United States of America in Congress assembled,

Section 1. Short Title.

This Act may be cited as the "Religious Freedom Restoration Act of 1993".

Section 2. Congressional Findings and Declaration of Purposes.

(a) Findings.—The Congress finds that—
  (1) the framers of the Constitution, recognizing free exercise of religion as an unalienable right, secured its protection in the First Amendment to the Constitution;
  (2) laws "neutral" toward religion may burden religious exercise as surely as laws intended to interfere with religious exercise;
  (3) governments should not substantially burden religious exercise without compelling justification;
  (4) in Employment Division v. Smith, 494 U.S. 872 (1990) the Supreme Court virtually eliminated the requirement that the government justify burdens on religious exercise imposed by laws neutral toward religion; and
  (5) the compelling interest test as set forth in prior Federal court rulings is a workable test for striking sensible balances between religious liberty and competing prior governmental interests.
(b) Purposes.—The purposes of this Act are—
  (1) to restore the compelling interest test as set forth in

Sherbert v. Verner, 374 U.S. 398 (1963) and Wisconsin v. Yoder, 406 U.S. 205 (1972) and to guarantee its application in all cases where free exercise of religion is substantially burdened; and

(2) to provide a claim or defense to persons whose religious exercise is substantially burdened by government.

Section 3. Free Exercise of Religion Protected.

(a) In General.—Government shall not substantially burden a person's exercise of religion even if the burden results from a rule of general applicability, except as provided in subsection (b).

(b) Exception.—Government may substantially burden a person's exercise of religion only if it demonstrates that application of the burden to the person—

(1) is in furtherance of a compelling governmental interest; and

(2) is the least restrictive means of furthering that compelling governmental interest.

(c) Judicial Relief.—A person whose religious exercise has been burdened in violation of this section may assert that violation as a claim or defense in a judicial proceeding and obtain appropriate relief against a government. Standing to assert a claim or defense under this section shall be governed by the general rules of standing under article III of the Constitution.

Section 4. Attorneys Fees.

(a) Judicial Proceedings.—Section 722 of the Revised Statutes (42 U.S.C. 1988) is amended by inserting "the Religious Freedom Restoration Act of 1993," before "or title VI of the Civil Rights Act of 1964".

(b) Administrative Proceedings.—Section 504(b)(1)(C) of title 5, United States Code, is amended —

(1) by striking "and" at the end of clause (ii);

(2) by striking the semicolon at the end of clause (iii)

and inserting ", and "; and

(3)   by inserting "(iv) the Religious Freedom Restoration Act of 1993;" after clause (iii).

Section 5. Definitions.

As used in this Act—

(1)   the term "government" includes a branch, department, agency, instrumentality, and official (or other person acting under color of law) of the United States, a State, or a subdivision of a State;

(2)   the term "State" includes the District of Columbia, the Commonwealth of Puerto Rico, and each territory and possession of the United States;

(3)   the term "demonstrates" means meets the burdens of going forward with the evidence and of persuasion; and

(4)   the term "exercise of religion" means the exercise of religion under the First Amendment to the Constitution.

Section 6. Applicability.

(a)   In General.—This Act applies to all Federal and State law, and the implementation of that law, whether statutory or otherwise, and whether adopted before or after the enactment of this Act.

(b)   Rule of Construction.—Federal statutory law adopted after the date of the enactment of this Act is subject to this Act unless such law explicitly excludes such application by reference to this Act.

(c)   Religious Belief Unaffected.—Nothing in this Act shall be construed to authorize any government to burden any religious belief.

Section 7. Establishment Clause Unaffected.

Nothing in this Act shall be construed to affect, interpret, or in any way address that portion of the First Amendment prohibiting laws respecting the establishment of religion (referred to in this section as the "Establishment Clause"). Granting government funding, benefits, or exemptions, to the extent permissible under the Establishment Clause, shall not constitute a violation of this Act. As used in this section, the term "granting", used with respect to government funding, benefits, or exemptions, does not include the denial of government funding, benefits, or exemptions.

Approved November 16, 1993.

Appendix H

Religious Freedom Restoration Act
State Version

A bill to be entitled
An act relating to religious freedom; creating the
Religious Freedom Restoration Act of
_____; providing that government may
not substantially burden the exercise of religion;
providing for attorney's fees and costs; providing an
effective date.

Be It Enacted by the Legislature of the State of _____:

Section 1. Short title. -- This act may be cited as the
"Religious Freedom Restoration Act of _____."

Section 2. Definitions. -- As used in this act, the term:

(1) "Government" includes any branch, department,
agency, county, municipality, instrumentality, or official or other
person acting under color of law of the state.

(2) "incarcerated person" means any person confined
within any correctional facility in the state.

Section 3. Free exercise of religion protected. --

(1) The government shall not substantially burden
the exercise of religion, even if the burden results from a rule of
general applicability, except that government may substantially
burden the exercise of religion only if the burden:

(a) Is in furtherance of a compelling
governmental interest; and

(b) Is the least restrictive means of
furthering that compelling governmental interest.

(2) The government shall not substantially burden
an incarcerated person's exercise of religion, even if the burden
results from a rule of general applicability, except that government
may substantially burden an incarcerated person's exercise of
religion only if the burden:

(a) Is in furtherance of a substantial
penological interest; and

(b) Is the least restrictive means of
furthering that substantial penological interest.

(3) A person whose religious exercise has been burdened in violation of this section may assert that violation as a claim or defense in any action or proceeding and obtain appropriate relief.

Section 4. Attorney's fees and costs. -- The prevailing party in any action or proceeding to enforce a provision of this act is entitled to reasonable attorney's fees and costs to be paid by the government.

Section 5. This act shall take effect upon becoming a law.

Appendix I

Freedom of Access to Clinic Entrances
18 U.S.C. § 248

Chapter 13 of title 18, United States Code, is amended by adding at the end thereof the following new section:

§ 248. Freedom of Access to Clinic Entrances.

(a)   Prohibited Activities.—Whoever—

    (1)   by force or threat of force or by physical obstruction, intentionally injures, intimidates or interferes with or attempts to injure, intimidate or interfere with any person because that person is or has been, or in order to intimidate such person or any other person or any class of persons, from obtaining or providing reproductive health services;

    (2)   by force or threat of force or by physical obstruction, intentionally injures, intimidates or interferes with or attempts to injure, intimidate or interfere with any person lawfully exercising or seeking to exercise the First Amendment right of religious freedom at a place of religious worship; or

    (3)   intentionally damages or destroys the property of a facility, or attempts to do so, because such facility provides reproductive health services, or intentionally damages or destroys the property of a place of religious worship, shall be subject to the penalties provided in subsection (b) and the civil remedies provided in subsection (c), except that a parent or legal guardian of a minor shall not be subject to any penalties or civil remedies under this section for such activities insofar as they are directed exclusively at that minor.

(b)   Penalties.—Whoever violates this section shall—

    (1)   in the case of a first offense, be fined in accordance with this title, or imprisoned not more than one year, or both; and

    (2)   in the case of a second or subsequent offense after a prior conviction under this section, be fined in

accordance with this title, or imprisoned not more than three years, or both;

except that for an offense involving exclusively a nonviolent physical obstruction, the fine shall not be more than $10,000 and the length of imprisonment shall not be more than six months, or both, for the first offense; and the fine shall be not more than $25,000 and the length of imprisonment shall be not more than 18 months, or both, for a subsequent offense; and except that if bodily injury results, the length of imprisonment shall be not more than 10 years, and if death results, it shall be for any term of years or for life.

(c)   Civil Remedies.—

      (1)   Right of action.—

           (A)   In general.—Any person aggrieved by reason of the conduct prohibited by subsection (a) may commence a civil action for the relief set forth in subparagraph (B), except that such an action may be brought under subsection (a)(1) only by a person involved in providing or seeking to provide, or obtaining or seeking to obtain, services in a facility that provides reproductive health services, and such an action may be brought under subsection (a)(2) only by a person lawfully exercising or seeking to exercise the First Amendment right of religious freedom at a place of religious worship or by the entity that owns or operates such place of religious worship.

           (B)   Relief.—In any action under subparagraph (A), the court may award appropriate relief, including temporary, preliminary or permanent injunction relief and compensatory and punitive damages, as well as the costs of suit and reasonable fees for attorney and expert witnesses. With respect to compensatory damages, the plaintiff may elect, at any time prior to the rendering of final judgment, to recover, in lieu of actual damages, an award of statutory damages in the amount of $5,000 per violation.

(2) Action by Attorney General of the United States.—

(A) In general.—If the Attorney General of the United States has reasonable cause to believe than any person or group of persons is being, has been, or may be injured by conduct constituting a violation of this section, the Attorney General may commence a civil action in any appropriate United States District Court.

(B) Relief.—In any action under subparagraph (a), the court may award appropriate relief, including temporary, preliminary or permanent injunctive relief, and compensatory damages to persons aggrieved as described in paragraph (1)(B). The court, to vindicate the public interest, may also asses a civil penalty against each respondent—

(i) in an amount not exceeding $10,000 for a nonviolent physical obstruction and $15,000 for other first violation; and

(ii) in an amount not exceeding $15,000 for a nonviolent physical obstruction and $25,000 for any other subsequent violation.

(3) Actions by state attorneys general.—

(A) In general.—If the Attorney General of a State has reasonable cause to believe that any person or group of persons is being, has been, or may be injured by conduct constituting a violation of this section, such Attorney General may commence a civil action in the name of such State, as parens patriae on behalf of natural persons residing in such State, in any appropriate United

States District Court.

(B)   Relief.—In any action under subparagraph (A), the court may award appropriate relief, including temporary, preliminary or permanent injunctive relief, compensatory damages, and civil penalties as described in paragraph (2)(B).

(d)   Rules of Construction.—Nothing in this section shall be construed—

(1)   to prohibit any expressive conduct (including peaceful picketing or other peaceful demonstration) protected from legal prohibition by the First Amendment to the Constitution;

(2)   to create new remedies for interference with activities protected by the free speech or free exercise clauses of the First Amendment to the Constitution, occurring outside a facility, regardless of the point of view expressed, or to limit any existing legal remedies for such interference;

(3)   to provide exclusive criminal penalties or civil remedies with respect to the conduct prohibited by this section, or to preempt State or local laws that may provide such penalties or remedies; or

(4)   to interfere with the enforcement of State or local laws regulating the performance of abortions or other reproductive health services.

(e)   Definitions.—As used in this section:

(1)   Facility.—The term "facility" includes a hospital, clinic, physician's office, or other facility that provides reproductive health services, and includes the building or structure in which the facility is located.

(2)   Interfere with.— The term "interfere with" means to restrict a person's freedom of movement.

(3)   Intimidate.—The term "intimidate" means to place a person in reasonable apprehension of bodily harm to him- or herself or to another.

(4)   Physical obstruction.—The term "physical obstruction" means rendering impassable ingress to

or egress from a facility that provides reproductive health services or to or from a place of religious worship, or rendering passage to or from such a facility or place of religious worship unreasonably difficult or hazardous.

(5)   Reproductive   health   services.—The   term "reproductive health services" means reproductive health services provided in a hospital, clinic, physicians' office, or other facility, and includes a medical, surgical, counseling or referral services relating to the human reproductive system, including services relating to pregnancy or the termination of a pregnancy.

(6)   State.—The term "State" includes a State of the United States, the District of Columbia, and any commonwealth, territory, or possession of the United States.

Appendix J

The Defense of Marriage Act
(Federal)

No State, territory, or possession of the United States, or Indian tribe, shall be required to give effect to any public act, record, or judicial proceeding of any other State, territory, possession, or tribe respecting a relationship between persons of the same sex that is treated as a marriage under the laws of such other State, territory, possession, or tribe, or a right or claim arising from such relationship.

Appendix K

The Defense of Marriage Act
(State)

A marriage licensed in any other country, state or territory, if valid where licensed, is valid in this state except that marriage between parties in which both parties are of the same gender shall not be valid in this state because such marriages are determined by the legislature to be contrary to the strong public interest of this state.

Appendix L

Declaration of Independence

In Congress, July 4, 1776
The Unanimous Declaration of the Thirteen United States of America

When in the Course of human events it becomes necessary for one people to dissolve the political bands which have connected them with another, and to assume among the Powers of the earth, the separate and equal station to which the Laws of Nature and of Nature's God entitle them, a decent respect to the opinions of mankind requires that they should declare the causes which impel them to the separation.

We hold these truths to be self-evident, that all men are created equal, that they are endowed by their Creator with certain unalienable Rights, that among these are Life, Liberty and the pursuit of Happiness. That to secure these rights, Governments are instituted among Men, deriving their just powers from the consent of the governed, That whenever any Form of Government becomes destructive of these ends, it is the Right of the People to alter or to abolish it, and to institute new Government, laying its foundation on such principles and organizing its powers in such form, as to them shall seem most likely to effect their Safety and Happiness. Prudence, indeed, will dictate that Governments long established should not be changed for light and transient causes; and accordingly all experience hath shown, that mankind are more disposed to suffer, while evils are sufferable, than to right themselves by abolishing the forms to which they are accustomed. But when a long train of abuses and usurpations, pursuing invariably the same Object evinces a design to reduce them under absolute Despotism, it is their right, it is their duty, to throw off such Government, and to provide new Guards for their future security.--Such has been the patient sufferance of these Colonies; and such is now the necessity which constrains them to alter their former Systems of Government. The history of the present King of Great Britain is a history of repeated injuries and usurpations, all having in direct object the establishment of an absolute Tyranny over these States. To prove this, let Facts be submitted to a candid world.

He has refused his Assent to Laws, the most wholesome and necessary for the public good.

He has forbidden his Governors to pass Laws of immediate and pressing importance, unless suspended in their operation till his Assent should be obtained; and when so suspended, he has utterly neglected to attend to them.

He has refused to pass other Laws for the accommodation of large districts of people, unless those people would relinquish the right of Representation in the Legislature, a right inestimable to them and formidable to tyrants only.

He has called together legislative bodies at places unusual, uncomfortable, and distant from the depository of their Public Records, for the sole purpose of fatiguing them into compliance with his measures.

He has dissolved Representative Houses repeatedly, for opposing with manly firmness his invasions on the rights of the people.

He has refused for a long time, after such dissolutions, to cause others to be elected; whereby the Legislative Powers, incapable of Annihilation, have returned to the People at large for their exercise; the State remaining in the mean time exposed to all the dangers of invasion from without, and convulsions within.

He has endeavored to prevent the population of these States; for that purpose obstructing the Laws for Naturalization of Foreigners; refusing to pass others to encourage their migration hither, and raising the conditions of new Appropriations of Lands.

He has obstructed the Administration of Justice, by refusing his Assent to Laws for establishing Judiciary Powers.

He has made Judges dependent on his Will alone, for the tenure of their offices, and the amount and payment of their salaries.

He has erected a multitude of New Offices, and sent hither swarms of Officers to harass our People, and eat out their substance.

He has kept among us, in times of peace, Standing Armies without the Consent of our Legislature.

He has affected to render the Military independent of and superior to the Civil Power.

He has combined with others to subject us to a jurisdiction

foreign to our constitution, and unacknowledged by our laws; giving his Assent to their acts of pretended Legislation:

For quartering large bodies of armed troops among us:

For protecting them, by a mock Trial, from Punishment for any Murders which they should commit on the Inhabitants of these States:

For cutting off our Trade with all parts of the world:

For imposing taxes on us without our Consent:

For depriving us in many cases, of the benefits of Trial by Jury:

For transporting us beyond Seas to be tried for pretended offenses:

For abolishing the free System of English Laws in a neighboring Province, establishing therein an Arbitrary government, and enlarging its Boundaries so as to render it at once an example and fit instrument for introducing the same absolute rule into these Colonies:

For taking away our Charters, abolishing our most valuable Laws, and altering fundamentally the Forms of our Government:

For suspending our own Legislature, and declaring themselves invested with Power to legislate for us in all cases whatsoever.

He has abdicated Government here, by declaring us out of his Protection and waging War against us.

He has plundered our seas, ravaged our Coasts, burnt our towns, and destroyed the lives of our people.

He is at this time transporting large armies of foreign mercenaries to compleat the works of death, desolation and tyranny, already begun with circumstances of Cruelty & perfidy scarcely paralleled in the most barbarous ages, and totally unworthy the Head of a civilized nation.

He has constrained our fellow Citizens taken Captive on the high Seas to bear Arms against their Country, to become the executioners of their friends and Brethren, or to fall themselves by their Hands.

He has excited domestic insurrections amongst us, and has endeavored to bring on the inhabitants of our frontiers, the merciless Indian Savages, whose known rule of warfare, is an undistinguished destruction of all ages, sexes and conditions.

In every stage of these Oppressions We have Petitioned for Redress in the most humble terms: Our repeated Petitions have been answered only by repeated injury. A Prince, whose character is thus marked by every act which may define a Tyrant, is unfit to be the ruler of a free People.

Nor have We been wanting in attention to our British brethren. We have warned them from time to time of attempts by their legislature to extend an unwarrantable jurisdiction over us. We have reminded them of the circumstances of our emigration and settlement here. We have appealed to their native justice and magnanimity, and we have conjured them by the ties of our common kindred to disavow these usurpations, which, would inevitably interrupt our connections and correspondence. They too have been deaf to the voice of justice and consanguinity. We must, therefore, acquiesce in the necessity, which denounces our Separation, and hold them, as we hold the rest of mankind, Enemies in War, in Peace Friends.

We, therefore, the Representatives of the united States of America, in General Congress, Assembled, appealing to the Supreme Judge of the world for the rectitude of our intentions, do, in the Name, and by Authority of the good People of these Colonies, solemnly publish and declare, That these United Colonies are, and of Right ought to be Free and Independent States; that they are Absolved from all Allegiance to the British Crown, and that all political connection between them and the State of Great Britain, is and ought to be totally dissolved; and that as Free and Independent States, they have full Power to levy War, conclude Peace, contract Alliances, establish Commerce, and to do all other Acts and Things which Independent States may of right do. And for the support of this Declaration, with a firm reliance on the Protection of Divine Providence, we mutually pledge to each other our Lives, our Fortunes and our sacred Honor.

	John Hancock
New Hampshire:	Josiah Bartlett
	Matthew Thornton
	Wm. Whipple
Massachusetts Bay:	Saml. Adams
	Robt. Treat Paine

	John Adams
	Elbridge Gerry
Rhode Island:	Step. Hopkins
	William Ellery
Connecticut:	Roger Sherman
	Wm. Williams
	Sam'el Huntington
	Oliver Wolcott
New York:	Wm. Floyd
	Frans. Lewis
	Phil. Livingston
	Lewis Morris
New Jersey:	Richd. Stockton
	John Hart
	Jno. Witherspoon
	Abra. Clark
	Fras. Hopkinson
Pennsylvania:	Robt. Morris
	Jas. Smith
	Benjamin Rush
	Geo. Taylor
	Benja. Franklin
	James Wilson
	John Morton
	Geo. Ross
	Geo. Clymer
Delaware:	Caesar Rodney
	Tho. M'Kean
	Geo. Read
Maryland:	Samuel Chase
	Thos. Stone
	Wm. Paca
	Charles Carroll of Carrollton
Virginia:	George Wythe
	Thos. Nelson, jr.
	Richard Henry Lee
	Francis Lightfoot
	Th. Jefferson
	Lee

	Benja. Harrison
	Carter Braxton
North Carolina:	Wm. Hooper
	John Penn
	Joseph Hewes
South Carolina:	Edward Rutledge
	Thomas Lynch, Junr.
	Thos. Heyward, Junr.
	Arthur Middleton
Georgia:	Button Gwinnett
	Geo. Walton
	Lyman Hall

Appendix M

First Amendment Outline

I. Identify The Parties.
    A. Governmental actor, and
    B. Private actor.
II. Identify The Forum.
    A. Traditional public forum.
        1. Streets,
        2. Sidewalks, or
        3. Parks.
    B. Limited Or Designated Public Forum.
        1. Any facility which the government intentionally opens for expressive activity.
        2. Government may open any facility for expressive activity but may also close the facility to preserve the facility for its intended purpose.
    C. Nonpublic Forum.
        1. Any government facility which is not intentionally opened for expressive activity.
        2. Examples include airports, transportation facilities, or utility poles.
III. Identify The Restriction.
    A. Content neutral,
    B. Content based,
    C. Viewpoint based, or
    D. Prior restraint.

Free Speech Clause

I. Content neutral restriction.
    A. Traditional public forum.
        1. Must be a substantial or significant governmental interest.
        2. Reasonable time, place, and manner restrictions must be narrowly tailored.
        3. Must leave open ample alternative means of expression.

B.   Limited or designated public forum.
    1.   Must be a substantial or significant governmental interest.
    2.   Reasonable time, place, and manner restrictions must be narrowly tailored.
    3.   Must leave open ample alternative means of expression.

C.   Nonpublic forum.
    1.   Must be a substantial or significant governmental interest.
    2.   Restrictions must be reasonable and rationally related to the governmental interest.

II.   Content restriction.
A.   Traditional public forum
    1.   Must be a compelling governmental interest.
    2.   Any restriction must be the least restrictive means available.

B.   Limited or designated public forum.
    1.   Must be a compelling governmental interest.
    2.   Any restriction must be the least restrictive means available.

C.   Nonpublic forum.
    1.   Must be a substantial or significant governmental interest.
    2.   Restrictions must be reasonable and rationally related to the governmental interest.

III.   Viewpoint restriction.
A.   Traditional public forum.
    1.   Prohibited.
    2.   Rationale is that government cannot take sides in any debate by allowing one viewpoint to the exclusion of another.

B.   Limited or designated public forum.
    1.   Prohibited.
    2.   Rationale is that government cannot take sides in any debate by allowing one viewpoint to the exclusion of another.

C.   Nonpublic forum.
    1.   Prohibited.

2.   Rationale is that government cannot take sides in any debate by allowing one viewpoint to the exclusion of another.
IV. Prior restraint.
  A.   Presumptively unconstitutional.
  B.   Must have specific time for granting or refusal to grant permit.
  C.   Must not permit governmental discretion to grant or deny speech without specific objective standards.
  D.   Must provide that the government has the burden to file suit to substantiate any denial of speech.

Symbolic Speech

I.   Symbolic Speech.
  A.   The regulation must be within the Constitutional power of the government.
  B.   The regulation must further an important or substantial governmental interest.
  C.   The governmental interest must be unrelated to the suppression of speech.
  D.   The incidental restriction must be no greater than essential to the furtherance of that interest.

Injunctions

I.   Content-Neutral Injunction
  A.   Heightened level of scrutiny stricter than the time, place, and manner test.
  B.   Must not burden more speech than necessary to achieve its objective.
II. Content Based Injunction
  A.   Presumptively invalid.
  B.   Must have a compelling governmental interest.
  C.   Must be the least restrictive means available.

Prisoner Rights

I. Prisoner Rights
    A. Government must have a legitimate penological interest.
    B. Restriction must be reasonably related to the governmental interest.

Free Exercise Clause

I. Pre-1990 Test.
    A. Sincerely held religious belief negatively impacted or burdened by some governmental rule or regulation.
    B. Must be a compelling governmental interest.
    C. Must be the least restrictive means available to achieve the governmental interest.
II. Post-1990 Test.
    A. Any general law of neutral applicability will be upheld.
    B. Pre-1990 test will be used only in the following circumstances.
        1. If the law specifically targets religion for discriminatory treatment; or
        2. The Free Exercise right is combined with some other constitutional right.

Establishment Clause

I. The *Lemon* Test.
    A. Must have a secular purpose.
    B. The governmental action must not primarily promote, endorse, or inhibit religion.
    C. The governmental action must not excessively foster governmental entanglement with religion.
II. Coercion Test.
    A. Does the governmental action coerce private individuals toward religion.
    B. Sometimes used during graduation prayer cases.
III. The Historical Test.
    A. Review history surrounding the First Amendment.
    B. Determine the original intent of the Amendment.

	TRADITIONAL PUBLIC FORUM (can never close) Street, Sidewalk, Parks	LIMITED OR DESIGNATED PUBLIC FORUM (can close or open) Any Government Facility Intentionally Opened	NONPUBLIC FORUM Airport, Transportation Facility, Utility Poles
Content Neutral	1. Substantial government interest 2. Reasonable time, place and manner restrictions must be narrowly tailored 3. Leave open ample alternative means of expression	1. Substantial government interest 2. Reasonable time, place and manner restrictions must be narrowly tailored 3. Leave open ample alternative means of expression	1. Substantial government interest 2. Reasonable restrictions
Content Based	1. Compelling government interest 2. Least restrictive means	1. Compelling government interest 2. Least restrictive means	1. Substantial government interest 2. Reasonable restrictions
Viewpoint Based	1. Prohibited *Example: Allow abortion speech but only pro-choice view.*	1. Prohibited *Example: Allow abortion speech but only pro-choice view.*	1. Prohibited *Example: Allow abortion speech but only pro-choice view.*

SYMBOLIC SPEECH	PRIOR RESTRAINT	INJUNCTIONS
1. Regulation must be within the constitutional power of the government	1. Presumptively invalid	1. Content-Neutral
	2. Valid only if	A. Heightened scrutiny above time, place and manner restriction
2. Must further an important or substantial governmental interest	A. Delay is brief	
	B. Specific time is given for granting or denial of speech	B. Must not burden more speech than necessary to accomplish the injunction's objective
3. Government interest must be unrelated to the suppression of speech	C. Specific guidelines prohibit government discretion by creating neutral objective standards	2. Content-Based
4. The incidental restriction must be no greater than essential to the furtherance of that interest*	D. Burden is on the government to file suit to support its denial	A. Since a content-based injunction is also a prior restraint it is presumptively invalid, with the burden to prove its validity on the government
		B. Compelling governmental interest
		C. Least restrictive means

* This four part test is essentially the same as the time, place and manner test with content-neutral restrictions. *See Ward v. Rock Against Racism*, 491 U.S. 781 (1989).

PRISONS	FREE EXERCISE	ESTABLISHMENT CLAUSE

1. Must have legitimate penological interest	1. Pre-1990 Test
	  A. Must show sincerely held religious belief is burdened by government
	  B. Must be compelling governmental interest
	  C. Must achieve interest in least restrictive means available
		1. *Lemon* Test
		  A. Must be a secular purpose
		  B. Must not primarily promote, endorse, or inhibit religion
		  C. Must not foster excessive governmental entanglement

2. Restriction must be reasonably related to penological interest	2. Post 1990 Test
	  A. Any general law of neutral applicability will be upheld
	  B. Pre-1990 test used only if
	    1. Law targets religion for discriminatory treatment, or
	    2. Free exercise right is combined with another constitutional right
		2. Coercion Test
		  A. Government must not coerce religious belief
		  B. Used sometimes in graduation prayer cases
		3. Historical Test
		  A. Determine historical meaning and intent of First Amendment
		  B. Used in legislative prayer cases

Table of Authorities
Cases

505

Table of Authorities
Constitutional and Statutory
Provisions and Other Rules

Table of Authorities
Books, Articles, and Other Sources

Index

550 Faith & Freedom

About the Author

Mathew Staver is an attorney who specializes in free speech and religious liberty constitutional law. He is board certified by the Florida Bar in Appellate Practice and Workers' Compensation. He is president and founder of Staver & Associates, a law firm based in Orlando and Tallahassee, Florida. He is editor of the firm's monthly newsletter, *The Advocate*, a legal publication dealing with insurance litigation.

In 1989, Mat became founder and president of Liberty Counsel, a religious civil liberties education and legal defense organization established to preserve religious freedom. Based in Orlando, Liberty Counsel provides education and legal defense throughout the nation. As president, Mr. Staver has produced many informative brochures, booklets, and monograms on religious liberty and free speech issues. He is also editor of *The Liberator*, a monthly newsletter devoted to religious liberty, free speech and pro-family topics. He hosts *Freedom's Call*, a two minute daily radio commentary, and *Faith and Freedom*, a fifteen daily radio program, both of which are dedicated to religious freedom, free speech and pro-family issues. In addition to hosting a weekly television program, Mat is a frequent guest on radio and television programs throughout the country.

In addition to receiving a doctorate of law degree, Mat graduated Summa Cum Laude with a Master of Arts degree in Religion. He reads Greek, Hebrew, Aramaic, and Syriac. While pursuing graduate study, he was an honorary guest lecturer at the American Society of Oriental Research at the University of Illinois.

He has numerous legal opinions credited to his work and has argued before the United States Supreme Court in the landmark case of *Madsen v. Women's Health Center, Inc.*, 114 S. Ct. 2516 (1994).

About Liberty Counsel

Liberty Counsel is a nonprofit religious civil liberties education and legal defense organization established to preserve religious freedom. Founded in 1989 by president and general counsel, Mathew D. Staver, Liberty Counsel accomplishes its purpose in a two-fold manner: through education and through legal defense.

Liberty Counsel produces many aids to educate in matters of religious liberty. *The Liberator* is a monthly newsletter reviewing various religious liberty, free speech, and pro-family issues throughout the nation. *Freedom's Call* is a two-minute daily radio program produced by Liberty Counsel providing education in First Amendment religious liberties. *Faith and Freedom* is a fifteen minute daily radio program dedicated to religious liberty, free speech and pro-family matters.

Liberty Counsel has produced many brochures, booklets and monograms outlining various aspects of religious liberty. Most of the cases in which Liberty Counsel is involved resolve through education, either by a telephone call, informative literature, or letters. Many individuals and public officials are ignorant of the First Amendment. Religious rights are often restricted or lost simply out of this ignorance. Liberty Counsel also has cassettes covering a variety of religious liberty topics.

Unfortunately, education will not solve all religious liberty issues. Some individuals are hostile and bigoted toward religion. If education does not resolve the issue, Liberty Counsel aggressively fights for religious liberty in the courtroom. Liberty Counsel represents individuals whose religious liberties are infringed, and defends entities against those trying to restrict religious liberty. Liberty Counsel attorneys frequently argue cases throughout the country, including the United States Supreme Court.

Liberty Counsel is a nonprofit tax-exempt corporation dependent upon public financial support. Contributions to Liberty

Counsel are tax-deductible. For information about Liberty Counsel, or to make tax-deductible contributions, please write or call:

Liberty Counsel
Post Office Box 540774
Orlando, Florida 32854
(407) 875-2100
(800) 671-1776
(407) 875-0770   Fax
www.lc.org   Internet Home Page
www.liberty@lc.org   Internet E-Mail